Maurice Nicoll

"In his usual elegant eloquence, Gary Lachman shines light on yet another seminal figure in twentieth-century Western esotericism. A must-read for anyone interested in Carl Jung, Gurdjieff, and other intellectual-spiritual streams of consciousness that have helped shape the world we live in today."

CARL ABRAHAMSSON, AUTHOR OF
OCCULTURE: THE UNSEEN FORCES THAT DRIVE CULTURE FORWARD AND
SOURCE MAGIC: THE ORIGIN OF ART, SCIENCE, AND CULTURE

"Gary Lachman is one of our surest guides through the forest of eccentric teachers and difficult teachings that constitute modern esotericism. This book displays again Lachman's rare balance, his luminous mind, and his constant turn of phrase, this time with intimate histories of Gurdjieff's Fourth Way through such figures as the master himself, the Russian P. D. Ouspensky, and the British teachers A. R. Orage and especially Maurice Nicoll and his esoteric Christianity. That Lachman includes an unflinching focus on Nicoll's 'unclean thoughts,' male masturbatory imagination, and related conviction that the erotic and the mystical are deeply intertwined makes this a very special book, indeed."

JEFFREY J. KRIPAL, AUTHOR OF *HOW TO THINK IMPOSSIBLY:
ABOUT SOULS, UFOS, TIME, BELIEF, AND EVERYTHING ELSE*

PRAISE FOR PREVIOUS WORKS
BY GARY LACHMAN

"Lachman writes about philosophical and mystical ideas with exceptional grace, forcefulness and clarity."

MICHAEL DIRDA, *THE WASHINGTON POST*

"Lachman is a writer with an elegantly readable style, a passionate interest in aspects of the world that history normally neglects, and a profound understanding of psychology."

PHILIP PULLMAN, AUTHOR OF THE *HIS DARK MATERIALS* TRILOGY

ALSO BY GARY LACHMAN

Dreaming Ahead of Time

Introducing Swedenborg: Correspondences

The Return of Holy Russia

Dark Star Rising: Magick and Power in the Age of Trump

Lost Knowledge of the Imagination

Beyond the Robot: The Life and Work of Colin Wilson

The Secret Teachers of the Western World

Revolutionaries of the Soul

*Aleister Crowley: Magick, Rock and Roll, and
the Wickedest Man in the World*

The Caretakers of the Cosmos

Madame Blavatsky: The Mother of Modern Spirituality

The Quest for Hermes Trismegistus

Jung The Mystic

Swedenborg: An Introduction to His Life and Ideas

The Dedalus Book of Literary Suicides: Dead Letters

Politics and the Occult

Rudolf Steiner: An Introduction to His Life and Work

In Search of P. D. Ouspensky

The Dedalus Occult Reader (Ed.)

The Dedalus Book of the Occult: A Dark Muse

A Secret History of Consciousness

*Turn Off Your Mind: The Mystic Sixties and the Dark Side
of the Age of Aquarius*

Two Essays on Colin Wilson

As Gary Valentine

New York Rocker: My Life in the Blank Generation

Maurice Nicoll

FORGOTTEN TEACHER

OF THE

FOURTH WAY

Gary Lachman

Inner Traditions

Rochester, Vermont

Inner Traditions
One Park Street
Rochester, Vermont 05767
www.InnerTraditions.com

Cataloging-in-Publication Data for this title is available from the Library of Congress

ISBN 978-1-64411-991-4 (print)
ISBN 978-1-64411-992-1 (ebook)

Printed and bound in India by Replika Press Pvt. Ltd.

10 9 8 7 6 5 4 3 2 1

Text design and layout by Virginia Scott Bowman
This book was typeset in Garamond Premier Pro with Cheltenham used as the
display typeface

To send correspondence to the author of this book, mail a first-class letter to the
author c/o Inner Traditions • Bear & Company, One Park Street, Rochester, VT
05767, and we will forward the communication, or contact the author directly at
gary-lachman.com.

Scan the QR code and save 25% at InnerTraditions.com.
Browse over 2,000 titles on spirituality, the occult, ancient
mysteries, new science, holistic health, and natural medicine.

❖

For James Hamilton,
essence friend, 1945–2022

Contents

Essence and Shadow

On November 4, 1922, Maurice Nicoll, the prestigious Harley Street physician, author, and, until only recently, British lieutenant of the psychologist C. G. Jung—second only to Sigmund Freud in fame—arrived at the Prieuré des Basses Loges in the forest of Fontainebleau, just outside of Paris. With him were his young wife, his infant daughter, her nanny, and two goats. His sister-in-law had gone ahead to help prepare the way; the goats were brought along to provide milk for the child. The thirty-six-year-old Nicoll had sold his successful London practice and borrowed against the inheritance he expected from his father, the eminent journalist and political thinker William Robertson Nicoll, in order to secure a place for the family at the newly opened Institute for the Harmonious Development of Man, a center offering a unique educational experience. This center had only recently been established at the Prieuré—after misfires in Berlin and London—by the redoubtable G. I. Gurdjieff, a mysterious teacher of esoteric knowledge and uncertain origin—(was he Greek, Armenian, Russian?)—who had emerged from the chaos of a collapsed Russia, bringing a message like nothing Nicoll had encountered before. It was stark, unsentimental, at times brutal. But according to Nicoll, it was what he needed.

For years Nicoll had been searching for a doctrine that could satisfy the conflicting demands of his head and heart, his body and soul, his scientific intellect and his religious faith, his sexuality and spirituality, a tussle not unfamiliar to many. Jung had taken him some way along that path, but as Nicoll explained in what we might call a "Dear Carl" letter, when he told his mentor that his allegiance had shifted, he needed someone to *force* him there.

The man into whose hands he was placing himself and his family would do just that. Nicoll had met him only briefly—if sitting in a tense silent room for an uncomfortable time because none of those present had the courage to ask the guru a question could constitute a meeting. But it was enough for the still impressionable doctor to feel he had been in the presence of power. He was, and he would feel it soon enough.

Nicoll observed the sign at the entrance to the institute, *Sonnez fort*—"Ring loudly"—and did. Not long after, as "kitchen boy," the doctor, who as a child had sat in on conversations between his father and eminent men like Winston Churchill and Lord Asquith, in an atmosphere of literature and politics—and who Jung hoped would champion him in England—was washing hundreds of greasy dishes in cold water without soap. This, after waking up before dawn to light the burners for the Prieuré's kitchen, where his wife slaved over huge cauldrons of soup prepared for the institute's other inmates, while her sister cleaned the toilets. (The nanny it seemed had the best of it.)

Nicoll was not alone in having given up a comfortable, congenial life for what seemed to be a work camp overseen by a mad Levantine foreman. When his friend A. R. Orage, suave editor of the *New Age*, a journal of ideas that included Bernard Shaw and H. G. Wells among its contributors, turned up at the Prieuré, he was given a shovel and told to dig. He did until his back ached and he was in tears; he was also forbidden to smoke, which nearly killed him. Nicoll himself was forbidden to read. It was quite a jump from the world Nicoll had known before. It is safe to say, I think, that it was the most meaningful time in his life.

In the years to come Nicoll would try to reproduce it on more than one occasion.

Nicoll had got to Fontainebleau by way of another Russian export, the writer and journalist P. D. Ouspensky, who had abandoned his own career to follow Gurdjieff, after a long and unsuccessful "search for the miraculous" in the East. In 1921, by what must certainly have seemed a miracle, Ouspensky had been rescued from a Turkish White Russia refugee camp by an unlikely savior. This was Lady Rothermere, wife of a London newspaper baron and reader of his book *Tertium Organum*, an exhilarating work of speculative metaphysics that had become a surprise bestseller. She wanted to talk to Ouspensky and, as money was no object, had him brought to London. Ouspensky had spent the past few years in Russia under Gurdjieff's tutelage, but by the time the flood tide of revolution and civil war had deposited him and his erstwhile teacher in Constantinople—soon to be renamed Istanbul—they had gone their separate ways. Yet, the Byzantine psychohistory of the Fourth Way—as the system transmitted by Gurdjieff to Ouspensky is called—is nothing if not complicated, and the relationship between the two very different men was never as clear-cut as it may have seemed. Although separated from Gurdjieff, Ouspensky taught his ideas in London and New York until shortly before his death in 1947, which followed a series of final lectures in which he repudiated the system itself.

In late 1921 Nicoll attended a lecture by Ouspensky—delivered in a clipped, fractured English—at the Quest Society in London's Kensington Town Hall. There he heard for the first time that he, and everyone else in the room, was "asleep," was only a "machine," that he was living mechanically, and that he possessed no stable, single, unified "I," as Gurdjieff's austere doctrine insisted. Nicoll was, we could say, electrified. Not everyone was happy about these grim tidings, which seemed to offer small prospect to, as Ouspensky told them, "awaken." But Nicoll knew he had come across a knowledge unlike any he had ever suspected. He was so excited by what he heard, he rushed home to his wife, still recovering from having their first child and told her all about it, forgetting about the baby. He insisted she hear Ouspensky too. She did, and became as fervent an apostle as her husband. For the next three decades, both husband and wife became students and then teachers of "the Work," a name for the practical side of Gurdjieff and Ouspensky's demanding system.

Some of the fruits of those labors are the five volumes of Nicoll's *Psychological Commentaries on the Teaching of Gurdjieff and Ouspensky*, a collection of the weekly talks Nicoll prepared for his groups, starting in 1941 and continuing until his death in 1953. Nicoll's *Commentaries* have garnered some significant readers, among them the economist E. F. Schumacher, the philosopher Jacob Needleman, and the comedian John Cleese.* These, along with Nicoll's short exegeses on the esoteric meaning of the Gospels, *The New Man* and the unfinished *The Mark*, present his particular approach to the body of ideas and practices he learned from his years with his teachers in the Work. Another work, started early in his career but only published much later, *Living Time*, is Nicoll's attempt to understand the mysteries of time and its relation to eternity, an obsession of Ouspensky's. One of its readers was the author J. B. Priestley, who counted Nicoll and Ouspensky among those who, like himself, were "time-haunted men."

To people familiar with the Fourth Way, Nicoll presents a rather more mellow approach to what is often a very serious business. He is not the unpredictable, startling "crazy guru" that Gurdjieff is often depicted as being—although how much of this was "acting" on Gurdjieff's part is, as always with that remarkable man, unclear. He was also not the dry logician, the stern taskmaster of the Work, the "Iron Man," that

---

*See Schumacher's *A Guide for the Perplexed* and "John Cleese's Six Favorite Books," *The Week*, February 5, 2017.

Ouspensky, initially a gentle, poetic soul, became after his years with Gurdjieff.* Nor was he a flamboyant esoteric mover and shaker in the style of Ouspensky's other long-term student, J. G. Bennett, who took the Work in some rather messianic directions.[1] Nor was he like his friend Kenneth Walker, who did not set up shop as a teacher of the Work, but who produced excellent introductions to its ideas.[2] Nicoll did not present himself in any public way as a follower of the Work; he did not, as Walker and Bennett did, produce accounts of his time with Gurdjieff or Ouspensky. He kept to the background, and word about his work traveled by way of mouth; we can say that he was one of those whom I have called "secret teachers."

The persona he showed to those who did come to him—the face, as Jung would say, that he presented to the world—was that of a convivial, congenial country doctor or preacher, someone you could sit with at a pub in a way you couldn't with Gurdjieff or Ouspensky and which was something people often did. There was a soft, gentle side to Nicoll, who liked laughter and song, and who played guitar and apparently had a good voice. He was fond of practical jokes, and more than once told his followers that "serious things can only be understood through laughable things," and that the secret to "transforming situations" was to "receive them with humor, and comment on them with wit," something Nicoll displayed often.[3] He liked to drink—an occupational hazard with some in the Work—to eat, to dance, and to play.

If Gurdjieff's teaching strategy was to "shock," and Ouspensky's to raise his students' awareness by sheer mental effort, Nicoll was more likely to coax his pupils into understanding, to make a serious joke, wink, and ask if they had "caught" the message he was trying to get across. And something else a reader of the *Commentaries* will find is that Nicoll gradually introduces ideas and themes that come from outside the system, something that, as far as I understand, is *verboten* among purists.

---

*This is the subject of my book, *In Search of P. D. Ouspensky*.

Yet a reader of the *Commentaries* who knows that Nicoll started out as a follower of Jung, and who also knows Jung's ideas, will find some of them thinly veiled and in close contact with ideas that are *echt* Ouspensky or Gurdjieff. What may not be as easily recognizable is that Nicoll also introduces themes and ideas originating in the eighteenth-century Swedish scientist and spiritual savant Emanuel Swedenborg. As an author of books on Jung, Swedenborg, and Ouspensky, when reading the *Commentaries* I was surprised to find notions about the shadow and synchronicity, but also about love, wisdom, understanding, and other Swedenborgian themes turning up in them.* As a "time-haunted man" Nicoll was fascinated with the kinds of meaningful coincidences that Jung called synchronicities and that often involve a kind of precognition. And although Gurdjieff and Ouspensky frowned on the study of dreams—something Ouspensky himself had written about extensively—throughout much of his life Nicoll kept a dream diary, in which the hand of Jung and Swedenborg, another deep reader of dreams, can be found.

Adding Jung and Swedenborg, as well as other ideas coming from the Hermetic and Gnostic traditions, to his teaching of the Work may have put Nicoll beyond the "genuine" Gurdjieffian pale. As the title to this book suggests, Nicoll has in some ways been sidelined by the "purist" strain of the Gurdjieffian tradition. There is even a story that, although she commended the *Commentaries* for presenting Gurdjieff's ideas accurately, Jeanne de Salzmann, for many years following Gurdjieff's death the main carrier of his teaching, said that Nicoll's way was not the way the Work would carry on. Certainly during my own time in the Work, in New York and Los Angeles in the 1980s, some years ago indeed, Nicoll's books were read but were not considered mandatory for the course.

---

*I point this out in my article "Maurice Nicoll: Working against Time," *Quest* (Spring 2018): 24–28, theosophical.org.

Diluting the system with outside teachings may have decided this. It may have been Nicoll's emphasis on Christian themes, picking up on Gurdjieff's remark that the Work could be thought of as "Esoteric Christianity." Ouspensky himself pored over multiple translations of the Gospels in order to decipher their hidden meaning, the secret knowledge transmitted through them. It was Ouspensky's belief that the Gospels were written by men with such knowledge and for the specific purpose of waking up those who could grasp it, producing the change in consciousness that Nicoll called *metanoia*, a Greek word meaning "change of mind," but a change much greater than what we usually mean by that deceptively simple phrase. These men were agents of what Ouspensky called "the inner circle of humanity," awakened men (and one assumes women) who aided mankind—or at least some of us—in its evolution.

Or what may have exiled Nicoll to the half-life of a Fourth Way fellow traveler was the fact that, unlike Bennett, Walker, and others, he did not go to Gurdjieff following the death of Ouspensky in 1947; Gurdjieff himself would die two years later. Nicoll declined the possibility of revisiting the master, deciding that he had already learned all that he could from him. To the true believers, such a statement is a bald impossibility: one could always learn from the master, and to think that one could not was proof positive that one very much needed to do precisely that.

BOOKS ABOUT NICOLL HAVE addressed some of these issues and have presented an idea of what being a student of his was like. They have shown what it was like to live in the atmosphere of a Work environment, like those created at Tyeponds—the name of the first Work community established by Nicoll—and other places. When he started teaching the system in 1931, Nicoll soon gathered a loyal group, many of whom more or less lived with him in the "special conditions" that Nicoll, trying to recreate his experience at Gurdjieff's institute, created for them. These books, by Beryl Pogson and Samuel Copley, are essential to any understanding of Nicoll and his work, and it is curious that both books present themselves as "portraits," Pogson's *Maurice Nicoll: A Portrait* and Copley's *Portrait of a Vertical Man*.

A portrait aims at capturing the essence of its subject, and "essence" is a central Fourth Way term. In the system it is seen as what is truly one's own, what we are born with, our true self, not like our personality, which, like Jung's "persona," is a face we acquire in dealing with the world. "Essence," Nicoll told his students, comes down from the stars—an idea not entirely in line with strict Fourth Way teaching. He also believed it is what we will bring back to them.

It is understandable that such close and devoted followers of Nicoll as Pogson and Copley would present their teacher in the best light, even if such illumination at times reaches a hagiographic glow that casts hardly any shadow—an important Jungian term. It is no mystery that their portraits are not of the "warts and all" variety. That type is usually left to critics of the subject, and often enough descend into caricature, or even character assassination, gaining in effect what they lose in objectivity.

The other kind of biographical book, one that is sympathetic but critical, is the kind I am aiming at here, and which I believe I have managed to produce, with some success, in the cases of Jung, Ouspensky, Swedenborg, and other figures in the history of Western esotericism. I do not go out of my way to discover my subjects' feet of clay—often enough they are obvious—but neither do I ignore any skeletons that may be stored in their closets. In some cases this has earned me the enmity of some true believers; at least some reviews of my books suggest as much. Others have appreciated a fresh, unbuttoned look at flesh-and-blood, complex human beings who are too often presented as infallible gods.

As a figure in the history of modern Western esotericism, Nicoll deserves attention. After all, how many people had Jung, Gurdjieff, and

Ouspensky for teachers? And as a figure in the history of the Fourth Way, he is, as far as I know, unique in bringing together what he learned from these remarkable men, and combining it in subtle ways with the teachings of Swedenborg, which more and more occupied Nicoll in his last years. This would be sufficient to warrant a new study. But something else has come to light—an apt phrase in this context—that adds a whole new dimension to any understanding of Nicoll.

In Jung's psychology the part of the psyche that most often adds a new dimension to one's and others' experience of oneself is, once again, the shadow. This is a kind of dark essence, a hidden self that we do not show others, or often even ourselves, but that nevertheless exists and that we must integrate in order to mature. In the case of Nicoll, it seems that this shadow is precisely what has come to light.

In 2017, a Ph.D. candidate at Edinburgh University, John Willmett, researching the life of Nicoll, came upon a collection of papers that were in the possession of Camilla Copley, Samuel Copley's daughter. Among the papers were typescripts, manuscripts, notes, bills, and other mundane items. But what were also found were several exercise books that contained a diary Nicoll had kept over the years. These contained accounts of his dreams (mentioned earlier), thoughts, reports of everyday events, random musings, stream of consciousness gibberish, but also what appear to be odd conversations he conducted with an "inner voice," as well as some sort of visionary experiences.

This would be enough to make the diaries interesting. But what these diaries also tell us is that for several years Nicoll had engaged in what seems to have been a kind of mystical autoerotic practice, producing what an unkind critic might call the kind of visions "one has with one hand." That at least is the conclusion reached by another researcher interested in Nicoll, Jeffrey Adams, who annotated the transcription Willmett made of Nicoll's diaries. Making this knowledge public may seem like an invitation to derision and may work to undermine whatever reputation Nicoll has. A teacher of an esoteric doctrine has a difficult enough time to begin with maintaining a good reputation, without any scandal. The sort of thing the diaries reveal could overshadow Nicoll's many positive achievements. "Everyman should be allowed to have his own private life," Nicoll once told his longtime friend and fellow follower of the Fourth Way, Kenneth Walker.[4] In light of this, Nicoll's spirit, wherever it may be, may look askance at the liberties being taken with his. Nevertheless Nicoll's remaining family have approved making the material available to researchers.

There is a long tradition, in the East and West, of a kind of mystical sexuality, a sacred eroticism, that employs the powers of sexual arousal for visionary purposes. Ouspensky wrote about the transformation of consciousness induced by sex.[5] Gurdjieff taught that "it is a very big thing when the sex center works with its own energy"—there will be more about these "centers" further on.[6] Jung had a *soror mystica*, a "mystical mistress," and, according to the research of Marsha Keith Schuchard, Swedenborg practiced a kind of "sacred sexuality" aimed at maintaining the "perpetual potency" needed to induce visionary states.[7] So Nicoll is not alone in his pursuit of an eroto-mystical muse, although one may ask why he pursued her, as it were, in a closet.

Having read the one-thousand-plus pages of Nicoll's diaries, a file of which Jeffrey Adams kindly sent to me, I commend Willmett on his perseverance in transfering Nicoll's hand-written notes to a computer. It shows his commitment to the significance of his find. He is of the opinion that Nicoll's diaries are of as much importance for an understanding of his life and work as the fabled *Red Book* is for an understanding of Jung.

This may be so. Other readers and scholars will have to decide. I can say here that Nicoll's diaries are not as accessible as Jung's record of his "descent into the unconscious." Where Jung writes a dream narrative, and, in essence, tells a story complete with images, Nicoll's jottings are more often than not fragmentary, disjointed, at times indecipherable because of his use of a private code. His dream record is frequently interrupted by his interpretation of the dream, and with references to other dreams, all in a kind of shorthand. There are long, purple poetic and evocatory passages. He also at times descends into sheer verbal gobbledygook, with long spurts of punning and alliteration, not infrequently of an obscene or even scatological nature, that tried my patience more than once. Of course Nicoll wasn't writing for publication, and so he can't be blamed for giving the readers of these diaries a hard time. Most writers write rubbish that they forget to throw away; according to their critics, that includes some of their books. But one can ask what prompted Nicoll to devote time to such ramblings.

Mixed in with his dreams are Nicoll's reflections on his family, his father, his colleagues, his teachers, his work, his students, and other similar concerns, and what he has to say about them is not always polite. But a great deal of the diaries is devoted to Nicoll's preoccupation, one could even say obsession, with sex, and with the psychological, spiritual, and existential issues surrounding it. Nicoll went so far as to say that if it weren't for the Work, he most likely would have devoted his life to sex. He may have been exaggerating, but he is certainly concerned with it in these diaries.

Needless to say this is not the impression one gets from the two portraits of Nicoll that have come down to us. I don't think sex in any way turns up in either of them, certainly not in Beryl Pogson's understandably hagiographic memoir, which treats Nicoll with nothing but the utmost respect and propriety. (She was, after all, asked by his widow to write it, shortly before her own death.) And it should also be apparent that none of Nicoll's sexual ideas entered his teaching or, as far as I can tell, involved any of his students.

Copley's portrait is slightly less sanitized than Pogson's, but given that the diaries were in his daughter's possession, one can only assume they were previously in his, and that they had come into his keeping after Nicoll's death. Did Copley read them? If he did, there is no sign of it in his book. Or is there?

This is no criticism of Copley, if indeed he did know of the diaries; conceivably they could have sat in a box untouched for years. But now that they have come to light, one can't help but ask how they affect our picture of Nicoll, our new portrait of this "vertical" man? Vertical, for Nicoll, had a special meaning: it pointed to the eternal dimension of our being, rather than the horizontal dimension of what J. B. Priestley called "tick tock" time. Entering that dimension and staying there—feeling his "time-body"—was Nicoll's aim. The diaries give us an idea of how well he achieved it.

They also show us a man deeply troubled by what seems a savage self-division between his desire for the life of the spirit, the second birth promised by the esoteric message of the Gospels, and his natural, fleshly drives, inhibited by his upbringing and by what seems some obscure reticence in his own psyche. They also show us how psychologically and emotionally demanding being the son of a famous father is, and the toll this took on Nicoll's sense of self-esteem and his self-image, his picture of himself. The joyful, cheerful, convivial Nicoll, who was always up for gaiety and laughter, had a shadow side that was full of self-doubt, very low on self-esteem, eager for acceptance, uncertain of the value of his work, and burdened with the presence of what he called, "unclean thoughts," and which he wrote about in a remarkable document of the same name. These were the erotic fantasies, often of a crude, raw, "transgressive" nature, full of desire for the "forbidden," that Nicoll had entertained since his childhood, and which he may have transmuted, through some inner alchemical operation, into the elements of a mystical illumination. This document strikes me as one of the most important things Nicoll wrote. Unfortunately, as was the case with many of his projects, he did not complete it.

The diaries also show us a man who had difficulty bringing himself to work, who'd rather talk than write, who had at different times to subject himself to a strict discipline, who had problems with drink, with food, with his temper, and all the other faults and foibles that make us human. When your target is the superhuman, these stains and blemishes of the soul stand out in stark relief. When you spend much time contemplating the light, your shadow grows behind you. What follows is a look at this vertical man, Maurice Nicoll, and at the depths and other dimensions that open up as we explore the shape of his time-body—that is, his life.

1

Unclean Thoughts

In the Fourth Way a distinction is made between what is called the "law of accident" and the "law of fate."[1] Each can rule one's life. The majority of people—"sleeping humanity"—live under the law of accident, or so Gurdjieff and Ouspensky tell us. The few who have struggled to awaken live under the law of fate, or at least have a better chance of doing so. We can say that the aim of the Fourth Way is to move its followers from one law to the other. Laws play an important part in Gurdjieff and Ouspensky's system, and there will be more of them to follow.

The law of accident refers to whatever conditions one finds oneself in, the general melee of life, the chaos, contingency, and chance that are the norm. Under this law, things happen haphazardly, with no aim or direction, "one damn thing after another," and we are pushed and pulled by a variety of forces, appetites, and desires. Under the law of accident, life leads nowhere. Under the law of accident, one can lead a full life with much success and yet, toward its end, wonder what it was all about. Readers familiar with Leo Tolstoy's story "The Death of Ivan Ilych" will have an idea of how devastating this can be.

The law of fate is different. It relates to our essence, which, as mentioned, is what is truly ourselves. Our personality is like a weather vane, moved this way and that by events. Our essence has a kind of intuitive sense of direction that may be aided by what is known as a "magnetic center," a kind of inbuilt homing device that causes us to look for the kind of knowledge and experiences necessary for our spiritual growth.[2] We can say that our magnetic center always points north, whichever way the winds of events may blow. In that sense, for people with a magnetic center, their weather vane becomes a compass.

Most people lack a magnetic center, and so never come across the knowledge that will indeed set them free. This means that most people live under the law of accident, taking each day as it comes, chopping and changing as needed to satisfy the appetites and desires that make up their lives, moving this way and that as events dictate. But if someone has a magnetic center, it can lead them to what in the Work are called "C influences." These are influences coming from outside life, that are not generated by the perpetual process of "getting and spending," the unavoidable pressures to live, which make up what are called "A influences." C influences arise from the "inner circle of humanity," and are cast into life where they are diluted into "B influences." When Jesus said that man does not live by bread alone, he may have had C influences in mind—or so the esoteric interpretation would have it.

C influences have their origin in "higher mind," the small circle of conscious humanity, such as those Ouspensky believed wrote the Gospels, and are thrown into the "general vortex of life," appearing in culture: in art, literature, religion.[3] A finely tuned magnetic center responds to the emanations sent out by the inner circle of humanity. If its attraction is powerful enough, it can lead to someone who can provide instruction, offering C influences undiluted, which can be transmitted only orally, from teacher to student. In esoteric tradition, this is the way the true teaching is taught.

Related to the law of fate is the notion of a "time-body," although the idea derives from Ouspensky and is not part of the system proper. This is the shape or form of one's entire life, from birth to death, what we could call our "four-dimensional" being, the *linga sharira* in Theosophical terminology.[4] Most of us live in a perpetual present, the here and now of the moment. Yes, we have memories and knowledge of our past, and have a sense of the future, although our attitude toward these poles changes over time. When we are young, the future seems an immense field of promise; as we get older, this field shrinks while our unalterable past accumulates. If we are conscious of our time-body, we would be aware of different moments in our life as clearly and as distinctly as we are of the present. Nicoll once told a student he hadn't seen in some time, that if they were both aware of their time-bodies, they would be able to pick up their conversation from where they had left it the last time they met. When drowning people see their "whole life flash before them," it is their time-body.

If we are aware of our time-body, we could feel our life as a whole, see its pattern, its *necessity*. And presumably having "worked on ourselves"—otherwise we would not be aware of our time-body—we would also have passed from the law of accident to that of fate. We could see how our lives were the working out of an invisible order, a teleology as definite as that of the acorn on its way to becoming an oak.

If we add to this another Ouspenskian trope, that of "eternal recurrence," the somewhat austere notion that our lives recur over and over, with little, if any, variation—think of it as reincarnating into exactly the same life—we arrive at the conceivable situation in which one could remember one's last recurrence, one's time-body as a whole, and know in advance the working out of the law of fate.

IT WAS SOMETHING ALONG these lines, I believe, that was in Maurice Nicoll's mind when he told Beryl Pogson that his time-body was "ever present to him." He could, she wrote, "see the way in which he was prepared during his early life for his destiny," that of becoming a teacher of the Work.[5] All that had happened to him in the years before he met

Ouspensky and then Gurdjieff counted for him "only as a necessary period of preparation for his work as transmitter of the teaching he received from them."[6]

Not all spiritual teachers necessarily see the period leading up to the beginning of their ministry as one unalterably zeroing in on that preeminent moment, although a sufficient number of them do. And in Nicoll's case that preparatory period included some powerful experiences, such as his encounters with Jung, which are difficult to relegate to the sideline. But most followers of spiritual teachers do see their teacher in this way. Somehow, the idea that their teacher spent his or her formative years as the rest of us do—exploring possibilities, making mistakes, taking detours, and entering dead ends—seems to undermine his or her authority. It makes them all too human and suggests that if things had been different, they might not have become a spiritual teacher at all. But because *you* were fated to become their student, they must have been fated to become teachers, and so that destiny must be with them from the start.

For Nicoll and for Pogson, it was Nicoll's fate to become her teacher, just as it was hers to become his student. Nicoll himself believed that he and some of his students had known each other in past lives—and if eternal recurrence is the case, they would have had to—and that they had found themselves together again. How much of this belief he shared with his group is unclear. It may have formed part of the "real teaching" that, as Pogson says, is always oral and secret.[7]

An "oral and secret" teaching sounds awfully close to how the system understands C influence. One might look at this as suggesting that Nicoll was fated to become a transmitter of C influence, which in the Fourth Way by definition means a member of the inner circle of conscious humanity.

Did Nicoll himself ever say as much? No. At least I can't think of any remarks of his that could be read in this way. He did not exhibit the self-aggrandizement or egotism that can be found in some teachers suffering from what Jung called "inflation," when their egos are enlarged by injections of archetypal power coming from the collective uncon-scious. What Jung may have thought of Gurdjieff, who had no qualms about boasting of his own unique achievements and qualifications, must be left to the imagination, although it is clear he was not happy about Nicoll's defection to a new teacher. According to Samuel Copley, Nicoll "did not suffer from the 'Heir Apparent' syndrome, which appears to have affected others who have written about their relationship" with Gurdjieff. Yet Nicoll did say that he thought he was the "subtype" of Gurdjieff, in contrast to Ouspensky's dry, professorial manner, and so in a sense he was in some way emulating the master.[8]

Yet Nicoll was actually quite the opposite of the spiritual mega-lomaniac. His problem was not one of becoming puffed up with self-importance and a sense of mystical destiny. It was more one of emptying out, of self-effacement and humility to what seems an inhibiting degree.

Why do I say this? Perhaps this may help. When I came across a reference by Nicoll to Franz Kafka's novel *The Castle* as an example of Work literature, I was at first surprised.[9] Early in his career, Nicoll analyzed the poet Edwin Muir, who translated the novel. Nicoll wasn't given to reading novels, and what he did read was more or less what used to be called middlebrow; this at least is the impression one gets from Pogson's book and the jottings about his reading that turn up here and there in his diaries. His favourite book was Boswell's *Life of Samuel Johnson*, a choice that suggests Nicoll's own preference for talking over writing.

Kafka's writings, like those of Samuel Beckett, have always struck me as exhibiting the height of paralysis, if I can put it this way. They both have a genius for it. The cramped, claustrophobic atmosphere of Kafka's world, with an anonymous authority issuing arbitrary edicts, leaving his characters the helpless victims of some inscrutable law, seems the furthest thing from the vivid sense of freedom and unknown pos-sibilities, of the immediate potentials of life, that I associate with "self-remembering," the awakened state of consciousness aimed at by the Work. In Kafka's universe, life has no unknown possibilities, except those of frustration, guilt, and suffering; Kafka seems never to have experienced the "all is good" insight that is the essence of any "awakening." We know he rejected his life work, and we have his friend Max Brod to thank for disobeying his request and not destroying his manuscripts.

Why would Nicoll feel an affinity with a writer who felt defeated by life from the start? But then I remembered that Gurdjieff taught a variant of Plato's myth of the cave. He said that we are in prison, something the ancient Gnostics, of whom Nicoll was fond, said as well. What does a man in prison want to do? Escape. Is this why Gurdjieff told Nicoll that esotericism, that is, the system, was a "rope?" Did he know that what Nicoll wanted most was *a way out*? Of what? In order to answer that question, we must turn to the time-body of Maurice Nicoll and see what it has to tell us.

HENRY MORRIS DUNLOP NICOLL, to give his full name, was born not long after midnight on July 19, 1884, in the Free Church Manse in Kelso, Scotland. Astrologically, this made him a Cancer. Such characters are known for their compassion, sensitivity, intuition, and optimism, traits not difficult to see in Nicoll. But they are also given to moodiness and a certain dreaminess. Nicoll was ruled by the Moon, which accounts for his intuition, but also by Neptune, which makes for a strong imagination and an attraction to all things spiritual. In fact, the imagination of such characters is so strong, that reality can often pale by comparison. The danger here is that one can resort to the imagination in order to escape from reality. Whether these reflections on Nicoll's general astrological makeup, taken at random from different sources, are in any way accurate, is debatable. But the friction between imagination and reality will certainly play a large part in his life.

Nicoll's father was the Reverend William Robertson Nicoll (1851–1923), of the Presbyterian Scottish Free Church, who was knighted in 1909 by King Edward VII, presumably for his literary work but more likely because of his long support for the Liberal Party. His mother, who would die when Nicoll was only ten, was Isa Dunlop. In later years he would speak to his students of her beauty and gentleness. Nicoll inherited the aesthetic, artistic side of his character from his mother; she was a musician and taught him to play the violin. His father remarried a few years after Nicoll's mother's death. Nicoll liked his stepmother, Catharine Pollard, although in later years he would voice some reservations about the company she kept and the kind of life they led, but the loss of his mother at an early age not surprisingly affected him deeply. It may be that the pursuit of a kind of "inner goddess," at least through the avenue of his imagination, that occupied Nicoll for many years, as evidenced in the "dream diaries," had its roots in the loss of this source of unconditional acceptance. That Nicoll needed such acceptance—who doesn't?—and that he didn't receive it, at least not in sufficient quantities, supplies the emotional and psychological backdrop to his early life.

Nicoll did not have much chance to get to know the world he was born into, although in later years he would return to the manse for holidays. (Nicoll's father had bought the place for *his* father, who had been the minister before him, so it stayed in the family.) From a description of the place, it sounds rather like the kind of environment in which Nicoll would spend his formative years. It was a tiny, cozy house crammed top to bottom with books.[10] Collecting books was an obsession of Rev. Harry Nicoll, William's father, and the 17,000 volumes that filled the Manse were bought at the expense of his children's health. The "Chinese obsession with paper" that William Nicoll saw in his father meant that he and his siblings practically starved; everything went to books, and there was no money left for food. Maurice Nicoll did not starve—hardly—but whether by design or accident, the house he would grow up in, although considerably larger, was similarly furnished.

A year and a half after Nicoll's birth, his father had to give up the ministry because of health. The tuberculosis that would eventually kill him was already a problem, and no doubt early malnutrition was a likely factor. He was advised to move south, and he and the family did. They first went to Dawlish on the Devon coast, then to Upper Norwood, in South London. Finally the Nicolls landed in Hampstead, North London, once a green, leafy, hilly suburb that has since been absorbed by the city.

It's curious that someone suffering a lung complaint would move to London for their health; by the 1950s, the pollution levels in London were so high that it gained the nickname "the big smoke." But in the 1880s, Hampstead would have been practically the countryside. A walk today on Hampstead Heath, a large area of uncultivated land, with fields of heather, gorse, and wild grass, over which the poet Keats and the painter Constable wandered, can give an idea of what Nicoll's new neighbourhood would have been like when the family arrived in 1889 and moved into their new home, Bay Tree Lodge, Frognal.* This was the gaslit London of Sherlock Holmes, Jack the Ripper, Madame Blavatsky, and *Dr. Jekyll and Mr. Hyde*. In fact, for a brief time, Robert Louis Stevenson, who wrote the classic tale of man's twin but warring souls, lived not far from the Nicoll home.[11]

Nicoll's father's exile from the ministry and move to London proved an excellent decision. He lived for several more years than may

---

*Interestingly enough, I live not far from Nicoll's old home, and pass it often on my walks. Hampstead has several connections with the Work. A. R. Orage is buried in Hampstead parish churchyard, a short walk from Nicoll's old address; his grave is marked by a stone with an enneagram, an important Work symbol, and a passage from the *Bhagavad Gita*, carved by the artist Eric Gill. A house in Hampstead would have been the setting for Gurdjieff's institute, had the Home Office allowed him to establish it in London; it did not. Nicoll's first groups met in a dance studio on Finchley Road, again very near to where I live. Fate? Accident?

have been expected had he remained in Scotland and continued eating a Scottish diet, or so at least Nicoll thought.[12] But he also started a new career, one that brought more success and prestige than he could have dreamed of had he remained in Kelso. William Robertson Nicoll had a literary bent, something his son and daughter—Nicoll's older sister Constance—would show evidence of too. But although according to Nicoll his father "looked like a poet," and even "was a poet"—as were his sisters, who wrote poetry—the Presbyterianism he grew up in had made its mark; it had, in fact, "ruined" him, as it would also damage Nicoll.[13] William's literary talent was commandeered by his faith, and he would become one of the most influential religious and political thinkers and analysts of his time. With help from the publisher Hodder and Stoughton, Nicoll established the *British Weekly*. He was also the editor of the *Exposition* and the *Bookman*, and it was not long before he became one of the most famous men of letters of his day—a literary animal that, in our overly specialized times, seems to have become extinct, or is at least on its way there.

Nicoll's earliest memories though, were not of the literary and political world of his father, although to be sure, this would soon come to dominate life at Bay Tree Lodge. Nicoll's teacher, Ouspensky, claimed to have remarkably vivid memories of his earliest days; he could, he said, recall a trip down the Moscow River when he was three, with the boats gliding by, the smell of tar, the hills, deep forest, and a monastery. Ouspensky believed that young children could recall their previous recurrence, and that as they grow older these memories fade. Ouspensky himself tells us that when his mother took him to school for the first time, she got lost in the long corridors trying to find the headmaster's office. Neither of them had been in the building before, but Ouspensky told her the way, even mentioning some steps leading to a window from which they could see the office. He was correct. On another occasion, when he was even younger, Ouspensky was taken to some site outside of Moscow; he said that it wasn't as it had been on his previous visit, some years earlier. Memory was important to Ouspensky, even before he had heard of "self-remembering," the essential aim of the Fourth Way.

One result of Ouspensky's memories of his past recurrence—if indeed this is what his remarkably vivid memories were—is that, as he told Nicoll, he "saw what life was like" from early on. Ouspensky told Nicoll that as a child, he didn't have the same interests as other children, and that a kind of seriousness about life was with him from the start. Nicoll, who didn't remember his past recurrence, was a more "normal" child, and so it took him longer to see what "life was like."

And what was life like? To Ouspensky, life in general was made up of "obvious absurdities" that for some reason no one noticed, except himself and his sister; the phrase came from a picture book called *Obvious Absurdities* that the two would look at as children, with illustrations of a cart with square wheels, or a man carrying a house on his back. What struck the young Ouspensky and stayed with him throughout his life is that these picture-book absurdities were just like ordinary things in everyday life, which was made up of similar absurdities. His later experiences "only strengthened this conviction."[14] With such a perspective, it isn't surprising that Ouspensky would be attracted to Gurdjieff's teaching, which promised a way of getting free of these absurdities, of getting out of "life."*

Nicoll might not have remembered his previous recurrence and so not known as early as Ouspensky what "life was like." But soon enough the feeling would come to him that, if nothing else, it was a trap and he needed to escape from it. Throughout his life, "life" was something about which Nicoll would remain wary and uncertain.

The early memories he did have were of a gentler character. He told Beryl Pogson that one of his earliest memories was of going fishing

---

*Another version of "life" for Ouspensky comes from Mother Russia. In writing about eternal recurrence, he speaks of people for whom "absolute repetition is inevitable." These are people of *byt*, a Russian word meaning "deeply-rooted, petrified, routine life." Ouspensky, *A New Model of the Universe*, 422.

while on holiday at the Old Manse. Nicoll also remembered a sun-dew plant that ate flies—a Venus flytrap. He had memories of mosses and asphodels, and of drawing and painting these; along with music, Nicoll's knack for illustration was something else that he inherited from his mother. There was also a velvet suit and a pair of scratchy socks.

Yet he was not to be spared the cruel lesson we all must face: that whatever it may be, life isn't fair. A boy who lived next door so enjoyed a toy steam engine of Nicoll's that when the unsuspecting innocent allowed him to play with it, he wouldn't give it back. According to Pogson he took the injustice stoically. "All through his life," she wrote, "he was to lose his possessions continually, and to accept each loss with-out taking action."[15]

This attitude of detachment is not one we usually associate with young children, and one suspects Nicoll reacted with a bit more indig-nation. But in later life he was known for giving away presents prac-tically as soon as he received them; how the givers felt about this is unclear. And an increasing interest in coincidences or what the Austrian biologist Paul Kammerer, a "collector of coincidences," called "seriality," when things of a like character, unconnected in any causal way, seemed to happen in a "cluster," led him to note when he would lose similar kinds of things in a row.[16]

But most of Nicoll's early memories centered around his father and the important people who made up his friends, colleagues, and acquaintances. William Robertson Nicoll seems to have been a highly dominant character, what we would call an alpha male. The admiration and respect that Nicoll felt for him were sincere, but they came with an admixture of "awe amounting to fear."[17] Nicoll found his father and his prestigious friends—Winston Churchill, Lloyd George, Lord Asquith among them—overpowering, so much so that he developed a stammer. He would later overcome it with help from Jung, but for much of his early life it was a handicap.

His father would hold court from his bedroom, where he would dictate to his secretaries while still in bed, surrounded by newspapers, manuscripts, and cats. The family was always worried that Father would set the house on fire; he was an inveterate chain-smoker, and there was always concern that, with so much paper around—"haystacks" of it—a forgotten cigarette would spark a blaze. Another important room in the house was the library, which was on the top floor and from whose windows one could see the Surrey Hills to the south. Here William carried on the family tradition and gathered a collection of some 25,000 books, part of which were 100 editions of the Greek New Testament, inherited from his father. Whatever professional exegetes may think of Nicoll's reading of the Gospels, he certainly had a solid grounding in the literature.

Part of his father's prolific output included the highly popular "Claudius Clear" articles, relating his latest readings, interests, and other musings. But William Robertson Nicoll's metier was religion, the Scots Presbyterianism that according to his son ruined him. He wrote an enormous amount about it. I suspect it is little read these days, and what is of central interest here is that Nicoll Senior's approach to scripture was the exact opposite of the one his son would spend decades trying to express. Suffice it to say that Nicoll's father took the word of the Bible literally, as many fundamentalists do today. Nicoll would reject this and argue that the true meaning of the Gospels can only be found by reading them symbolically, that is, as an expression of esoteric knowledge. In many ways, and even against his own desires, the son echoed the father; after all, the *Psychological Commentaries* can be seen as Fourth Way sermons. But in this regard, they were antipodes.

But such subtleties would come later. The first effect the religion of his father had on Nicoll was to put in him the fear of the devil. This took precedent over the love of God. Nicoll spent much of his childhood in fear. "I was brought up," he told his group, "with the sense that only the conviction of sin was important."[18] For him, religion meant sin, and the awareness of one's propensity for it, and the watchfulness necessary to avoid it. Nicoll grew to hate this kind of religion. Yet is it too much to see here a pre-echo of another kind of watchfulness that would occupy Nicoll in later life, when sin became, as it is in the original Greek, "missing the mark," that is, the failure to achieve the change of mind, or *metanoia*, that was needed to awaken in the esoteric sense? Perhaps. But what this awareness of his sinfulness induced in the young Maurice was a deep sense of his unworthiness, or, as we would say today, low self-esteem.

Late in life he told his group at Great Amwell House that "Sitting in Church as a boy and looking around at the congregation, I used to think that I did not really want to go heaven with such worthy people." They may belong there, but not his sinful self. But he knew that if he remained a Christian he would have to accompany them past the pearly gates.[19] This created a "difficulty" in his mind, "one of those strange early difficulties one is aware of perhaps all of one's life but does not mention."

The difficulty, which Nicoll does not explain directly, may have been the dim recognition that if Christianity meant what he saw in the "good faces" of the congregation, then either he did not belong with them, or it *was not real Christianity*,[20] which naturally raises the question of what "real" Christianity is. If Christ's teachings were not about what he saw going on in church, then what *were* they about? Many people brought up under the puritanism that Nicoll endured recover from its effects by rejecting religion all together. Nicoll instead wanted to escape the false religion of his father and to discover what Christ was really saying.

The young Nicoll took his religion seriously. It "really mattered" to him.[21] This seriousness later led him to say that he didn't claim to be a Christian, because one becomes a Christian by being "born of the spirit," and Nicoll must have felt that he hadn't had this second birth yet, although it was the aim of his esoteric practice and interpretation of the Gospels.[22] Early on he had a profound moment when he realized he held a deep love for Christ.[23] At an Easter service, hearing the story of Peter's betrayal, Nicoll felt a powerful conviction that he would never betray or deny Christ, no matter what, a vow that would be sorely tested and briefly found wanting by his experiences in World War I. As it was, the Sunday services he attended as a boy were for him such an ordeal that in later life Sundays would always seem dreary and depressing.

We can guess the source of Nicoll's sense of unworthiness from an experience he had on the first day of his Latin class, at the college preparatory school he attended in Hampstead. His age at the time is uncertain; the context suggests that he was around nine or ten years old. Because of his stutter, Nicoll hated to be asked questions in class, and this time was no exception. It seemed as if the headmaster zeroed in on him. The headmaster looked at him and asked, "What is sex?"

A tough enough question for anyone at any age, but for the young Nicoll it was a shock. The headmaster, of course, meant what is sex, that is, gender, grammatically, but the young boy, new to the class and conscious of his stammer, didn't know that. Pogson writes that Nicoll told his group that at that moment he thought the headmaster had "seen into his young, dark, and secret soul" and that the awe and terror of the moment "always remained in his mind."[24] Nicoll managed to control himself and master his stammer enough to answer honestly that he didn't know. Some of his classmates giggled and the headmaster moved on, but for Nicoll it was a moment that stayed with him. Why?

What did he think the headmaster might see in his "young, dark, and secret soul" that so terrified him? One suggestion is offered by the essay found among the collection of papers containing his dream diaries, mentioned in the introduction. "Unclean Thoughts," written sometime after Nicoll had set up in practice, is a remarkable document. In it Nicoll penetrates into some of the deepest and darkest aspects of not only his own sexuality, which was a lifelong concern, but, to my mind, of male sexuality itself. "Ever since I was a boy," Nicoll writes, "my mind has been occupied with what uncleanness meant."[25] He writes that he heard things being said: "She is a clean woman," or "Although he is queer in his ideas he is quite clean," or "There is nothing unclean about him," or "He is a clean man."[26] (Conversely we have all heard of "dirty old men.") Such things made him wonder if he was clean, and he soon came to the conclusion that he was not. Why?

Because he found himself "full of unclean thoughts," and he couldn't understand other people "because I fancied they never had unclean thoughts as I had continually," and so they must have been different from him. They were "fine and wholesome and clean," and this left him with "a constant feeling that I was strange and unusual and not normal," a notion not unfamiliar to adolescents, and which Poe captures in his poem "Alone," and which as a young reader I found echoed in Kafka's *Metamorphosis*.[27]

Nicoll's unclean thoughts "always centered on women," and were always involved with his feeling for religion. How much this was so for the young boy asked a question about the place of gender in Latin is debatable, but it was certainly true of his older self. Nicoll discovered that he felt an "excessive impulse at times toward religion," that he couldn't understand, except that it seemed that the "unclean thoughts and the religious impulse seemed the same thing." Although this seemed "quite wrong and impossible," nevertheless, it was so. Nicoll writes: "The cravings I felt arising from my unclean thoughts and desires and the tremendous momentary impulse toward a life other than conventional life, that I felt strongly as religion, seemed inextricably interwoven and hopelessly contradictory."[28]

This last sentence needs to be read a few times and thoroughly assimilated, as it is the key to the inner struggle Nicoll engaged in for decades, between the demands of his sexuality and his aspirations to the "second birth." It suggests to me that what Nicoll is talking about here is the desire for the forbidden, or, as we might say today, the "transgressive," that is a powerful element in male sexual desire. As Nicoll rightly points out, this is in some strange way related to the mystical or religious impulse, the "tremendous momentary impulse" toward some way of living other than "conventional life." How is this so? We will return to this question later. Suffice it to say here that the mystical and the sexual impulses are both attracted to the "unknown" and the possibility of penetrating it. And it can be said that the power and *certainty* of the sexual orgasm is closely related to the same sense of "Of course!" that accompanies mystical insight. Both raise us above our ordinary selves, our limited egos, as we are temporarily gripped by some power seemingly outside us.

BUT NOT EVERYTHING WAS DARK and terrifying in the Nicoll household. There was Connie, his sister, described as "very clever, a real booklover," with whom he played and whom he scared with a kind of mechanical spider he had made. Nicoll was handy with mechanical things and with the new power, electricity, that was just then coming into common use. He had a den in which he carried out experiments with electricity and chemicals, and he rigged electric bells throughout the house; he was also good at photography and mending toys. Like Gurdjieff, the young Nicoll was a handy Mr. Fix-It, and this talent came to good use when he set up his Work communities where, again like Gurdjieff, he would set out to repair broken machines: his students.

This hands-on technical talent was lost on his father; he described Nicoll at thirteen as "stupid" and "slow at his lessons." To his stepmother he was "handsome, smiling, friendly . . . small for his age and not over strong." He was a "dear boy," though, mostly because he was obedient. If told he could ride his bicycle only up to a certain spot, Maurice would do just that, and turn around.[29] In later life, Nicoll regretted that he hadn't crossed the line more often. Eventually he would, but it would take some time.

The most important moment of Nicoll's early life again happened in school, and we can say that it set him on his life's work. At thirteen, Nicoll starting attending Aldenham, a boarding school not far from Hampstead. Here the musical side of his character that he inherited from his mother came out. He sang in the choir, and was a soloist at St. Albans Cathedral. But a single moment at the new school marked a break with everything that had gone before. Later, telling his group about his loathing for the kind of Christianity he was being forced to swallow, the "gloomy business" about sin and continence, the weight of guilt, which induced in him a state of perpetual fear and anxiety, he shared with them the moment he first felt free of the "power of external life," the vortex of events he wished to escape.[30]

It happened in class while discussing the parables in the Gospels. Nicoll remembered the setting vividly: it was a moment of "self-remembering." The headmaster sat in front of the class, and Nicoll recalled his "scholarly, thin face, the nervous habits of twitching his mouth and jerking his hands."[31] The young Nicoll was put off by what he knew of the Old Testament, which presented a "violent, jealous, evil, accusing" God. The New Testament was less violent, but it's meaning was in no way clearer. Nicoll could not understand what Christ was saying in the parables, and it seemed that no one else knew or even cared to know. Summoning up the same effort he had made to answer his Latin teacher, Nicoll controlled his stammer and asked the headmaster what one of the parables meant. The answer, Nicoll wrote, "was so confused that I actually experienced my first moment of consciousness."[32] This consisted of the sudden insight that *no one knew anything*," that is, anything of any real value. Certainly not the headmaster. They were in exactly the same position as he was. Even worse: in "Unclean Thoughts," Nicoll remarks that "someone must know," yet he discovered that a "droopingly moustached, large, bland, tweedy" uncle with a lisp, thought to be some kind of authority, was even more ignorant than he was.[33] Nicoll said that it was from that moment of insight into the ignorance of others, that he began to think for himself.*

The second revelation to come from this insight was that "no one knew what I was thinking," which must have come as some relief to a boy worried that the "unclean thoughts" lurking in his "dark and secret soul" were apparent to Latin headmasters. The liberating effect of knowing that his headmaster knew nothing, convinced Nicoll that the revulsion he felt toward his father's religion was justified. It also established in him a conviction that would stay throughout his life: that in essence, our true life, that is our inner one, is invisible.[34] For Nicoll this meant that our real life is not in outer events, but in inner states. This "authentic perception" of "the only source of real knowledge" would lay in Nicoll's soul like a seed, germinating over many years.

It's unclear if Nicoll engaged in any discussions with his father about his insight. One suspects that if he had, William Robertson Nicoll would have rejected his son's doubts over the meaning of the Gospels, and would have corrected him about the character of the God of the Old Testament. There is a parallel here with Jung's relation with his father, who was a Protestant clergyman, as Nicoll's father had been,

---

*Nicoll's moment of awakening has parallels with similar moments experienced by his teachers Jung and Ouspensky. In *Memories, Dreams, Reflections*, Jung writes of walking to school one day when "suddenly for a single moment I had the overwhelming impression of having just emerged from a dense cloud. I knew at once: now I am *myself*!" This insight awakened Jung to his own will, his own "authority" (49). In *A New Model of the Universe*, Ouspensky writes of the effect of grasping the principle of the lever had on him. Oddly enough, it happens in his Latin class. Instead of his lesson, he is reading a book on physics, and as he understands it, "horizons infinitely remote and incredibly beautiful stand revealed" (3). When the teacher sees what he is reading, he confiscates the book. But Ouspensky consoles himself with the insight that the teacher is "all made up of large and small levers" (4). It is interesting that in both Nicoll's and Ouspensky's case, the awakening involved a teacher whose authority is reduced by being seen as "mechanical." In Ouspensky's case, the teacher is made up of levers, and in Nicoll's he specifically draws notice to the headmaster's "nervous habit of twitching his mouth and jerking his hands," precisely the sort of unconscious "automatic" behavior Gurdjieff would point out to his students.

and the clashes the two had over religion. Jung's increasingly inquiring mind was met by his father's bald refusal to debate any religious issue, banking on a tenacious grip on a faith that in truth he no longer had. We might also mention that Swedenborg's father, who was eventually made a bishop, also held very strict and literal views on Scripture, and held himself up as an exemplar of the true Christian life, with an unselfconsciousness that for our sensibilities can come across as self-parody. Swedenborg's father gave his children copies of his 1,012-page-long autobiography as instruction books on how to live a spotless life. Nicoll's father seems not to have been quite so satisfied with himself as a paragon of virtue, although he did subscribe to the Protestant work ethic—which his son also accepted—and did suggest that his worldly success was a sign of approval from higher up. If people did well in this life, it surely must be a sign that they are doing something right. In different ways, Nicoll, Jung, and Swedenborg had to overcome the faith of their fathers in order to discover a faith that each would devote their lives to communicating to their followers.

IN 1903, NICOLL HEADED to Caius College, Cambridge, with thoughts of becoming an engineer. He had rejected his father's designs on a life for him in religion or politics; his natural scientific bent was coming out. His father had asked Kenneth Walker, a neighbor in Frognal already at Caius, to look after his son. Walker and Nicoll would remain friends for life, under both the law of accident, and the law of fate. Walker was often at Bay Tree Lodge, and he spent some holidays at the Old Manse. When Nicoll changed his allegiance from Jung to the Work, one of the first people he took along with him was Walker.

Walker was born in Hampstead in 1882, and so was two years older than Nicoll. He would outlive him as well, dying in 1966. Of the two, he seems the more sober and stable. He was also a prolific writer, one of the first to make known his involvement with the Work, once the ban on public disclosure had lifted with the death of Gurdjieff. At this time he was charged with being a kind of older brother on the lookout for Nicoll's benefit. Nicoll's step-grandfather had said it was cause for gratitude that Nicoll had "escaped the dangers attendant upon youthful life," more proof if needed that Nicoll's inner world was invisible to others.[35] It was also ironic, because once let loose in Cambridge, Nicoll became something of a party animal. Walker did his best to keep him on the straight and narrow, but the "gaiety" and "high spirits" that Nicoll craved meant that his buttoned-down teetotal chaperone was often left behind.

For all his later interest in human psychology, higher states of consciousness, and the true meaning of Scripture, in his university days Nicoll seemed intent on having a good time. This love of parties would carry on into his Work life. Along with accounts of his eroto-mystical practices, in his diaries Nicoll noted dozens of evenings spent drinking, singing, dancing, and generally having a "gay" time, often into the wee hours, so many that I began to think of his group as a Fourth Way version of J. B. Priestley's *The Good Companions*. At Caius Nicoll sought out "those who would give him the gay companionship, which was a necessity for him all his life."[36] These were "simple, jovial types," who were fond of "drinking and laughter."[37] Nicoll did not mix with intellectuals or literary people, put off perhaps by life with father. He was also keen on the horses, a pastime that later he and some of his flock would engage in. Nicoll cut a jaunty figure, rolling into Newmarket in his "steam car," to catch the races; he would also take it on trips to London to see the family.

One gets an idea of Nicoll's "high merriment" from a story his sister tells. At one point Nicoll carried on a debate in the *Times* about bell ringing, taking both sides, a literary joke worthy of G. K. Chesterton. One prank sounds worthy of Gurdjieff himself. One of Nicoll's Cambridge wags handed one end of a tape measure to a passer-by, asking if he could hold it, then turned a corner and did the same with

another.[38] Yet one can't help but ask if Nicoll's high spirits were a coun-
ter to his dark thoughts, or if the kind of youthful pranks he got up to
can tell us anything about his later interest in the ancient image of the
puer aeternus, the "eternal boy" of Greek mythology, the Peter Pan who
never grows up.

Yet, although his academic work took a back seat to his social life,
Nicoll did manage to score a first in natural science. He told Samuel
Copley about a method he had devised for passing his exams. It consisted of being able to grasp the central points of a lesson, its essence
one might say, rather than trying to memorize by rote.[39] Whatever his
method, Nicoll earned a result that pleased his father, who set high
store by achievement and excellence, virtues Nicoll himself would value
highly. As his father disliked slackers and any sign of waste—a temperament rooted in the austerities of his upbringing—so too would Nicoll
keep his later charges on their toes, seeing hard work as a virtue in itself.

Of hard work there was plenty. After Cambridge, Nicoll studied at
St. Bartholomew's Hospital in London from 1906 to 1910, where his
method of passing exams was put to the test. "Medical exams," he told
Pogson, "were a nightmare" that leave a man "without a mind." Nicoll
was never one to swallow dogma whole, whether religious or medical.
He told Pogson that one "needs to be able to see through and not accept
blindly all that is said and claimed."[40] In later years, Nicoll would be
quite vocal in his criticism of the state of medicine and how it was practiced, a forthrightness that earned not a few criticisms itself. In 1910 he
qualified and could practice.

But Nicoll was yet to settle into a single groove, if indeed he ever
did. In 1910, Nicoll went to visit his sister who was recovering from an
illness at her mother-in-law's house in Boscombe, on England's south-
ern coast. While there they decided to try to write a novel, just for fun.
Naturally, it would be filled with gaiety and charm. As children they
had written and edited a family newspaper, with stories of local life
and such.

It turned out to be a very good idea. For one thing, the effort involved cured Nicoll's sister of her illness. In a way, this was rather like the "work therapy" Jung had employed as a doctor at Zürich's Burghölzli Clinic. But more than that, the book they wrote turned out to be a great success. *Lord Richard in the Pantry* (1911), written under the pseudonym "Martin Swayne" that Nicoll would use for other work, became a bestseller. It was made into a stage production and a film, although no print of the film exists today and it is on the British Film Institute's list of "most wanted" films.[41] The plot involves an aristocrat fallen on hard times who has to take employment as a butler; it sounds reminiscent of the American screwball comedy *My Man Godfrey* (1936) with William Powell and Carole Lombard.

Not wanting to depend on their father's prestige for their book to secure a publisher, they avoided Hodder and Stoughton, who published their father's works, and took it to Methuen. They and Methuen were glad they did. Not only were book sales good, for a time the stage production was a West End triumph—London's equivalent to a Broadway hit—and if my calculations are correct, they were receiving the equivalent in today's money of £1,200 a week in royalties, nearly $1,700 at the time of writing. This was another occasion when Nicoll's father was pleased with his children's work. It was also around this time that Nicoll met Maud Hoffman, an American Shakespearean actress, with whom he collaborated on a stage version of the book that eventually wasn't used.

Hoffman was an enthusiastic Theosophist, a member of the Theosophical Society, founded by the redoubtable Madame Blavatsky in New York in 1875. Blavatsky died in London in 1891, and the society was then led by Annie Besant, the former suffragette, "planned parenthood" proponent, and mistress of Bernard Shaw. Through Hoffman, Nicoll met Mabel Collins, author of the spiritual classic *Light on the Path* and onetime housemate of Blavatsky herself, although their association ended acrimoniously.[42] Nicoll would wind up sharing a house with Hoffmann and his friend and brief workmate—in the Gurdjieffian sense—James Young on prestigious Harley Street. And it was through Hoffman that Nicoll would first step over the boundary from the law of accident to that of fate. But that was in the future.

Now what lay before him was a voyage to Buenos Aires, where he would meet Walker, who was working there as the resident medical officer at a British hospital. Nicoll was on his way to join him, as ship's surgeon, a job that Arthur Conan Doyle, with whom "Martin Swayne" would share pages of the popular *Strand* magazine, had done himself.[43] Conan Doyle's voyage was to the Arctic, and he passed the time harpooning whales and gazing at the sublimity of endless ice; Nicoll says that on his voyage, going in the opposite direction, most of the time he played poker. What he recalled most of his adventures on the pampas was staying at Walker's sister's ranch, and getting his fastidious friend to experiment with eating armadillo.

By the time Nicoll returned from his South American adventure, he had a considerable amount of "life," whatever it may be, under his belt. But as the law of fate would have it, he would only really begin to live when "the tremendous momentary impulse toward a life other than conventional life," that combined the dark delight of his "unclean thoughts," with his desire for mystical illumination and spiritual rebirth, was satisfied.

2

The Sins of the Father

When Nicoll returned from Buenos Aires, he asked his father if he could finance a trip to Europe, so that he could study the new psychology that was emerging in Vienna and Zürich. His "versatile mind" that could "never limit itself to one field alone," was bored with general practice.[1] The opportunity he had to practice medicine on his ocean voyages was minimal, but even if it had been more extensive one suspects Nicoll would have still been dissatisfied with a career as general practitioner, which indeed he turned out to be. But perhaps more to the point, Nicoll's own fascination with his "unclean thoughts" may have led him to want to explore his inner world more seriously. The dream diaries found among his papers suggest as much. If so, he wouldn't have been alone. By the time he packed his bags and left London for the Continent, Sigmund Freud and C. G. Jung were on their way to becoming household names, with Alfred Adler not far behind, and psychoanalysis was all the rage.

This isn't to say that deciding on a career in psychoanalysis wasn't considered something of a risk. The strange ideas coming out of Vienna, full of sex and other unmentionable things, at least in polite society, did not appeal to Nicoll's father's generation, and Nicoll would soon be caught up in the battle between the old school of psychiatric medicine and the new. But Nicoll could be persuasive, and it's to his father's credit that he agreed to his son's wish. It is ironic that one result of the trip would be Nicoll's partial liberation from the person who made it possible.

The person responsible for introducing Freud to the English speaking world was Ernest Jones, a Welsh neurologist who had first come upon Freud's work in 1905, introduced to it by the surgeon Wilfred Trotter. Although he is little read today, at one time Trotter was famous for his work on crowd psychology and the "herd instinct," popularized in books like *Instincts of the Herd in Peace and War* (1916); his name appears a few times in Nicoll's diaries. Jones read Freud's account of the Dora case, in the original German, and was impressed by it. It led him to believe that there was "a man in Vienna who actually listened to every word his patients said to him."[2] Oddly enough this was even more true of someone who became for Jones a personal *bête noire* and enemy of his new true faith, Carl Gustav Jung.

At the time Jones was reading Freud, Jung was working at the Burghözli Clinic in Zürich, where he listened to schizophrenic patients' ramblings, convinced there was some message mixed in among the word salad. It was out of this attentiveness that his idea of the "collective unconscious," an inner reservoir of psychic images to which we all have access in our dreams, emerged.[3] While Freud's experience was limited to the neurotic patients who visited Bergasse 19, Jung was up close and personal with patients suffering from schizophrenia, catatonia, and other more debilitating mental disorders. In the strange streams of unconsciousness he encountered every day with his patients, Jung began to see links to the mythologies of the past, portals into the history of the human psyche, beyond the merely familial skeletons in the individual's personal unconscious that were Freud's area of expertise.

In 1907, Jones met Jung at a conference in Amsterdam and was impressed by the Swiss doctor's charm and personal strength. He was also impressed by his account of his recent visit to Freud in Vienna.

On that occasion, their first meeting, the two talked for thirteen hours straight, Jung unleashing a torrent of ideas and observations, Freud patiently organizing and clarifying the welter of Jung's thoughts. At that point Jung, the younger man by some twenty years, was happy to sit at the master's feet. In a few years, however, he would no longer be so comfortable in that position.

Jones spent some time with Jung at the Burghözli and then soon sought out the master himself. He met Freud in 1908 at the first congress of the International Psychoanalysis Association, in Salzburg, organized by the indefatigable Jung. That same year, however, Jones had to leave England for Canada, after a scandal in which he was accused of inappropriate behavior with some underage girls he was treating. The details are murky. Jones was acquitted and later claimed that the girls had projected their sexual feelings onto him. This is a complaint known as the "transference," that more than one psychoanalyst, Jung included, has had to contend with; at the time, Jung himself was involved in his own scandalous affair with Sabina Spielrein.[4] While in Canada Jones became convinced of the truth of psychoanalysis, and from there he became "the most energetic of Freud's advocates, first in North America, then in England, in the end everywhere."[5] In 1912, Jones's *Papers on Psychoanalysis* became the first psychoanalytical work in the English language.

Jones's energetic advocacy of Freud's ideas would contribute to a breakup among the psychoanalytic elders that almost put an end to the movement in its infancy. By the time Nicoll headed to Europe, in 1911, Freud and Jung were on their way to severing their relationship, and the growing psychoanalytic fold was fracturing into warring factions. One of the agents of this fracture was Jones, who took it upon himself to protect the master from any criticism and his work from any deviation. When Nicoll arrived on the Continent, in search of psychoanalytic enlightenment, the biggest deviationist around was Jung, who painfully and with much reluctance was nevertheless making known that

Freud's theory of the sexual basis of all neuroses simply didn't cover all the bases. This was a point he made with as much delay and camouflage as possible in his first major work, *The Psychology of the Unconscious* (1912).* (Alfred Adler had already made the same observation, and by 1911 had broken away, defecting before Freud had a chance to excommunicate him.) To Jones this was heresy, plain and simple, and had to be stopped.†

Nicoll would not be caught up in the psychoanalytical civil war that was about to break out until he returned to England, and the battle lines would be drawn, with Jones the strategist who was more royal than the king, determined to crush Jung. The account of his grand tour of Europe's psychological centers that Nicoll gave to his students sounds like more of a holiday than hard work. He often talked of his time in Vienna, where he studied with some of Freud's students but not the master himself. Yet what he related were his memories of the riding school he attended and the "many happy hours" he passed with Georgette, a Viennese girl who taught him German.

Sehr gemütlich, no doubt: Georgette remained a pleasant memory for Nicoll, and she would later reappear in his dreams and also in the post. During World War II, Georgette wrote begging letters, telling of the scarcity in Vienna, and asking Nicoll for help. As synchronicity would have it, her husband's measurements just happened to be the same as Nicoll's; one suspects Nicoll had filled out since last they met. Suits that languished unworn were quickly wrapped up and dispatched to enemy territory, evidence that Nicoll felt no enmity toward the Boche, and also that his father's dictums about waste had hit home.

---

*Jung worked on and revised the book many times over many years. It is now published as *Symbols of Transformation.*

†Jung's opinion of Jones was not particularly flattering, but then he didn't think much of the circle around Freud. In a letter to Freud in July 1908, he calls Jones an "enigma," unsure whether "there is more in him than meets the eye, or nothing at all," an "intellectual liar," with "too much adulation on one side, too much opportunism on the other."[6]

When he wasn't falling off his horse at the Spanish School—an equestrian establishment with a tradition of dressage going back centuries—or dallying with the delightful Georgette, Nicoll did manage to study. He did in Berlin—with whom is unclear. And he did in Paris, where Freud and Jung had studied before him, Freud with the great Jean-Martin Charcot, and Jung with Charcot's equally illustrious student Pierre Janet. We don't know if Nicoll attended Janet's lectures at the Collège de France, but it is likely. If he did, he may have heard ideas that he may have believed originated with Freud, but which Janet had promoted some years before Freud had made them popular—insofar as Freud was popular at that time.

Janet coined the terms "subconscious" and "dissociation," and was the first psychiatrist to suggest that past experiences could be the source of current mental problems. He did pioneering work in multiple personality, hypnosis, and hysteria. Janet believed that the psyche was capable of "splitting," of breaking up into separate, autonomous segments, like icebergs breaking off a great ice shelf and floating freely in the sea. These autonomous chunks of psychic material can become so independent that in severe cases of what we can call "reality withdrawal," they become individual personalities. One of Janet's central ideas is what he called the "reality function," an individual's psychic "grip" on the world. Janet saw that schizophrenia was essentially a "scattering" of attention, an inability to focus the mind, to concentrate, a kind of splintering of thought. We recognize something of the sort when we say of an empty-headed individual that he is "not all there." Where? *There*, "in his head," where his mind should be focused.

Janet called this act of focusing "psychological tension," and he believed that mental illness results when an individual has allowed this tension to go slack, through a lack of use of the will. It was Eugene Bleuler, Jung's superior at the Burghözli, who developed the idea of work therapy, getting his patients to take some responsibility for their upkeep, and make use of their will; I mentioned earlier that a form of this seemed to have helped Nicoll's sister over her illness, when the two decided to write *Lord Richard in the Pantry*. Jung would later prescribe creative work as therapy for his clients.

Janet saw that if the patient was faced by a challenge that *forced* him to "pull himself together" and reestablish his "psychological tension," then contact with reality can be made and that this was always beneficial. Jung was influenced by Janet's ideas, but given Nicoll's later tutelage under Gurdjieff, we can see how the idea of a "challenge" forcing an individual to "get a grip"—to, in other words, face reality and not avoid it—would make good psychological sense. In a very real sense, we are all in the position of the patients who came to Janet, Jung, even Nicoll himself. We are all "neurasthenic," as William James said, subject to "the habit of inferiority to our full self," like the patients James treated who found it impossible to take any action, even as simple as getting out of bed, until he *forced* them to, using what he called the "bullying treatment."[7] When they finally did act, after much distress, the "contracted self" opened up, and suddenly realized it was much bigger than it believed, and contained possibilities it wasn't aware of. But it isn't only such individuals who suffer from this constriction of the self. We are all to some extent "partial personalities;" we all, as W. B. Yeats wrote, want to "complete our partial mind."[8] And Yeats, like James, knew that this often requires "some sort of violence."[9] As Nicoll will find, the "bullying treatment" he would receive under Gurdjieff's care was aimed at providing just that.

THE HEIGHT OF NICOLL'S EUROPEAN adventure was his encounter with Jung. He said it was "the first important event of his life."[10] This sounds a similar note to Jung's own estimate of Freud on their first meeting. "Freud," Jung said, "was the first man of real importance I had encountered."[11] For both Jung and Nicoll, these meetings marked a new stage in their lives. Nicoll said that his time in Zürich with Jung marked the end of his youth. He was twenty-eight.

At the time of Nicoll's visit, Jung was going through a difficult patch, and soon enough things would get worse. It had taken enormous efforts to complete *The Psychology of the Unconscious*, the book that made unambiguous his disagreement with Freud, especially about the usefulness of the sexual theory as a kind of all-purpose answer to the mysteries of the psyche. The first, less offensive half of the book had already been published in the *Psychoanalytical Yearbook* in 1911. It was written in more or less appropriate Freudian terms, and covered new but not yet threatening ground, but the master knew that it was only the overture to the main event. Its one major deviation from the party line was to reject the idea of the libido as a specifically sexual energy or drive, that, as Freud argued, is sublimated into other currents: aesthetic, religious, spiritual, and so on. Jung instead believed there was one basic energy, an *élan vital*, as Henri Bergson called it, that aims at different targets. Sex is one of them, but so are things of a higher, spiritual character. We have a religious or spiritual drive just as we have a sexual one—or one for food and drink, for that matter. The "life force," or "interest"—a term Nicoll would use—propels us toward the satisfaction of those appetites. This was not how Freud saw it. With him, it was sex, period.

Emma Jung had tried to pour oil over the soon-to-be-troubled waters by writing to Freud directly, asking him to be favorable in his response to Jung's book; she had already consulted him about her husband's infidelities. He offered faint praise, saying what he had read so far was good and suggested that his esteemed colleague would surely produce something much better. His esteemed colleague didn't, at least not in the way that Freud had meant. When Jung finally summoned the courage and will to finish the book, he knew his days as the heir apparent of the psychoanalytic movement, as Freud had hoped he would be, were numbered.

What was the offense? In a nutshell, where Freud took the Oedipus complex as evidence of a desire in the psyche for literal incest with the mother—engendering the fear and hatred of the father who prevents this—Jung argued that it instead should be understood symbolically, as an expression of a hunger for spiritual rebirth, the "second birth" that Nicoll understood as the true meaning of Christ's message. The mother, in this case, is not the actual person from whose womb we emerge, but the Great Mother, the unconscious, which for Jung was increasingly looking like something far more vast and profound than the personal unconscious, full of provincial family matters, stored via repression, that Freud would have. It was the matrix of all life, the *anima mundi* of the ancients, the soul of the world.

At the word spiritual, Freud's nostrils would have flared, as he sniffed out the true, sexual root of such nonsense. Jung could not accept Freud's reductionism, which was the dominant tone of the nineteenth-century science on which Freud's thought was based. The central idea was this: reduce the higher to the lower, whether it was spirituality to sex, or human consciousness to atoms. It still holds today. When Jung told Freud that if the sexual theory was true, then all culture becomes a mere façade, a charade, masking sublimated sexual desire, Freud shook his head and said stoically, "Yes, so it is, and that is just a curse of fate against which we are powerless to contend."[12] It was this belief that led to Freud's late work, *Civilization and Its Discontents* (1930), which argues that we are inescapably neurotic, because civilization makes us so. It was this belief that led Freud and his many epigones to "explain" works of art as sublimated expressions of "free smearing," or literature as motivated by the desire to get admirers in the sack.[13] Which is not to say that no artists or writers use their talents for base or purely personal ends, just that such aims or motivations are not the essence of culture. Freud, however, would have none of it.

Even more explosive were arguments the two had over "occult" phenomena, what we would call the paranormal. The public Freud was a confirmed skeptic, although in private he did accept some forms of telepathy and, like Jung, was fascinated with the kinds of coincidences Jung called synchronicities.[14] Jung grew up with the occult all around him. His mother was given to speaking in strange voices, and as a child her job was to shoo away the spirits who were trying to distract her father, the Reverend Samuel Preiswerk, from writing his sermons. She also attended séances and so did Jung. On one visit to 19 Bergasse, Jung and Freud got into a heated argument about the reality of the spirits. Freud was dismissive, and as Jung became more frustrated, he felt his diaphragm begin to glow, as if it was becoming red hot. Suddenly a loud bang exploded in Freud's bookcase; both of them jumped up, thinking it was about to fall. "There," Jung said, "that is an example of a so-called catalytic exteriorization phenomenon," which was Jung's long-winded circumlocution for a poltergeist or "noisy spirit." "Bosh" replied Freud, to which Jung said it was not and promptly announced that another such bang would happen immediately. It did. From that moment, Jung said that Freud became wary of him, and that he seemed to have taken the experience as a kind of personal affront.[15]

Jung had voiced his reservations about Freud's sexual dogma from the start, and had early on spoken of what he called the "prospective tendencies" of the psyche, its forward-looking character. This suggested to Jung that the psyche was motivated not only by causal forces operating from *behind,* as it were—instincts, appetites—but *purposes* drawing it forward. In other words, the unconscious was purposive, it had an aim. These prospective tendencies would eventually become for Jung what he called "individuation," the process by which "one becomes who one is," that is, a true individual, differentiated from the mass, dominated neither by collective forces without (society) or unconscious forces within (the archetypes).

ONE PERSON WHO WANTED to individuate just then was Nicoll. And the force that he wanted to free himself from was his father. He had been a good boy for long enough; now it was time to go past that point he should have trespassed against on his bicycle long ago. To say that Nicoll was afraid of his father is not to judge him or his father, but merely to state what Nicoll himself would later make clear to his students and what Jung would have picked up early on in their conversation. Nicoll told his students that he always felt "fear" and a "lack of confidence" in the presence of his father; the physical manifestation of this was the stammer that expressed his sense of "inner restraint."[16] It is curious that in later life, Nicoll made his greatest impact as a speaker, or rather, talker; that is, not as an orator but as a partner in a kind of Socratic dialogue, carried on, more times than not, at the village pub. But is it too much to suggest that in later life his *writing* took on a kind of stammer, with many starts and stops and much hesitation, and great effort needed to complete a book? The trouble he had bringing together the material making up *The New Man*, an important but slim work, would suggest as much.

Jung had written on the subject of the father's impact on the psychology of the individual. The title of the work, "The Significance of the Father in the Destiny of the Individual" (1909), says it all, and if it doesn't, the Latin tag Jung put at the heading brings it home. *Ducunt volentum fata, nolentem trahunt*: "The Fates lead the willing; the unwilling they drag." For the ancients, the Fates were the offspring of Zeus and Themis, the goddess of justice, and their edicts were final. They wove man's destiny, and even the gods could not prevail against their decisions. For us, they are the neuroses we carry around in our heads. And of those neuroses, ones pertaining to the father, Jung tells us, echoing Freud, "are of overwhelming importance" to one's life.[17]

For Jung, the father represents the archetype of masculine power; he provides the model and energy needed to break away from the seductive embrace of the Great Mother, the warm, buoyant, but also restrictive waters of the undifferentiated unconscious. Some actual mothers, and not just the archetypes, may smother their son with love, emasculating him, preventing him from cutting the umbilical cord and apron strings, and facing life on his own. Some sons may wish to remain a *puer aeternus*, an eternal child, the Peter Pan who never grows up. But each of us faces the same challenge in our own psyches. Life is hard. Freud was not fully wrong when he placed the "reality principle" against the "pleasure principle." It isn't difficult to guess which one is more attractive to most of us. Floating in the warm, ouroboric embrace of the unconscious is a lot more pleasant than facing the harsh edges of a difficult world. But staying in those buoyant amniotic waters is tantamount to psychic death, or at least castration. So the father kicks us out and forces us to face reality. And not only that but to master it, with any luck.

But this doesn't always happen. And when life confronts us with "too great an obstacle," with a task too unpleasant, Jung writes, "we draw back," and the energy needed to face the challenge flows backward along an "infantile channel," dredging up memories and patterns of our childhood. In a word, we regress, and react to the obstacle in ways that we have long ago jettisoned as inadequate. Life presents us with disappointments we must overcome. Not everyone does. "He who has missed the happiness of woman's love," Jung writes, "falls back, as a substitute, upon some gushing friendship, upon masturbation, upon religiosity; should he be neurotic he plunges still further back into conditions of childhood which have never been forsaken."[18] The rest of the paper relates case studies of various neuroses in which the patient's early relationship to the father, seen in terms of Freud's psychosexual theory, is revealed to be paramount. Just as the Fates drive men to their destinies, one's early psychosexual orientation toward one's parents lays out the path of one's life. Toward the paper's end Jung arrives at a summary: "*in essence our life's fate is identical with the fate of our sexuality.*"[19]

Nietzsche said something along the same lines when, in *Beyond Good and Evil*, he wrote: "The degree and kind of a man's sexuality reaches up into the topmost summit of his spirit."[20] This insight into the total contribution of sexuality to the formation of character—and character, we know, is fate, as Heraclitus said long ago—will be a necessary guide when we look at Nicoll's diaries.

THE FATHER, THEN, IS AN IMPOSING, dominating figure in everyone's life, at least in terms of our psychic development. In Nicoll's case this was doubly so. The picture we get of William Robertson Nicoll is of an old-school *paterfamilias*, given to treating his family with a strict, unsentimental discipline, and holding them up to stringent standards of thrift and efficiency, with high expectations of productivity. He could be "harsh, dominating, and overpowering," and one suspects he issued orders to his children as he did to his secretaries.[21] As a public intellectual, he was accustomed to being listened to and having his opinion respected. He stood for tradition, what today would be called the "patriarchy." He was capable of "violent anger," as later Nicoll would be, and did not care to be contradicted.

More knowledge about his private life, especially his treatment of his wives, is needed, but even with what we know, we can see that Nicoll's father displayed at least some of the characteristics of a psychological profile known as the "Right Man."[22] The Right Man is so-called because he is always right, always knows better, and is uninterested in the opinions of others, character flaws that Nicoll would berate himself for in later life. Full-on Right Men are given to violence and to a tyrannical rule of their family, particularly their wives, and are capable of murder if their judgment is contravened. William Nicoll wasn't of this sort, but the pressure of being his son must have been considerable. When he told his group that "it was a very great handicap to be the son of a famous father," Nicoll spoke from experience.[23] He would later advise those of his students who had children to keep them free of "parental tyranny." Nicoll apparently followed this wisdom himself, having a hands-off relationship with his daughter, although one suspects this left her mother, or at least the nanny, with a very hands-on one.

We don't know exactly what Jung said to Nicoll, but we do know the effect it had on him. It cured him of his stammer. This was the visible sign that he had been freed from the psychological domination of his father that he had lived under for many years.[24] Whatever Jung told Nicoll, it broke the hold that Nicoll's fear of his father had on him.

Nicoll returned from the Continent with new self-confidence, with a renewed sense of the "I" he had felt when the insight that his New Testament headmaster knew nothing had come to him, and when he realized for the first time that he was in truth invisible, that his real life was his inner one. He was beginning to feel, as he so much wanted to, a "man among men." Yet the liberation he had reached through his conversations with Jung was only partial. Nicoll's father would remain a dominant figure, certainly in his son's psyche. And as his students would say in later years, as he got older Nicoll began to resemble his father, and he would behave in ways that were like him, too. More than one of his students admitted to being afraid of Nicoll. Nicoll told his group that he was unlike his father, the very antithesis of him.[25] Yet the apple doesn't fall far from the tree, and how free of his father's shadow Nicoll actually became is debatable. Jung later said that the most crucial psychic influence on children is the unlived life of their parents. How much, if at all, this was true in Nicoll's case is an open question.

HOWEVER MUCH NICOLL WAS PSYCHICALLY freed from his father, in other ways he was still dependent on him. One was financially. Out of gratitude for the year abroad he had financed, Nicoll accepted his father's offer of a house in Golders Green, north of Hampstead in one of the new garden suburbs where he could set up a practice. His heart really wasn't in it, but he had little choice. Nicoll's whimsical side came out when he insisted on having a frieze of Noah's ark and its animals painted in his consulting room. The ark would become an important symbol for him and for his friend Kenneth Walker, who wrote a children's book

about it. For both it would symbolize the safety they found in the esoteric teaching that protected them from the floodwaters of history.

Nicoll shared his practice with a friend, Gordon Moore. The
demands were light, and in his free time Nicoll began to write stories
under his pseudonym Martin Swayne. With the success of *Lord Richard
in the Pantry*, Nicoll had produced some light comedies, *The Sporting
Instinct* (1912) and *Cupid Goes North* (1913), but neither were a hit. Yet
his "versatile mind" which couldn't limit itself to "one field alone" was
not satisfied with waiting for patients to knock on his door, and for a
time he was a regular contributor to the *Strand* magazine. The *Strand*
was famous for its accounts of the world's first consulting detective,
Conan Doyle's Sherlock Holmes. Other contributors numbered the
novelists Arnold Bennett, H. Rider Haggard, and Talbot Mundy, the
last two, like Nicoll, having an interest in mysticism.

Nicoll contributed several stories to the *Strand*, some of which
appeared in later anthologies.[26] It's unclear if he signed them Martin
Swayne in order to profit from whatever exposure his pseudonym garnered from the success of *Lord Richard*, or if he thought it unseemly
for a doctor to write fiction, or if he wanted to avoid any connection
to his father. Or, simply, if he liked being someone else for a while.
What I've read of Nicoll's fiction shows him as inventive and able to
tell a story. He tended toward tales with a bizarre angle. One, "Life
Like," is about a director who captures people to serve as prey in his
wild animal films. Another, "A Sense of the Future," concerns an
investor who has a vision of a coming oil shortage, a theme that would
go over well with today's concerns about fossil fuels and renewable
energy. Nicoll continued to contribute to the *Strand* for several years;
later, when he had begun teaching the Work, he submitted some stories to some magazines, but they were rejected. We will look at his science fiction novel, *The Blue Germ,* further on. Another novel, *Pelican
Hotel*, about time travel, recurrence, and an attempt to change the
past, was left unfinished; the outbreak of World War II, which Nicoll

in some way wanted to prevent by writing it, making it redundant.

Even with his writing, Nicoll found he had time on his hands. He joined Dr. Hugh Crichton-Miller who was then working at Bowden House in Harrow-on-the-Hill, a nursing home specializing in nervous diseases, which he founded in 1912. Like Nicoll, Crichton-Miller was a student of the "new psychology." In 1920 he would found the Tavistock Clinic, where both Jung and Nicoll would lecture. His specialty was hypnotism, about which he wrote a book, and he became a staunch supporter and longtime friend of Jung. Yet even collaborating with an esteemed colleague didn't satisfy Nicoll's restless spirit. He was also out of sympathy with using hypnosis, which was part of the treatment at Bowden House. Freud had worked with it, and of course Janet and Charcot had astounded their colleagues with the spectacular results they had achieved with their hypnotic techniques. But Nicoll found it too exhausting and unreliable.

He had applied some of what he had learned on his trip to some of his cases. But it was still hit or miss, and the self-confidence he had brought back from Zürich had fairly soon become an awareness of his "inadequacy" and the urgent need to "get a better grip of things." Among the things on which he needed to improve his grip was himself. And he could only get a grip on *that* by "going through the process oneself that one is constantly putting others through."[27] That is, by being analyzed. He needed to go back to Zürich and to see Jung again.

Yet Nicoll's reasons for returning to Jung so soon after coming back to England were more than professional, the need to keep his "brass plate bright," which he no doubt hoped would convince his father that a second trip was worth the investment. They were even more than personal. In the letter to his parents thanking them for the money, he speaks of his "line of work," that is, Jung's psychology, in something just short of messianic tones. It is, he says, a "very extraordinary thing, so completely remarkable and curious that one finds it difficult to talk about and quite impossible to explain."[28] This reminds us of the "difficulty created in his mind," by his youthful sense of alienation from his congregation at church. "It is," Nicoll goes on, "an experience and not a teachable thing," something with which Jung would agree, and something that Nicoll will also feel about Gurdjieff's system. If everyone had this experience—of undergoing a Jungian analysis and experiencing a living, breathing unconscious—there would be, he informed his conservative God-fearing parents, a "complete social turnabout," that would be nothing short of an "impulse" toward a "universal newness" in the same way that Christianity had produced such an impulse. (Jung himself felt something of the sort, although he thought more along pagan than Christian lines.[29])

Yet the link with Christ's glad tidings is made even stronger. Nicoll explains that he is convinced that Jung's psychology will produce this "newness," precisely because it concerns itself with "the last place that a man would look for such an impulse," that is, in the rejected realms of the unconscious, rather as the stone that was rejected—scorned, ridiculed—became the cornerstone.[30] Nicoll said this was his "confession of faith," and he could not have thought that his father would not have got the hint. "Know thyself" was his motto, and he was on his way to doing just that.

Someone else who was knowing himself just then was Jung. He had in fact been forced to. By the time Nicoll wrote to his parents from Zürich, updating them on his journey, telling them that he was "too lazy to make plans yet"—a sign of problems to come—Jung had tumbled down more than one rabbit hole following his breakup with Freud. Nicoll told his parents that he had found "an instrument that is of comforting value in the direction of one's own affairs" as well as that of his patients, that is, dreams. For Jung, that instrument had got quite out of hand. In October 1913, on the train from Zürich to Schaffhausen, a journey of little more than an hour, Jung looked out the window, and was surprised by what he saw. Shocked is more like it. Rather than the familiar scenery, Jung saw an immense wave covering Europe, a flood reaching from the North Sea to the Alps. Bodies and debris floated in the churning waters that soon turned to blood. The vision lasted most of Jung's journey and by the time he reached Schaffhausen he was worried that he was losing his mind.

Other visions assailed Jung. The publication of *The Psychology of the Unconscious* had turned the widening seams in his relation with Freud into fissures, but Jung's friendship with his erstwhile mentor and his standing within the psychoanalytical community were not the only things that were cracking up. Jung was himself. Like Nicoll, for much of his life, Jung had felt like an outsider, and once again he found himself cast out and alone. The movement that he had worked relentlessly to establish had turned against him. He was no longer the crown prince that Freud had primed to inherit his throne; now he was the "brutal and sanctimonious" Jung, blackballed by former colleagues and friends. By April 1914, shortly before Nicoll arrived, Jung had resigned as president of the International Psychoanalytical Association, thereby making his departure from Freud's camp official. His exit had been facilitated and indeed planned by one man, Ernest Jones.

Jones had heard Jung speak of the "prospective tendencies" of the unconscious once too often, and he had taken it upon himself to nip those tendencies in the bud, or at least to make sure that any prospecting they did took place outside of psychoanalysis. When he returned from his ignominious exile in Canada, Jones approached Freud and suggested that he form a "secret committee," whose task it would be to ensure that Freud's teachings remained pure and unadulterated—a concern with what we might call "ideological cleansing."* The most offending adulterer at the time was Jung—in a more than ideological sense.†

---

*Freud was delighted with the idea. He especially liked the notion of "a secret council composed of the best and most trustworthy among our men," a kind of psychoanalytical Knights of the Round Table. Their task would be to examine the desire to "depart from any of the fundamental tenets of psychoanalytical theory." This sounds rather like a self-imposed form of testing for "unconscious bias" or any deviationist tendencies. Peter Gay, *Freud: A Life for Our Time*, 229–30.

†Jung had by this time started his long relationship with his *soror mystica* Toni Wolff. See my *Jung the Mystic*, 94–95.

Jones took steps to segregate Jung and his followers so that their contribution to conferences, journals, yearbooks, and any other avenue of psychoanalytic dissemination would be seriously limited. Jung held on, but
eventually the pressure to leave was too great, and he gave up. He was
strong and could take a lot of punishment, but the emotional turmoil
threw him. Depending on your perspective, the crisis opened Jung's
psyche to the archetypes of the collective unconscious, who began to
pay him visits at all hours, or he had a psychotic breakdown—if, indeed,
there is much difference between the two.

Jones was as energetic a psychoanalytic mover and shaker as Jung
had once been, and in fact still was; it was only with great reluctance
that Jung resigned as editor of the movement's yearbook a year before
giving up its presidency. On his return from Toronto, Jones had organized a small band of Freud's English followers; in November 1913, he
could tell the master that the "London Psychoanalytical Society" was
up and running. Among its nine members were Nicoll, David Eder, and
William Mackenzie. Eder translated early works of Jung and Freud, and
he would be among those interested in psychoanalysis who attended
Ouspensky's lectures. Mackenzie was a doctor whose work focused on
public health; he wrote an introduction to Eder's translation of Freud's
short popular work, *On Dreams*. Eventually Nicoll and the others would
form the "Jung rump" that Jones would work tirelessly to exorcise from
what would become, following the interruption of World War I, the
100 percent *echt* Freudian British Psychoanalytical Society.

Jung was in a highly stressed and embattled state, with incursions
coming in all directions, from without and within, when his young
British disciple arrived to consult him. How much Jung spoke with
Nicoll about his own psychic turmoil is unknown. But we do know that
he did speak with him about dreams, and especially about one in particular. Nicoll told Jung of a dream he had had of his father holding a rifle
and a bullet with Nicoll's name on it, and that this dream had made
him angry.[31] The symbolism here is not too difficult to decipher. Years

later Nicoll told his group how Jung interpreted the dream. It showed, Jung said, that Nicoll didn't understand his father. Nicoll needed to see him objectively. "You must begin to understand all the difficulties your father had in bringing you up," Jung told him; by that time Jung himself was a *paterfamilias* in his own right. Jung asked "How would you have liked to bring up yourself?" a question that effected a state of what Gurdjieff would call "external considering" in Nicoll, when we forget about our own needs and desires and try to see things from another's perspective. Apparently through Jung's help, Nicoll was able to see his father objectively, to detach himself from his infantile reactions. But even more important for Nicoll's career as a Jungian psychologist, he had discovered the "instrument of comforting value," that would help him in his work with his patients and himself. He had discovered dreams.

We will look at Nicoll's book, *Dream Psychology* (1917), further on. Suffice it to say here that it holds a place of importance in Jung's reception in the English-speaking world similar to that which Ernest Jones's *Papers on Psychoanalysis* holds for Freud's. For Jung and for Nicoll, the most important thing about dreams are the "prospective tendencies" that so troubled Freud and Jones. Where Freud saw the unconscious as a nasty cellar into which we throw a lot of emotional rubbish, which creeps back into our awareness in our dreams, and the analyst as a kind of dustman come to clean out the psychic trash, Jung instead saw the unconscious as containing, in a latent state, the possibilities of our future psychological development. And it was in the strange language of dreams that our fate, our destiny, could be read.

IN THE MEANTIME, Nicoll was absorbing all he could from his time with Jung. In a letter to his parents, he spelled out how he saw the immediate future. He was not looking forward to returning to Bowden, where he and Crichton-Miller would be taking on another partner. He was also, as mentioned, unhappy with using hypnotism. He didn't see himself as running a sanatorium, but wanted to pursue "more illuminating directions." Exactly what those were was not clear. His strategy was to just "work quietly . . . for a year or two" and then perhaps to push out "feelers in the journals and in reading papers before outside societies."[32] Jung had been helpful in this regard.

Nicoll's assurances to his parents suggest he had a vague, general idea of what lay ahead for himself for the rest of 1914. And like many notions of the immediate future held at the time, these promising possibilities would suddenly be blown away by a stiff wind coming from the east. On June 28, 1914, Archduke Franz Ferdinand of Austria and his wife, the Duchess of Hohenberg, had been shot dead in Sarajevo, Bosnia. Their assassin was Gavrilo Princip, a Bosnian Serb, Yugoslavian nationalist, and member of the secret society known as the Black Hand. For weeks everyone in Austria, Russia, Germany, England, and France, as well as many other places, had been holding their breath waiting to see what would happen. A little more than a month later, they exhaled. The guns of August were firing, and Europe, and then the world, was at war.

Nicoll reacted to the news patriotically. He immediately enlisted, and even got some of his "better patients" to do the same, thinking it "would do them good," perhaps intuiting the benefits the "bullying treatment" they would receive might have on them.[33] Nicoll seemed to have been caught up in the initial jubilation with which many in England greeted the declaration of war. For many it promised to be a fantastic outing. There was the sense that it would "clear the air" and dispel a sense of ennui and apathy that had come over Europe in the early twentieth century. We can get an idea of this feeling from Rupert Brooke's poem "Peace," in which the poet thanks God "who has matched us with his hour," and "wakened us from sleeping"—a rather different perspective on "wakefulness" and war than the one Gurdjieff would present. The young men going off to the conflict were "as swimmers into cleanness leaping / Glad from a world grown old, and cold, and weary."[34] Weary of a sense of pointlessness, perhaps, which the discipline and challenge of war would dispel. Many who went off to the battle thinking it would be something of a lark were very likely feeling the effect that a sense of purpose has of energizing the will—remember Janet?—and of tightening our "psychological tension" and increasing our "grip" on reality. This is why philosophers like Nietzsche, who knew the importance of the will, could praise war, not for its bloodshed—Nietzsche was a vehement anti-militarist—but for its invigorating effect on the spirit.

From our perspective in the third decade of the twenty-first century, we can see the outbreak of World War I as the true end of the nineteenth century; certainly after the war, the world was not the same, and the optimism and sense of progress that had informed the nineteenth century had turned into the kind of barren spiritual landscape depicted in T. S. Eliot's *The Waste Land*. Indeed, it was precisely that barren landscape that would lead many to Gurdjieff and Ouspensky.

At the moment though, Nicoll was eager to go. "These blighters must be smashed," Nicoll told his father from his station in Limerick, en route to the "cleanness." This was one occasion when father and son felt the same. William Nicoll was an enthusiastic supporter of the war, which he saw as a holy cause and into which he threw all the rhetoric he could muster. He had "worked indefatigably to secure victory for his country."[35] As his biographer made clear, to William Nicoll, a Christian patriot, "nothing else seriously mattered." The war had showed him his calling. His existence as a journalist was nothing but preparation for it—as his son's existence prior to becoming a teacher of the Work had been for him. The war was righteous and necessary, and by God they would win.

Someone who experienced a paradoxical relief at the outbreak of the war was Jung. It was relief not in the sense that Rupert Brooke or Nicoll felt, as an excuse for high spirits and a release from lethargy and indecision but in the sense that it assured him that he wasn't going mad. The visions, portents, and premonitions that had invaded his waking consciousness and filled his dreams the past several months were not, he decided, evidence that the good doctor would soon be joining his ex-patients at the Burghözli. No. They were precognitive experiences of the war, which had now become a reality. And although Switzerland was neutral, Jung would spend much of the war as the Commandant de la Région Anglaise de Internés de Guerre in Château d'Oex, overseeing English soldiers interned in Switzerland. (Jung was an Anglophile and spoke fluent English.)

It was there that he began the practice of sketching out a mandala each day, seeing in the formation of these "magic circles" a clue to his own psychic state. He came to the conclusion that the mandala, a circular symbol used in Hinduism and Tibetan Buddhism, symbolized the Self, the larger totality of the psyche, of which the ego, our sense of "I," was only a part. Jung began to see that the unconscious seeks expression; it seeks to balance out the lopsidedness of the ego, which blindly believed it was the sole occupant of our inner world, and to achieve a state of wholeness. The process toward that wholeness Jung called individuation.

SOME 1,500 MILES FROM ZÜRICH, someone else, as deeply interested in the human psyche as Jung, and who also saw the "I," or ego, as only one occupant of a much more richly inhabited mind, was struck by the sudden announcement of war. He had hoped it would not break out, and had even denied the very possibility of it, at least to himself. But there was no escape. *"We were in it,"* a chastened and somewhat weary Peter Demianovich Ouspensky, journalist and *habitué* of St. Petersburg's Stray Dog Café, said to himself as he disembarked the ship that had returned him to Russia after a long and unfruitful "search for the miraculous" in Egypt, India, and other mystic ports of call.[36]

He was not surprised. The war was yet another "obvious absurdity" in a world of many, and in the face of it he was stoic. He would look at it as "one of those generally catastrophic conditions of life in the midst of which we have to live and work," and, perhaps more important, "seek answers to our questions and doubts."[37]

Questions and doubts Ouspensky had. In fact, their number had increased, as he had returned from his long voyage in search of knowledge "unlike anything hitherto known or used by us" empty-handed and not a little jaded.[38] After all, he knew what "life was like." Yet the knowledge he sought and those who possessed it—they must exist. Perhaps he would make another search. In the meantime, he would write and give talks about his travels. There was much to tell.

Ouspensky might not have had much luck in his search for the miraculous. What he didn't know was that the miraculous would soon come searching for him.

3

Shell-Shocked

Nicoll's enthusiasm to get to where the action was, so he would have a chance to "smash the blighters"—an eagerness shared by many of his generation—was dampened when he found himself stuck in a field hospital in Limerick, Ireland, complaining about lack of equipment and worried that the war would be over before he even got to it.[1] He had told his father that whatever happened, "one way or another, it will be destined," and that he would be "perfectly tranquil and serene" about it.[2] The stoicism that had fortified him as a child against suffering the loss of a toy would now be put to a greater test. But it would not be on the battlefields of Flanders, Ypres, or the Somme that Nicoll's serenity would be challenged but beneath the blisteringly cloudless sky and on the sun-scorched sands of the Middle East, or, as it was called then, the Near East. Here Nicoll would meet a challenge to his powers of endurance that in many ways prepared him for the "intentional suffering" he would experience under Gurdjieff. He never got to smash a blighter, but one suspects that the physical, emotional, and mental wrecks that he and his colleagues patched up as best they could, under almost impossible conditions, put him off the idea soon enough.

Nicoll hoped that he would soon be shipped out to France, and he had braced himself for the trenches. Toward the end of July 1915 word came that he would finally be heading out, but toward a different destination. By August his parents knew where he was: Suvla Bay, on the Aegean coast of the Gallipoli Peninsula, in Ottoman Turkey. He was part of the amphibious landing that the Entente powers hoped would turn the battle of Gallipoli in their favor. It didn't, and Gallipoli is remembered today as one of Winston Churchill's—Nicoll's father's friend—worst mistakes. The losses were enormous and the campaign a failure. Nicoll himself didn't see much of the offensive. His main complaint in a letter home was that he was stuck with only one book, *Jane Eyre*, which he didn't like. The situation didn't last long. Nicoll soon contracted dysentery and in September he was sent back to England to recover. His stay at his next port of call would be longer and more taxing.

In February 1916 Nicoll and the rest of the 32nd Field Hospital of the RAMC found themselves in Mesopotamia, the ancient land between the two rivers, the Tigris and the Euphrates, an area that, if we are to believe him, Gurdjieff had wandered through in his youth with some of his fellow Seekers of Truth.[3] Today, much of the area is part of Iraq and Kuwait. Here Nicoll would be stationed for nearly a year. At the beginning of his account of this time, *In Mesopotamia* (1917)— written again as Martin Swayne—Nicoll tells us that "There is nothing to suggest that you are approaching the gateway to the Garden of Eden when you reach the top of the Persian Gulf," as he did that winter, one of the worst in the war.[4] Local legend suggested that Kurna—or Al-Qurnah—where the Tigris and Euphrates meet (the name means "juncture"), is where the archetypal garden might have been located. Yet the landscape was so featureless that there was nothing to suggest that Nicoll's true destination was something closer to hell, which, in fact, it was. Nothing, that is, except the heat.

The inescapable, relentless, desiccating heat that Nicoll lived under during this time was, by his account, often a worse cause of sickness and death in the soldiers in his care than the bombs and bullets of the

Turks. At an average temperature of 120° in the shade, this should not be surprising. Nicoll saw malaria, dysentery, "sandfly fever," jaundice, and scurvy, not to mention the wounds caused by shrapnel, bullets, and bomb blasts. But nothing was as bad as the effects of heatstroke. "I do not know of any other malady so dramatic," he wrote, " or so painful to witness as heat-stroke."[5] Coming from someone who had seen some of the worst effects of war at firsthand, and who was responsible for the lives and welfare of hundreds of patients, one hesitates to contradict him.

In Mesopotamia is a short, clear, sober account of Nicoll's part in the Mesopotamia campaign, which was aimed at knocking the Ottoman Empire—the "sick man of Europe"—out of the war. It lacks the literary power and psychological depth of another account of a similar effort, the Arab Revolt, led by T. E. Lawrence, and recounted in his masterpiece *The Seven Pillars of Wisdom*, which Churchill ranked with "the greatest books ever written in the English language."* Nicoll did not have Lawrence's passionate commitment to the Arab people, which crushed him at the end of the war, when he saw that the European powers had no interest in a united Arab nation. *In Mesopotamia* is more a work of reportage, with Nicoll's watercolors helping to evoke a sense of place. The work strikes me as an attempt by Nicoll to write about where he was and what was taking place in front of him. He would later tell his group that he had missed an opportunity to do this during his time in Vienna; instead of writing stories that took place in England, which he did while there, he should have set them in Austria (and perhaps featured Georgette.)

In Mesopotamia shows Nicoll as a competent travel writer, attuned to local color and atmosphere, what there was of it, and refraining from

---

*It's curious that, in assessing the Arab mentality and its "fatalism," Nicoll remarked that "A man who expected to throw a spell over the country and act as a stimulant on everyone would truly need to possess a prodigious character," which is exactly what Lawrence of Arabia had. I don't know if Nicoll ever read *The Seven Pillars of Wisdom.* Swayne, *In Mesopotamia,* chapter 6, "Day's Work."

giving way to any impulse to embellish or romanticize. He was in the land of flying carpets and Harun ar-Rashid, but neither he nor any of his companions had a copy of the *Arabian Nights*. Indeed, there was nothing magical or mysterious about Nicoll's time in the East, unlike Gurdjieff and Ouspensky's sojourns there; and the only thing paradisical about it was that Adam and Eve could be excused their nakedness— not because of their innocence but because of the temperature. Ice, a necessity when dealing with heatstroke, was almost impossible to find. "Mesopotamia," Nicoll wrote, "welcomes no man."

It is difficult to read Nicoll's account now without seeing in it some unintentional pre-echoes of what he would encounter in his time with Gurdjieff. Yet if it was true, as he told Beryl Pogson, that everything that happened to him up to that time was "mere preparation" for that encounter, then perhaps these pre-echoes were not as unintentional as we might think. One of the first things that Gurdjieff impressed upon Nicoll was the idea that he did not build to last but to meet a present need. When erecting the Study House at Fontainebleau, put up at top speed, Nicoll asked Gurdjieff why he did not build more solidly. Everything seemed a bit jerry-rigged. Gurdjieff replied: "This is only temporary. In a short time everything will be different. . . . Nothing can be built permanently at this moment."[6] One of the first things that struck Nicoll as he reached the field hospital where he would be working was the makeshift, temporary character of everything. He and his colleagues had to make do with what they had, and that was not much. (A theme running throughout the book is the lack of equipment at the field hospitals, and the lack of foresight on the part of those in command.*) "An immense hammering and shouting filled the stifling air," Nicoll tells us, as large sheds, housing fifty beds each, were put up on stilts pounded into the marshy, spongy soil that would regularly be flooded.

---

*The original MS was heavily censored, cutting out much of Nicoll's criticisms of the mishandling of the campaign.

Of course, the reason to "get it up quick and dirty" was different in each case. Yet we can find a similarity even here. No one would think to erect a hospital on such terrain under normal circumstances. It was only because of the exceptional circumstance of a war that one was needed. Gurdjieff created a set of exceptional circumstances of his own. One of the axioms that Nicoll would bring back from Fontainebleau and that would guide him with his own groups was "overcome difficulties." Gurdjieff may have gone out of his way to create difficulties for Nicoll and the others who had put themselves under his command, but here in the Fertile Crescent they were everywhere at hand.

Drinking water was scarce, and what there was of it had to be heavily chlorinated. Food was equally bad, and without refrigeration, soon rotted. Vegetables were practically unheard of, and the meat they did get was stringy and unappetizing. Medical supplies were also difficult to obtain, and this at a time when Nicoll was tending to hundreds of badly wounded men. Along with the absence of ice, there were also no fans, nothing to break the stifling heat with the slightest breeze. Yet, in these conditions, the appalling heat was in some ways a benefit: it induced a "spirit of indifference" that soon ordered one's priorities, and accounted for the Eastern "fatalism" that left everything in Allah's hands. Nicoll told his group that he soon adapted to the environment, which gave him an opportunity to display the "Nicoll spirit of knowing how to do a thing with the least possible physical exertion," thus making a virtue of his own predilection for laziness.[7]

Nicoll learned about the need to make peculiar efforts some years in advance of his tutelage in Fontainebleau. Each day under the Mesopotamian sun was an endurance test. Even here, waking up was hard to do. "The business of getting up," he wrote, "is one of infinite weariness." Mental exertion of any kind was almost impossible. Being stuck with *Jane Eyre* was less of an annoyance here, given that reading "was not easy, writing was a burden, and thinking a matter of extreme difficulty."[8]

The heat, along with the "peculiar effect of a landscape that is entirely flat and uniform," combined to produce a state of unreality.[9] Gurdjieff would later tell Nicoll that "impressions"—our perceptions of the world—are a kind of food, and that without them a man would die in seconds. Nicoll's tenure in Mesopotamia was like being on a strict "impression-free" diet, or like being dropped into an open-air sensory-deprivation chamber. This led him to remark that in such an environment one has two choices: that of becoming either a sensualist or a mystic. The one relief that everyone found absolutely necessary was alcohol. "The mind was exhausted, food was unattractive, conversation was impossible, the passage of time immeasurably slow, and a restless irritation pervaded one until a dose of alcohol was taken." Nicoll would later write an article on the virtues of alcohol and its power to annul the criticisms of "the father"—or superego—thus allowing for a renewal of energy through contact with the unconscious. (William James had praised alcohol's "yea-saying" power, linking it to mysticism.) Gurdjieff and Ouspensky, in different ways, used alcohol as part of their teaching "strategy," and Nicoll himself would rely on it at different times in order to get over a particular "work" hurdle.

The physical lethargy did not prevent Nicoll from making some psychological observations. One was on the efficacy of opium, which was the only medication of any use in many cases, especially those of sandfly fever, a kind of fast-acting intense influenza that could incapacitate a man in a matter of moments. Like alcohol, but stronger, opium—obtained locally—produced a sense of detachment that enabled one to sleep, even with the attentions of the "most successfully maddening insect ever designed by the Lord of Flies." The psychology of rumor also interested him. His group had little information about anything, and rumors of the fall of this city or that, or of the advance or retreat of troops, spread easily. Nicoll likened the effect to that of a woman: charming on some days, unpleasant on others. Jung had written a paper on the subject, and one suspects Nicoll had read it.[10] Mirages fascinated him, and he came to suspect that the mirage one sees might have some inner relation to one's psychology in the way that the images we see in dreams do. Nicoll also observed something that the psychologist Viktor Frankl would as well, years later during his internment in a Nazi concentration camp: that discipline, or a sense of purpose, plays an important part in staying healthy.[11] One's physical condition was not as important a factor as one's morale. The collapse that led to serious illness, Nicoll saw, always came from within: in essence one *allowed* oneself to get ill.*

Some of Nicoll's observations are less noteworthy; his remarks about Arab women, for instance, would not pass muster with today's politically correct brigade. But some would find an echo in his later reflections on what Jung would call synchronicity and the Austrian biologist Paul Kammerer seriality, when occurrences of a similar character seemed to follow one another. Nicoll became attuned to this when he noticed that similar cases seemed to turn up at the same time, usually after a period when there were none at all. He saw that this was also true in other contexts. "It is the same way with everything," he wrote, "whether it be cardplaying, or business, or war, or love, or thinking, or sport. There are phases in which something seems to overshadow the scene."[12] Something, that is, other than the causality we usually look to in order to explain events. Nicoll had expressed similar ideas in a letter published in the *British Weekly* in which he reflected on a question that occupied many at the time: the fate of the dead in the afterlife.

The war of course had turned many minds to this question. It had turned some soldiers into atheists and driven some mad. It brought Nicoll to the belief that the afterlife does not "solve the great mystery," that of our own individuality, and the problems involved with it. We continue to deal with these in some form in the next world, and "the

---

*This was something that T. E. Lawrence recognized in his Arabs. During the revolt, Lawrence saw men "push themselves or be driven to a cruel extreme of endurance: yet never was there an intimation of a physical break. Collapse rose always from a moral weakness eating into the body." Lawrence, *The Seven Pillars of Wisdom*, 477.

great plan is still that of progress by conquest of self." If we have left the world with unfinished business, we are "sent back again to learn our full lessons and complete our labours," a strange belief for a Christian, sounding awfully like reincarnation, or even, at a stretch, recurrence.[13] To make his point clear, Nicoll thanked the paper for printing "the message of Sir Oliver Lodge," the great scientist and former president of the Society for Psychical Research, whose book *Raymond* (1916) is an account of spirit communication with his son, who died at Ypres in 1915.*

It was bold enough for a doctor of psychiatry to admit to believing in an afterlife—and if Ernest Jones had read the letter, proof positive that the Jungians were off their collective rocker—but bolder still to envision an afterlife where we are faced with the same existential questions that plague us here. No wonder Nicoll believed that he was "condemned by Christians at home already." Yet by now he no longer wished to be a member of a congregation to which he did not belong.

TOWARD THE END OF 1916, not long before returning to England, where his active service would end and other wartime work begin, Nicoll wrote to his father to tell him once again of his plans for the future. The break between Zürich and Vienna was complete. Jung had found a new name for the work he was doing. He had christened his approach "analytical psychology" to differentiate it from Freud's "psychoanalysis," and Nicoll had joined with other British Jungians to "cut entirely away" from the latter and adhere to the former. To laymen, the different terms suggest a certain amount of hairsplitting: both posit a psyche in need of analysis. Yet while Nicoll admits that the two have so much in common that tracing a definite dividing line between them

*Raymond's account of the spirit world, as recounted in Lodge's book, has a concrete, robust character similar to the full-bodied heaven and hell of Swedenborg. See my *Introducing Swedenborg: Correspondences,* 10–11.

is difficult, in essence they are as far apart as one could imagine.

Freud and his circle, Nicoll told his father, are pessimists, descendants of "Schopenhauer and Co.," the nineteenth-century German philosopher whose *World as Will and Representation* (1818) depicts a blind, insatiable, unconscious "will" behind existence, an echo of which can be found in Freud's notion of the id. Schopenhauer's philosophy leads ultimately to a kind of nihilistic negation of life; salvation comes only with abnegation of the will, with giving up desire (in Freudian terms, a psychic homeostasis or "death wish"). It was this Buddhistic life-rejection that turned Nietzsche, an early follower of Schopenhauer, against his onetime "educator." In contrast to this, "our theories," by which Nicoll means Jung's, are "in their ultimate outlook . . . spiritual."* The problem is that both schools use the same material: the dark rejected matter of the unconscious.

That there *was* a dividing line between the two schools there was no doubt, but it often seemed flexible, and Nicoll would find himself more than once moving back and forth across it. One way he sought to establish a clear demarcation was by writing a "simple non-technical volume" spelling out his own attitude to the matter. It was, he said, "an offshoot of Zürich but independent." We will look at this independent offshoot further on. He didn't "propose to join any school," at least not yet, yet his use of "our theories," in opposition to those of the "pessimists," and the clear sympathy for Jung's "prospective tendencies" over Freud's reductionist methods, suggest he was in the analytical psychology camp whether he liked it or not. That was certainly how Ernest Jones saw him. Nicoll rallied to Jung's side, or would do so, in the days ahead.

Because of the war, the pessimists would be popular, Nicoll told his

---

*Jung, of course, was a reader of Schopenhauer, as was Freud. "He was the first to speak of the suffering of the world, which visibly and glaringly surrounds us." Jung, *Memories, Dreams, Reflections*, 88.

father, and it was strange to think that *their* work, that of Nicoll and his colleagues, "in which lies the germ of something very wonderful" could be traced back to Freud and the pessimists. Nicoll makes a point of saying that most if not all of Freud's followers were Jewish, and that he, like the other Christians who had become "entangled" in what he sees as "a kind of revival of Jewish thought," have "broken free" of it, but not "empty-handed." One wonders if these observations—not uncommon among those participating in the psychoanalytic civil wars—suggested to his father, and perhaps to Nicoll himself, a parallel with the early Christian movement, rising up out of its "archaic" Jewish past?

Nicoll's first work back on home ground, however, would be caring for officers who suffered mental and emotional trauma in the war. At 10 Palace Gardens, near the north side of Hyde Park on the west side of London, Nicoll cared for officers suffering from "shell shock," prolonged exposure to bombardment. The effects of "the excessive impact of reality on the individual"—a remarkable understatement, considering that the reality in question consisted of high explosives—included hysterical paralysis, blindness, deafness, a general helplessness, and "retreat from life."[14] Many became like William James's neurasthenic patients who were unable to get out of bed. Their "psychological tension" had grown slack, their "reality function" overworked, and the methods and treatments in place at the time were, Nicoll saw, worse than useless.

The electric shocks, hot and cold baths, and variety of tonics designed to treat an ailing body had no effect on the mind of these individuals. Or it had a counterproductive effect, forcing the patient further into the withdrawal from reality that offered the only respite from its oppression, when what was needed was precisely the opposite, to reawaken one's *interest* in reality. Nicoll's contempt for the inadequacies in the treatment of mental and psychological ailments associated with the war and his suggestions for their improvement found voice in an article for the *British Weekly*, "The Need for Psycho-Pathological Hospitals." At the time, there were no facilities designed to deal with these specific cases, and more often than not, patients already suffering from an overdose of reality were put into mental asylums. Predictably they got worse. Nicoll's campaign had some success. When he was appointed to the staff of the Empire Hospital for Officers, he managed to convince the senior members of the need for change. After months of lobbying, dinners, and meetings, Nicoll could report that the "orthodox medical reactionaries have been smashed and psychology has been born."[15]

The central psychological effect of shell shock, Nicoll found, was that it caused the patient to *regress* to an earlier time in their life, to childhood, or further still to infancy. This, as we've seen, is the same point Jung made in his paper on the significance of the father on the destiny of the child. When faced with "too great an obstacle" we draw back, and the energy needed to face the challenge flows in the opposite direction, into the past, activating behavior patterns we long outgrew, or at least thought we had. This regression was also something that happened with advancing age. In another letter to the *British Weekly* Nicoll had written that, "A man is old just as soon as he shows by his conversation that he looks wholly into the past for his greatest and best." Nicoll refers to that "large and ever present class of men whose thoughts dwell continually on their school or college days." As a contemporary expression of this we might consider the American penchant for seeing one's high school years as the best time of one's life.

The preventative to this tendency to nostalgia is the "sacrifice of old ways of thought." "Those whose physical bodies are full of years, but who still look forward, are men who have the courage to undergo continually these inner sacrifices." Age and its psychological consequences was a pet theme of Nicoll's, and he would return to it. The need to undergo inner sacrifices, too, would become more insistent.

Nicoll's public profile was growing. He published in the *Lancet*, Britain's premier medical journal, and started a publication himself, the *Journal of Neurology and Psychology*. He gave lectures in London, attended those of others, and at Birmingham University he spoke on psychotherapy to postgraduate students in a course in criminology. He was, or was becoming, a "man of standing and promise in the worlds of medicine and letters."[16] He was also becoming something of an authority on a rather obscure subject. At a symposium jointly held by the British Psychological Society, the Aristotelian Society, and the Mind Association, Nicoll was asked the question why the unconscious *is* unconscious. Nicoll's answer was to compare the unconscious to a womb: in both, something gestates until it is time for it to be born, for it is "only the comparatively adapted form that is born into life." A thought and a child born prematurely are both not ready for life. The unconscious, he said, is an "inexhaustible source of our psychic life," and not "a cage containing strange and odious beasts."[17] If there was any doubt as to which side of the indistinct dividing line between psychological pessimists and spiritualists Nicoll was on, this should have ended it.

SOMETHING THAT HELPED NICOLL'S RISE on the London psychological scene was that "independent offshoot of the Zürich school" that he had brought back with him from the Near East. During the war Nicoll had passed his free time writing. *In Mesopotamia* was one result. The other was the first of his books to which he put his own name. If Nicoll is the "forgotten teacher of the Fourth Way," as I'm suggesting he is, then *Dream Psychology* (1917) is his forgotten book.[18] It has been forgotten by most readers of Jung, and left out of the huge body of literature that has grown up around him and his work. Most readers who know the book come to it through their interest in Gurdjieff and Ouspensky; at least that is how I became aware of it.

This is a shame. *Dream Psychology* has little to say to someone who comes to it thinking it may contain some nuggets of Fourth Way knowledge. But Jungians who are unaware of it will find a clear, straightforward exposition of the basics of Jung's early approach to dreams. It is, as mentioned, the first book in English to articulate Jung's ideas, and according to more than one Jung scholar, it achieves its aim of presenting a "highly effective introduction to analytical psychology."[19] This is a Jung without the shadow, or anima, or any of the cast of archetypal characters that we associate with him and Jungian psychology today. Some readers may find this disappointing. Others will appreciate a simple exposition of Jung's constructive approach to dreams, spelling out its differences from Freud's reductive one.

As the Jungian analyst Ean Begg remarks, the book is "a good deal more Jungian" than Nicoll's comments about his independence would suggest.[20] But Nicoll himself is clear about his reasons for writing it. He will have been justified in doing so, he tells us, if the book "enables its readers to regard the dream, in some degree, from Dr. Jung's standpoint."[21]

And what is that standpoint?

Fundamentally it is the difference between seeing dreams in terms of their *cause*, and seeing them in terms of their *purpose*. Jung's "constructive approach" assumes that the dream rises into consciousness *for a reason*, that is, it has an *aim*, and is not a mere by-product of physiological factors—bad digestion or agitated neurons—or the work of a dream-censor, camouflaging our secret desires so we can get a good night's sleep. For Jung the dream presents some knowledge about ourselves that *wants* to become conscious: the unconscious seeks expression, for ultimately it aims to compensate for the conscious mind's one-sided, incomplete point of view. This is the exact opposite of Freud's view, which sees the dream as a way of keeping us ignorant of our true desires. Freud's "reductive approach," aims to "explain" the dream in terms of the factors leading up to it, which for him were always repressed wishes. We can say that while Freud looked for where the dream came from, Jung and Nicoll are more interested in where it is going, its "prospective tendencies."

Nicoll begins by making a point with which anyone who has paid serious attention to their dreams will agree: that they can be so involved and detailed that no one could consciously come up with them each night. They emerge, Nicoll suggests, from a kind of inner "workshop" that produces the dream spontaneously and effortlessly. What drives the workshop is what Nicoll calls "interest," a term he uses to differentiate what he considers our motivating force from Freud's libido, which carries with it an explicit sexual connotation.* A dream, Nicoll says, is "a patchwork of interests."[22]

Jung struggled to find a neutral term to express this general character of the *élan vital*, or life force, the energy that "animates" us to take an interest in life—exactly what Nicoll's shell-shocked patients needed to do. (He later personified it in the contra-sexual archetypes of the "anima" and "animus.") Nicoll admits that "interest" lacks scientific precision, but such precision, he suggests, has its own drawbacks. Freud's libido may seem more specific, perhaps even measurable. We know some people are more highly sexed than others; Nicoll, it turns out, is one of them, and Freud would say he had a lot of libido. But it requires some rather strenuous contortions to have a specifically sexual libido account for the "interest" we take in spiritual or religious matters.

"Interest," on the other hand, does not need to be sublimated. We can be interested in radically different things, without the force behind one interest needing to be sublimated to account for our interest in another. Our interest in spirituality need not be a sublimation of our interest in sex. We can be interested in both and at the same time. As we will see, such was the case with Nicoll.

Nicoll then makes a distinction that, it strikes me, will set the foundation for his later life's work of unpacking the esoteric meaning of the

---

*We may say that Nicoll's "interest" serves the same purpose as what Swedenborg called one's "true affections" or "abiding love." This, as the Spice Girls used to say, is what one "really, really wants."

Gospels, although that is not on his agenda here. This is the difference between what he calls "focused" and "unfocused" meaning. The difference between the two is very important. The terms themselves may not be that useful, being imprecise, but that, in fact, is Nicoll's point. They arise in a discussion of symbolism and the "condensed and latent meaning" in the symbols in a dream. It is the language of the dream, and what it is trying to say, that interests Nicoll most. It is not a language of precision, of the sort of explicit statements logic and the scientific mind find most appealing, but one of analogy, metaphor, suggestion, even a kind of poetry.

By "focused" meaning Nicoll means any easily identified object. "A bottle of ink or a lamp," Nicoll tells us, "are things with a certain clear circle of focused meaning within which no argument occurs." But not everything enjoys such clarity. "The expression of a face, the configuration of the stars, a poem or a dream are things that contain no clear circle of focused meaning. Their meaning is blurred or unfocused."[23]

A lamp is a lamp is a lamp, while a poem or the look on someone's face needs to be *interpreted*. Their meaning cannot be expressed in the same way as the meaning of a word or of a mathematical formula. We might say that they have an *implicit* but not *explicit* meaning, one that can be implied—suggested or shown—but not stated unequivocally. What we can call the "focused meaning" approach to the parables, the literalist approach that set Nicoll on his path that day in class when he knew the headmaster knew nothing, was what his father dedicated his life to communicating.

We will return to this further on. I mention it here to show that what we might call the roots of Nicoll's interpretation of the Gospel parables—his "hermeneutic" we might say—were planted in the soil of his study of dreams, even if he was not necessarily aware of this. This should not surprise us. Both the dream and the parable speak to an awareness that is other than our rational, conscious mind, just as poetry and music do, and both convey meanings that we *feel,* rather than give intellectual assent to. If we grasp the meaning of a dream, it *affects* us, or at least it should. (If it doesn't, then we haven't grasped its meaning, however cleverly we may have "interpreted" it.) The same is true of a parable: we *see* what it means in a flash, rather than arrive at its meaning through a process of deduction. The difference, we might say, is that the dream is a parable written by our unconscious self, while the parable is a kind of dream created by a mind—so Nicoll will argue—*more* conscious than our own. Yet both kinds of parables have the same intent behind them: to open our limited consciousness to "unexpected and unthought-of" possibilities, to realities of life of which we are unaware. Both, we can say, offer the possibility of change.

What this tells us, Nicoll suggests, is that "dreams have a kind of intelligence behind them concealed under a curious and fantastic symbolism."[24] If we assume the presence of this intelligence, and are sympathetic to its expression in images containing unfocused meaning, we can try to discern the "motive of the unconscious." We can try to learn what it—really a deeper part of us—wants us, the top tip of "it," to know.[25] As Jung would later say, a dream is a kind of postcard sent from one part of ourselves to another, with the sender and receiver being the same person. The trick is to find out what the deep I, who sent the postcard, wants the superficial me, who received it, to know. Or we can see a dream as a kind of game of charades that we play with ourselves.

Often the message is a criticism or commentary on our conscious, usually one-sided attitude for which the dream tries to compensate to achieve a better balance between our two selves. Another way of receiving these messages is by paying attention to our fantasy life. Fantasy, Nicoll writes, "intervenes between what is conscious and what is seeking consciousness."[26] It is a kind of bridge between the unconscious and conscious minds, and within it can be found indications of future life. In this sense, fantasy should be taken seriously. Nicoll spells this out with a warning. "It is impossible to over-estimate the danger of destroying an individual's fantasy." The "prospective tendencies" of a future self can be found here, just as much as the debris and remains of an unadapted past. Yet the dangers of destroying an individual's fantasies are complemented by those of allowing fantasy too loose a rein.

A LOOK AT NICOLL'S *DREAM PSYCHOLOGY* should be followed by a look at his dream diaries. But the diaries require some introduction, and so rather than have this chapter be overlong, I have left them for the next. Here I want to take a look at another work by Nicoll published under the name Martin Swayne, his last full-length novel and the last book written under his pseudonym to see print.

The Blue Germ (1918) is an entertaining, inventive, and thought-provoking parable—one hesitates to call it infectious—about what would happen if humanity were suddenly granted the gift of longevity, if not immortality. It's a shame the book isn't better known. It's well written and moves at a quick pace, and fans of early science fiction would enjoy it; in many ways it is a close relative of H. G. Wells's *In the Days of the Comet* (1906), in which gasses in the tail of a comet trigger a radical change in human behavior. I thought it was something of a synchronicity to be reading the book during our own COVID-19 pandemic, although the infection in the novel is altogether beneficent.

The theme of *The Blue Germ* is one that Bernard Shaw would take up in his "metabiological Pentateuch," *Back to Methuselah* (1921), and that the science fiction writer John Wyndham would explore in *Trouble with Lichen* (1960). All three works recognize that one thing wrong with human beings is that it is only toward the end of our lives that we begin to achieve the kind of detachment from them, the freedom from trivialities, that allows us to get an idea of their meaning and of that of life in general. Old age, of course, is no guarantee of this: many of us never grow up, or we become more narrow-minded and petty as we get older. But in some of us, a wisdom comes with age, but also a regret that we are now too old to do anything with it. But what if humanity could live long enough to gain this wisdom, and still have sufficient time ahead in order to put it into practice?

Shaw suggested that three hundred years would be a decent tenure on earth. Shaw did not say how an increased life span would come about. He believed that if the need for it became absolute, it would just happen. Wyndham and Nicoll are more specific. For Wyndham, a rare form of lichen contains the *elixir vitae*. For Nicoll it is a germ, a form of bacteria that can't be seen even with the strongest microscopes. It can be detected only by its effects, one of which is to turn its carriers a subtle shade of blue. Hence its name: the blue germ.

The idea that a germ can be beneficial to our health was itself unusual, but as the story goes on, the benefits the germ provides lead to developments that all but wreck society. With the old no longer dying off when they should, and hence leaving no room for those who come after them, the young begin a campaign of eradicating their elders, doing themselves what nature had taken care of before.* When Nicoll wrote the book the possibilities of life extension were limited. Today the increase in life span of people in the twenty-first century has led to serious crises in social care, housing, pension schemes, and a number of other concerns. And no small part of the increasing popularity of "transhumanism," the belief that humanity will soon transcend its biological limitations through a physical union with computer technology (producing something like *Star Trek*'s Borg), is its promise of an extended life span, if not a technologically based immortality. As do the transhumanists, the scientist responsible for the discovery of the blue germ declares that "death is only a failure of human perfection."[27] As with his story "A Sense of the Future," which depicts the effects of a coming exhaustion of fossil fuels, in *The Blue Germ* Nicoll again seems to have caught a whiff of what was on its way.

---

*M. P. Shiel used a similar theme in his eccentric novel *The Young Men Are Coming* (1937). Shiel, like Nicoll, was a contributor to the *Strand* magazine.

The plot is too complicated to run through here, but this is the basic idea: Professor Sarakoff, a "tall, lean, black-bearded and deep-voiced" Russian, possessed of "immense energy," has discovered a germ that eliminates all other germs, that, in essence, makes one healthy. It eliminates disease, leaving accident or violence the only sources of death. It also radically retards the aging process.

Sarakoff is an eccentric. He takes notes on the shell of a gigantic tortoise, is "careless of public opinion and prodigious of ideas." He looks like an anarchist, "huge, satanic, inscrutable."[28] He is an absolute materialist, who sees the germ as an opportunity to create a heaven on earth, a hedonistic, humanistic one. "Can't you see," he tells Harden, Nicoll's alter ego who tells the tale, "that as soon as the idea of Immortality gets hold of people, they will devote all their energy to making the earth a paradise?" It is interesting that Sarakoff is Russian. Nicoll himself will meet an eccentric Russian thinker a few years hence, and the philosophy Sarakoff spouts is very much like that of the Cosmist school of Russian thought, an obscure movement that was engulfed by the Bolshevik Revolution, which was taking place as the book was published. Some of the ideas of the Cosmists are remarkably similar to those of the system Ouspensky learned from Gurdjieff.[29]

Harden is not sold on Sarakoff's vision, and his misgivings are confirmed when he meets a young doctor who is stricken with an incurable disease that the germ cannot affect. He tells Harden that there is something more than matter; there is spirit, and that a world without suffering, as Sarakoff envisions, would be one in which there would be no spirit. Harden finds himself between the two, the spirit and the flesh, as Nicoll was himself and indeed we all are. The story raises the question: What would we *do* with immortality, which is only another way of asking what we do with our lives now? As the parable unfolds, the blessings and curse of the germ are presented until the disastrous end with the war of the young against the old, and the moral is made clear that mankind is not yet ready for such miracles.

With Nicoll's belief in mind that everything that happened to him prior to meeting Gurdjieff was mere preparation for that encounter, it is difficult to read the book without seeing it in this light. Some of the most interesting parts of the book are when Nicoll describes the effect of the germ. It has remarkable tonic qualities. One's perceptions achieve a new clarity. Harden notices these changes after he becomes infected. "I seem to see twice as many things to what I used to, and everything seems to have a new coat of paint."[30] He says that the effect was rather like having a glass of champagne after a long day. The results, though, are more far-reaching. "The patterns of the carpet glowed in colours more brilliant than I had ever seen before," he says, a remark that would not have been out of place in Aldous Huxley's account of his experiment with the drug mescaline *The Doors of Perception*.[31]

One of the few questions an intimidated audience asked Gurdjieff when he came to London and Nicoll saw him for the first time was what it would be like to perceive the world in "essence." Gurdjieff answered: "Everything more vivid," a concise summing up of the effects Nicoll describes above.

The sense of time and space of those infected with the germ is also seriously altered. One's sense of *scale* is widened—and the notion of scale will play a large part in the system Nicoll will learn from Ouspensky. One thinks in terms of centuries rather than years. It takes some time to adjust. But Harden soon feels as if he had "entered a world of new perspectives, a larger world in which space and time were widened out immeasurably."[32] This widening of space and time was accompanied by a lack of anxiety, of any sense of need to do anything at all. With the prospect of immortality, the rush and worry to get things done and to "save time," dissolves, and one feels an "extraordinary sense of freedom" from care or concern, somewhat like the "fatalism" prevalent during Nicoll's time in the Middle East. One can enter one's thoughts as one could a comfortable room, close the door, and stay there, undisturbed by the irrelevancies outside. Harden and Sarakoff reach a "level of consciousness that is undisturbed by any craving," experiencing a kind of bacteriological Buddhism, in which they reach nirvana.[33]

Reading Nicoll's description of these states of profound detachment, I remembered his remarks about opium in *In Mesopotamia*, and wondered if he had tried it himself. He had experimented with hashish, as had Ouspensky, and Gurdjieff had a considerable knowledge of the effects of certain drugs. The main effect of opium or its more powerful refined versions, heroin and morphine, is to induce a state in which nothing troubles one, nothing matters, and there is no reason to do one thing rather than another—something that Huxley, under mescaline, also experienced. Hence its appeal. The will is completely relaxed, the need to concern oneself with the outer world annulled. Harden finds that he has "a prodigious, incalculable amount to think about," and he sinks into a state in which he "was not asleep and yet at the same time I was not awake," the intermediary state between sleeping and waking mentioned earlier. He finds that he can focus his thoughts for hours at a time, and that they seem to take on a strange *plastic* character. He remarks that he has become "acquainted with a doctrine that teaches that thoughts are in the nature of things," that they are a "formation in some tenuous medium of matter just as a cathedral is a structure in gross matter."[34]

The doctrine Nicoll refers to is the notion of "thought forms" presented by Annie Besant, head of the Theosophical Society, and her associate Charles Leadbeater in their book of that title.[35] By this time Nicoll had moved into a house at 146 Harley Street, which he shared with James Young and Maud Hoffman, an ardent Theosophist. This idea of thoughts being a form of fine matter will form part of Gurdjieff's system, but it will also emerge years later in the exercises in mental visualization that Nicoll will perform with some of his groups, in which he used thought forms to protect members of the group, or relatives of members, during the war years. Harden also finds that his thoughts have taken on a more dreamlike character, as if "the magic of dreams had in some way become attached to thought."[36] His thoughts became more stable, and formed themselves into "clear images, which had a remarkable permanence," another characteristic of the liminal state between sleep and waking.

Nicoll seems to prefigure his own future experience in the book. At one point Harden sells his house on Harley Street, just as Nicoll would sell his practice, and he also buys a cottage by the sea, just as Nicoll would rent one. And Sarakoff can be seen as a combination of Ouspensky, Gurdjieff, and even Jung, at least in the capacity of a father figure. At one point he tells Harden that he has "taken life too seriously. You have worked too hard. You are stunted and deformed with work."[37] This is rather like Jung's interpretation of a dream Nicoll presented to him, in which he was carrying cushions. Jung told him that the dream was saying that he worked too hard, that he needed to take a softer approach. The fact that Nicoll was on his way to enter the Work may even qualify this dream as prophetic.

4

A Taste for the Forbidden

With the war over and the world getting back to normal—which meant, in effect, gearing up for the war that would erupt twenty years later—one might think that Nicoll finally had good reason to think well of himself. He had come through some extraordinary experiences in the war and had saved men's lives. He was a popular author, even if under a pseudonym. He was an increasingly respected younger member of the growing if contentious psychoanalytical community. He had a thriving practice on prestigious Harley Street. And he was the intimate associate and all but officially appointed English representative of the second most famous psychologist in the world. Even his father would have nodded in acknowledgment if not approval at worldly achievements like these. Yet, with all this, Nicoll still felt that something was missing.

What was it?

To answer that question we will need to take another look at the "unclean thoughts" that Nicoll never stopped entertaining, and at the diaries in which he recorded their often crude appearances in his dreams. Nicoll took very seriously—perhaps a little too seriously, as Jung believed—the idea that through our dreams we can become aware of aspects of ourselves of which we are usually unaware, parts of ourselves missing from our conscious attitude and that need to be integrated if we are to become whole. Nicoll applied Jung's ideas and terminology in trying to understand his own dreams. As many people interested in their dreams know, this can be a risky business. Jung himself points out that we are rarely objective enough about ourselves to be able to catch what a dream, which is an objective assessment of our current state, may be trying to tell us. We lack the detachment that another may possess; hence the virtue of an analyst, or even a friend. (Gurdjieff would make a similar argument, insisting that one man alone can do nothing.)

Nicoll's diaries are full of references to the shadow, the anima, and the other archetypes that were encountered by Jung during his shattering "night sea journey" into the unconscious following his breakup with Freud. Jung recorded his encounter with the psyche's depths in his *Red Book*. We can say that an account of Nicoll's own introduction to these depths is presented in his diaries. If nothing else, they reveal a man struggling to understand his dreams and to glean from them the self-knowledge he believes and hopes they can provide. That is to say that Nicoll's interest in recording his dreams is not to prove Jung's theories or disprove Freud's, although at one point he considered writing a book to do just that, but never got around to it. His interest is not academic and has much more to do with his salvation.

There are two sets of diaries, covering an "early" and a "late" period. The early diaries contain a few entries from 1913, but the main body begins in 1919 and continues until Nicoll switches his allegiance from Jung to Ouspensky and the Work toward the end of 1921. The later diaries cover the 1940s until shortly before Nicoll's death in 1953. The Work dismisses dreams, but Nicoll may have continued recording his, or he may have merely jotted down a daily account of his activities, which is what many of the entries we have amount to, throughout the 1920s and '30s. I would not be surprised to find that he had kept other diaries, but so far, to my knowledge no other notebooks have come to light.

The diaries are without doubt a remarkable source for anyone interested in what was going on in Nicoll's life and in his conscious and unconscious mind during two important but very different periods in his career. They are not, however, the easiest documents to decipher. As mentioned, Nicoll rarely wrote a clear dream narrative, and what a reader of these diaries finds is a series of fragments, jottings, frequently merely a sentence or two—or, conversely, a torrent of word salad—and often in a kind of shorthand and accompanied by various symbols, the meaning of which we will get to shortly, and often with illustrations. There are also invocations, strange dialogues with a kind of inner guide or spirit, and purple poetic passages. Nicoll moves in and out of noting down mundane affairs and archetypal encounters, often in the same paragraph. As Willmett remarks, reports of personal events and meetings easily shift into "cosmological dramas, orotund hymn-like paeans, interrogatory catechisms, invocations or great hieratic prayers," without much warning. Nicoll's dream records may play the same part in his development as Jung's *Red Book* played in his, as Willmett and Adams contend, but they are not as readable, and they lack the striking watercolors of mandalas and dream images with which Jung illustrated his account, which is odd, given Nicoll's talent with the brush.*

This, of course, is not to criticize Nicoll; he is not in competition with Jung, although at times in the diaries more than a note of conflict enters their relationship. Nicoll didn't think of publication when keeping his notebooks; they were entirely private and for his own use, and only ravenous scholarship has brought them to light. And although Jung kept the *Red Book* a secret known only to a few close colleagues and friends, he treated it like an illuminated manuscript and did privately publish at least part of his account of his experience at the time of his "descent into the unconscious," his *Seven Sermons to the Dead*.[1] Jung played his esoteric cards very close to his chest, and while clearly he did

---

*I am basing my remarks on the annotated file of Nicoll's diaries sent to me by Jeffrey Adams. It is a work in progress, and the final edited version may be rather a different affair.

want to share his experience with others, he was circumspect about the *Red Book* and half dismissive of it on more than one occasion. This was a kind of protective coloration the scientist in Jung assumed whenever he felt the mystic in him was getting a little too vocal.

Another account of an inner journey with which we can compare Nicoll's diaries are the *Dream Journals* of Swedenborg. Like Nicoll's, Swedenborg's dreams were often frankly sexual, and we know that, although Swedenborg never married, he did have mistresses. We also know that Swedenborg engaged in a form of spiritual sex or erotic mysticism similar to Nicoll's pursuit, at least according to the researches of Marsha Keith Schuchard.

Nicoll's early diaries cover a relatively short period, only a few years, while the later ones stretch over a decade. But the early notebooks document a time of intense psychological and spiritual tension in Nicoll's life. They relate to Nicoll's growing uncertainty about Jung's work, his increasing sense of inferiority to his father and alienation from his world, his nagging sense of unfulfillment, of not "taking his place as a man among men," and his introduction to and gradual acceptance of Ouspensky and the stern message of the Work. But what they are occupied with mostly is sex and its relation to spirituality and religion. There is little to suggest that these two concerns were not on Nicoll's mind for any length of time. In fact, if what he says about his and everyone else's "unclean thoughts" is true, they were on his mind constantly, if in the background. It's a toss-up, but if I had to choose between them, I'd say that sex was on his mind most of the time, with spirituality a close second.

IT IS ODDLY TYPICAL OF NICOLL that one of the most important things he wrote, at least to my mind, is also something that he didn't finish and that most likely would have remained unknown if it hadn't surfaced in the batch of papers John Willmett unearthed from Sam

Copley's daughter. At least I have come to see it as typical of him. Something I've come to recognize in Nicoll over the course of writing this book is a frustrating habit of not finishing projects and a strangely casual attitude toward any written work. Not infrequently he shows an outright reluctance to do it, a manifestation, perhaps, of the "Nicoll spirit of knowing how to do things with the least possible physical exertion." He seems to lack the power of sustained intellectual effort. If *inability* seems too strong a term, we can say that Nicoll certainly displays a tendency not to complete writing projects, that he lacks a certain staying power, a stick-to-itiveness.*

If I can jump ahead a bit, the difficulties he had in finishing what we know as *The New Man* make up a good many of the entries in the later diaries. Nicoll himself recognized this, saying he had no "will to life," meaning to succeed, to conquer as his father had—a not uncommon sentiment of his generation, who blamed the war on their fathers—and that he tended to work in fits and starts. When his enthusiasm in some project lessened, he tended to look for something new to get it going again. (This may account for his "versatile mind" that could "never limit itself to one field alone.")

Yet what we have of his account of his "unclean thoughts" is enough to give us some idea of what he was pursuing in his imagination in the years leading up to his break with Jung and his commitment to the Work. It will also help us to understand what it was that Nicoll felt was missing from his life.

What excited me—I use the term advisedly—when I read Nicoll's

---

*It was curious that while reading Nicoll's diaries I was reminded of another writer who also had difficulty finishing projects and whose large body of work is for the most part made up of fragments and incomplete pieces of writing. This is the Portuguese poet Fernando Pessoa, whose work Nicoll would not have known. Aside from an interest in esotericism, there is little in common between them, except for the fact that Pessoa was, like Nicoll, a costive writer and that, also like Nicoll, he carried on extensive inner dialogues with a voice that often reprimanded him about his sexual proclivities. See my *A Dark Muse*, 229–36.

essay on "unclean thoughts" was that, as mentioned, in it he hit on what seems to be essence of the male sexual impulse: the attraction of the "forbidden." This is not, of course, wholly limited to males. Women like to be "naughty" and to have a "dirty weekend" too. But these adjectives give the game away. We *know* that sex isn't naughty or dirty, in the way that Nicoll was brought up to believe it was. The whole "modern" attitude toward sex is to see it as a perfectly normal, natural part of human life. The message is that we all need to get rid of our "hangups" about it, to get rid of our "guilt trips" about practically any sexual practice at all, in order to be happy. (This is what Freud hath wrought.) The "sexual revolution" of the 1960s was supposed to bring this about, and there are tributaries of it carrying on today.

So why do we still get a tittle out of pretending sex is something deliciously wicked and taboo, as the many sex websites online encourage us to do? Because it excites the imagination, and sex without imagination is about as exciting as any other bodily function. What most excites the imagination is the forbidden, the *verboten*, the strange, just as it has ever since the first bite of the apple. We can say it is a powerful lure for our "interest," indeed the most powerful one. As Colin Wilson writes in his phenomenological study of sex, *Origins of the Sexual Impulse*, "The major component of the sexual urge is the sense of sin . . . the sense of invading another's privacy, of escaping one's own separateness." "Without the sense of violation . . . sexual excitement would be weakened, or perhaps completely dissipated."[2]

This sense of violation, of going beyond the limits, excites the imagination. And as Nicoll points out in his essay, men have a relationship to their imagination that is different from a woman's. It assumes, as he says, a strange "fixative" quality in men that easily forms into a compulsion; hence the power of fetishes, to which men are as a rule much more prone. Our imagination rules us, we can say, in a way that women don't experience. We are driven by it to seek out new conquests. Even the act of penetration is a kind of assault on a castle under siege. As

Shaw pointed out long ago, men are the dreamers, women the realists.

We can say that as a sex, men are subject to what is known as "the Coolidge effect," the name coming from a story told about the American president, Calvin Coolidge. During an inspection of a government farm, the president and his wife were shown around by different guides. At the chicken pens, Mrs. Coolidge asked if the rooster mated more than once a day. The man in charge replied, "Dozens of times." Mrs. Coolidge said "Please tell that to the President." When the president arrived at the pen, he received the message. He then asked the man "And does the rooster choose the same hen each time?" "Oh no," was the answer. "A different one each time." Coolidge smiled and said "Tell that to Mrs. Coolidge."[3]

A similar phenomenon is known to cattle breeders. A bull will not copulate with a female it has already mated with. He loses interest and will only perform with a new, *strange* female. Mrs. Coolidge's remarks suggest that the female sees sex as a way of keeping the male. Mr. Coolidge's remarks suggest that the male is interested in mating with as many desirable females as he can. This seems a fair estimate of their different attitudes toward sex.

Animals are at a disadvantage in this. The male's sexual response is dependent on the female being in heat; the smell of the estrus sets him off. But once the objective has been achieved, the male ignores a female he has mated with, even if no other females are around. Human females are no longer cyclical; they are sexually receptive year-round, their non-receptive sisters being sidelined by evolution. Now it is no longer estrus that stimulates the male, but the female's appearance; hence the development of full lips, breasts, buttocks, and other curves. And by now these are accentuated by any number of erotic accoutrements, from fishnet stockings and black underwear, to PVC, chains, and whips. We can say that with sex, the imagination performs an alchemical transformation that results in the wrapping becoming more important than what's inside. All roads lead to Rome, but with sex, it's the getting there that matters.

This means that, with a little ingenuity, a woman can keep her man sexually interested, in a way that a cow or a hen can't. The cow or hen can't resort to their imagination to stimulate the male, for the simple fact that neither he nor they have one. A woman can buy sexy lingerie or even "dress up" as a nurse, French maid, or schoolgirl, so that, at least for the crucial moments, she can appear to her man as "different." She can even wrap herself in half-torn clothes, as they "make believe" a rape. This is how businesses like Victoria's Secret turn a profit.

It is from this need to spice up sex so that it achieves "strangeness" that all sexual perversions arise. And the simple fact that we have sexual perversions shows that sex isn't like our other natural functions; no one needs "strangeness" in order to stimulate digestion or excretion. This is why the Russian existential philosopher Nicolai Berdyaev can remark that, "It is quite possible to say that man is a sexual being, but we cannot say that man is a food-digesting being."[4] (As Nietzsche has already told us, "The degree and kind of a man's sexuality reaches up into the topmost summit of his spirit." We can't say the same about his digestion.) Perversions work by stimulating the imagination, because, unlike estrus, "the forbidden" isn't a thing, but an *idea*. It works by focusing the mind, in the same way that Janet's "psychological tension" focuses our "reality function." You have to *know* you are transgressing to get the *frisson* that comes from breaking the rules. ("Aren't we naughty?") The reality that the sexually jaded individual wants to "grip" is the sexual act itself, having let it slip through his mental fingers because he—or she—has allowed his "reality function" to go slack. "The forbidden" acts as shock, jolting the imagination awake, which then focuses the mind, and with any luck other parts, on the business at hand.

As WE'VE SEEN, Nicoll's "unclean thoughts" troubled him as a young boy, and like other young boys at the time, he read pamphlets on the dangers of "polluting" oneself through masturbation. These, of course, were of little help; as we see from his diaries, he carried the practice on into later life.

After relating the feelings of loneliness and isolation he experienced because of his "unclean thoughts" that set him apart, or so he believed, from those around him, Nicoll begins to explain exactly what he means by these thoughts. Yet he never becomes explicit about them. That is to say, he never goes into any detail about any particular unclean thought; he is never graphic, as a work of pornography would be, nor does he harp on a single obsession, as a fetishist would. He is trying to understand his thoughts, to arrive at what they mean. The repertory of possible "unclean acts" is as limited as that of pornography, so although Nicoll may never tell us of any specific unclean thought, we nevertheless get the picture. It isn't the case that there is one obsessional thought that dominates his mind, in the way that the minds of patients suffering from obsessive, compulsive thoughts who sought out Freud or Jung were so dominated. At least there seems no evidence of this. The simplest way to put it is that Nicoll had what we could call a "dirty mind"—where else would unclean thoughts abide?—although it was a bit more complicated than that. He thought about sex a great deal, and mixed in with his notions of ecstasy and excitement were fantasies of violation, of treating embodiments of utmost purity—women—in ways that degraded and debased them.

"My unclean thoughts were always centred on women," Nicoll writes.

> While on the one hand I had every conceivable—as far as I know— unclean thought about women, I had beyond doubt ideals about them. Woman seemed to present herself to me as the lowest and the highest simultaneously. And I could never understand why this was so. Depth and height seemed to go together. The seeming purity of the face, the sweetness of the lips, the delicateness of the body, the extraordinary softness, the wonder of the very fact of woman,

seemed always to meet and merge with the most unclean thoughts and desires, the lowest impulses, the most impossible imagination about her and her body and her natural functions. I remembered that I tried to be good. . . . I tried to think that my unclean thoughts were really wicked and that I should not have them. But I could not believe in all I was trying to do. My unclean thoughts seemed to have a life of their own, which I could not do without. I wanted to satisfy my unclean thoughts—to realize them.

I remember how rarely those unclean thoughts fastened on any actual woman. Occasionally they did—and usually on a woman below me socially—that is, on a woman of whom I felt less afraid. But they seemed to be always about an *imaginary woman*—one who changed as I wished and became anything I wished. And I do not think it was long before I understood that man meets woman first in imagination and forms, in that medium . . . all sorts of scenes that become stereotyped in a general sense, but remain open in regard to detail. And I believe that this is stronger in a man than in a woman, because I believe that the relation of a man to his imagination is not the same as in the case of woman, who seems always more flexible and less caught and held than a man in every respect. . . . I do not think that a woman's imagination is like that of a man, which has a very powerful fixative quality.

What interests a man most deeply, whether he permits himself to acknowledge it or not, is the possible realisation of his unclean thought. That part of man is always near him and full of energy. It causes him to travel, to go about, to mingle with crowds, to see people. I noticed that always, whatever offered itself, this factor came in, sooner or later into my thoughts . . . in the background this interest was present—a possible realisation, a possible adventure, something unknown and new and tremendously urgent and powerful . . . this element is always present and . . . it is always influencing [a man] all through his life. And it does not diminish with passing years.

On the contrary it may increase and become more marked, more quickly acknowledged, more unhesitatingly accepted. But what is most interesting is that these unclean thoughts *are never satisfied*, whatever the age or experience. Neither in man nor in woman do they ever lead to reality.[5]

These few paragraphs make up the bulk of Nicoll's essay on "unclean thoughts." It is unfortunate that Nicoll didn't finish the essay; it trails off in reflections on how it is much easier for men than for women to enter into casual affairs, experience of which Nicoll may or may not have had. Although Nicoll's diaries show that he had sex on his mind practically all the time, it is difficult to tell whether he ever tried to realize any of his "unclean thoughts"—which, according to him, are always eager to become real—or if he even engaged in any more ordinary sorts of affairs. His diaries, especially the early ones, are full of references to women, but is never quite clear exactly how far he got with them. There is little evidence that his wife satisfied his desires, or that she was even aware of them. There is little mention of their sex life in a diary that is focused almost exclusively on sex.

One reason for that may be that early on in their relationship, which began as doctor and patient, Catherine Jones admitted to Nicoll that she had a "horror of physical sex." Why a man obsessed with sex would marry a woman who found it revolting is one of those questions biographers simultaneously love and hate. If we can assume that marriage did not assuage his obsession with his unclean thoughts—and going by what we can tell from the diaries it didn't—it seems that rather than enter into affairs in order to seek out an actual partner who might satisfy his desires, Nicoll decided that the best way to approach the question was through his imagination. The practice that troubled him as boy remained in later life as means of satisfying the urges of his "unclean thoughts."

Nicoll may not have known it—I suspect he didn't—but he was not alone in indulging in a practice that, although no moral stigma attaches to it now, is still regarded as a rather disreputable habit, like taking drugs or drinking. A short list of Nicoll's contemporaries of comparable stature—indeed of a greater eminence—that shared his devotion would include the poet W. B. Yeats, the novelist John Cowper Powys, and the creator of Narnia and fellow Christian C. S. Lewis.* Alan Watts, the popularizer of Zen and other forms of Eastern wisdom, was an ardent masturbator.[6] Jean-Jacques Rousseau is perhaps the first to publicly sing the praises of self-pleasure, rating it higher than the real thing in his *Confessions*. By now magazines carry articles on it, instructions and "how to" guides are available, and the health benefits of orgasms have been articulated far and wide, so that we can say there is a new meaning to getting your "five a day."

A few things jump out from the extracts from Nicoll's essay. One is his remark that "While on the one hand I had every conceivable—as far as I know—unclean thought about women, I had beyond doubt ideals about them. Woman seemed to present herself to me as the lowest and the highest simultaneously." This is a pretty clear presentation of what at the time Nicoll was writing—most likely before World War I—was a new and disturbing idea, but which today, more than a century later, we toss about in conversation without batting an eye. This is the notion of the madonna/whore: woman as the embodiment of the Eternal Feminine, the ever-virginal inspirer of ideals, who, as Goethe tells us, "leads us upward," and woman as a sex object, a plaything for men's desires, the lascivious slut who gives herself to all and sundry to be used and abused. The devotees of this feminine yin and yang are subject to a

---

*Yeats writes of masturbating himself into exhaustion in his *Autobiographies*. Like Nicoll, John Cowper Powys, a writer of mythic stature, entertained "unclean thoughts" throughout his life, although his were more along sadistic lines. In later life he praised masturbation as a means of purging oneself of any such desires. Powys maintained that he never indulged in his desires in any "real" way, only through the mind. C. S. Lewis shared Powys's taste for sadism, and according to David Holbrook in *The Skeleton in the Wardrobe* (Lewisburg, PA: Bucknell University Press, 1991) evidence of this can be found in the Narnia series.

peculiarly exquisite masochism, the revulsion at knowing that this paragon of beauty and the ideal is capable of giving herself to any stranger. (And indeed, some men are sexually excited by watching their paragon so give herself.) This feminine double act—at least from the male's point of view—is at the root of many of problems between the sexes, and its ostensible eclipse with the rise of feminism has evidently done little to eradicate them. Freud had introduced the idea into the psychoanalytical vocabulary, but it had been present in the minds of romantic poets long before him.

Nicoll points out another incompatible polarity in men's vision of women, when he speaks of how "The seeming purity of the face, the sweetness of the lips, the delicateness of the body, the extraordinary softness, the wonder of the very fact of woman, seemed always to meet and merge with the most unclean thoughts and desires, the lowest impulses, the most impossible imagination about her and her body and her natural functions."

Again the ideal and the real—or the pure and the natural—clash and throw him into an emotional turmoil. Nicoll seems to have had a morbid fascination with women's bodily functions, an interest not as unusual as it may appear.* As we might expect, the natural functions Nicoll mentions appear in his dreams, as they do in most people's. Here Nicoll is experiencing what Jonathan Swift had expressed in his poem "The Lady's Dressing Room," which has a suitor entering his lady's chamber when she is absent and discovering, among other nasty things, that she defecates.† The knowledge shatters the suitor, as the educator

---

*James Joyce liked to carry a pair of his wife Nora's soiled underpants with him and believed that "It is wonderful to fuck a farting woman." Quoted in Colin Wilson, *The Misfits*, 211.

†Swift, of course, is more graphic:
Thus finishing his grand survey
Disgusted Strephon stole away,
Repeating in his amorous fits
"Oh Celia, Celia, Celia shits!"

John Ruskin famously was shattered at the sight of his wife's pubic hair. But it is precisely this vision of woman, not as an ideal or delicate creature of beauty, but in the raw, that the Hindu holy man Sri Ramakrishna urged on his disciples if they were ever lured from the path by feminine charms. They should reflect, he told them, that women were made up of disagreeable things like blood, gristle, and bones, and not, as they may have believed, sugar and spice and everything nice.[7]

This objective, unsentimental view has cured many a besotted calf of his romanticism, but ultimately it seems just as unsatisfactory as the affliction it relieves. Bernard Shaw's quip that women are just men in petticoats is bracing and refreshing, yet even he knew that there was more to it than that. What exactly that *more* is, remains something of a mystery. It was a mystery that Nicoll wanted to grasp, and many entries in his dream diaries are evidence of how he went about this.

Something else that jumps out from Nicoll's fragment is the fact that his unclean thoughts and his vision of woman have a great deal to do with his imagination. This may seem obvious, but as we've seen it is in fact the essential point. It is curious that Nicoll admits to being afraid of women, at least of the women of his own social rank. Nicoll remained something of a snob throughout his life, and it is ironic that the revival of interest in esoteric teachings that characterized the 1960s and our "New Age" led to many people Nicoll would have turned his nose up at becoming readers of Gurdjieff and Ouspensky. The hippies who read *In Search of the Miraculous* and *Meetings with Remarkable Men*, and took the journey to the East in search of enlightenment, would not have got past his door.

The only actual women who served as targets for Nicoll's unclean thoughts—meaning he may have fantasized about them—were those who were his social inferiors, and we have no evidence to suggest that he acted out his thoughts with any of them. (John Willmett practically insists that he didn't.) This was not uncommon at the time. Aside from the prostitutes many men visited, while maintaining a respectable family life, another source of sexual liaisons without attachment were shopgirls. We don't know if Nicoll took this path, but it would have been an easy one for him to take.

Yet the essence of his unclean thoughts was this: that they were focused on an "*imaginary woman*—one who changed as I wished and became anything I wished." This, of course, is woman's age-old complaint against men: that they do not want a real woman, but a fantasy, an infinitely plastic erotic doll that will assume whatever shape and character they desire. Nicoll's remark that "man meets woman first in imagination," may sound like textbook Jung, a nod to the anima, the feminine archetype in the male psyche that prepares him, as it were, for his encounter with women. But she is also that element in his unconscious that *animates* him, arouses his "interest," lures him into life, with all its rewards and dangers, with the promise of her conquest. Without her approval, nothing seems worth the effort. And we meet her first in our imagination. As William Blake wrote in *Visions of the Daughters of Albion,* "the youth shut up from the lustful joy shall forget to generate, and create an amorous image / In the shadows of his curtains and in the folds of his silent pillow." She is simultaneously the Eternal Feminine and the Great Whore, the mother bestowing love, acceptance, and security, and the concubine brazenly offering herself. This was a dual personality Nicoll would come to know, or at least would try to get acquainted with.

I've said that imagination is the key to understanding Nicoll's fascination with his unclean thoughts and the imaginary women with whom we can assume he satisfied them. I've also asked, if obliquely, *why* he chose to fulfill his desires in this way: why, that is, he was afraid of "real" women and so reluctant even to try to satisfy his cravings in the flesh, as it were. This part of the question is not too difficult to answer. The sense of inferiority that living in the shadow of his domineering father had instilled in him would have made him insecure and apprehensive, certainly not confident. Nothing gives a man more confidence than sexual conquest. But, as with the art of making alchemical gold, to secure this one needs some confidence to start with. Nicoll also was insecure about his appearance; the portliness that came with middle age—his insecurity about it fills the later diaries—began to show itself early. And even with a successful practice on Harley Street and his other achievements, Nicoll still felt that he was not yet "a man among men," but boyish. In photographs he tended to look chubby, and he retained the "schoolboy" appearance for some time. This youthful character gave Nicoll his light touch, the taste for gaiety, his sense of humor, and his versatility, but it also gives the impression of a character that is fundamentally lightweight, flighty, lacking solidity, lacking, Jung would say, a *shadow*. Again, it is interesting that in later years the figure of the *puer aeternus*, or eternal youth, would occupy Nicoll's attention greatly.

Yet, as we've seen, there is another aspect to Nicoll's seeming preference for an imaginary woman with whom he could pursue his unclean thoughts, one that isn't rooted in his insecurity and lack of confidence, but in the nature of the male sexual impulse itself. This is the fact that, as mentioned, with men, sex has much more to do with imagination than with any purely physiological or "natural" need.* We say that we "hunger" or "thirst" for sex if we've been without it for some time. But no one has ever died from lack of sex, while we know that without food or water we succumb fairly quickly.

Yet one of the strangest things about human sexuality is that if sex *is* a hunger, it is one we can satisfy purely through the mind. If I am hungry, no matter how vividly or in what detail I imagine a meal, I cannot eat it and it will not fill my stomach. If I am thirsty, I can visualize a tall, cool drink, with drops of moisture sliding down its side,

---

*I am, of course, speaking from a male perspective. This would ordinarily go without saying; only our highly sensitive time requires pointing it out.

but I can't swallow it and it will not quench my thirst. But if I feel sexually aroused, I *can* imagine a sexual object to the degree that I can satisfy my appetite to the same extent I could if I had a "real" partner. From the evidence of his diaries, Nicoll was doing this practically all the time. That is, I can achieve an orgasm this way, which physiologically is equivalent to filling my stomach or quenching my thirst.

My imaginary meal and drink may only serve to heighten the absence of anything "real" on the table. That is, they may make me only more hungry and thirsty. But my imaginary sex partner *will* quench my erotic thirst, at least for the time being. In fact, it is not uncommon that satisfying my sexual urge in this way is often more effective than the usual route. It avoids preliminaries. One can quench one's thirst directly; the male sexual impulse has an urgency and immediacy to it that can rarely be "acted out" in normal relations, as the male delight in conquest feeds the will. There is more control, more focus, and the other person's personality does not become a postcoital problem. But the important point is that, as odd as it sounds, masturbation is one of the clearest examples of the remarkable power of the imagination. It is, as Colin Wilson writes, "one of the highest faculties mankind has yet achieved."[8] How so? Because it displays a power to create reality, to endow our experience with it—that is, to "make it real"—*with the mind alone.*

THIS IS NOT, LET ME ASSURE the readers of this book, a call for them to put it down and pleasure themselves, or even to read it with one hand. But it may be taken as a suggestion that there may be more to that activity than we realize. In fact, "realizing" is the key here, for that is what the act of masturbation does: it "realizes" an imaginary object to the degree that we respond to it exactly as we would were its real counterpart present. Again, the point here is not to argue that solitary sex is preferable, or, conversely, that "there's nothing like the real thing, baby."

There is more to sex than satisfying orgasms, although clearly they are an important part of it. As Wilson writes, the power of the orgasm suggests "an intuition of some deeper, more 'god-like' state of satisfaction for the individual."[9]

For most of us, the orgasm is the closest we come to a mystical experience. It is an experience of tremendous power, beyond anything in everyday life, what Nietzsche called "the Dionysian," referring to the ancient Greek god of drunkenness, ecstasy, and abandon. It is a sudden explosion of "power, meaning, and purpose." Hence its popularity. The sexual orgasm seems to offer a taste of some more powerful, unified consciousness, an intensity of being we rarely feel. Because of this, Wilson writes that "A satisfactory notion of 'ultimate sexual satisfaction' *must* be bound up with some larger mystical vision about the purpose of human existence."[10]

What is important is to understand exactly what the imagination is achieving here. The point is not to celebrate or promote masturbation but to recognize a clear instance of the ability of imagination to "focus" on a reality that at the moment happens to be absent, to the degree that our response to it is "as if" it were present—that is, on the imagination's ability to "create reality." For if imagination can create a sexual reality, or endow a flat two-dimensional image with a reality equal to that which it represents (which is the point of pornography), to which we respond as if it were the real thing, then there is no reason, Wilson suggests, why it cannot endow other aspects of our experience with a similar reality—(which is what art does)—or even the *whole* of reality with an extra dimension, which is what seems to happen in mystical experiences.

That is to say, if imagination can bring a *Playboy* centerfold "to life" to the degree that I respond to it "as if" it were the "real thing"—I have an orgasm—can I not direct this same focus to my "real" experience, and likewise "bring it to life" in ways that would be the equivalent of my making a two-dimensional image three-dimensional, at least momentarily? The centerfold is a good example in the sense that my "real" response to it is unmistakable: I get sexually aroused. And as Wilson says, in this case imagination is "subsidized" by the sexual urge. But I can also direct my focus to, say, a photograph of Paris. I can see it as just that, a flat image. But if I "add" to it my memories and knowledge of Paris in a process Wilson calls "completing," it can "come alive" in the same way that the centerfold does (and the centerfold "comes to life" because I am "completing" it as well). My response to it is not sexual, but the *reality* I evoke from the photograph can generate a similar physical response: I recall a particular scent that I associate with a visit there, I remember the taste of the coffee and croissant I would get at the small *tabac* near my hotel, I recall the feel of the zinc table top, the smell of Gauloise, and so on.

We rarely exercise our power to evoke reality in this way, although it can happen of its own; the madeleine that sets Proust off on writing *Remembrance of Things Past* is the classic example. Or, we may dredge up the memory on purpose. The point is that because it concerns sex, and we feel faintly embarrassed to consider it, we fail to see that the power of focusing imagination that we experience in masturbation is really a crude use of a forgotten power we possess to *endow our experience with a reality it otherwise lacks*. (And it isn't surprising, as Wilson points out, that one of the earliest results of the Romantics' discovery of the imagination in the late eighteenth century was pornography.) And it is precisely because our experience lacks "reality" that Gurdjieff and Ouspensky say we are "asleep." We suffer, as the philosopher Heidegger says, from "forgetfulness of Being," a forgetfulness that is shaken off whenever our imagination receives a jolt and focuses our concentration.

EXCEPT FOR CERTAIN MOMENTS, the reality we experience most of the time and accept as the "real thing" is the equivalent of the centerfold without a sexually aroused consciousness "bringing it to life"—that is, flat and two-dimensional. If we want to say that the flat two-dimensional image *is* "real," and my "completion" of it via my imagination a "falsification" of reality—as some materialists would—I can only say that in this case, we seem to prefer the false to the genuine, as the "falsified" reality triggers the "real" response; the "real" reality leaves us cold. But because we can maneuver through this two-dimensional world and prosper in it, we never think to direct our imagination at it in the same way that we *instinctively* do when looking at the centerfold.

The people who do direct their imagination in this way we call poets and mystics. Their "interest" is aroused as energetically as my sexual interest is by the centerfold, but by a wider range of stimuli, and not for the relief of a specific appetite. They can get excited over a tree or flower in the same way that a sexy picture excites me; indeed, the novels of John Cowper Powys, mentioned earlier, can be seen as long exercises in depicting the fundamentally erotic relationship his consciousness has with nature and inanimate objects.* We can say that the whole world becomes a centerfold for them, with their poems and visions being not too far from "orgasms" but of a higher type. (Incidentally it is this kind of power over their experience that Shaw's Ancients in *Back to Methuselah* achieve and which Shaw believed would eventually make the sexual orgasm old hat.)

We could say that "reality" is a factor of the focusing of consciousness, and very little focuses men's consciousness in the way that sex does. This is a power inherent in human consciousness about which we know very little. It is a power that we experience in our dreams, which also present a purely mental world that we respond to as if it

---

*See especially *A Glastonbury Romance* (1932), and his philosophical book *In Defence of Sensuality* (1930).

were real.* It is a power that is enormously liberating because it tells us that reality has much more to do with the mind than with the senses, something that Nicoll believed and would tell his students. It is a power, I think, that Nicoll sought and that, going by how I read his diary entries, he achieved on at least one occasion.

It is this power, I believe, that he alludes to when he speaks of a "tremendous momentary impulse toward a life other than conventional life," that he felt both as religion and as the *satisfaction of his unclean thoughts*. The two were inextricably entwined. That is, he had a dim intuition that the "lure of the forbidden," the hunger for the strange, the new, the unknown, was in some way the same as his religious need. Jung himself said as much when he posited a religious instinct that was as fundamental as a sexual one, then set about to show how this instinct could manifest in dreams in sexual symbolism.

This desire, this hunger for a life *more satisfying* than "conventional life," is at the root of both a spiritual quest and the worst sex crimes, the difference being that the man on a spiritual quest starts from a position that the man prone to sex crimes doesn't occupy. He is in a far lower position and hence needs to perform radically transgressive acts in order to tighten his "grip" on reality, and suffers from the "law of diminishing returns" in the process.[11] But in essence the urge is the same: to break out of the stultifying lukewarm consciousness of everyday life, to make the centerfold come to life. This is why Nicoll can refer to the itch to

---

*Perhaps even more to this point are the visions and audial hallucinations we experience on our way to sleep in the hypnagogic state, in between sleeping and waking. In this state we can slip into a half dream and respond to it in more directly physical ways than we do in dreams, when our muscles are torpid and we enter what is called "sleep paralysis." I often experience as I fall asleep the vision of a ball being thrown at me, which causes me to duck, which then wakes me up. Or I will enter a dream of walking down stairs and missing a step, which has the same effect; my leg regaining balance will jerk me awake. We should note that while the rest of the body is paralyzed in dreams, the sexual organs become active. Men have erections and women lubricate. Freud was right in one sense: dreaming does have something to do with sex. Erotic dreams can result in "real" orgasms and ejaculation. This seems another link between sex and imagination.

satisfy his unclean thoughts, not in some wicked way—although, to be sure, he will fill pages of his diary with self-recriminations—but as "a possible realisation, a possible adventure, something unknown and new and tremendously urgent and powerful." It is so "urgent and powerful" that it "interests a man most deeply" and is "always near him and full of energy." It *animates him*, it "causes him to travel, to go about, to mingle with crowds, to see people."

Yet Nicoll tells us that the satisfaction of his unclean thoughts, at least in some real sense, is impossible. "Neither in man nor in woman," he writes, "do they ever lead to reality." Does this mean that people never try to satisfy their unclean thoughts? Hardly. There are multi-million dollar businesses aimed at doing just that. I would suggest that what Nicoll is alluding to here is the fact that except on some rare occasions, sex is more times than not a letdown, a disappointment. We all know of postcoital sadness. "Man is sad after sex," Aristotle tells us, and many have echoed his remark down the ages. Why? Because the dream has suddenly shifted to reality, of the everyday kind. The fairy gold of sexual excitement—which makes the woman a prize worth every effort, or the man a dashing adventurer come to ravish her—vanishes, and we are faced with a woman, just a woman, like most others. (Needless to say, women feel the same about the brute they have woken up with.) Imagination has left the building, and in its wake we wonder what the fuss was all about. Yet I believe that postcoital sadness is not inevitable. If we could manage to focus our minds voluntarily, in the same way that the sexual urge focuses them instinctively, we would not feel it.*

---

*Postcoital sadness is also not a factor of satiety. In his novel *Ritual in the Dark* (1961), a study of a sex killer, Wilson has a scene that illustrates perfectly how the "strange" is the central attraction to the male sexual imagination. The hero has spent the morning making love to his girlfriend, and feels sexually exhausted, his desire spent. He has a basement flat, and when he goes to retrieve the milk bottles left outside his door, he catches a glimpse up the skirt of a woman passing by. Instantly his desire revives. Why should a fleeting glimpse up a skirt electrify him, when the woman he has just made love to for hours, is lying in bed, naked and most likely willing to carry on? Because the passing skirt is *strange*. Whatever postcoital sadness he may have felt is dissipated by it as a thin mist is dissipated by a stiff wind.

But if we could do that, we would be among the poets and mystics.

Nicoll was a reader of Dr. Johnson, but I wonder if he understood the true import of this passage from his *Rasselas, Prince of Abyssinia*? The protagonist gazes at the beautiful scenery of the Happy Valley, and can't understand why he can't share the kind of happiness that the sheep and cows seem to enjoy. He reflects that "Man has surely some latent sense for which this place affords no gratification, or he has desires distinct from sense that must be satisfied before he can be happy."[12] This "latent sense" and these "desires distinct from sense" refer to the imagination, whose power is to focus reality. When the imagination is caught up in the sexual excitement it transforms the sexual object into a magical source of power and fulfillment. Going by the range of fetishes men are prone to, this can be anything from a rolling pin to a pair of soiled underpants, with much in between. For most men, it's a woman; she is fetish enough. Once the fever has passed, the object reverts to its everyday reality: the coach becomes a pumpkin, and we wonder where Cinderella went to.

This is why individuals obsessed with the idea of some ultimately satisfying sexual experience never seem to achieve it, no matter how much they pile on the stimulants—perversions—to get there, as any reader of de Sade's *120 Days of Sodom* soon discovers. The satisfaction is not in the sex, or in the enhancements they add to it, but in the tightening of the focus of consciousness that the sexual imagination stimulates. It was this tightening that I believe Nicoll was after, albeit instinctively, when he pursued, through his dreams and fantasies, the imaginary woman who would administer to his unclean thoughts.

How far did he get in his pursuit? Let us see.

5

Dark Nights of the Soul

On June 18, 1919, Nicoll recorded a dream involving a woman named Laura, some horses, and a broken ankle.

"What are the horses that dash so wildly after they break away from the lorry, which is so primitive?" he asks in his account, presumably referring to events in the dream that he does not record. And he receives an answer. "They are the horses that are led by your primitive feelings."[1]

Who responds to Nicoll's query about the meaning of the symbolism in his dream? That is a good question. We can say it is an inner voice with whom Nicoll will carry on many of these internal dialogues over the next few years. It is his soul, we might say, although it is difficult to determine how independent and objective this voice is, and how much it is Nicoll simply talking to himself. He seems to have picked up the practice from Jung, who engaged in a similar dialogue with his unconscious during the psychic turbulence following the breakup with Freud. Jung called this practice "active imagination," and the results of his inner dialogues fill the pages of the *Red Book*. Jung kept the idea to himself for a long time, committing it to print only obliquely—and Jung is not always the clearest writer to begin with—and speaking of it only to his closest followers; understandably, as it advises talking to people in your head. One assumes Nicoll was among those Jung trusted.

Nicoll doesn't say as much, but we can say that *stylistically* his inner dialogues bear a resemblance to Jung's, which suggests he was among those of the inner circle who heard about this means of accessing inner worlds from the master himself.

Nicoll will ask his inner voice for guidance and advice, which he won't always take. He will seek its approval and forgiveness and, on occasion, will even argue with it. But in general Nicoll will address this voice with respect, occasionally fear, sometimes passing into guilt-ridden self-abasement as if he were prostrating himself before a deity. He will offer it praise and submit to it entreaties, pray to it, and invoke its protection and strength. For the most part though, he will ask it for help, something that throughout this period Nicoll was sorely in need of. If nothing else these diaries present a record of a deeply troubled man. On the whole the voice will respond positively, but on occasion one gets the impression that its patience has been sorely tried, which a reader of these diaries may find understandable. But let us return to the dream.

"On passing the bus and going before you they"—the horses—"fall into disorder and terrible disaster and cause you to fall with Laura," Nicoll's inner voice tells him. "Where they fall is the road along which you seek to travel."

> Beware because you bring with you many terrible forces. You saw the horse dashing madly about and lying mangled and while this happened you were in safety with Laura, but because the horses were in confusion you had to come off the high place and leap to earth with Laura in your arms. Know that this is to come and that you are in the Power of Instinct who goes before you but I am with you and because you prayed to me you will be saved though the scene seemed terrible. Do not be guided by the Horses of Desire or by the Primitive Feelings for there is already something fastened to Laura which will guide you best of all. It is the descent from the perilous and the temporary to the permanent. When you reach the Earth the

horses have vanished. The problem has now changed. But the Ankle is broken and because you are concerned too much with eating and drinking do not see this.

The account breaks off into gnomic phrases—"Live the life that is the Path and trust to the Few"—and ends with a poem about the Cabiri, ancient Greek chthonic gods who presided over the orgiastic rites of Samothrace. "Ho, little men, Mighty Ones, what do you," Nicoll asks, and in reply they tell him. "In the valley we work . . . weaving golden cloth." Yet one stanza of their song seems to refer to Nicoll himself. "Who is the Puppy? / Ho, I am the puppy, playful and foolish." Similar self-recriminations will fill diary entries throughout this time. He asks the voice to "Free me, for I am enslaved with things that I loathe." He needs its help in order to "free myself from the hollowness of my life." He is "quite vile," "despicable," and other reprehensible things. "There is need for steel in thy psychology," the Cabiri tell him, perhaps intuiting that Nicoll will soon find his source for this. He will meet his fate. He is in search of it. He asks only "to know the way." The account then dissolves into some gloomy reflections on the fate of the man who has shot the albatross and breaks up into scattered fragments. "The mist is dark. He downs the Black Night and laughs. I am a poor thing, cringing." For all his gaiety and laughter, Nicoll was not a happy man.

His inner voice thought well of Laura. She turns up in quite a few dreams. In the very next entry, for June 19, another girl in Nicoll's dream is jealous of Laura, because she and Nicoll are engaged to be married.[2] Nicoll notes in the diaries that they *are* engaged, and it seems that he means in the "real world." But aside from his remarks there seems no evidence that they were "really" engaged, nor in fact do we ever find out who Laura was or what happened to her. (As far as I know, we still don't know.) And the fact that six months after noting down this engagement, Nicoll does get married, but not to Laura, does raise some questions, and not only of chronology.

Was Nicoll in some way desperate to marry? One thing that came to me while writing this book is that it seems that Nicoll never lived alone. He spent time alone; the later diaries record times when he went off on a kind of "private retreat," and in this early period he has a cottage he can get away to. Yet even this was not much. There doesn't seem to be a time when he was not either living at home, sharing a flat, living with his wife and child, or leading the more or less communal life he adopted once he set up shop as a teacher of the Work. He seemed to want and need to be surrounded by people, an observation that could be made about Gurdjieff and most gurus, in fact. We remember his need for gaiety and parties. Whatever this may say about Nicoll's psychology, it is not the best environment for creative work.

What is surprising is that Nicoll *did* get married in what seems something of a rush, not to Laura but, as mentioned, to a woman who almost upon meeting him confessed to a horror of physical sex, a revulsion Laura seems not to have shared—at least as far as I can tell from the diaries. What makes this even more surprising is that his inner voice told him that he should marry Laura, advice it (she?) gave Nicoll a week after his dream about the horses and lorry. The voice practically insisted that he did. "Marry Laura and follow me," it told him, which leads one to wonder *why* the voice wanted Nicoll to marry Laura and why in fact he didn't.[3] If, as the voice told Nicoll, "I am the fair one and thy beloved for whom thou yearnest," and if she would come to Nicoll as part of a package deal which included marrying Laura—who, as far as we can tell from Nicoll's remarks, was attractive and not averse to sex—then one wonders why he didn't marry her. Of course, it wasn't all up to him, and there is some suggestion that the question did come up and Laura turned him down. But as with quite a bit in these diaries, it is not quite clear.

What is clear is that Nicoll's inner voice did expect a lot from a union with Laura. After Nicoll asks a question about his sexuality—"what is this sexuality of mine, is it horrible?"—the voice explains why

Laura is the right choice for him.⁴ "Nay," his sexuality is not horrible it tells him. But he desires the "feeling which absorbs me and makes you forget yourself"—the escape from personality Nicoll craves and that at times manifests as a kind of masochistic humility. He can only achieve this now, the voice seems to tell him, by plunging "into the sensations of sexuality which is Me in my lowest form of love and union." But is it mere sex that is the problem? Or is it Nicoll's way of approaching it?

Later the voice will tell him that because he fears sex with another person—that is, actual intercourse—he always lets his instincts out "alone."⁵ That is, he masturbates rather than sleeps with a woman. Did Laura frighten him? Was she too open about sex, too forthright? After all it was the time of the Bright Young Things, Britain's equivalent of the Roaring Twenties. Sexual mores were changing. Free love and the New Woman were making sex political and progressive. Indeed, one of Jung's colleagues and patients, the unfortunate Otto Gross, was a notorious sexual profligate, promoting free love in places such as Monte Verita, the "mountain of truth" rising over Ascona, Switzerland, home to one of the first "nature cure" communes.⁶ It was Gross who, while a patient of Jung's at the Burghölzli clinic, encouraged the buttoned-down doctor to submit to the sexual advances of his patient Sabina Spielrein, first of his *sorors mystica*. And people whose company Nicoll would soon keep—like Havelock Ellis and A. R. Orage—were pursuing sexual freedom in print and in deed. Orage was a notorious seducer, and Ellis practiced his own form of sexual fetishism, apt for the author of the six volume *Studies in the Psychology of Sex*.*

We remember that the only actual women Nicoll would ever allow himself to fantasize about were those who were his social inferiors, and from what we can gather, he never approached a shopgirl or waitress for

---

*Ellis practiced urolagnia: he enjoyed watching women urinate, a habit he developed as a young boy after seeing his mother do so outdoors, when she was "caught short." Wilson, *The Misfits,* 178–83.

sex (although how far he got with Georgette is unclear). From Nicoll's remarks Laura comes across as a dominant woman, something that, from most accounts, the woman he will marry was not. He speaks of Laura as "enigmatic," and that in her presence he felt "as if I were a poor crawling insect whose ups and downs she regards with distant sympathy."[7]

Yet the inner voice was sold on Laura. She tells Nicoll that "I have had union with thee for endless limits and I have transformed into forms of lust that have made thee forget thyself and cling to me as woman," which I presume refers to Nicoll's sexual fantasies, the imaginary woman of his "unclean thoughts" who "changed as I wished and became anything I wished." "But now there are wings to be grown and manhood to be won . . . because with Laura you will cease to live in the pocket mirrors of other people."

So with Laura he will cease to let his sexual instincts out alone— that is, stop masturbating—and grow wings and become a man. (We should remember that Nicoll is thirty-five at the time, the age when, according to Jung, the "midlife crisis" hits.) He will also increase his self-respect and self-esteem and no longer worry about what other people think. (And "living in the pocket mirrors of other people" is a description worthy of Gurdjieff.) His inner voice is telling Nicoll that it is time to grow up leave the nest. Why doesn't he listen?

As we will be encountering it throughout this chapter, I should perhaps point out here that the stylistic resemblance between Nicoll's diaries and Jung's *Red Book* mentioned earlier is the high-flown, orotund, kitschy classical language in which both are written, redolent of "thees" and "thous" and "thys." This pastiche biblical cadence, Jung tells us, is the language in which the archetypes speak, and if this is so, one is grateful that they more often communicate through symbols. Exactly why the archetypes must express themselves in verbose stentorian periods—which in Nicoll's case, often peter out in random alliteration—is not clear, but it is curious that Jung and Nicoll both had a solid grounding in the Bible, something that they share with another visionary who produced his own strangely inspired text.

The notorious magician Aleister Crowley, a contemporary whom Nicoll may have known about through the sensational press of the day, or through his interest in mystical literature, claimed to have received the text of *The Book of the Law*, the sacred scripture of his self-styled religion, from an extraterrestrial source, an "other dimensional" entity named Aiwass.* Oddly enough, *The Book of the Law* is written in something like the same overblown language that we find in Nicoll's diaries and the *Red Book*, with helpings of Oscar Wilde and Algernon Swinburne.† It and Crowley's religion as a whole are focused on a kind of sacred sexuality similar to the sort that Nicoll pursued, albeit Crowley's devotions were altogether more forthright and newsworthy, involving drugs and orgies, the sort of thing Nicoll got up to only in his dreams.[8]

This may suggest that Crowley too was channeling the archetypes, but a more mundane reason may be that like Jung and Nicoll he grew up with the Bible. Crowley's parents were Plymouth Brethren, a severely fundamentalist Christian sect whose apocalyptic outlook—they anticipated the imminent end of the world—makes Nicoll's Presbyterian upbringing seem like a rave-up. For a good deal of his youth, the only book Crowley had to read was the Bible, which he knew very well. (And we can see Crowley's rip-roaring reaction to his oppressive, repressive childhood as the polar opposite of Nicoll's.) It isn't surprising that when communicating with some supernatural entity, the high style of

---

*Crowley also produced a record of a series of visionary experiences, *The Vision and the Voice* (New York: Weiser Books, 1972). A Jungian reading of his account would prove interesting.

†Another example, and one that Jung clearly draws on in the *Red Book*, is Nietzsche's *Thus Spoke Zarathustra*. Nietzsche, too, grew up in a Bible-rich family—his father, like Jung's and Nicoll's, was a pastor—but his use of the pseudo-biblical style is conscious and ironic and lightened by a sense of humor that his more solemn interpreters, among them Jung, miss.

King James would make itself available to men who had it stored away in their psyches.

Laura lingered on in Nicoll's dreams—and life—for a while longer, and shared space in his psyche with Jung. On July 13 Nicoll recorded a dream in which he, Laura, and Jung were "working on the 3 branches of a tree as it were and Jung got something valuable from his and was excited about it."[9] This was, Nicoll noted, a "big" dream, one Jung would have said had bubbled up from the collective unconscious and had an archetypal meaning beyond that of Nicoll's personal life. Jung figures often in Nicoll's dreams, as one might expect. He is a father figure, a status he shares with Nicoll's actual father, and which he will have to share for a while with Ouspensky, once Nicoll comes into contact with him, before he, as it were, graciously bows out. Ernest Jones appears as a kind of shadow figure—and what he and Freud would have made of these diaries one can only imagine; whatever prospective tendencies Nicoll's unconscious might harbor, they certainly shared top billing with sex. Other women move through the diaries and Nicoll's life too. There are Helene and Joan, to name just two.

Jung had appeared in Nicoll's real life too. Jung was a dedicated Anglophile. He spoke excellent English, took to dressing in an English style when he could, and in 1903 had come to England on his first visit just before settling down to marriage with Emma Rauschenbach. With the end of World War I, travel in Europe was possible again, and one of the first places Jung visited was England. The occasion was an invitation to lecture to the Society for Psychical Research, which was founded in 1882 by Fredrick Myers, Edmund Gurney, and other late Victorians interested—as Jung was—in psychic phenomena. Jung's topic was "The Psychological Foundations of the Belief in Spirits." His argument, which was rooted in his earliest work with his mediumistic cousin Helly Preiswerk, was that ghosts were "unconscious projections" or "exteriorizations" of the psyche, rather like the one that had turned up in Freud's bookcase. Exactly how someone's unconscious can "project" an image of a wraith that can be observed by others Jung does not explain. But it was the more or less acceptable "scientific" way in which the public Jung, concerned with his professional status, spoke of occult phenomena. The private Jung held slightly different views.

Jung's projection theory was sorely tested during his visit when he spent a weekend in a cottage in Aylesbury, southeast of London, that Nicoll had rented with James Young and Maud Hoffman. They had got the place at a bargain because, Nicoll said, it was supposed to be haunted. Jung had been staying with Nicoll at Harley Street, and the group headed to the cottage one weekend. Decades later, in 1950, after years of having no communication between them—a radio silence precipitated by Nicoll's defection to Ouspensky—Jung wrote to Nicoll to ask for his account of the strange incident that occurred during Jung's stay. Jung's reason for breaking their thirty-year silence was that he had been asked to contribute to a book about apparitions—ghosts—and he wanted to check his memory against Nicoll's. "The purpose of this letter," Jung wrote, "is really to ask you whether you still remember the noteworthy adventure we went through in your weekend place . . . during that summer I spent with you."[10]

Nicoll did remember. In his reply he reminded Jung that they had no motorcars then and that they had to walk through several large fields to get to the place. He mentioned them observing the "ceremony of the Bull surrounded by the cows at the full moon." Nicoll recalled that he, his sister, her husband, and Maud Hoffman were "fascinated" by Jung's talk, for which some "twisted orchard trees" served as backdrop. Nicoll also mentioned that he was "furious" with Jung because he had divined that he, Nicoll, was in love with someone whom Jung believed was "typically English." (Was this Laura?) He also recalled the strange symbolic painting Jung had instructed them in doing, on the whitewashed walls of the indoor garden. Jung painted a Mithraic temple, as well as an allegorical scene of a soul "taking the Middle Way." Nicoll tried his hand at a Tree of Life. Kenneth Walker, who met Jung around this time, visited the cottage too, and also dabbed a brush on the wall, leaving behind a centaur peering into a valley.

Jung impressed his hosts with his cooking, frying up a steak in olive oil. (Like Gurdjieff, Jung was a good cook.) But the most impressive event of the weekend was the ghost. One morning Jung came down to breakfast and asked Nicoll if there was "anything wrong" with the house. Nicoll reminded him that they had got it cheap because there were "things said" about it. Jung replied "There is a woman with half a face in my room and she put it on my pillow and I felt horrible."

The half-faced woman had rattled Jung—she was accompanied by strange noises and unpleasant odors—and he had spent the rest of the night in an armchair. Apparently this was one "unconscious projection" or "exteriorization" too many for the Herr Doctor. Which is surprising, given the visions and utterly weird phenomena that had accompanied his recent confrontation with the unconscious, with the "seven dead" knocking on his door to deliver their sermons, and spirits tugging at his children's blankets.[11] But more to the point it was something of a refutation of his theory. Jung went on to give his account in the anthology of ghost stories, and in it he more or less accepts that, at least on this occasion, his unconscious might not have been the culprit.*

Nicoll had felt something in the cottage too. But we could say that if he did, he seems to have gone out of his way to make himself available for it. His account is a bit unclear; he speaks of "loathing" Jung for "the time being" and sending him to town, and staying at the cottage

---

*Fanny Moser, *Spuk* (Baden bei Zürich: Gyr-Verlag, 1950). Jung's understanding of ghosts, however, remained ambivalent. In a footnote to his lecture to the SPR, printed in his *Collected Works* in 1947, Jung is no longer sure that an "exclusively psychological approach can do justice to the phenomena." Yet in a later postscript he again hedges his bets by saying that he couldn't decide on the reality of spirits, because he had no experience of them, conveniently forgetting the ghost of Aylesbury. Yet in a letter of 1946 written to Fritz Kunkel, a psychotherapist, Jung admitted that "metapsychic phenomena could be explained better by the hypothesis of spirits than by the qualities and peculiarities of the unconscious." C. G. Jung, *Letters, Volume I: 1906–1950*, 430–34.

alone. (Why he loathed Jung isn't said. Was he disappointed that Jung had been scared by a ghost? Or was he still angry about his divining his infatuation with that "typically English" woman?) Nicoll says that he stayed in an upper room, not the one that Jung had slept in, and that he was "at the time trying to serve Hecate," the goddess of magic and witchcraft.

Such devotion might well entice a spirit to make itself manifest, but by name-checking Hecate, Nicoll gives a misleading idea of the number of gods and goddesses that he invoked and with whom he sought to curry favor at this time. One might say that Nicoll was taking no chances and that he had decided on offering his obeisance to as many deities as he could, a kind of buckshot approach appropriate for polytheism. A reader of these diaries finds him petitioning Gnostic, Hermetic, Orphic deities—Abraxas, Hermes, Mithras, Rhea—and seeking their guidance as did the ancient participants of the sacred mysteries. Along with these there are a number of figures of spiritual import that are peculiar to Nicoll's own personal mythology: the Great Ones, the Shining Ones, the Mighty Ones. These and others seem to be involved in some impending fundamental shift in things that Nicoll refers to variously as the Great Hope or the Great Time or the Time of the Great Coming or the Great Relief, which he firmly anticipated was on its way. Whether this was some transformation in himself or in the outer world is difficult to say.

What this meant at the cottage that weekend was that Nicoll felt the "presence round me of evil" and that he had to get out fast. He didn't feel panic, but there was some kind of "pressure" that made itself felt and that he couldn't ignore. Whatever it was it was enough to have him pull a camp bed out into the garden, where he spent the rest of the night. He stayed there another night too, only retreating back into the house because of rain. Whether any future occupants had similar experiences once Nicoll and his friends' lease ran out, isn't known. What is known is that the cottage was eventually pulled down.

FOR ALL HIS INVOCATIONS TO THE GODS—"Hertha, Rhea, Dark
Mother who stands at the Roots, I have seen and feel thee and know
something of thy deep mystery"—Nicoll still felt held back by his
upbringing.[12] He personified this in a type he called "Pussyfoots." His
soul was "in danger" from them. They were "unclean, hypocrites, nasty,
fanatical, tight-lipped bigots—narrow folk without imagination—
puritans." The Pussyfoots "pretend" that they do not have "primitive
feelings," as Nicoll clearly did, and become "glib, solemn, portentous
little liars" in the process. They are criminals, he says, because they
"destroy the soul in man which feeds on Imagination."[13]

It isn't clear exactly who Nicoll had in mind, but we can recognize the type: the conventional Babbits, afraid to stray from the path
of respectability, who deny the vital, animal powers and so desiccate
their lives. Nicoll would have met quite a few of them among his
father's friends, his stepmother's dinner guests, and the parishioners
at his church. Yet if we can go by what he has recorded in his diary,
Nicoll did not suffer a diminution of his imagination at their hands.
His dreams, his invocations to the goddesses, his fantasies and various
streams of consciousness collected in his diaries argue vocally if not
always eloquently to the contrary. Nicoll's imagination was in no way
diminished by any Pussyfoot, unless said feline-footed individual was
Nicoll himself. That is to say, any inhibitions placed upon Nicoll came
from his own hand.

As a reader goes on with Nicoll's diary he soon becomes aware that
Nicoll is engaged in what will become an exhausting struggle with himself, not over sex per se but over his habit of expressing his sexuality, as
his voice had cautioned him, "alone." In an entry for July 29, 1919, after
feeling "savage and resentful" over some message from Laura—was it
her rejection of marriage?—Nicoll records the following note. "μ With
feeling much better than last time, but little spent on drawing. If much
libido is spent on drawing, then little should be available for the act.
During act tried to get devotional absorption in the act right, the sheer

delight and wonder. Oh that is wonderful, oh how marvellous—that is the real mystery of God in sexuality—it is the Great Wonder."[14]

The Greek letter μ—mu—seems to be a symbol for Nicoll, one of the ones that I mentioned in the previous chapter. Along with σ— sigma—it seems to stand for sex, but it is unclear if by this Nicoll means intercourse or masturbation. I am inclined to think it means masturbation, given that in some entries concerning his dreams, Nicoll explicitly refers to intercourse without this symbol, or in such a way that it is clearly differentiated from his experiences of having sex "alone," either in reality or in his dreams.

It is curious that Nicoll speaks of Freud's libido here, given that in *Dream Psychology* and elsewhere he is more inclined to Jung's notion of some all-purpose "life force"—what Nicoll calls "interest"—than to Freud's notion of a specific sexual energy. Nicoll seems to have made a habit of drawing erotic images to help focus his imagination, a kind of do-it-yourself form of spiritual sexual stimulation. At least this is how I read some of his entries. If he did, he would be in some esteemed company. William Blake, like Nicoll a reader of Swedenborg, filled his notebooks with images that are frankly pornographic, the definition of which "is pictures or written material aimed at stimulating sexual excitement," rather as glossy advertisements depicting sumptuous meals are designed to stimulate our appetite. Nicoll will hem and haw over Freud vs. Jung in several entries, and, as suggested already, one can only wonder what Freud would have made of Nicoll's habit of having sex "alone."

The important thing here is that Nicoll is using "sex alone" to experience the Godhead. What is necessary for this is to get the "devotional absorption in the act right." That is, to have the proper focus. Something that obscures this is the guilt that often accompanies his devotions. One source of this guilt is his father, or the archetypal father that Nicoll's biological one embodies. Another seems to be some kind of inner organization—the "devotional absorption" that he wants to get right—an arrangement of his psyche that makes all the difference between "sex alone" leading to an experience of "the Great Wonder" or to a guilt-ridden post-onanistic hangover. As he noted in an entry for August 10, "μ is a question to be solved by the Inner Man [a Swedenborgian term] and thus a question of attitude within. . . . With the right attitude to sexuality it becomes the right force."[15]

Here it isn't a question of whether "μ" is acceptable in itself, and not merely a poor substitute for an actual relationship with a woman, but of the right attitude toward it, what in other entries Nicoll will speak of as "sincerity" and "intention." Yet this tolerant, what we could even call "progressive," view of "sex alone" does not always win out. Nicoll never settles this question; that is to say, he will be troubled by guilt over his devotions for years to come, as the many entries about it in his later diaries show. There are times when his entries in the early diaries suggest that, as had happened to Jung, Nicoll was heading toward a nervous breakdown. Many of his dreams are about being back at a school and having committed some crime, which left him to "wander about school as a Culprit or Criminal."[16] He had done something that had cut him off from others irrevocably, but he couldn't remember what it was, rather as the protagonists in Kafka's paranoid fables are the perpetrators of crimes they are unaware of committing and about which no one informs them. He submitted himself to a dream court martial and at one point seems to identify his "outsider" status with that of Christ.[17] More than anything else, it may have been the crisis stirring in Nicoll's psyche that led him to abandon Jung and hitch his wagon to Ouspensky.

As LAURA WALKED OFF THE SCENE, Nicoll turned his attentions to Helene, but his luck with her wasn't much better. He asks the voice if his feelings for her were wrong. Not wrong, the voice replies, but Nicoll's problem is that with her "you would not be yourself but were many people," a concise expression of Gurdjieff's indictment of humanity in general: we possess no "real I." Nicoll at this point certainly didn't, or at least not one that he felt comfortable enough with to relax and be himself, something it seems he found difficult to be around women. When the voice points this out to him, typically he asks, "How is it that I am so despicable?" After his evening with Helene he spoke with James Young ("Jimmy") about it. He told Young that spending time with Helene was "not the Way" and yet he felt no disgust at it, which suggests that Nicoll had vaguely accepted the standard spiritual dictum, generally associated with the theosophy he had come into contact with, that to achieve enlightenment the desires of the flesh must be repressed. From all we know about him, this is an axiom he was constitutionally incapable of adhering to. It was "difficult to be content with the path" he told Young—hence the attraction of Helene. Yet his interest in her was not out of "lust" but out of a need for "stimulus," an appetite for which we have already recognized in Nicoll. Nicoll will meet and dine with Helene a few times, but from the diaries it seems to amount to little more than flirtation.

His spiritual appetite seemed to be doing no better. On October 20 Nicoll noted that he "longed for a more physical contact with the powers" and that even "marvellous experiences like dreams and casting the Yi"—the *I Ching*, a Chinese method of divination, which Jung had already been working with—do not "keep the fire burning within."* Nicoll needed stronger stuff; hence the invocations to Hecate et al. It may seem unspeakably mundane, but in a word, Nicoll was bored, and he went to Helene for distraction.

Nicoll himself is aware of this tendency. In a later entry, where he is discussing with the voice his difficulties in directing his libido at spiritual rather than sensual targets, he remarks on his temperament,

---

*Nicoll consults the *I Ching* throughout his diaries, often about his devotions. He used the James Legge translation, which was largely superseded by Wilhelm/Baynes edition (Princeton, NJ: Princeton University Press, 1950) to which Jung contributed a foreword.

which is "easily impatient and easily weary." This suggests the lack of staying power I remarked on earlier. Nicoll symbolizes his task as that of making himself a "perfect container" for the "Blue Jewel," an emblem of spiritual fulfilment that suggests an echo of Novalis's elusive "blue flower," the search for which sets his fictional pilgrim, Heinrich von Ofterdingen on his quest.[18] The notion of making himself a "vessel" is an early sign of the mystic path that Nicoll will wish to tread in his later years, that of the "negative theology" of Meister Eckhart and the anonymous author of *The Cloud of Unknowing*, which sees *kenosis*, or the emptying out of the ego, as the means of spiritual fulfilment. Nicoll's already low self-esteem and craving to escape his personality suggest that this is a path for which he is well suited. And as he will note at the time, it is radically different from Gurdjieff's.

Let me say here that Nicoll's desire to become a "perfect container" tells us something about him, and it is something that a reader of these diaries comes to see about Nicoll fairly early on. It is that Nicoll is essentially *passive*. He desperately wants the gods and goddesses of his fantasies to *possess him*. He is always waiting for something to *happen*, for something to be *done* to him. He is in this sense a romantic. Several entries attest to this. "Oh my soul redeem me—prompt me in my speech and actions," "Fill thou the Empty Space in myself whereby I have to crave for lust to fill it," "Guide me, hold me, pour love into my heart," "make me fit to receive thy In-pouring," "I crave for penetration," which in the context of the diary should really read "I crave to be penetrated." In fact, there is more than a hint of homoeroticism in several dreams, and when we first hear of Nicoll's inner voice, he asks it to "Turn thy face and thine eyes to me—those boy's eyes that are bright and glad and strong and fill me with thy being."[19] There is a kind of rapturous ecstasy that he wants and he waits for it—impatiently at times—to arrive.

Petitions for this rapture to appear can be found throughout the diary. They suggest that the Nicoll of this time felt an inner emptiness that apparently his devotions alone could fill; at least nothing else mentioned in the diaries seems to come close. Someone whose only satisfaction came from masturbation would generally not be considered to be living a full life. But when "sex alone" is wedded to a form of spirituality, as it was with Nicoll, the situation is a bit more complicated.

IT WAS AROUND THIS TIME that Nicoll crossed paths with A. R. Orage, a well-known figure on the London literary scene. According to Bernard Shaw, Orage was a "desperado of genius." Orage would also convert to Gurdjieff's teachings, and he would spend several years of his life in America trying to convert others. Orage had met Ouspenky years earlier, during the Russian's "search for the miraculous," and recently he had published a series of Ouspensky's "Letters from Russia" in his magazine the *New Age*. In these letters, written from "the most God-forsaken place one could imagine"—Russia in the middle of its civil war—Ouspensky depicted the grim reality of what communist sympathizers in the West called the "Bolshevik experiment." For Ouspensky, a virulent anti-communist, this meant "the dictatorship of the criminal element," a political antipathy Nicoll would share.[20]

At the moment, Orage, an omnivorous imbiber of ideas, was putting together a group of interested minds to look at the possibility of what he called "psychosynthesis" as a counterbalance to the psychoanalysis he had written about so eloquently in the *New Age*.[21] Jung had used the term, and another early student of Freud, the Italian Roberto Assagioli, had developed an entire system of psychology based on it, which incorporated elements from Theosophy and Rudolf Steiner's Anthroposophy.* As early as 1904 Orage had lectured to the Leeds Theosophical Society on higher states of consciousness, and suggested

---

*Jung mentions "psychosynthesis" in a letter to Freud dated April 2, 1909, following the incident of the poltergeist in Freud's bookcase. William McGuire, ed., *The Freud/Jung Letters,* 216; Roberto Assagioli, *Psychosynthesis* (New York: Penguin Books, 1977).

that human consciousness was capable of achieving a kind of "superman consciousness," borrowing the term from Nietzsche, about whom Orage wrote some perceptive books, the first in English in fact.[22] The basic idea was that if the psyche could be analyzed—that is, taken apart— why couldn't it be put back together more coherently and effectively and so achieve a level of integration beyond that of being merely "well-adjusted," which was all psychoanalysis could hope for? That such a notion spoke more to Jung's "prospective tendencies" than to Freud's reductionist ones should be clear. It was certainly something that would interest Nicoll.

Although Orage was an "enthusiastic student of the new psychology," he placed it within an unusual context, discussing the Oedipus complex alongside "St. Thomas Aquinas, the Hermeticists, and Patanjali," the great fourth-century Indian yogi and sage.[23] This unlikely juxtaposition, one suspects, gives an idea of the atmosphere of the group. It met at Harley Street, and eventually included members from the psychoanalytic and medical world (the Freudian David Eder, James Young, Nicoll, Havelock Ellis, J. M. Alcock) and the press (Rowland Kenney was a former editor of the *Daily Herald*, and Clifford Sharp was the editor of the *New Statesman*). One mystic was in attendance, at least for a time. This was the Serbian Dmitri Mitrinovic, who filled the "World Affairs" column in the *New Age* with a peculiar utopian politics while serving as guru to Orage. He did so until Orage left him for Ouspensky, just as Nicoll would leave Jung. A good many of the psychosynthesists would attend Ouspensky lectures. And when the time came, they too would cross the channel and head to Fontainebleau to submit their psyches to Gurdjieff.

It seems that Nicoll did not care for Orage. This is understandable; in many ways, Orage was what Nicoll was not, or at least felt he wasn't: suave, self-confident, able to express ideas with a clarity that sparkled like champagne, physically large, and sexually successful. In a dream recorded on October 16 in which a gorilla and a Pekinese were involved,

Orage turns up. Nicoll is the Pekinese, or at least the Pekinese symbolizes a character trait in Nicoll. The Pekinese is "sentimental" and "foolish"; it is extroverted and likes to "please people."[24] Nicoll felt that in Orage's presence he had talked too much, had made too much of an effort to impress and be liked. He worries that he had spoken too much "even of mysteries," which I assume means his invocations to Hecate et al.[25] Orage, on the other hand, is the gorilla, which Nicoll read as a warning not to be sentimental in the face of a brute. Orage had a vitality that didn't care about the impression it made.

It was through Orage, though, that Nicoll practiced his analytical skill on an individual with whom he felt more at home. In early 1920 Orage sent the poet and translator Edwin Muir, who was then working as an assistant editor for the *New Age*, to Nicoll to be analyzed. Muir's wife had urged him to seek help in dealing with the neurotic fears and guilt left over from his difficult childhood in Glasgow. Orage heard of this and suggested to Nicoll that he analyze Muir gratis, in return for professional experience with someone more interesting than the run-of-the-mill neurotics that made up much of Nicoll's clientele. (And on the salary he earned at the *New Age*, Muir couldn't have afforded to pay anyway.)

Nicoll accepted the idea, and Muir began his sessions on the couch. It turned out to be a good experience for them both. In his autobiography, Muir recalled how it came about. He writes that Orage "saw that I was not in a good state, and with the mixture of active benevolence and diplomacy which characterised him, spoke about me to an analyst, a brilliant and charming man who one evening invited me round to see him." Muir visited Nicoll, not "suspecting any plot for my good," and was shocked when the kindly doctor asked him some blunt questions. Then Nicoll told Muir that he would like to "analyse me for the mere interest of the thing, and without asking for payment." Muir was not immediately sold on the idea. He had still to admit to himself that he was "a neurotic needing the help" Nicoll freely offered. In the end Muir did accept Nicoll's help. With it, he was able to overcome the feelings that had paralyzed him. It was an important turning point for him, and he would "always feel grateful for the kindness of the analyst."[26]

Muir wrote his autobiography years after his analysis, when both Orage and Nicoll were dead. He did not remember his analyst's name and was unaware of Nicoll's later life as a teacher of the Work.

Someone else who came to Nicoll for help would eventually have a longer-lasting relationship with him. With Catherine Champion Jones, whom he would marry, we may say it was a case of third time lucky. Catherine first met Nicoll in 1917, at the home of her uncle and guardian, Dr. Leonard Williams, Nicoll's neighbor on Harley Street. She arrived at her uncle's when Nicoll was there. He had only recently returned from Mesopotamia and was working on an article with Dr. Williams. A year later, she turned up at Dr. Williams's again when Nicoll was visiting. When she spoke of that evening years later to Beryl Pogson, Catherine recalled that "Dr. Nicoll said some rather extraordinary things and did not speak as the others did."[27] Their third meeting was prompted by Catherine being "on the verge of a nervous breakdown." She remembered the extraordinary things Nicoll had said and felt convinced that he was the only person who might be able to help her. She went to his rooms on Harley Street but was told by Nicoll's secretary that he had appointments all day and would not be able to see her. Disappointed and distraught, she left.

The next morning Dr. Williams's butler informed her that Dr. Nicoll was downstairs waiting to see her. When he saw her Nicoll said "If I had known it was you I would have seen you at once." She then returned with him to his consulting room.

According to Beryl Pogson, during that consultation the two discovered that they shared the same aim in life. They both sought the "peace which passeth all understanding." From that day they dined together practically every evening. Their life's purposes were so aligned that Nicoll later said that he was convinced that they had married in a previous life.[28]

All of which sounds like a match made in heaven, which it may very well have been. Nicoll's diaries, however, suggest a somewhat different story. They record that after he and Catherine recognized each other as kindred souls, he was still seeing Laura and Helene; as mentioned, in what capacity is unclear, but they were still on his mind and in his dreams, as were other women. He notes on November 14 that, "C. C. J. came to see me re: phobia."[29] That night he had a dream in which he was with Laura in a room, where they watched Georgette—his Austrian girlfriend—and another woman making love; I omit the graphic detail Nicoll's dream provided. He and Laura then attempt to have sex, but it doesn't work out. For November 15, the following evening, he notes that he visited "H," whom we can assume is Helene, and that they had a "less sensual time."[30]

By early December, he is being philosophical about marriage. He sees it as "the giving up of a certain bright infantility," and as the work of "a steady task" before him. Life will no longer be a "bright insolent adventure," which leads him to conclude that "love must be coming to me."[31] This means an acceptance of "routine" and a purging of the "infantile."[32] Yet, Catherine appeals to him so "enormously" that he doesn't have "the heart to go for her weakness."

What was Catherine's weakness? Perhaps more to the point: What was the phobia she came to see him about, that had her on the verge of a breakdown? On December 13 Nicoll recorded that he looked at Catherine's horoscope—as Jung did, Nicoll sometimes used astrology with his patients. It is unclear if the stars shed much light on this occasion. But we do discover what led Catherine to see a psychiatrist. Nicoll noted that she "has a horror of physical sex."[33] It seems that she had had some bad experiences with men, which left her suicidal, as well as bad-tempered, suffering from insomnia, and drinking too much. Nevertheless she is "something very beloved" to him. Catherine's remark, which he recorded, that he loves her only "out of pity," may suggest some psychological insight.[34] It may also suggest the dependable ploy of getting a man to insist that he loves you by pretending to refuse to believe that he does.

Catherine had an interesting background. She was born in 1891 in Mexico, where her father was a banker. The family then moved to Lima, Peru, where she and her siblings grew up. She would later speak to her Work groups of the colorful tropical flowers and birds she remembered from that time, as well as of the lepers that passed through the town and the earthquakes that shook it. In 1899, she and her sister rounded Cape Horn on their voyage to England, where they went to boarding school. With her exotic background, she felt something of an outsider, something she had in common with Nicoll. Her father died in 1910, and her uncle Dr. Williams became her guardian.

Catherine was described as "very beautiful and very quiet." She dressed well and had an air of self-command. When Nicoll brought his fiancée to the family home in Hampstead, she received their unanimous approval. By January of the New Year it was settled, and the two were married at the parish church in Marylebone. Nicoll was thirty-six; Catherine was twenty-nine.

THE NEWLYWEDS SPENT THEIR HONEYMOON in Switzerland, part of which included a visit to the Jungs in Küsnacht, their home on the shores of Lake Zürich. Carl and Emma found Nicoll's bride "charming," or at least Emma said she did, in a letter written years later, after Nicoll's death.[35] The honeymoon must have kept them busy, as there is a break in Nicoll's journal for about a week. In the entries we do have he refers to Catherine as "Eo," "the dawn" in ancient Greek. She is named in some fragmentary notes about some dreams: of sleeping in a strange room, of being on a train, of a dark haunted valley, and of Nicoll's sister becoming very ill. There are long entries later in the month, then nothing until mid-March. What one doesn't find are any entries concerning "μ," nor anything about his sexual relations with Catherine. Modesty and propriety may have ruled in this case, or Catherine's phobia may still have been firmly in place. Nicoll may have been too busy to make any notes, and if he did, perhaps those pages have gone missing. Whatever the reason, we find nothing.

One might be excused for thinking that a man who had sex on his mind as much as Nicoll did, would have jotted down a word or two in his journal about the nights of bliss with his soulmate, in which they both achieved the "peace which passeth all understanding" in each other's arms. Or if not that, then perhaps a short note of disappointment. Yet the only reference to sleeping with Catherine that I came across in the diaries occurs toward the end of their first year as husband and wife. Nicoll reports that he has been impotent for several weeks, and that Eo made some disparaging remarks about the single-mindedness of the male sexual appetite.[36] These notes are sandwiched between a dream of sleeping with Eo and a "dark haired girl" with whom he went at it "savagely" while his wife lay passive—he was stuck in the middle between instinct and duty—and long lamentations about our "filthy and abominable sexuality."* It seems the "Scotch teachers of divinity" had got it right after all, when they condemned his "unclean thoughts." They knew "how difficult a thing it must be for God to endure our humanity." "We have only to force our thought," Nicoll writes, "for one shuddering moment to the horror of our sexual organs (and then recoil with heartfelt relief) to feel an over-whelming sense of gratitude that God tolerates our existence a moment longer upon the radiant and happy earth."[37]

---

*Nicoll recorded several dreams in which he and Eo are sharing a bed with another woman, with whom Nicoll "talks dirty" and has sex, while Eo is otherwise occupied. This of course isn't unusual, but it suggests that their marriage was one founded on common beliefs rather than strong physical attraction.

This hits the pure, unadulterated Gnostic note of the rejection
of the flesh. Yet one might ask why, if our sexual organs are so horrible, God had made them that way in the first place? Presumably he's
responsible for them? And if we are "made in his image" then perhaps
he should have used a different model? But let this pass. What is interesting is that this horror of our sexual organs—one perhaps informed
by his wife's horror of sex—comes only a short while after Nicoll
engages in a long and "archetypally written" dialogue with his inner
voice. Appearing as a Mother Goddess, she asks, "Wouldst thou lie on
my breast and suck at my teats and wring the milk from my cunt and
wallow in my dung, thou brat?" "Wouldst commit incest in my lap?"
To which Nicoll replies "Yea, mother."[38] There is a passage in which
a dream about rain becomes, by way of a stream of associations, an
exhortation to "seek in thy penis the wonder of the circle of magic and
the strange low song of the incestuous mother." He is urged to do this
because "By semen all things are possible."[39]

The "incestuous mother" here is the Jungian symbolic one, not the
Freudian literal one. And the incest suggested by the mother's "strange
low song" is the way to conquer and possess her, the unconscious, our
dark, vital roots, and to integrate their energies into consciousness. The
danger is that the force of attraction, the seductive power of the mother,
can be too great. One may not achieve escape velocity, as it were, and
remain a satellite, pampered and pleasured by her, yet never becoming a
star of one's own.[40] Forms this orbit can take vary from that of the *puer
aeternas*, the Peter Pan who never grows up, to alcoholism, drug abuse,
and addiction to sex. As we've seen, Nicoll looked at marriage as "the
giving up of a certain bright infantility." It was a move to maturity, yet
the path had more than a few bumps in it.

In April 1920, the Nicolls bought their new home at 36 Chester
Terrace, near the Regent's Park, not far from Harley Street, although
they wouldn't move in until July. It was a prestigious and expensive
neighborhood, and Nicoll would soon feel the pressure of having to

keep up appearances. With all his rejection of the "successful" life of his father and his friends, Nicoll nevertheless felt the pull of convention. The necessities of making a living were unavoidable. "Life" would not let him get away. He began to feel that "the inevitability of life seems overwhelming," that there was "no escape, no way—just the Great Wheel of Existence."[41] And if there is no way, then why not "Sheer sensuality and greed and death before suffering?" Either way, Nicoll concludes that he will "go on, come what may, and if there is nothing, then there is Nothing."

But right now Nothing wasn't the problem. The Great Wheel of Existence had brought him to having to support a wife who would soon enough provide him with a daughter. Maintaining the new house would not be easy, even with the help of his father. He had a name in his profession but it was easy to lose status. One dream recorded soon after Nicoll bought the new house involved an encounter with his shadow "other," Ernest Jones. Nicoll had been reading Freud's account of his "Irma" dream, which led to his theory that dreams are wish fulfillments, an idea that Nicoll never completely rejected. He thought of giving a paper on it before the Royal Society of Medicine. In Nicoll's dream, he meets Ernest Jones, Freud's "hitman," and in the course of recounting the analysis of a dream to Jones, Nicoll becomes confused and intimidated, believing Jones knows it is really one of Nicoll's own "infantile" dreams.[42] This suggested to Nicoll that he had to turn his libido—his life force—away from Jones and aim it toward himself.

Nicoll's reflections lead him to make some interesting observations regarding the link between "attitude," "intention," and "sincerity." Thinking about what actually happens in analysis, Nicoll reflects that "Analysis concerns attitude by examining intention, and without the gaining of sincerity . . . there is no true Attitude and no true relationship to the unconscious."[43] He defines sincerity as "growth out of the Unconscious." It is rooted in us and "appears in the world as something based on itself." That is, it is not lured by an outside value or approval, but remains as an interest coming from the self, not the persona. Or, as Gurdjieff would say, from "essence." The problem in the modern West is that all value comes from outside. It is "outer" not "inner" directed. "The preoccupation with the Object has become so great, that subjective growth, without which sincerity is impossible, has been dwarfed."[44] Under such conditions, "neurosis is inevitable," unless "interest" can be pointed inward and "the power taken into ourselves." Nicoll remarks that he would much rather deal "with a patient who sincerely expressed his sexuality, than with a hypocrite," and one can't help but wonder if he ever spoke with any of his colleagues about his own struggles with μ? If so there seems no sign of it in his diaries.

The struggles went on, however, both over μ and the more immediate business of making ends meet. A long entry in the diary begins with Nicoll asking "pardon for not drawing to thee"—not attending to the voice of late, the Great Wheel of Existence having turned his attentions elsewhere. This leads to a fantasy based on the Mithraic ritual of the slaying of the bull. He must slay the bull with his sword because "out of the bull will come the blood of new life." New life must have been on Nicoll's unconscious mind; in a dream not long after this, Eo tells him she is pregnant (she will become so, but not until the next year). In a dream Nicoll recites the last lines from Ibsen's *Ghosts*, a play about hereditary madness and an incestuous relationship between siblings. The lines, "Mother, give me the sun," are spoken by Oswald, the son, who is syphilitic, as Ibsen was himself. Nicoll asks the voice to interpret the dream. It is not encouraging. "It is thy death and end. Here lies the end of all human endeavour. Yea in vanity." With gloomy thoughts like these, it's not surprising Nicoll had not drawn near to the voice for a while.

Not long after the move into the new home, Nicoll had a dream in which Jung pulls a knife on him and tries to stab him. Jung takes the knife from a sideboard cupboard, and by the look in his eyes,

Nicoll knew he was mad.* Afterward he was "haunted by vague anxiet-
ies re future and money, also of sex." He wrote about "Sexuality and
Religion"—one assumes it is an unfinished essay, perhaps among his
papers—but thought it "poor." "After all," he asks, "who am I to write
about these things? Can we help ourselves?" He has sexual dreams
involving his patients in which he "talks dirty"; at one point the voice
will encourage him to sleep with them (he was, after all, married to
one of them). Yet his troubles did not occupy Nicoll all the time. In
August he experimented with a pendulum, using it to try to detect the
male and female aura—a method he borrowed from Conan Doyle—
and he notes that Walter John Kilner, a doctor who claimed to have
developed glasses that would make the human aura visible, had died.†
Nicoll, it seemed, was keeping abreast of things in what we would call
the "alternative" world. And the swing of the pendulum will become an
important metaphor for him when he begins his ministry in the Work.

Yet the pressure to keep up appearances and maintain a spiritual
life were taking their toll. Pendulums, auras, and smoked glass did not
allay his worries. "I am not a saint in the desert with nothing to distract
him save the contemplation of hidden mysteries," he informs the voice,
who has been berating him for backsliding. "I am constantly involved
in making enough money so that my household can live."[45] What Nicoll
might have given for another *Lord Richard in the Pantry* just about then
we can only imagine. The tension of his struggle with μ begins to eat
away at his energies. He slips into a "flat and dreamy state in which I

---

*The mention of Jung and a knife from a "sideboard cupboard" reminds one of another
knife in another sideboard. This involved one of the psychic experiences Jung recounts
in *Memories, Dreams, Reflections*, when he returned home to find his mother and sister
in a state because of a loud report they heard coming from the sideboard. In it Jung
discovered a breadknife that had inexplicably shattered into discreet sections (126). Did
Nicoll know of this story?
†In Theosophy, the aura is a kind of subtle energy field that surrounds the human
body. Psychics are said to be able to perceive it, and there have been several "scientific"
attempts to capture it.

lose everything." A "haunting fear of failure" pervades his conscious-ness.[46] His patients have become burdens. He fears he will "sink into sensualism," and asks "Thou Unknown whom I address here" for help.[47] Toward the end of August he wonders if he is jealous of Jung. He asks if he must "humble my desire of ambition and be nothing," something we can say he has been working at. "Must not man have a strength and fire of his own?" "I have to force my strength into action and come what will."[48]

Some of this action included a book that Nicoll notes he has just begun to write; this may be the Freud vs. Jung book he had been con-templating but never completed. This unexpected gumption even leads Nicoll to tell the voice off, complaining that it should "block not the way always with thy arrant words and booming emptiness."[49] A reader who has followed Nicoll this far in his diaries can only remark, "Finally."

This defiant attitude will not last, but while it does, Nicoll gets some things off his chest. The most pressing of these is his rejec-tion of Christianity, at least the Christianity of the church he knew. In a dream in which he argues with his father over money, a Jew, Shakespeare's Shylock, turns up, and a meditation on him leads to his condemnation of the church. It begins when the voice chides him for feeling pity toward his patients, who are sick "because of the times rather than through deliberate choice."[50] The voice says pity is wrong because everyone has their own fate, and it is through this that the soul grows. Nicoll reminds the voice that the "greatest Teacher of all on the Planet"—Christ—taught that we should have pity for others.[51] To speak of the need for suffering in order that the soul should grow was all well and good, but somehow that explanation no longer sufficed. "There is everywhere a feeling of vexation against Christ's teaching," Nicoll writes, "a polite feeling of having been let down a good deal and that what he said wasn't as good and satisfactory as was hoped. People are anxious and have been anxious for his teaching to work, but it does not work and the best thinkers who call themselves Christians admit that a compromise is all that we can really make."[52] As for the vicarious atonement: "thousands were crucified before and after Christ—victims were skinned alive for the sake of religious custom, in Mexico for example, every year . . . Christ's suffering was in no way unique and has been equalled and surpassed by hundreds of thousands."[53]

The fact that Christ knew he was the "son of God" and would be sitting at his right hand relatively soon after the Crucifixion, subtracts any real value that his suffering and death might have had. Given this, "the average soldier who got buried in a fallen trench or went over the top at dawn with his limbs numb and his eyes frozen . . . behaved more nobly than did Christ."[54] And as for saving the souls of sinners, "You cannot produce evidence to show that Christianity had done anything of the kind." But perhaps Nicoll's most damning remark is this: "Christianity in the hands of every Christian authority . . . has been used quite calmly as a personal thing. . . . Now that means an identification. . . . No man can work the Christian game unless he unconsciously identifies himself with Christ," something we've seen Nicoll do, if only briefly and in passing. Such identification is "really pathological power lunacy"—what Jung would call "inflation"—or "a private conviction that he is in special favour with Christ and God."[55]

Nicoll's estimation of Christ and his teachings would recover from this all-time low. But his relations with other guides and teachings would not remain secure.

6

Breaking Up Is Hard to Do

In the early autumn of 1920, Jung was again invited to England, this time to give a seminar on analytical psychology to a small group of people interested in his work. It was held in Sennen Cove, at Land's End, the very tip of Cornwall, and according to one source it was the "first proper seminar" on Jungian psychology ever held.[1] Jung had given informal talks to small groups in Zürich, under the auspices of the Psychology Club, which had started in 1916, but the two weeks at Sennen Cove were something more extensive and intensive. The seminar was organized by Constance Long, one of Jung's earliest English supporters; her translation of Jung's *Collected Papers on Analytical Psychology* had been published in 1916. According to Jung's biographer Barbara Hannah, who attended, Long was helped by H. G. Baynes, another of Jung's early translators.[2]

Details of the seminar are few; there is no written record of the talks themselves, and the number and identities of the attendees vary depending on the references one reads. There were probably not more than twenty people assembled there to hear what Jung had to say. He preferred the intimate atmosphere of small gatherings, and was, after all, just beginning to stick his head above the parapet again after his breakup with Freud and the shattering "night sea journey" that followed. Among those attending were Long, Baynes, Hannah, Eleanor Bertie (a doctor from Bellevue Hospital in New York), Beatrice Hinkle (a feminist and early Jungian, again from America), James Young, Nicoll, and Catherine. Emma Jung, a student of Jung's in her own right as well as his wife, had come with Carl.

The seminar was devoted to Jung's interpretation of a series of dreams collected in an odd book entitled *Authentic Dreams of Peter Blobbs and of Certain of His Relatives*, published in 1916.[3] Peter Blobbs was the pseudonym of Arthur John Hubbard, about whom little is known; apparently he acquired the nickname during his time as a medical student. Hubbard wrote books about history, prehistoric man, and the rise of civilization. The Peter Blobbs book is a record of what the author calls "proleptic dreams," dreams in which some knowledge, unknown to the conscious mind, is given in advance of the events it refers to taking place. In other words, what we can call "precognitive dreams," of the kind recorded in the once famous book *An Experiment with Time* by J. W. Dunne, which Jung and Nicoll read. It isn't known if Jung spoke of them in this way at the seminar, but these are the kinds of dreams that he would later refer to as examples of what he would call "synchronicity," the experience of "meaningful coincidence." Jung himself had dreams of this sort at the start of his "night sea journey," when he saw the flood covering Europe on his train to Schaffhausen in advance of the outbreak of World War I. It was the archetypal character of the Peter Blobbs dreams that attracted Jung to them.

Hubbard dreamed a great deal, as did other members of his family, and if the dreams recorded in his book are indicative, they were very creative dreamers indeed, composing, among other things, whole sonnets and songs while fast asleep. Hubbard does not offer an explanation for the dreams he recorded, and he dismisses the explanation often given at the time to account for the related sensation of déjà vu, the feeling that one has experienced something before when in fact it is the first time. It was suggested that this happened because "various centers in the brain are not acting in harmony," and that when we experience déjà vu, or a proleptic dream, "one part of the brain is asleep while another part is awake."[4] This hints of the "split-brain" psychology that will fascinate Nicoll shortly before his death, not to mention that it offers an early use of a term, "centers," that we will hear more about. Hubbard did believe that when the solution to the problem of proleptic dreams comes, it "will be found to carry with it the solution to some of the most profound problems of philosophy and psychology."[5] Jung would think something similar about synchronicity and what it suggested about the nature of reality.

The setting for the seminar must have been to Jung's liking. According to one account, everyone stayed at the same boardinghouse, and there was a fluid character to the proceedings, with Jung holding analytical hours with the attendees, as well as the seminar and social gatherings, all under the same roof. That area of Cornwall was "steeped in mysteries," and was said to be "frequented by mermaids." It had the reputation of being the habitat of a "living mist."[6] According to Nicoll, whose diary entries during the seminar are one of the few sources of information about it by someone attending, Jung also held some analytical sessions in a "coastguard's castle" at the edge of a cliff, overlooking the sea.[7] It reminded Nicoll of Jung's "hut in the reeds at Küsnacht." (This must have been Jung's hideaway before he built his own castle at Bollingen.)

Jung had experimented with a kind of "group psychology" back in Zürich with the Psychology Club, throwing analysts, analysands, and students together to see what happened, in ways that by today's standards would seem hazardous. The club had been started by Edith McCormick, one of Jung's wealthy clients (she was a Rockefeller), and she had spared no expense in providing it with a well-appointed setting. As I remark in my book on Jung, he was doing what Gurdjieff was doing around the same time in St. Petersburg and Moscow, although in less lavish settings. The idea was to bring people together and have them clash, so that they could get past their "personas" (Gurdjieff would say "personalities"). The sparks created by the friction would shake them out of their usual selves. Jung may have had a similar idea here. He was in any case in an "apparently rather mischievous mood," something Nicoll's future master was also known for. Whatever Jung may have thought of Gurdjieff, or vice versa, in some ways they had much in common.

Yet not everyone was happy. According to Nicoll, when he and Catherine arrived at the Sennen Cove Hotel on that September 20, he was feeling "very disturbed and cross—crossed with conflict." Catherine was "wonderfully calm and cheerful."[8] James Young was "desperate," about what we don't know. But we do know why Nicoll was out of sorts. He mentions his "infantile transference," which was expressed in his need to recognize his own ambitions and growing envy of Jung, and wonders if this meant that he couldn't go on with him. He had been having doubts for some time, both about Jung's ideas and their usefulness in his own case. Was he getting anywhere with them? Did he understand his dreams? His diaries are evidence that he certainly *tried* to understand them; whether he did or not must be left to conjecture.

For example, on arrival at the seminar Nicoll recorded a dream— one assumes it was from the night before—in which Jung asks him what was wrong, and he replied that he didn't know. Jung then tells him that the problem is that he takes analysis too "earnestly" and is "too anxious" about it, something a reader of these diaries may agree with.[9] "Analysis," Jung said in the dream, "is something very big and not personal. Do not be so over anxious." Given what we've seen of Nicoll's struggle, this seems like his unconscious trying to compensate for his exhausting soul-searching, and giving it to him straight from the horse's mouth, no less. But Nicoll *was* anxious, and part of his anxiety came from his growing dissatisfaction with himself and with Jung's approach. It took him only so far, he felt, but he needed to go further. And wherever that was, according to Nicoll, he couldn't get there by himself.

He and Jung had some conversations though. Nicoll described Jung as "very mystical yet in life very ordinary." Jung "says extraordinary things as if they were ordinary," but he is "no paragon in behaviour," something that could, and would, be said about Gurdjieff. He is "affable, with a store of illustrations," and "quite courteous at times." Jung could be "greedy at cards—is no chicken with his food—gets bored at times" and was not immune to sulking if he is "taken beyond his reach." Nicoll noted something that others would remark on too: that Jung liked to be the center of attention and was not above being petulant if he wasn't.

Nicoll mentioned that his "sexuality had got far away since coming here"—to the seminar, one assumes. Jung said his had as well. Yet a look at Nicoll's diary entry for that same day shows that his sexuality hadn't gone all that far away; one dream involved him "talking dirty" to a patient who had come to him for an examination. Jung talked about something he called "*Beziehung* analysis," dealing with relationships.[10] It was a way of looking at what happens to us in the outer world in the same way as we would look at it if it happened in a dream. Emma was not that keen on it, as it meant discussing "intimate things" with others. As one does this already in analysis, I suspect this "relationship analysis" was carried on in a group; if so, by this time such a group may have included Toni Wolff, Jung's mistress and *soror mystica*, who had more or less become part of the family. He also spoke of what he called "the Church Invisible," by which Jung seems to have meant some kind of unseen partition, separating us from others, a kind of see-through protective bubble.* When we are "walled up" in it, "we are each in our right place, fulfilling our respective positions."[11] Nicoll records Jung making a comparison to cells in the body. "If a brain cell is in the kid-

---

*The term "Invisible Church" is reminiscent of what the eighteenth-century Christian mystical writer Karl von Eckartshausen called the "Interior Church," a mystical body of true believers, linked by spiritual experience rather than by doctrine. See Karl von Eckartshausen *The Cloud upon the Sanctuary* (Berwick, ME: Ibis Press, 2003).

ney, it is unhappy," Jung said. "But if it is in the brain it is happy and realises itself properly."[12]

Oddly enough, Ouspensky will use a similar analogy when talking about the possibilities of waking up: that some individuals, those who can wake up, are destined for a higher purpose, just as the cells in the brain serve a higher purpose than those in the stomach. Both Jung's and Ouspensky's analogies seem an echo of Swedenborg's idea of the Homo Maximus, the Grand Man making up all of the universe. Jung in fact referred to Swedenborg's Homo Maximus, when Nicoll showed him a drawing he had made of "the orientations of scales of worlds as figures within figures."[13] As Jung mentions the "demiurge," the idiot "craftsman" whom the true God put in charge of creation, this seems to have been some sort of Gnostic emanationist diagram, depicting the "descent" from the unmanifest One to the natural world.

Without the diagram it is difficult to grasp exactly what Jung means by the comments that Nicoll recorded. Pointing to the diagram, Jung told Nicoll that getting to "the Son upon the Demiourgos" was a "point in one's development."[14] Upon achieving it "there is great liberation, something extraordinary," and Jung pointed out that in the hero myths, that generally meant "an orgy," something that might have appealed to Nicoll, if his diary is anything to go by. But from the "Son," Jung told Nicoll, one gets to "the Mater Gloriosa, behind whom stands the Homo Maximus."[15]

The Mater Gloriosa, the Heavenly Mother and Eternal Feminine of part 2 of Goethe's *Faust*, associated with the Virgin Mary, will appear a great deal in Nicoll's diary. It is no exaggeration or misreading of his diary to say that Nicoll was intent on performing some sort of act of "sacred incest" with her. Jung remarked that he had not tried to go beyond this, "not to the Son upon the head of the Mater Gloriosa." Again, it is unclear exactly what Jung means, but he speaks of "Intensities," of "greater and greater intensification," and he remarks that the Homo Maximus "is also a point, very intense—the smallest most intense thing as well as the greatest, most infinite thing."[16] Readers of Jung will note that this is very much along the lines of the famous definition of God, as an "infinite sphere whose center is everywhere and whose circumference is nowhere," that he often quoted. (The definition has been attributed to different people—among them, strangely, Voltaire—but seems to have originated with the fourth-century philosopher Marinus Victorinus.)

Jung passed on some of his analytical insights into Nicoll's personality, this time in "real life," and not in a dream. He told Nicoll that he was an "introverted intuitive" type, who was easily "tired of the actual" and who was "intrigued by the possible," and that the "inner" attracted him, rather than the "objective." Jung was working on *Psychological Types*, the first book he wrote after his breakup with Freud, and no doubt was performing some impromptu typology on Nicoll.* Nicoll noted that he had a "resistance to types" and wondered if one could believe one was this type or that. But Gurdjieff's system uses its own typology, and it was one that Nicoll would have no problem accepting. We might also wonder if Nicoll's resistance was in part motivated by what seems, to this writer at least, a fairly good assessment of his character. Going by his diary entries, Nicoll does tire of the actual and often leaves it for something else, one example of this being his habit of starting a writing project but losing interest in it and, more often than not,

---

*Jung's typology arose from his recognition that people can be differentiated into two basic types: those who are more attentive to the outer world—whom he called "extroverts"—and those whose interest is in their inner world, the "introverts." Extroverts are happy to attend any social gathering; introverts prefer to stay home with a book. A similar differentiation comes from William James, who spoke of "tough" and "tender" minded thinkers. Jung added to his basic polarity four different "functions": thinking, feeling, sensation, and intuition. We develop one function, through which we deal with the world, but allow our other functions to remain undeveloped. It is through these "blind sides," as it were, that our psychological growth must begin. The "inferior function" appears in dreams, often personified by someone who has developed this side of themselves. Nicoll's dreams are full of individuals who are much more extroverted than he was, and of people who are able to express their sexuality openly.

leaving it unfinished. And his devotions to sacred sexuality are more focused on an inner object of desire than an outer one.

What Jung might have thought of the others at the seminar—what types they were—remains unknown, although we do have an idea of his general estimate. "These people here," Jung said "learn analysis by heart, like a lesson. They will tire of it."[17] He was certainly accurate when it came to Nicoll. Jung didn't think much of Beatrice Hinkle, who was his first advocate in America, translating *Symbols of Transformation* in 1916, after switching her allegiance from Freud, abandoning his "patriarchal" psychology for Jung's more "matriarchal" variety. Of her Jung said that "she always knows too much," and that she was "perfectly adapted to the American situation."[18] (Nicoll found her a "small nice bright glare of a woman, with a shrilling laugh."[19]) Jung's remark came after Jung tried to get across to Nicoll that in order to understand his psychology, he must "know how to be stupid," something many Freudians would no doubt agree with. What Jung meant by this was that "The God in yourself is always the least thing—the idiot—the stupid—the lowly," a statement whose meaning Nicoll must have recognized was the same as that about "the stone that was rejected." What Jung meant was that it is through our undeveloped side, our "inferior function," that the possibility of growth appears. And for most of the people at the seminar, and in modern society in general, it was their intelligence, their intellect, that got in the way of the unconscious—the most rejected thing of all—making itself known. "You can't be too simple," Jung told Nicoll. "Everything real starts with something very simple that everyone can see."[20]

But Jung didn't have everything his own way with the group. Toward the end of the seminar, in early October, Nicoll recorded that there had been an argument in the group, "all nagging at Jung and his God-instinct doctrine."[21] "Much of what Jung says about evil, the instincts and the chthonic (earthly) rouses in people here a feeling . . . of doubt and irritation," Nicoll noted. Jung himself remarked that he talked about the unconscious in a "negative way" to avoid people accepting it in an "ecstatic, aesthetic, or Christian-sentimental way." (And if this troubled Nicoll, compared to Gurdjieff, Jung was wearing kid gloves.) Everything had to be related to "life as man can know it and live it"; they were faced with the challenge of what Nietzsche in *Thus Spoke Zarathustra* called "the ugliest man," he who has killed God. Because of this, Jung told Nicoll that, "Heaven and Hell must no longer be things beyond man. Heaven must be pulled down and Hell pulled up and united in man."

Nicoll himself had difficulty with this; he was troubled by what he saw as the need to "drop all ideas of heavenly destinies and accept a painfully crude dynamic law," which seems an early expression of a complaint that theologians would make against Jung: that he reduced the divine to something in our psyche. It was a form of this complaint that would eventually force Nicoll to cut ties with Jung. Nicoll was unsure where following Jung would take him, and he was uncomfortable with the idea that Jung knows "more than he will say." "He certainly talks simply in public about things he talks about more fully in private."[22] Nicoll has got the public/private Jung dissonance in a nutshell. Later he will compare Jung to Socrates. For Nicoll, both the ancient philosopher and the modern psychologist remain enigmatic because of their relation to the unconscious. One might also add that in his own way, Jung, too, was something of a gadfly.

Nicoll also had a conversation with Mrs. Jung. He describes her as "tall, dignified, graceful, dark," with "child-like eyes" that often turn "fiery."[23] She spoke English slowly, and although it was apparent that Jung spoke to her about his work, Nicoll was surprised to find that she didn't know Jung's ideas as well as he assumed she would. She remarked that after practically pleading with Freud to say something about the second part of *Symbols of Transformation*, the book that made unavoidable the split between the two men, he refused but finally mustered the opinion that it was "an infantile revolution against the father," and little else. She recalled that when she and Carl visited Freud in Vienna, Freud "sat at the head of the table talking almost in a whisper with the children all around him," which she found "unnatural." Freud told her that all his children were neurotic—no surprise there—but that he had no idea what to do about it.[24] She also had some harsh words about the Freudians, whose treatment of her husband was "villainous."

It may not have been the best moment to mention it, but Nicoll took the opportunity to confide in Emma something that had been on his mind for some time: his reservations about Jung's approach to dreams. There was, he felt, something missing in it. Through analyzing dreams, he told her, we only get to see the problem; their analysis doesn't provide the solution to it—at least Nicoll was having difficulty finding any solution to his problem in his dreams, as a look at his diary confirms. He was also troubled by the lack in Jung's approach of something *outside* the psyche, some "orientating principle," a "crown," by which we can only assume he meant a deity, a god, something more than human, what today we would call the "transpersonal." Perhaps something like the Great Mother he had been consorting with in his devotions? Or simply God? We know God was a reality for Nicoll, a sometimes very harsh one. Nicoll added cryptically that there were "methods about which Jung knew nothing," by which he presumably meant ways of reaching a solution, although he did not name any and would not come into contact with Ouspensky for another year, so it is unclear to what "methods" he referred.

We don't know if Emma asked the obvious question: solution to what? What is the problem you want to resolve? We don't know if Nicoll confided in her about his dilemma, or if he ever spoke of it with Jung. There is no evidence that he did, or that he spoke with anyone else about it. We don't know Emma's response to his confession, or if she had one at all. She might have said that individuation wasn't about getting the solution to your problems in a dream, handed to you on a plate, although often enough they do present insights we are unaware of. The aim of individuation, she might have said, is to *grow beyond* your problems by becoming more conscious, and understanding what your dreams may be saying to you is one way of doing that. But a reader of these diaries may accept that Nicoll was not making much headway with that. This could mean that Jung was wrong, or rather that like most of us, Nicoll was not the best person to analyze his own dreams. That he was not detached enough is clear from the diary. I've pointed out at least one instance where Jung himself in a dream was giving him some very good advice, which it seems slipped by him.

About his second reservation, a lack of "orientating principle," Jung would make it a point throughout his career to say he was a psychologist, not a theologian or metaphysician. He had nothing to say about the "objective" existence of God—at least insofar as he was a psychologist—but of the *archetype* of the divine in the human psyche, what he called the Self, he was convinced. That was his "orientating principle." And as for the absence of anything "outside" the psyche, in later life Jung would often point to this fragment from Heraclitus in response: "You cannot discover the bounds of the psyche even if you walked off every step, so deep is its meaning." This means that whatever "objective" crown or orientating principle you may choose, you know of it through the mediation of your psyche. We cannot escape from our own minds, so in a sense, this makes everything "psychological."

Would any of these responses have satisfied Nicoll? I doubt it. His dissatisfaction with Jung's approach was real, not merely theoretical. Someone else in a similar situation might have gone to see a psychiatrist, perhaps even to Nicoll himself. He was in a crisis, to be sure. It did not, however, interfere with the seminar, which on the whole Nicoll seems to have enjoyed. And it was not a one-man show. One evening Emma contributed by reading some stories from Celtic folklore about the original inhabitants of Ireland. This was a nonhuman species who tried to fend off the humans when they finally came, battling them with magic. They were eventually defeated and became "archetypes" in the "collective unconscious."[25] After this, Jung spoke about metempsychosis, when a human soul passes into that of an animal. And it was during this seminar that Jung painted a "Sphere and Serpent," that later appeared in *The Art of C. G. Jung*, a herald of what the later *Red Book* would bring.

SOME CURIOUS DREAMS followed Nicoll's time in Cornwall. In one he is with a party of men who have got together "to kill an Old Man."[26] He has a rifle and is given a strange bullet in order to shoot him, but can't load it and eventually there is a mix-up and in the end the Old Man isn't shot. Jung interpreted the dream to mean that the Old Man represented "the habitual way of taking life" taught to Nicoll by his education. By shooting the Old Man he can free himself of this—oddly enough the scene of the aborted murder in the dream was Liberty's, a famously expensive department store in London (liberty doesn't come cheaply). But Nicoll can't fire his bullet, which Jung read as the need not to kill the Father; instead "one must find a way to overcome and harmonise all he represents in one's psyche."[27] Was the Father here Jung? Was Jung advising Nicoll not to commit one-half of the Oedipal sin?

A few days after this dream, Nicoll spent several hours at work on a "drawing of the Great Mother."[28] He wanted to "blend with her" and wrote hymns that "took symbolic form though grossly sexual." A toss of his *I Ching* coins produced "Restraint—accumulation through holding in," hexagram 26, Ta Ch'u—and Nicoll notes "thus did not." One can only suspect that this "holding in" referred to his devotions. He was curious what effect this restraint would have on his dreams, after a day of "absorbed instinct." It seemed not to produce much, at least going by Nicoll's account. He dreamed of "endless black lines" that were like "black hairs," and records little else. Yet on another occasion when "the libido is tremendously stirred and pours out as it did in my drawings," he remarked that if he deferred his devotions and refused to allow them a physical release—did not allow μ—then the anima, the feminine aspect of his psyche, "is tamed" and appears in his dreams as a "high symbol."[29]

He notes that Jung spoke about the necessity of sincerity in order for the compensatory effect of a dream to be realized. "Unless the attitude is sincere," Jung said, "the compensatory function cannot work."[30] This is, of course, a generally valid dictum, but did Jung mean it for Nicoll in particular? The compensatory power of dreaming about "endless black lines" seems ambiguous, unless we take what seems a rather dull dream as compensation for Nicoll's "compulsion" in spending an entire day at an erotic drawing of the Mater Gloriosa. But then, perhaps dreams are not always compensatory. But Jung's remarks seem appropriate, whomever they were directed at: "The Unconscious—that is, the psychic background on which our conscious life floats, is full of many forces. Sincerity brings those forces useful to man."[31]

Something else that Jung related to Nicoll was beginning to have more than a professional interest for him. At Sennen Cove Jung had spoken of marriage as "the beginning of relations" and that "relationship is impossible save through both sides acting on their subjective states. People do not understand what relationship depends on."[32] This was something about which Nicoll was beginning to ponder. From some of his diary entries I get the sense that the trouble that had brought Catherine to see him in the first place was making an appearance again. One entry notes that she "seemed to show some of the old reactions," which, presumably, meant her revulsion to physical sex.[33] In one dream, Nicoll is on a train with Catherine and Jung. Jung tells him that because Catherine was pregnant, with a boy, she had no libido for him. Catherine wasn't pregnant at that time, and when she will be, it will be with a girl. (Was the "boy" then her embryonic animus, her unrealized masculine side?) But whether she had any libido for Nicoll is an open question. When in the dream Jung advises Nicoll to seek some libido elsewhere, he is repelled by what he takes to be Jung's "ruthless" point of view, yet he sees that part of the problem in relationships is a kind of "sick sentimentality" that makes a real exchange impossible.[34]

Nicoll was beginning to see marriage, or at least his marriage to Catherine, as a kind of analysis in itself. "Marriage," he noted, "is nature's process of psychological analysis."[35] Nature may be a clumsy analyst; nevertheless, she was effective. One thing his marriage was producing were what he called "soul tensions," something that analysis did as well. One of these tensions was a recognition that most men come to sooner or later after marrying: that casual affairs, "sexual adventures," are very different from the relationship between man and wife. The affairs have a single aim in view—sex—and the personalities of the people involved do not necessarily have to be a part of it. In fact, people have affairs precisely in order to get away from themselves, at least from the self they find themselves saddled with in their marriage. They have a fling and do something wild. These sexual adventures don't come with all the baggage that people bring to a relationship. They come with no strings attached. Marriage is different, and it brings quite a lot of baggage and enough strings to find oneself tripping over them fairly often.

"These mutual tensions of the soul," Nicoll noted, "still form the starting point of adult psychological growth at this point in human evolution."[36] Nicoll hits on a phrase that Jungian therapists will get a great deal of mileage out of in the 1980s and '90s. He calls marriage "the first school of the soul," jumping the gun on the many books about "soul making" and such that have come from people like James Hillman and Robert Johnson and their epigones.[37] It is not a state of "stationary comfort," something anyone who had been married for some time could have told him, but a process in which is produced "a continual crop of problems which are only partially objective"—that is, originating in some problem or need in the outer world; money, for example, which Nicoll, resident on Chester Terrace, knew all about. The real problems are those that arise between the subjectivities of the marriage partners. If these are not engaged, "a husband and wife may be amiable and courteous to each other . . . simply because it pleases their idea of what husband and wife should be," but there is no real relationship.[38]

We've seen that Jung's psychology suggests that there are contra-sexual archetypes in men and women; that is, a man's psyche has a feminine archetype, what he called the anima, and a woman's has her male equivalent, the animus. This arrangement means that when a man and a woman get together, they are really a foursome, and that much of the action that goes on has to do with how his anima reacts to her animus, and vice versa. And this psychological sussing out takes place at levels about which both parties are generally unconscious, and of which they only know the effects, which often enough can be disastrous.

A long section in the diary in which Nicoll looks at the problems created in the "psycho-sexuality" of women because of their relationship to their father leads one to wonder about Catherine's relationship with her father. Interestingly enough, she lost her father at a young age just as Nicoll lost his mother. Unfortunately, given our highly impressionable psyches, we seem to enter the mating game with the cards stacked heavily against us. Nicoll is speaking about women's psychology but the same remarks apply equally to men and their relationship to the mother. If "the love of the father has been too well satisfied," he writes, then the woman will remain fixated on that relationship to the detriment of any she might make with another man.[39] No man will ever match up to that paragon of excellence, and she may come to hold all other men in contempt, of which she will be unconscious, perhaps consciously trying to make things work and having no idea why they don't. But if her relationship to her father was bad, if he was "unlovable," then her future relationships will also be affected, because she did not have a model of positive male figure to help her choose her future mate. Either way, her "psycho-sexuality" will be traumatized in ways that her possible future mate will find less than appealing. One wonders if this scenario was coming home to Nicoll in ways that reached beyond his consulting rooms.

NICOLL MAY HAVE BEEN QUESTIONING his relationship to Jung and his ideas, but this did not prevent him from having him as a visitor to Chester Terrace. In late October Carl and Emma came to dinner at the Nicolls; the evening before they had seen a play by J. M. Barrie, famous for *Peter Pan*; Barrie was a friend of Nicoll's father. Nicoll confided in his diary that "taking my place with men in life once more," entailed the "sacrifice of the idea that I am anything very special."[40] Jung had told him that his ambition was "dangerous" to him; it led him to the "wrong situation." What he needed to do, he told himself, was to find his place and be content to remain there, an admonition that seems reminiscent of the injunction he received as child to ride his bicycle only up to a certain point and no further, which he dutifully obeyed.

Yet this decision to accept his lot did not stop Nicoll from pursuing the incessant self-analysis that makes up a great deal of the diary entries. The earnestness that Jung had warned him about remained. So did signs that all was not well in the Nicoll household. Catherine was suffering from migraine—a psychosomatic ailment—and Nicoll noted that she had displayed "no temper" since she had returned from Cornwall.[41] This suggests she had displayed some while there. An entry some weeks later has her "holding her balance," and at one point he is angry with her for buying some hats on a shopping spree, which he found "vulgar and common."[42] The sexual dreams continued, as did his devotions. It would be tedious and pedantic to go into detail about each one. Nicoll had some peculiarly insistent and consistent sexual fantasies that his unconscious returned to frequently, something not uncommon in men. "Talking dirty" to a dark sensuous woman was one; the others involved engagements with the more or less "acceptable" perversions, oral or anal sex, occasionally with some curious partners. In one dream he is having sex with Emma Jung, while she confesses her unhappiness with Carl. During the act she appears to have a penis.[43] In another dream, he meets Jung at a café in a seaside town. Jung is in drag, wearing a dress and "his face is evil." He has just come from some sexual affair, and he is "steeped in the magic of it." This shows not in a "spiritual radiance," but in a kind of crude sensuality.[44] It seems that in Nicoll's dreams, the anima and animus of Mr. and Mrs. Jung got around.

Again, we must wait for a fully edited and annotated edition of the diaries for a proper interpretation of Nicoll's dreams, but we can see them broadly as a kind of compensation for Nicoll's waking life. In one entry he notes that "I am not easily coarse with people," yet he recognizes that "I am coarse enough in my phantasy, but then it is very rich and satisfying, and even the magic words are magical."[45] One wonders what "magic words" Nicoll had in mind? Were they the ones he used when "talking dirty"? He contrasts his nocturnal coarseness with "this goodness in me," sounding rather like Mr. Hyde complaining of Dr. Jekyll, and remarking that something about him must give people the impression that he is not sexual, an odd remark coming from the author of this diary. Yet given that Nicoll's sexuality was profoundly introverted—not to say inhibited—it isn't surprising that he may have come across as asexual to the people who knew him. Perhaps it was this that got in the way of anything happening with Laura, and why the woman who would have him was one who had admitted to a horror of physical sex.

Nicoll kept up his studies, reading widely in mystical literature; his entries during this time mention Jakob Böhme, Swedenborg, William Blake. His patients had him working long days, and another group, the Analytical Society, had started meeting at Harley Street, perhaps as a riposte to Ernest Jones's strictly Freudian British Analytical Society.[46] Money troubles plagued him. And his dreams began to speak of his "resistance to Jung," although in one he and Jung are in bed.[47] It was around this time, in late November, that Nicoll records the fantasy, mentioned earlier, of performing an act of sacred incest with the Great Mother and being admonished by her to seek in his penis for the "wonders of the circle of magic." Yet, as we saw, not long after this he is cursing "our filthy and abominable sexuality," paying special attention to

our generative organs, and being grateful to God for tolerating his existence a moment longer in spite of them. By December he is impotent,
and in a dream Jung concurs with Freud that "there is plenty of wish
fulfilment scattered about in dreams."

THINGS SEEMED TO PICK UP in the New Year. There are no entries
for January and February, and only a few for late March. But on
April 2, 1921, Nicoll noted "(s.i. 4 times in week—great freeing of
forces)"; the parentheses are his. His "s.i." is another code, standing for
"sexual intercourse," so to differentiate it from μ.[48] Yet the passage that
follows—another exchange with his inner voice—ends in the usual
quandary, "How can there be pure sexuality and impure?" a question
that has troubled him for some time. He knew that the "direct control of the instincts is not the real solution."[49] That only leads to an
impoverishment of the soul. But they must also not be let loose through
the ego. If the "fire" of the libido passes into the personality, "it simply obsesses it and there is no freedom." We can assume Nicoll knew
this from experience. What is needed, he felt, is a kind of "jiu-jitsu"
method whereby the opposing forces of spirit and sexuality can meet
without actually fighting each other. Yet Nicoll still hadn't found this,
and he felt that he was increasingly "in danger of meeting with impersonal forces and being torn." We can say that he was concerned that the
archetypes might get him as they had almost got Jung.

Help was coming though, and from some unusual places. In a dream
Winston Churchill helps Nicoll drag some boats out of the water and
onto shore. Nicoll took this as a symbol of retrieving elements of his
psyche from the unconscious—the shoreline is the meeting place of the
conscious and unconscious minds, whose juncture Nicoll's "jiu-jitsu"
would effect—and notes that Churchill, " a sensualist," has his "own
interpretation of life" and possesses "dash and courage."[50] He seems
a symbol of a man "doing" with panache and ease—rather as Orage

was—something that Nicoll still found difficult. There still remained "the plaguing question" at the back of his mind: "the conflict between spirit and sense and the doubts about Jung's teaching."

An evening out with Catherine and James Young at the Trocadero, an entertainment palace near Piccadilly Circus, left him depressed and caught in the same conflict. He was afraid of being considered a "flannelled fool" or "sick Christ," that is, an ascetic unable to enjoy sensuous life. But he was just as much in fear of "being a disgrace to the unconscious," which one assumes means failing to integrate his anima. He is in anticipation of the coming "New Church," a nod to Swedenborg's vision of a new age, and asks his guide to "redeem me, liberate me, cleanse me from the filth of modern life."[51] He prays for help in this difficult moment. Apparently he did not get it, because not long after this he is feeling suicidal. On May 12, Nicoll notes that he no longer knows "what anything means." He is "tired, weary, worn" and wants only "obliteration and peace." "I am getting bitter, suicidal, ill . . . and awfully tired." "I have no strength by myself to go on. . . . I shall never know anything for certain. . . . I cannot go on with the most difficult task—I might as well lay down my arms and rest . . . there is no hope for man if man is going to find it always so hard as I . . ."[52]

This was a low point, just as the despair that had led to his rejection of Christ had been some months earlier.

NICOLL'S DESPAIR, HOWEVER, did not prevent him from noting down some reflections on two of our "functions," as Jung called them, feeling and thinking, and our need to develop them to achieve psychological maturity. Both are necessary—as are sensation and intuition, our two other functions—and both can be under- or overdeveloped.* In

---

*For Jung, thinking and feeling are our "rational" functions, in the sense that we weigh their evidence and come to a decision based on it. Sensation and intuition are "irrational" in the sense that we simply have a sensation or intuition. They are "given" and that's that.

the modern world, thinking is the function we've come to prize, but this does not mean that everyone thinks properly—far from it. Yet, just as an overweening intellect can obscure the messages from the unconscious because it has difficulty in being "simple"—as Jung had pointed out in Sennen Cove—so too can dependence on thinking interfere with the proper function of feeling.

"Christ sought to develop the feelings," Nicoll noted.[53] Why? Because it is through feelings that "we affirm the existence of other people and relate ourselves to humanity. Through them we sit at the common table of mankind and identify ourselves with the human race."[54] This is because the feelings make "the demon of power impotent." Thinking is important because without it "psychology remains blurred and chaotic," that is, a swarm of feelings.[55] Thinking makes possible discrimination and realization, without which we are left to the vagaries of "impulse" and a "continual inundation of the ego."[56] This is because "what remains undeveloped feeds the Titans," that is, the dark, undifferentiated unconscious.

The urge to differentiate, to become an individual, is "the deepest need of humanity," Nicoll wrote. Without it "the hero myth would have never sprung out of the universal imagination."[57] Yet there are forces at work that inhibit the hero in us. We are brought up to believe that "someone knows" and that at every difficulty "someone should come forward . . . with advice, comfort and guidance," whether it is our parents, teachers, doctors, scientists—or psychotherapists and gurus, for that matter. This "infantile attitude has to be left, and the adventure of life entered upon." Yet "we have done our best to make life as little like an adventure as possible."[58] Nicoll would later note that the hero "is the spirit of dangerous adventure." He is the one who "easily oversteps the limits of ordinary precedence."[59] Yet this was a challenge that Nicoll still found difficult to meet. His "conventionality," his inner voice told him, was "very, very strong" and "difficult to break."[60]

One adventure Nicoll decided to set out on just then was to write a book comparing Freud's ideas with Jung's. This would be as detailed and closely argued a comparison as he could make it. We've seen that although he considered himself a Jungian and was seen as such by people like Ernest Jones, Nicoll still retained more than a little of Freud's views. His use of "libido" as a specific sexual energy runs throughout the diary; his own term "interest" is used considerably less. And we've seen that even in a dream Jung told Nicoll that he could find plenty of wish fulfillment in in his dreams. Although the real Jung never denied that some dreams perform that function, it is odd to find a dream Jung arguing his opponent's position, at the same time as he compensated for Nicoll's conscious attitude. And the fact that Nicoll's problem, whose solution he had sought unsuccessfully in his dreams, was focused almost exclusively on sex, speaks for itself. The idea of a detailed comparison between the two different systems may have seemed to Nicoll as a way of finally settling the "spirit vs. sensuality" tussle that had troubled him since his adolescence and had brought him to a psychological crisis.

Unfortunately, this was another writing project that never got off the ground. Aside from *Living Time*, which Nicoll researched during his first years with Ouspenky but that wouldn't see print until 1952, Nicoll would not complete another book until he finished *The New Man* not long before his death; or, to be more precise, allowed what he had written of it to be published. He would, of course, write the sermons that would be collected as the *Psychological Commentaries*, but these were never conceived as a book and were collected long after most of them had been written. Now, in the summer of 1921, he was still "plagued by uncertainty," bemoaning his "lack of root and weight," his "nothingness." He was "so soon spent, exhausted . . . failing."[61] Not long after announcing the project, at least to himself, in the diary and sketching an outline, he was confessing his inability to do it. In early July, Nicoll wrote that he was "trying to get started on my book again—writing as simply as possible—yet immediately I begin to block and cover to veil myself—to hint at profundities that I do not understand myself."[62]

Yet Nicoll's writer's block had as much to do with his increasingly equivocal feeling toward Jung as it did his natural tendency toward laziness. At one point he writes petulantly, "Here have I been slaving and toiling to help forward Jung and his work and I get no reward."[63] In another diary entry he records a dream in which he and Emma Jung enter into an affair, and Nicoll wonders what Jung would think about that. (In the dream Jung is sarcastic.)[64] Yet at the same time, Nicoll contrasts Jung's "individuation" positively against what he sees as the "dissolution" of the self in a "sea of emotions" that is the essence of Christianity. "Christianity does not teach uniqueness. Jung teaches Individuation."[65] And at least in this entry Nicoll sets quite great store by this. "Through uniqueness you touch life magically. Through the sense of uniqueness, you produce an effect without effort. Through uniqueness you transform everything."[66] And the opposite is also true. "Through lack of uniqueness everything becomes commonplace and weariness arises," a weariness that yearns for "dissolution."

It's unclear if Nicoll realized this, but he seems to be suggesting that Christianity is a religion for those who are weary of life and seek a "dissolution" of themselves into "uniformity" and "collectivity." This, in essence, is the argument Nietzsche makes against Christianity as a religion of *ressentiment* in *The Antichrist*. Nicoll would later call Nietzsche's assessment of Christianity as an antilife religion of slaves "insane," yet his reading of it here is not far removed from this. In a later entry, Nicoll will equate much of "Christian love" with a kind of "hate," that spouts the "highest spiritual lies," which is not far different from Nietzsche's characterization of Christianity as a "curse" against life.[67] Nietzsche too, I might point out, argued for a form of individuation. His call for *amor fati*, "love of fate," and to "become who you are" are to all intents and purposes the same as Jung's.

Yet Nicoll is honest enough to recognize his ambivalence to Jung. He writes that "Everything I do, I seem to do in orientation to Jung. He is the Father and I am the one who shall please him and gain his approval."[68] Yet he acknowledges that he "is jealous of Jung" because he wants to "be Jung." He writes "I wish him to love me, to establish and confirm me, to accept and applaud me, to encourage me." Yet at the same time he doesn't want Jung to see that "on the sly I hate him because he is bigger than I am."[69] (Here Nicoll might have noted an Adlerian touch; Jung was a large man and Nicoll comparatively short, so his feelings of inferiority could be accounted for through purely physical factors.) This ambivalence can be seen in a dream in which Nicoll gets into an argument and finds himself fighting someone named "Allman" (the collective), yet soon after he and Constance Long are jumping up and down on a copy of her translation of Jung's *Collected Papers on Analytical Psychology.*[70]

IT ISN'T SURPRISING THAT THROUGHOUT all this, Nicoll continued to seek help from higher forces. On one occasion, that has become well known within the world of the Fourth Way, he petitioned the Greek god of magic and communication, Hermes, for help. "O mighty teacher," Nicoll begins his prayer, "teach me—instruct me—show me the path, so that I may know certainly—help my great ignorance, illumine my darkness. I have asked a question."* Given that Beryl Pogson highlights this petition as especially significant, it has stood out as a unique request from Nicoll for assistance from the gods.[71] But as we've seen, Nicoll was liberal in his petitions to higher forces, addressing many gods and goddesses as well as spiritual powers of his own naming. (Again, I have only referred to a small selection of these.) Yet his interest in Hermes was most likely stimulated by a reading

---

*There is some ambiguity about the date of this prayer to Hermes. Pogson has it as taking place on August 9. In the diary it appears in the entry for September 8. Jeffrey Adams suggests the confusion may be because of the difference between the English and American way of writing the date. The English put the day before the month; in America it's the opposite.

of G. R. S. Mead's monumental three-volume survey of the *Corpus Hermeticum*, the collection of writings attributed to the ancient sage Hermes Trismegistus.

Although for centuries thought to be an actual person who lived before the flood, Hermes Trismegistus was a mythical amalgam of Hermes and the Egyptian god of magic and writing, Thoth, that arose in the heady esoteric climate of Alexandria, in the early years of the Christian era. Mead's *Thrice-Greatest Hermes: Studies in Hellenistic Theosophy and Gnosis* (1896) was one of the first works to present the ancient Hermetic teachings in a modern light, following the lead of his late teacher, Helena Petrovna Blavatsky, whose secretary Mead had been. Mead had been a member of Blavatsky's Esoteric Section of the Theosophical Society, as well as of her Inner Group, reserved for her more advanced students. He left the society in 1909 when Annie Besant, its head—Blavatsky had died in 1891—reinstated C. W. Leadbeater, who had been excommunicated in 1906. Leadbeater's expulsion followed allegations that in the occult training that he was administering to the young sons of some American Theosophists, he had included some "hands on" lessons in masturbation. That same year Mead established his own group, the Quest Society, as an open association dedicated to studying religion, philosophy, science, and the mystical teachings of the ancients. They held their meetings in the old Kensington Town Hall.

Mead would be important in Nicoll's life in a very direct way. It would be through his intervention that his prayer to Hermes would be answered.

In the meantime, Nicoll struggled on. He was interested enough in the sex scandal surrounding the American silent film star Fatty Arbuckle to note it in his diary. "We read about Arbuckle's case . . . it speaks of his sexuality plainly, in a way that anyone who <u>knows</u> can understand," Nicoll wrote.[72] Arbuckle was a silver-screen star famous for his comedies; he was enormous, weighing some 330 pounds, and this added to his persona of "cherubic innocence." At a three-day party in San Francisco in early September 1921, celebrating a lucrative contract he had just signed, Arbuckle enticed a young model turned actress, Virginia Rappe, whom he had been pursuing for some time, into a bedroom. Rappe disliked Arbuckle but wanted to advance her career and so was willing to show him some favor. She had needed to use the toilet since she had arrived at the party, but all were occupied. A few minutes after Arbuckle closed the door—with a salacious wink to his friends— screams were heard from the room. They went on for a few minutes, then Arbuckle came out with a sheepish smile and did a little dance in the hallway. Inside, Virginia was groaning in pain, her clothes torn. She died in the hospital three days later. It turned out that in his excitement Arbuckle had flung her on the bed and thrown his full weight upon her. This caused her full bladder to burst; she died of peritonitis. Rumor soon got to work embellishing the story. One account had it that Arbuckle's penis was so large that it had caused the damage. Others said she had died from the objects he had used to penetrate her, among them a huge piece of ice and a champagne bottle. In the end, Arbuckle was acquitted of any charges—her death had been an accident—but his career was in ruins.[73]

One can't help but wonder why Nicoll considered this worth jotting down, and how the account of the incident that he had read had related the affair. What is interesting is that the remarks in his diary following this note all relate to how a too-protective attitude toward women spoils sex. In essence, good sex requires a bit of violence, of taking without permission. Were Nicoll's thoughts prompted by reading the account of Arbuckle's "rape" of Virginia Rappe, as the first sensational reports had it? (Arbuckle was only acquitted after three trials.) Nicoll was never as large as Arbuckle, but he was on the chubby side, a fact that would trouble him in later life. Did he identify in some way with the incident? Unlike other silent stars—Charlie Chaplin, for example—Arbuckle did not have a reputation as a sexual predator. He was described as "protective and 'big brotherly'" by the women who worked with him. One reason his career went down in flames is precisely because he presented an image of innocence and harmlessness. The public felt they had been betrayed, and that someone they had seen as jolly and childlike had turned out to be a "sex fiend." Did Nicoll feel that in some way this was also true of him?

"The attitude of protection spoils the sexuality," he wrote, noting the fundamental aggressive character of the male sexual drive. "Repression of the sexuality produces the desire to protect overmuch. Sexuality is an outburst, an adventure [again, 'the forbidden'] . . ." "When the protective attitude can be laid aside, sexuality comes at once forward." He reflected that he sought a woman whom he did not have to protect—a woman, that is, toward whom he could be honestly sexual. Yet he suppresses this "brutal idea," and through this its opposite arises, an extreme sense of protection, which inhibits the sex. His self-consciousness adds another layer of inhibition. His "fear of criticism" makes him "vulnerable."[74] Yet a few days after making these notes, following an account of a dream in which he and Ernest Jones achieve some reconciliation, Nicoll wrote that "If nothing else, I will devote myself only to the joy of my wife so that she is well and has a good time."[75]

The simplicity of that remark suggests a sincerity, but also a weariness, a tiredness with the struggles he has been through. There is a sense that he is ready to give up. He holds on, "for there is nothing else to do," but he fears that in the end he will just have to be "grim, respectable, hard-working" and make his way up that "old dreary ladder" of success. "Life" had got him after all.

Yet everything was just about to change.

At the time, in fact, Catherine was pregnant with their daughter, Jane, who would arrive only a few weeks later, on October 12. Jung served as godfather, Dame Katherine Furze, an administrator in the Red Cross and Royal Navy Service, as the godmother. But his daughter was not the only new person that would enter Nicoll's life just then. Soon after her arrival he would meet someone else whose importance to him would overshadow even that of his newborn child. The teacher he had long prayed for was in town, and the law of fate was arranging a meeting.

7

Finding the Miraculous

The law of fate works in mysterious ways, and not all of its agents are aware of their part in its plans. When, in 1918, Nicholas Bessaraboff, a young Russian émigré living in the United States, knocked at the door of the author, publisher, and Theosophist Claude Bragdon, he knew that his action would affect the life of at least one other Russian. But of the impact it would have on the life of a spiritually troubled Harley Street neurological specialist, he could not have known, or even have suspected. Yet it was through his action that a series of events were set in motion that would lead to the god Hermes answering Nicoll's prayer.

Bessaraboff, a draftsman and engineer, had been sent to America to help with the shipment of military equipment to Russian forces during World War I. When Lenin came to power, he stayed behind in the States, where he eventually became an authority on ancient musical instruments. Back in St. Petersburg, Bessaraboff had read Ouspensky's early, pre-Gurdjieff work *Tertium Organum,* the "third organ of thought" following Aristotle's and Francis Bacon's, and was stunned by its power and scope. His reading had awakened a burning hunger to know more about philosophy, science, religion, and the mystery of being itself, a reaction that the book's twenty-first-century readers often have as well. *Tertium Organum* is an exhilarating metaphysical *tour de force*, setting off speculative fireworks in a number of directions, most of them having to do with "higher space," "cosmic consciousness," the "fourth dimension," mysticism, and a variety of ideas and insights into the mysterious nature of time. It's general aim was to show the inadequacies of the reigning positivist, reductionist, scientific outlook. Its overall effect was to spark in its readers a riveting sense of wonder.

Ouspensky had been a popular and influential figure in Russian Theosophical circles—which is precisely why Gurdjieff had sought him out—and Bragdon had published books on "higher consciousness" and "higher space." Most helpful, he could read Russian. Bessaraboff wanted Bragdon to translate and publish Ouspensky's extraordinary work, and he had showed up on his doorstep with a copy in hand to tell him so.

Bragdon was soon convinced Bessaraboff had knocked on the right door. He quickly saw that Ouspensky was "the Columbus of that uncharted ocean of thought in which I and others had indeed adventured, haunted by dreams of rich argosies from virgin continents."[1] Bragdon found Ouspensky's thought so congenial that he felt readers might accuse him of plagiarism, if they didn't know that his own *Four-Dimensional Vistas* (1916) had been written before he knew of Ouspensky's work. Both he and Ouspensky had been influenced by the speculative fantasies of Edwin Abbot, author of the "romance of many dimensions," *Flatland* (1884), and Charles Hinton, whose *Scientific Romances* (1885) influenced H. G. Wells's *The Time Machine* (1895), which brought the fourth dimension into many households.

Hinton had developed a way of peering into the fourth and several other dimensions, an artifact he devised that came to be known as the "Hinton cube." This was a 36 × 36 × 36 block of cubes, to each of whose 46,656 units he had given a Latin name. Hinton then taught himself to visualize this "hypercube," and to memorize all its possible positions. This purely mental image—remarkably anticipating Picasso and Braque's Cubism—was made available to the average person in the form of a stripped down version of twelve cardboard cubes, decorated in different colors, that one could memorize. By moving the cubes into different combinations and visualizing them, one was supposed to be able to perceive "higher space," and the practice became for a time a party favorite.

Ouspensky used the metaphor of one-, two-, three-, and four-dimensional beings in order to show how the incursion of something from a "higher" dimension into a lower one, would seem something of a miracle to its inhabitants. So a plane would appear incredible to a line, having a strange "extra" dimension, just as a cube would seem impossible to a plane. We inhabit three dimensions, the length, breadth, and height of the positivism Ouspensky wanted to overthrow, but are constantly experiencing incursions of the fourth dimension into our world. But while most writers on the fourth dimension saw it as time, for Ouspensky it was a kind of all-purpose term to designate the source of what he was really in search of: the miraculous.

Bessaraboff's determination to have Ouspensky's work on the possibilities of human consciousness made available to English speaking readers paid off—literally. The book was a success, so much so that Bragdon's Manas Press was unable to meet the demand and he had to sell the copyright to Alfred Knopf.* The new edition sold even more, becoming something of a metaphysical bestseller, and reached important readers like the poet Hart Crane. Ouspensky's royalties amounted to a tidy sum. But Bragdon had no idea where Ouspensky was or how to

---

*The Manas Press edition of *Tertium Organum* is now a rarity. Among other things, it contains an error about Ouspensky that continues to be repeated even today. In his introduction Bragdon refers to Ouspensky as an "accomplished mathematician," and says that he "holds the position of instructor in mathematics in Petrograd Institute of Ways of Communication." Neither of these remarks was true. Ouspensky was a high school dropout who never earned a degree. His father was an amateur mathematician, which is how Ouspensky most likely first heard about the "fourth dimension." Though interested in science, Ouspensky was really more of a poet, as his early book *The Symbolism of the Tarot* (1909)—now a chapter in *A New Model of the Universe*—shows. In my book on Ouspensky, I argue that it was after his time with Gurdjieff that he shed his earlier gentle and poetic character, to become the iron taskmaster of the Work.

reach him. With a civil war tearing Russia apart, the prospects of find-ing out anytime soon seemed slim. He came across a copy of Orage's *New Age* with one of Ouspensky's "Letters to Russia" in it, and wrote to him, asking about Ouspensky's whereabouts, but by then Orage didn't know either. Yet the law of fate seemed to be working overtime.

Around the same time, during a visit to London, an American Theosophist visited the headquarters of the Theosophical Society, and asked for a copy of *Tertium Organum*. A Russian woman overheard him and explained that she was a friend of Ouspensky. She told him that he was languishing in a refugee camp in Constantinople, and wanted des-perately to get to England.* The American got word of this to Bragdon, who immediately sent Ouspensky three copies of the book as well as a much appreciated check for some substantial royalties.

The books and the money were welcome, without doubt. But what Ouspensky was most excited by was the prospect of getting out of the refugee camp on the island of Prinkipo, off the coast of Constantinople, that he and his family had been trapped in for some time. He had arrived there in January 1920, swept across an exploding Russia by waves of violence sent out by "the history of crime," known more locally as the Russian Civil War. He had been earning a crust as, among other things, a hotel porter, and was now teaching English to other Russians, like himself hopeful of somehow getting to England. Ouspensky wrote to Bragdon, expressing his thanks, and asking if he could in any way help him secure the visas needed to travel. Bragdon couldn't, but just as Ouspensky's hopes were beginning to fade, fate stepped in once again.

One reader of *Tertium Organum* was so taken with it that she was determined to meet its author, regardless of the cost. Lilian Rothermere, wife of Harold Harmsworth, the first Lord Rothermere, the newspaper

---

*Exactly who this Russian woman was is unclear. In my book on Ouspensky I raise the possibility that it was Anna Butkovky-Hewitt, with Ouspensky a member of Gurdjieff's early groups in St. Petersburg. See Anna Butkovsky-Hewitt *With Gurdjieff and Ouspensky in St. Petersburg and Paris*.

baron, had a weakness for subjects mystical and spiritual, and *Tertium Organum* had moved her deeply. She cabled Bragdon telling him so, and then decided to take no chances, and like Bessaraboff, showed up at his door in Rochester, New York. From this meeting emerged another cable, this one to Ouspensky in Constantinople. She was deeply impressed with his book indeed. "WISH TO MEET YOU NEW YORK OR LONDON" the cable said. "WILL PAY ALL EXPENSES."

One could excuse Ouspensky for wondering for a moment if Lady Rothermere's telegram had been sent from the fourth dimension. For surely the miracle had arrived. And to prove the point, there was even another check.

If these ostensibly chance events have not yet persuaded the reader that there may indeed be something in this idea of a "law of fate," one last link in this miraculous chain may do the trick. Obtaining the necessary travel visas was not easy in a Constantinople that was still recovering from a war and just about to start its new life under the secularizing administration of Kemal Ataturk, as the moribund Ottoman Empire went under. Ouspensky was one among thousands trying to leave the country; White Russians were twelve to the dozen. Counts and countesses were reduced to washing dishes, if they were lucky enough to find the work. Yet it just so happened that Ouspensky had recently met the one person in all of Constantinople who could help him, and more to the point, would.

John Godolphin Bennett, a member of British intelligence with an interest in higher dimensions, among many other things, had been introduced to Ouspensky by a former colonel of the Russian Imperial Guard, who was now earning his keep as a shoemaker. Mikhail Lvow had been living under a staircase in the White Russian Club in Pera—the European part of Constantinople—when Mrs. Beaumont, Bennett's companion, took pity on him and offered him a room in her flat. Lvow then asked if it were possible to use her drawing room once a week for some talks a brilliant countryman of his was planning to give.

The generous Mrs. Beaumont agreed. One afternoon, Bennett heard a ruckus coming from the room. When he asked what was happening, he was introduced to Ouspensky, who explained that they were discussing the "transformation of man," something in which Bennett himself had much interest. His interest was piqued even more when Ouspensky explained that the difference between one man and another can be greater than the difference between a sheep and a cabbage. The two became friends, and Bennett would visit Ouspensky in Prinkipo.

Six months after Ouspensky's arrival in Constantinople, Gurdjieff too showed up, by way of Tiflis, where he had acquired new students, among them Alexandre and Jeanne de Salzmann. He and Ouspensky had fled the deluge by different routes, but had each been funneled to this point. By a strangely circuitous path, Bennett met Gurdjieff without knowing that he and Ouspensky were acquainted and only became aware of this when he attended a performance of some of Gurdjieff's "sacred dances," at which Ouspensky was also present. Like practically everyone else who met him, Bennett was impressed with Gurdjieff, who possessed "the strangest eyes he had ever seen." Less impressive were the reports Bennett received from military intelligence that Gurdjieff was suspected of being a Russian agent, a suspicion based on perhaps equal parts conjecture and fact. Gurdjieff's dark, mysterious past, seeking out ancient, forgotten wisdom in politically volatile regions, would prove a hurdle he was unable to clear in his attempts to set up camp in England.

Ouspensky, however, had no murky past, and any Home Office official who had read his "Letters from Russia" would have known he was in no way any shade of pink. When the cable from Lady Rothermere, which Bennett assured Ouspensky was almost as good as a visa itself, failed to do the trick, Bennett explained to the authorities that Ouspensky was an important figure—perhaps the mathematician of Bragdon's introduction—and that his presence in London would be of value to England. And although Bennett had convinced the authorities that Mrs. Ouspensky should be allowed to accompany her husband,

Sophie Grigorievna—Madame Ouspensky perhaps only by name—had other plans. She preferred to remain with her teacher, Gurdjieff, who, having failed to get to England was now intent on reaching Berlin. The miracle, it seemed, was for Ouspensky alone.

AND IT CONTINUED ON HIS ARRIVAL. Lady Rothermere may not have been made of gold, but the plates on which she served dinner at Ouspensky's London debut were, as were the knives and forks. The audience for his talk was sterling too. For the brief time Ouspensky was the "intellectual flavor of the month," her patronage assured him a good crowd.[2] T. S. Eliot, Aldous Huxley, his friend and guru Gerald Heard, the writer of weird fiction—and member of the Hermetic Order of the Golden Dawn—Algernon Blackwood were among the intelligentsia that attended Ouspensky's talks at Lady Rothermere's St. John's Wood studio. Also present was another important figure on the London literary scene, Orage. He had met Ouspensky during his "search for the miraculous," and had been in contact intermittently during his subsequent escape from a collapsing Russia. Like everyone else, he was excited at his arrival. The buildup was a publicist's dream: the author of a philosophical bestseller, having survived a perilous trek across a country torn by civil war, was miraculously rescued from a refugee camp by the beautiful and rich young Lady Rothermere, and was here in London, to tell everyone about how they could perceive "higher dimensions." What more could you ask for?

Yet the message that Ouspensky brought was not the one he had presented so effectively in *Tertium Organum*. That work he now considered his "weakness," although it was a weakness that had helped him out of a desperate situation. He had been through Gurdjieff's mill, and although he now worked independently of his former teacher, it was *his* teaching and not the metaphysics of "higher space" that he put across to an audience who were at first surprised, then stunned at what he had to say. It was not a message that went down lightly.

It went something like this.

You are asleep. You, and everyone you know, is a machine. You have no free will, no stable, true "I" but many "I's" all at odds with one another. You have no power to "do," and are really nothing more than a contrivance on the part of the cosmos to transmit necessary energies among the planets. You are filled with the illusion that you are awake, conscious, and in control of your life. You are none of these things. You are a puppet, pulled by cosmic strings, no more conscious when awake than in your dreams.

But—there is a way to wake up. And I am here to tell you about it. There is a system—a system that Ouspensky would eventually spell out in lucid detail in his masterpiece, *In Search of the Miraculous*, which, at the time of his death, he left instructions to leave unpublished.

Such, more or less, was the gist of what was heard by those attending Lady Rothermere's salon, or the lectures Ouspensky later gave at 38 Warwick Gardens, Earl's Court—a very different neck of the London woods from those named after St. John—when Lady Rothermere's interest in Ouspensky inevitably faded. Some were quite taken with it. Others were less so and not that impressed with the messenger either. The writer David Garnett spoke of Ouspensky's "aura of high thinking and patent medicines," and said his false teeth made him think of Woodrow Wilson.[3] The poet Paul Selver, a friend of Orage, found him an "exasperating Russian."[4] Rowland Kenney, editor of the *Daily Herald* and one of Orage's psychosynthesists, thought Ouspensky looked like "a dejected bird huddling up in a rainstorm." And Algernon Blackwood, who knew a thing or two about "higher space," as his many stories about conditions there make clear, was more than a little disappointed. He was a great fan of *Tertium Organum*, but was put off by what seemed Ouspensky's tight-lipped, dismissive oratory. Blackwood had listened attentively, but he "never heard an intelligible question receive a satisfactory answer." What was worse, "The questioner was made to feel that his or her question was rather silly."[5] Ouspensky, who had elicited wonder in his wonderful book now shut it down "behind doors of common sense."

This last was a tactic that many Work teachers took on board, with Nicoll being a conspicuous exception, although he, too, at times could be a severe headmaster. Our mechanicalness showed through in everything we did, even in the questions we asked about it. This often left people paralyzed, afraid to speak lest they show how fast asleep they were. Ouspensky, who had run Gurdjieff's obstacle course and more or less survived, had no patience with speculation about higher space or anything else, and would not suffer fools gladly. His English was limited, yes. But his belief in the system was so strong—or, rather, his conviction that it alone offered any possible hope, slim at that—that he presented what he had to say in a gruff, "take it or leave it" manner that offended some but convinced others.

One so convinced was Orage. After hearing Ouspensky lecture, Orage wrote to Bragdon, telling him that Ouspensky was "the first teacher I have met who has impressed me with the ever-increasing certainty that he knows and he can do."[6] (Curiously, when, in America, Orage tried to recruit Bragdon to the cause, he gently but firmly declined.) Others of the psychosynthesis group had different reactions. Dmitri Mitrinovic, Orage's current guru, understandably did not care for the competition. But Orage was smitten and Dmitri was out. Yet one other psychosynthesizer was not at these revelatory first lectures. It is curious that Nicoll did not attend Lady Rothermere's salon. Did Orage not tell him? Was he not considered important enough? A brilliant psychologist, Jung's lieutenant, a contributor to the *Strand*, with a famous father, and a psychosynthesizer to boot?

Or was he busy?

WHILE OUSPENSKY WAS SETTLING into London, Nicoll, unaware that his prayers had already been answered, decided to renew his petition to Hermes. "I renew my faith. I go forward. I shall not fear," he wrote in his diary on September 24, 1921. "I ask for aid. I pray to Him for help. I go forward, seeking aid. Help me, O thou Hermes!"[7] Soon after this, in what seems an intuition of what lay in store for him, Nicoll noted that "contact with the Unseen must not be 'thrilling.'" It must not elicit a response of "how exciting" or be "casual or romantic or magical." Instead, "It must be so absolutely real that there is no sentiment attached to it other than a matter of fact recognition—as real, that is, as the fact that we must pay our rent or catch a train."[8] This seems a remarkable anticipation of the kind of message with which Ouspensky was disappointing some, like Algernon Blackwood, and enticing others, like Orage. His eminently practical approach, which shut down wonder in the name of common sense, was determined to stick to hard fact and the possible. After all, it was called the Work, and it was focused on getting down to business.

Yet Nicoll's interest in Hermes did allow for some imagination. He had become quite interested in a notion in the Hermetic philosophy that was known as the "Fate Sphere," or "sphere of fate." The similarity to the Work's "law of fate" is clear, although in fact, the meaning in each is completely opposite. For the Work, one wants to pass from the "law of accident" to the "law of fate." In the Hermetic tradition, one wants to escape the "sphere of fate," which in its view serves the same function as the Work's "law of accident." In the Hermetic creation myth, the "sphere of fate" is the realm given over to the planetary forces that were involved in the creation of the earth, that is Moon, Sun, Mercury, Venus, Mars, Jupiter, and Saturn. While we remain ignorant of their influence we are "sleepwalkers" in "the procession of fate." It is by becoming free of their influence that one "rises through the planets" and reaches the "Eighth Sphere," beyond the planets, and a further "Ninth Sphere" that embodies a level of mystical gnosis that words cannot describe. Those who do not strive to achieve gnosis—a direct, immediate intuition of reality—are destined to remain slaves to the cosmic forces that control them.[9]

In its concern with the "Ray of Creation" and escaping the laws one is subject to by rising up its "ladder of being," and the idea that humans are subjected to cosmic forces that inhibit their freedom—elements of the system Ouspensky was introducing to his London audiences—we can see much that is similar to the Hermetic "journey through the planets" with the intention of becoming free of their influence. What this similarity might suggest is debatable. Gurdjieff was no stranger to occult and mystical literature, and that he would have come across the Hermetic teachings is quite probable—it would, in fact, be hard for him to miss them—so it is entirely possible that he may have simply incorporated his own variation of it into his system. Or, conversely, the Hermetic account could have its source in the mysterious ancient Sarmoung Brotherhood, from whom Gurdjieff claimed to have learned the system in their hidden monastery in Central Asia. Or, it could be an inherent trope of the psyche, an archetype, as Jung saw in his suggestion that the *archons* and other planetary demons that the Gnostics—contemporaries of the Hermeticists—fought against were, in psychological terms, the neuroses and complexes that prevent our individuation.

Perhaps more to the point, Gurdjieff told Ouspensky that Christianity itself "was not invented by the fathers of the church," and that it was "taken in a ready-made form from Egypt," a "pre-historic Egypt" that was Christian "many thousands of years before the birth of Christ."[10] He also told Ouspensky that the Work could be seen as "esoteric Christianity," a description that would resonate well with Nicoll. This, of course, could be merely a good sales pitch, puffing up your product by making incredible claims. But as students of the history of Hermeticism know, for a time during the Renaissance, Hermes Trismegistus, who was believed to have lived before the flood, was seen as a fellow traveler with Christ, if not his actual teacher. Hermes Trismegistus was known as "the Egyptian" and was believed to have received his wisdom at the dawn of time, and there were many within the church who wanted to bring the

Hermetic teaching into its fold, and who saw the ancient Hermeticists as precursors to and heralds of Christ's coming.

In Nicoll's case, he was concerned with "those who dwell content in the Fate Sphere," satisfied with the gratification of the senses and of ambition and desire, the "sleepwalkers" making up the "procession of fate." He wondered: Was his father one of these? He had worked to fulfill his ambition and had prestige and influence. These reflections drifted into a waking dream or fantasy à la Jung's active imagination, in which Thoth, the Egyptian god of magic, tells Nicoll to enter a cave, where he will find a piece of paper on which is written something that will put him "beyond the power of the Fate Sphere."[11] What is written isn't clear, but Nicoll relates it to the Gospel trope of turning "water into wine," a miracle at the marriage of Cana, a transformation that will become increasingly important to him. To do this, Nicoll notes, is to turn "the Fate Sphere psychology into Individuality," that is, to move from being pushed about by other forces—whether those of the planets or of your complexes—and to "individuate" in Jung's sense. "Then," Nicoll notes, "you are near to the Tao indeed," the Chinese term for the Way or Logos that runs through all existence.

How near to this was Nicoll himself? The tensions that had been pulling at him all along had not dissipated, nor had his obsession with the Mater Gloriosa and other imaginative embodiments of the elusive sacred and profane feminine he pursued, often in very graphic detail. Not long after his dream of Thoth, Nicoll was remarking that he had "too exalted an idea" of his mission, and that he was "a coward."[12] He would hold on and not despair, but he did this only because there was "nothing else to do." He too, it seemed, was unable to escape the Fate Sphere. There was no one to show him the way. He had "no faith in his deductions," and "no clear Teacher," Jung's guidance notwithstanding.[13] His disappointment with Jung's approach, and with psychoanalysis in general, had reached a new low.

"Does it all boil down to this—is $\pi. \alpha$. Wrong or not?" he wrote in the diary.[14] "π. α." or *pi alpha*, is a code for "psychoanalysis," that Freud often used. Nicoll seems completely disenchanted with it, yet he seems to have no idea of what else he could do. "Is it a question of giving up something I don't want to do?" But if he gives it up, "there is nothing that leads me on." "Career, Ambition? Ah, there I fail." He admits to an "ambition for sensualism," which he sees as a "longing to understand" and to "break through Dagon," the fertility god of the Philistines in the Bible.

Following this there is a passage in his diary where Nicoll explains exactly what he gets out of his devotions, what we can see as his "ambition for sensualism." It suggests that Nicoll's absorption in his practice was motivated by something more than sexual gratification, although that was certainly a part of it, and the means by which this "something more" came into his grasp. It was nothing less than the "unified being," the sense of a unified consciousness that he had been seeking for some time. It belonged, he noted, "to the Individuation."

He writes: "In the Vice—in the act. Absolute concentration, quietness, absorption." Then he, or his inner voice, asks "What do you find in the vice?" He answers, "Complete satisfaction for the time. Absolute union with something. Something overpoweringly needful, real, compelling. Something where I alone am creative, undisturbed, reflective." Through the vice he can "escape from the uncertainty of collective life," from the "sense of burden and effort" and, most telling, he can become briefly free of his sense of "weakness, ineffectiveness, sickness." In the act, he participates in "a Union that I cannot reach otherwise."[15]

It is clear from these remarks that what Nicoll is talking about is something along the lines of what I have suggested earlier about the sexual orgasm: that, in Colin Wilson's words, it conveys "an intuition of some deeper, more 'god-like' state of satisfaction for the individual."[16] It provides a sense of "power, meaning and purpose" that dissipates any ambiguity and, if only momentarily, lifts us above our limited, everyday selves, the self that Nicoll was all too aware of. The act freed him of uncertainty, relieved the sense of life as a burden, blew away his sense of weakness and ineffectiveness. This last is key. In the act, Nicoll felt *more real*, more substantial, more solid, less inconsequential. We can say that what he got out of his devotions was an increase in his "psychological tension"—concentration—leading to a sudden boost in the effectiveness of his "reality function." It is precisely the desire for this effect that in less gentle but equally existentially challenged souls can lead to sudden acts of sexual violence, in an attempt to achieve the sense of reality that Nicoll seems to have reached in an altogether more innocuous manner.

We may think it unfortunate that Nicoll seemed unable to achieve this in his sexual relations with women, not even his wife, which, based on the evidence of his diaries, strikes me as a fair assumption. Or that he was unable to achieve it in any nonsexual ways, through some creative activity. Yet Nicoll often seems unable to maintain a creative momentum beyond the initial inspiration. And we've also looked at the suggestion that in some cases, "sex alone" may be a more powerful and gratifying experience. Nicoll seems to have felt this to be so. Yet he, or his inner voice, was unable to simply accept this. No sooner has he made clear what we can call the benefits of his practice, than his inner censor is on his back about it, leading Nicoll to make adolescent assertions of his independence and freedom from guilt. "What I do, I do and do not miserably seek pardon for it as soon as I have done it." But of course that is exactly what such an outburst is doing. To which the voice replies, calling him a "self-pitying, sententious fool," "is there any form of egoism worse than this analysis? Is not analysis simply a gigantic egoism?" "Are you any good whatsoever," the voice exasperatedly inquires. To which Nicoll answers, "I can at least μ well."[17] If his account of the effect of his μ is anything to go by, we can say he was right.

WHEN NICOLL DID FINALLY HEAR of Ouspensky, sometime in late October, the man he had been waiting for had been in London for two months, and it was not through Orage or any of the other psychosynthesists that word of his presence came. Maud Hoffman, with whom Nicoll shared space on Harley Street with James Young, had heard through the Theosophical grapevine that Ouspensky was giving lectures to G. R. S. Mead's Quest Society, and passed the information on. Lady Rothermere's infatuation had cooled to sober respect, and the dinners served on golden plates had stopped. Ouspensky had met Mead during his "search for the miraculous," and although Mead had reservations about *Tertium Organum*, and voiced them in his review of the book for the *Quest*, the two shared a common respect for their individual approaches to the mysteries. Oddly enough, Mead would also become a close acquaintance of Jung's, who found his knowledge of ancient religions invaluable during his exploration of the Gnostics.

The audience for Ouspensky's lectures at the Old Kensington Town Hall was made up of independent seekers of wisdom, or at least of an evening's intelligent entertainment. Nicoll hadn't read *Tertium Organum*; at least there is nothing in his diary to suggest he had, although he was interested in many of the same things that Ouspensky had written about: the mysteries of time and space, higher consciousness, ancient wisdom. Ouspensky had even written a chapter about sex, in which he likens its mystical character to that of nature, and speaks of love as a "cosmic phenomenon." (It may have been this sort of thing that he later felt was his "weakness.") So Nicoll had no chance to be disappointed with what he would hear, unlike the occult scholar A. E. Waite who, after listening to one of Ouspensky's lectures, stood up and informed him that there was "no love" in his system, and walked out. Nicoll was at his wit's end and had no idea what to do.

It is at crises like these that Jung said the "transcendent function" would activate, and the tension between the opposites could be resolved by the unconscious throwing up of a symbol that would unify them at a higher level. The prospective character of the psyche would then indicate a way forward. We know that Nicoll kept a detailed record of his dreams, and he mentions the transcendent function here and there in them. But either it was not working or he could not grasp the unifying and transcending symbol. Hence his despair and doubt about π α.

Yet according to the law of fate it is at crises like these that one's magnetic center, recognizing the seriousness of the situation, may lead one to *someone who knows*. That evening, Nicoll was convinced that, whatever it was that had got him to that lecture, Ouspensky was someone who knew. He was so convinced that afterward, he rushed back to Chester Terrace, where Catherine was still recovering from having their daughter, Jane, and, ignoring the baby, told his wife that she must come and hear Ouspensky. Shaking the bed he insisted that he was nothing short of a prophet and "the only man who has ever answered my questions."[18] The nurse was nonplussed. Yet Catherine understood. His prayers had been answered. Her husband appeared "transformed, as though irradiated by an inner light." And dutiful wife that she was, as soon as she could, she attended one of Ouspensky's lectures, and became as convinced of his knowledge as her husband was.

Nicoll saw quite a bit of Ouspensky over the next few months. Soon after seeing him at the Quest Society, they met again when Ouspensky paid a visit to the Psychosynthesis Group at a meeting on Harley Street. What Ouspensky thought of psychosynthesis can be assessed by an account of an earlier meeting, between Ouspensky and Orage and Rowland Kenney. Kenney tried to get a conversation going by expressing his views on "certain recent developments in psycho-analysis" and the need to reevaluate certain of its principles. Before he could get much further, Ouspensky interjected. "Why waste time, Orage? Tell Kenney what we are meeting for."[19] What they were meeting for was not to discuss psychosynthesis or any developments in psychoanalysis. It was to "establish a group to be taught, not a forum for discussion," a proposition that the loquacious Orage himself no doubt found daunting. Orage was a few years older than Ouspensky and could hold his own with Shaw, Wells, and other London literary luminaries. To be told he was there to listen, not talk, must have been a big pill to swallow. But this was exactly the sort of thing that Nicoll would be glad to hear. Jung had been too "suggestive" for him; he left too much up to him to interpret and do for himself. Ouspensky presented his facts, which required no interpretation. He could take them or leave them.

Nicoll decided to take them. Ouspensky began to dine at Chester Terrace where he, Nicoll, Catherine, and sometimes Orage and Clifford Sharp, would "talk on for hours by candlelight."[20] This, at a time when Nicoll was concerned that he was condemned to follow the "respectable path" of a Harley Street practitioner in order to appease the "Spirit of Chester Terrace," evidently without recognizing that were he not that practitioner he might not have ever heard about Ouspensky or be able to wine and dine him.[21] The talks that filled those candlelit evenings must have reached into Nicoll's psyche. He notes in his diary a dream in which Jung saves him from some shadow creature, and he is then with him in a library filled with alchemical books. Later in the dream James Young speaks to him about Abraham's sacrifice, and then he is with Ouspensky in a cave, and Ouspensky asks him if Jung knows about "the sleeping man," trying to gauge his level of knowledge.[22] After another evening with Ouspensky, Nicoll noted in his diary that he felt "puzzled" and "pulled."[23] He noted that Ouspensky emphasized the need to be in contact with a "real teacher," suggesting, perhaps, that Ouspensky did not consider himself one, or, conversely, that he was letting Nicoll know that one was in town. Oddly enough, that night Ouspensky appeared in Nicoll's dream as a bird, suggesting that Rowland Kenney's comparison of Ouspensky with a bird "huddling in a rainstorm," was apt.

What appealed to Nicoll about Ouspensky was precisely the "dominant if not domineering type of character" that Kenney had noted and that put off not a few individuals who might otherwise have been open to what he had to say.[24] Nicoll wanted to be dominated, and although the real ringmaster was yet to make his appearance, his herald brought with him an atmosphere suggestive of submission, something Nicoll notes in his diary.[25] "I need bracing," he confessed. "O braces me." It would not be long before Nicoll would be noting that "only the strongest souls can survive" and that "the more the lash is on you, the better. It means you are transforming." These were paeans to the "bullying treatment" and the salutary effect it would have on him, yet they hinted not a little at the tendency to masochism that Nicoll shared with not a few practitioners of the Work.[26]

Ouspensky returned Nicoll's hospitality and invited him to visit him at his flat at Gwendyr Road, Baron's Court. This was a far cry from Lady Rothermere's well-appointed Circus Road studio, or Nicoll's house in Chester Terrace. During the first flush of her excitement, Lady Rothermere had put Ouspensky up at a hotel in Russell Square in fashionable Bloomsbury, then the byword in all things chic and avant-garde. When her attention turned elsewhere she found him an unpretentious bolt-hole in a less reputable part of town. It was a basement flat, what is called a "bed-sitting room," which is fundamentally a single room with a small kitchenette. Dark, dreary, warmed by an unreliable gas heater, after a later visit Kenneth Walker described the place as displaying a "nice disregard for the inconveniences of which life is chiefly composed."[27] A bed, a table, two chairs, books, papers, a typewriter, a collection of lenses and cameras—Ouspensky was very shortsighted and fond of binoculars and such—bread, cheese, sardine tins, unwashed dishes: the décor could not have been much different during Nicoll's visit, although he did note that the room lacked a fire. They talked about the magnetic center, and the other centers—intellectual, emotional, moving—whose working must be harmonized in order for man to awaken. They talked about drugs—Nicoll mentions his experience with hashish. And they talk about sex. Sex, Ouspensky told him, drives many centers, a dictum he will hear again. "A man may write a book on economics," Ouspensky said, "and it is really sex behind it," something Nicoll had surely heard before; it is of course one of the earliest lessons in $\pi \alpha$ 101.

Their meetings continued, at Harley Street, or Gwendyr Road, or at the candlelit dinners at Chester Terrace. Yet as Nicoll got to know Ouspensky and heard more about the strange system he was presenting in his lectures, his initial enthusiasm began to shift into something less unquestioningly positive, into an uncertainty that seemed more to add to his dilemma than resolve it. The difficulties involved in "waking up," and the suggestion that not everyone could meet them or, if they did, actually benefit from the Work, troubled him, and went against his Christian sensibility. The system was not for everybody. Not everyone could wake up; in fact, it was a cosmic necessity that they didn't. But *some* can. The prison of our personality, secured by what Ouspensky called "buffers," psychological shock absorbers that prevent us from ever seeing who or what we really are, was impossible to escape without a certain necessary *force*. As we are, Ouspensky assured him, we cannot produce this force, but there were ways in which it could be produced. Nicoll knew all about this. Even with the new sense of purpose Ouspensky's talks had stimulated in him, Nicoll still felt that he had to "continually take myself in hand to produce a feeling or action." Otherwise he felt a kind of "vacancy."[28]

His appreciation of Ouspensky himself underwent some odd transformations. He noted in the diary that Ouspensky's "rat like smile"—an impression made, one imagines, by his false teeth—made Nicoll think of Dracula, the vampire of Bram Stoker's classic novel. The Bela Lugosi film version of the story had yet to be made, and Nicoll might have been thinking of a stage production, of which there had been many. But Dracula? He writes of the "numerical occultism" that the system is based on—one assumes he means the Ray of Creation and the different "laws" operating at its different levels—and wonders if what Ouspensky is teaching is really "black magic" and "moon stuff." Given the role the moon plays in the cosmology of the Fourth Way one could say that it was. Yet at the same time Ouspensky is also a fountain of common sense, whose ideas are "very practical and real" with no "mystical nonsense." But the severity of the system did affect him. He writes of waking up with a heaviness, thinking of Ouspensky, and of feeling an anger and bitterness about him.

He had by then begun to practice some of the Work exercises aimed at "waking up," trying not to express "negative emotions," and to "remember himself," to keep a vivid sense of his being in the midst of the distractions of life. This last produced a range of sensations, from a "power or massiveness" to a "slenderness or fragility," to a "lightness in the head." The diagrams Ouspensky used to convey his ideas at times stimulated him like "breaths of fresh air." Yet overall he writes of feeling a kind of "apprehension or fear or anxiety," as if he were waiting to hear when he was to go into battle. The tension entered his dreams, which he began to try to understand in Fourth Way terms, even asking Ouspensky about them. Ouspensky had much experience of dreams, but whatever he said to Nicoll about his seems lost. But whatever Ouspensky might have said, Nicoll had good reason to be tense. And the battle would commence soon enough.

Yet it was not all so serious and weighty. On December 30, Nicoll noted that there was a party at Harley Street and that Ouspensky was there until well after midnight. This seems an early taste of the festivities Nicoll would put on with his own Work groups, and the late night revels Ouspensky would engage in years later, when he established himself in Lyne Place, a stately mansion with extensive grounds outside of London. It was almost New Year's Eve, so there was cause for celebration. Soon enough Nicoll and the others would see what the New Year would bring.

GURDJIEFF DID NOT HAVE GOOD LUCK in Germany. He managed to give a few lectures in Berlin, but was unable to establish his Institute for the Harmonious Development of Man in the city of *Cabaret* and a fledgling Nazi Party, and which was already filled with indigent White Russians. He had been trying to establish this institute for some time, ever since he, Ouspensky, and some members of his original groups had fled the Bolshevik deluge. He had tried and failed in Tiflis, then in Constantinople, where he and Ouspensky had a brief reconciliation and revival of their early collaboration. Now Berlin proved unsuccessful. He next tried in Dresden, where an attempt to purchase the Hellerau, a former center of the Dalcroze Eurhythmics Institute, led to bizarre legal proceedings, in which Gurdjieff was charged with using his hypnotic powers, Svengali-like, to get his way. The owner had already leased part of the building to other tenants, among them the educational theorist A. S. Neill, a friend of Wilhelm Reich, the psychoanalyst who was more Freudian than Freud, taking the master's dictum about sex and neurosis so seriously that he would proscribe lessons in masturbation to his patients (one wonders what Nicoll might have thought of that). Gurdjieff is said to have hypnotically persuaded the owner to break his contracts with the other tenants; when this came out in court, he lost the case.

It is altogether possible that Gurdjieff did try to "persuade" the owner of the Hellerau in ways that a judge might find less than honest. There is evidence that for some years he had made a living as a hypnotist, curing alcoholics and drug addicts. What is interesting here is that earlier in his career, Gurdjieff had made a vow never to use his powers for his own benefit. This "artificial life," as he called it, would act as a constant "alarm clock," preventing him from "falling asleep."[29] If indeed he did make use of hypnosis in order to secure the Hellerau, it suggests that Gurdjieff's situation must have been desperate enough for him to break his vow.

Ouspensky had run into no such difficulties in London. In fact, he had attracted some very well heeled and influential followers. There was, of course, Lady Rothermere, who continued to provide financial support. Another was Ralph Philipson, a coal-mining millionaire from the north. In general, the audience for Ouspensky's lectures came from the better part of town. Gurdjieff got wind of Ouspensky's success—how, is unclear—and decided to pay his erstwhile student a visit. His real reason was to scout out the possibilities for having his institute develop harmoniously in London—insofar as anything developed harmoniously around Gurdjieff.

In February 1922, Gurdjieff arrived in London. By this time Ouspensky's lectures had moved to the Theosophical Hall at 38 Warwick Gardens, a location closer to his own neighborhood in Baron's Court. It was there that the people who had heard Ouspensky speak of the mysterious teacher from whom he had learned the system, saw the master in question for the first time. From all accounts it was quite an appearance. Some sixty people sat in silence for most of the meeting, Gurdjieff's sheer presence inhibiting them from speaking. With his shaved head and dark moustache he cut a strange, Asiatic figure. Gurdjieff spoke of how, when we are young, our "impressions" of the world are fresh, but as we grow older, they dim, and we become more mechanical; as Wordsworth had said in "Intimations of Immortality," "shades of the prison house close in" and with them departs "the glory and the freshness of the dream." We can, however, revive the freshness, through effort. Similarly, we have energy but use it mechanically. But there is a way to produce new energy and use it non-mechanically. After a brief talk about our many "I's" and our inability to "do," Ouspensky, who was interpreting for Gurdjieff, asked for questions. After a long, painful silence, a venturesome individual threw caution to the wind and braved a word. "What would it be like to be conscious in essence?" he asked. "Everything more vivid," was the master's reply.

Things certainly became more vivid after that. Ouspensky must have known it would happen. His dry, professorial approach was no match for Gurdjieff's dominance, the sheer power that seemed to surround him, like the aura the Theosophists were always on about. Orage, something of an esoteric impulse buyer, quickly recalibrated his magnetic center and declared that he now "*knew* that Gurdjieff was the teacher." Most of the flock that Ouspensky had gathered felt the same.

And when Gurdjieff said that he intended to establish his institute there, in London, Ouspensky considered relocating to Paris, a city he knew and loved. Yet, as he had done in Constantinople, he dutifully assisted his ex-teacher in every way he could, collecting funds to ship Gurdjieff's dependents over from Germany—something, to Ouspensky's relief, that would not happen.

But to shear Ouspensky of his flock was not all that Gurdjieff had in mind. In a private meeting he informed Ouspensky that the work he was carrying on was useless, utterly worthless, and that if he was serious about waking up, he would have to return to the fold and, as his wife was, once again become his student. And when it was clear that Ouspensky intended to do no such thing, Gurdjieff took advantage of another meeting to do his best to undermine the authority of his ex-student. Here he again spoke about our many "I's," our inability to control our emotions, and the need to harmonize our centers in order to apply our will. After the group had absorbed this, Gurdjieff landed his bombshell. He told the group that Ouspensky was neither authorized nor qualified to teach *his* system; so much for the Sarmoung Brotherhood. And when Ouspensky corrected a translation by Frank Pinder, a Work stalwart, Gurdjieff slapped him down, saying "Pinder is interpreting for me—not you." One can't avoid thinking the obvious thought: that having failed to get his institute going on his own, Gurdjieff decided to take advantage of the groundwork Ouspensky had already laid down, and he would do it by *force majeure*.

Yet, once again, it was not to be. The British would allow the institute—plans were made for a house in Hampstead—but refused visas for Gurdjieff's troupe, which included several Russians he was keeping alive. In a climate of paranoia about Bolshevik intrusions, Gurdjieff was suspect. Kenneth Walker tells of the attempt he and Nicoll made to convince a "bored Home Secretary how essential it was to the welfare of British Medicine that Gurdjieff . . . should be granted permission to settle in London."[30] Walker had no idea who Gurdjieff was at the time, and had only vaguely heard of Ouspensky, and had been swept along to the meeting by his excited friend Nicoll, who pushed him into a cab and explained their mission on the way. In the end, Gurdjieff was not allowed to settle in Britain—his murky past once again getting in his way—and Ouspensky breathed a sigh of relief. But his ex-master was not done with him just yet.

THE PRIEURÉ DES BASSES LOGES, in Fontainebleau, is some forty miles southeast of Paris. It was originally the home of Madame de Maintenon, mistress of Louis XIV, then had been a Carmelite monastery, and more recently was the property of Fernand Labori, the lawyer for the defense in the famous Dreyfus case. After his death, it became the property of Labori's widow, who had let it fall into neglect. No one had lived in it since before the war. It had languished in that condition until July 1922, when, after considerable negotiations by Madame de Hartmann—wife of the composer Thomas de Hartmann and a long-time student of the Work—it was leased with an option to purchase by a Mr. G. I. Gurdjieff. The Institute for the Harmonious Development of Man had finally found a home, although its students would not be able to move in until October. The place was run-down, the extensive grounds, some two hundred acres, were a mess, and to get it in shape and inhabitable would require a lot of work. It sounded perfect. Just the set of conditions for the kind of activities Gurdjieff had in mind.

Gaining possession of the Prieuré had been made possible by Ouspensky, or at least by some of his followers. The money had come from Lady Rothermere and Ralph Philipson, and the man-power needed to get the place in a decent condition would come from Ouspensky's groups. Once word had got out that Gurdjieff's institute was becoming a reality, practically all of Ouspensky's students started to make plans to cross the Channel. Ouspensky thought they were rash, but he was not going to argue. As he told Orage, who came to speak with him about it, "You have already made up his mind, so why ask?"

He must have known something like this would happen. He may even have planned on it. After all, Gurdjieff's other attempts to set up his institute had not panned out, and it would be curious to see what happened to the "motley company" that would be living there. Followers from St. Petersburg, Tiflis, Constantinople, and now London would be rubbing elbows in an unusual environment. Yet even with his misgivings, Ouspensky traveled to Paris, where Gurdjieff was staying while work was done on the Prieuré, and offered what help he could. One sign of his loyalty was the speed with which he quashed rumors that had circulated in London about Gurdjieff seducing some female followers. Ouspensky was the soul of tact, but he no doubt wondered how false the reports were. He knew Gurdjieff had no qualms when it came to sex and that his attitude toward women was, as J. G. Bennett would remark, that of a sultan toward his harem. Yet he made clear that he would not stand for any gossip.

Gurdjieff had thrown himself into his usual frenzy of activity in order to make money to meet the Prieuré's upkeep. According to one report, he "leased two restaurants, went into the oil business, and set up as a psychiatrist specialising in drug addiction and alcoholism."[31] As one account of Gurdjieff's knockabout life has it, whatever else he was, he was "essentially a tough, worldly-wise street urchin who excelled in looking after himself," and was possessed of "an almost magical ability to survive."[32] One of the most remarkable characteristics of this remarkable man was Gurdjieff's ability to find funds and raise money in almost any situation at almost a moment's notice. If nothing else, this certainly qualifies him as a magician. But there was much else. And the eager students of Ouspensky's odd system, Nicoll among them, making their way to France, would soon find that out.

8

Sonnez Fort!

The Fourth Way gets its name because of its radically different approach to the "psychology of man's possible evolution"—as Ouspensky calls it in a series of lectures of that title—from the three so-called traditional ways, those of the fakir, the monk, and the yogi.

The way of the fakir is "the way of struggle with the physical body."[1] These are the individuals who lie on beds of nails, stand motionless for days or months on end, fast continuously, contort their limbs into complicated positions, and generally submit themselves to various sufferings and tortures, in order to subdue their bodies, to have them obey their will. People who spend an inordinate time at the gym or in yoga class might qualify as "fakirs" these days.

The way of the monk involves the emotions, the feelings, which he strives to keep focused on God or whatever symbol of the divine he is enraptured with. Sri Ramakrishna, the nineteenth-century Hindu saint, who could fall into a swoon of ecstasy at the mere mention of the name of the Divine Mother, and whose *Gospel* Nicoll would later read, is an example of this. The monk strives to lose all sense of himself in his love of God. Where the fakir achieves a kind of unity of being through his physical exertions, the monk achieves it through unifying his feelings around his faith.

The way of the yogi is the way of the mind, the way of knowledge, of meditation and mental concentration, the mastery of *dhyana*, the stilling of thoughts. What the fakir achieves through the body and the monk through the emotions, the yogi does through the mind.

Through all three ways one can gain some ground on the path of our "possible evolution," that is, toward "waking up," but each also has drawbacks. The fakir develops his body, but he does so at the expense of his emotions and mind. The monk develops his emotions, but compared to the fakir and the yogi, he is hopeless when it comes to his body and has little or no control of his mind. The yogi is master of his mind, but is out of touch with his body and at a loss about what to do with his emotions, a condition common to many intellectuals. Each masters his own particular field, but this development is out of balance. If the fakir wanted to achieve the control over his emotions that the monk possesses, or the mastery of the mind enjoyed by the yogi, he would have to go through a long process of reeducation. He would, in fact, have to become a monk or a yogi, which means that he would have to submit to the years of training this required, and he has already spent years learning mastery of his body. This is one reason why an individual who has passed through all three of the traditional ways is a rarity indeed.

These traditional ways differ from the Fourth Way in another regard. In order to follow the traditional ways, one must he prepared for a "complete change of life." As Gurdjieff told Ouspensky, one must renounce worldly things; a man must "give up his home, his family . . . renounce all the pleasures, attachments and duties of life, and go out into the desert, or into a monastery, or a yogi school." He must, as tradition says, "die to the world."[2]

In other words, becoming a fakir, a monk, or a yogi is not something you can do at home via a correspondence course or online classes.

Not so the Fourth Way. In the Fourth Way, one works on the body, the emotions, and the mind simultaneously, and one does this in the conditions of life in which one finds oneself. That is, to follow the Fourth Way, one needn't abandon one's ordinary life and enter a monastery or cave or *ashram*. It is possible to work and follow the Fourth Way "while remaining in the usual conditions of life." You can live as you do, keep your day job, continue to see your friends; there is no need to don a yellow robe and enter a *sangha* or get a tonsure. In fact, one's current situation in life will supply the best possible conditions for a candidate for the Fourth Way. "A man's life and its conditions correspond to what he is," Gurdjieff told Ouspensky. And "any conditions different from those created by life"—such as one would find in a monastery, *Zendo*, or cloister—"would be artificial for a man."[3] For the Fourth Way, life, ordinary, mundane, implacable life, full of its boring difficulties and frustrations, is all the *ashram* or hermit's cave an applicant needs.

Yet one of the first things that most of the first and second generation of Fourth Way teachers did was to find some place in which they could arrange conditions that were precisely *not* those "created by life." As Gurdjieff did, they wanted to and did establish an "institute" of some sort in which very artificial conditions could be created in order to "speed up" the Work, practicing what Gurdjieff called "haida yoga," *haida* being a Russian word for "quick." We might say that they suffered from what we could call "institute-itis." Ouspensky, who was initially doubtful about setting up a "school for supermen," Bennett, Nicoll, and others like Ouspensky's ardent student Rodney Collin, all established at different times and places something along the lines of Gurdjieff's Prieuré. The only one of the Fourth Way pioneers who seems free from this itch was Orage, who spent most of his tenure in the Work in America, drumming up financial support for Gurdjieff's projects. He continued to do this until Gurdjieff's relentless demands for money, and his unmistakable dissatisfaction in Orage's marriage to Jessie Owen—a woman with her own mind and no interest in Gurdjieff—led to him abandoning the Work in 1931.

But in the late summer of 1922, that was a long way off.

ONE OF THE FIRST PEOPLE to pull up stakes in London and head to Fontainebleau was James Young. His first stop, however, was Paris, where Gurdjieff was staying while waiting for the Prieué to be made ready for his arrival. Gurdjieff had taken a house in Auteuil and, as he had in Dresden, was teaching the "movements" using a space in the Dalcroze Institute on rue de Vaugirard. These were the complicated, difficult positions, postures, and gestures that made up the "sacred dances" that now formed the heart of the Work. Young arrived in August to find Gurdjieff's students sewing. They were making costumes for a public performance of the movements, to be given at the Théâtre des Champs-Elysées. They were to perform dances from Gurdjieff's perpetually un-staged ballet, "The Struggle of the Magicians," which last saw a possibility of performance in Constantinople. (Separate dances from the ballet were performed, but to the best of my knowledge, never the entire ballet. It is unclear if Gurdjieff actually ever finished choreographing it.) Among the skills a Work hopeful needed to master now were metalwork, shoemaking, and embroidery.

As Olga de Hartmann recalls, Gurdjieff had purchased "thread, needles, scissors, thimbles, and a sewing machine."[4] When candidates for waking up arrived, they were surprised at what awaited them. "There was no philosophical conversation, just sewing."[5] Those who came prompted by Ouspensky's austere lectures were a bit put out, but this kind of "hands on" work would become increasingly familiar as their acquaintance with the Work grew, and it would form a great deal of Nicoll's own tutorial when he set up shop as a teacher of it. The aim of such efforts, according to Young, was to overcome "one's awkwardness and diffidence, and sometimes, be it confessed, one's indifference or even dislike."[6] Young found himself fumbling away with needle and thread "with feverish activity," spending "thirteen or fourteen hours every day" preparing for the performance as well as submitting to various exercises doled out by Gurdjieff. The overall assignment was to "Overcome difficulties—Make effort—

Work." Young and those who followed him certainly did that.

By October the Prieuré was open for business. One of the first to arrive was Orage, who kept his luggage to a minimum: he turned up with his toothbrush and a copy of *Alice in Wonderland*, appropriate reading material for the rabbit hole he was about to enter. Digging holes in one form or another was the order of the day for the forty-nine-year-old editor and intellectual desperado. Unlike James Young, who upon arrival in France was handed a sewing needle, when Orage reached Fontainebleau he was given a shovel and told to dig, which he did, until he was told to stop and to fill the hole in again. As mentioned, he was also not allowed to smoke, which, as he told C. S. Nott, another student of the Work, "almost killed him."[7]

Orage's Sisyphean task was embraced, not happily, as Albert Camus would have had it, but with a determination that did not prevent tears of exhaustion from flowing as he drifted off to a welcome sleep each night, only to begin his labors again early the next morning. Orage had exchanged the fashionable dress of the Café Royal literary man for the corduroys and calloused hands of a navvy, and for the first months of his stay in Fontainebleau, he was not entirely sure why he was there, a perplexity shared by several of his fellow inmates. He hardly saw Gurdjieff, or anyone else, and he returned to his room each evening— what he called "a sort of cell"—after hours of digging, dazed and confused. While his back ached and nicotine withdrawal symptoms kicked in, Orage wondered "Is this what I've given up my whole life for?"[8]

His literary associates on the other side of the Channel wondered about that too. When Orage announced that he was leaving the *New Age* and putting it up for sale, his secretary asked why he *had* to go, as he had made it clear that his exodus to Fontainebleau was an irrevocable necessity. Orage answered that he was going to find God. To the *literati* who shook their heads at the once brilliant editor, socialist, and all-around cultural mover and shaker, Orage's pilgrimage seemed more of a wild-goose chase. Yet the real reason Orage crossed the

Channel that autumn was that he had come to a dead end. The *New Age* had become old hat, and the various causes he had championed— Theosophy, Nietzsche, Fabian socialism, social credit—had not made the impact he had hoped they would have, although one has to say that his world-famous contributors Wells and Shaw had not made much of a dent in the *status quo* either. His love affairs had soured, and he was finding it harder and harder to fill pages with anything worth saying. He was at a crossroads and crisis, the preeminent prerequisites for entering the Fourth Way.

Yet friends who visited Orage at the Prieuré during his first months there were amazed at the transformation that had taken place in him. The hard work and strenuous healthy living paid off, at least from the perspective of personal appearance. Aside from special occasions, such as Christmas, when Gurdjieff would go "the whole hog, including postage," meals at the Prieuré were fairly austere, made up, for the most part, of bread, soup, vegetables, coffee, with meat a rarity.[9] Orage's diet of coarse dark bread and beetroot soup had the portly essayist dropping several pounds, slipping from a state in which he was "almost fat" to one in which he was "almost emaciated."[10]

But the hard labor was not an end in itself. It was, in fact, part of Gurdjieff's version of the "bullying treatment." With his interest in psychology and psychosynthesis, I am surprised that Orage—and Nicoll— seemed unaware of William James's important essay "The Energies of Men," in which he writes about the phenomenon of "second wind." This is when an athlete, pushed to the limits of endurance, suddenly discovers fresh energy he *did not know he possessed*. In this case, the athlete bullies him or herself into making one last effort; when he does, the floodgates open and a rush of new life makes the exhausted runner fresh as a daisy and able to do another marathon. In the case of a doctor, he or she bullies the neurasthenic patient—for whom life has become a "tissue of impossibilities"—until they reach what James calls "the extremity of distress," the equivalent of the athlete's exhaustion.

And just as the athlete on the brink of collapse is suddenly filled with new energy, the helpless distraught patient discovers that what he thought undoable is child's play.

Orage learned the wisdom of pushing himself to the breaking point. He told C. S. Nott that when he "was in the depths of despair, feeling that I could go on no longer, I vowed to make an extra effort." When he did, "something changed" in him. He began to *enjoy* the hard labor. A week after this miraculous renewal, Gurdjieff, who had been keeping his eye on Orage, came over to him. "Orage," he said, "I think you dig enough. Let us go to café and drink coffee."[11] Another account has Orage being woken at the middle of the night after a day of digging, and being sent back to the trench he had dug that day and told to continue until he should be permitted to stop. Determined to stay the course, Orage went, and worked until he could barely conceal his anger. He was about to give up when Gurdjieff appeared and took him back to his room where he treated Orage to "marvellous food" and "the finest of wines."[12] Gurdjieff had other plans for Orage than ditchdigging. He would in fact become his most eloquent and persuasive front man.

This last version of what we might call Orage's "revelation" suggests some embellishment, but it also seems an example of the "good cop/bad cop" psychology that some gurus employ, subjecting their students to harsh treatment, then rescuing them from it and bestowing their approval, with the student thankful for the crumb of acceptance. Yet other accounts of experiences like Orage's suggest that wherever he got his insight, from the Sarmoung Brotherhood or from his own psychological observations, Gurdjieff knew what William James did: that if pushed to the limit, human beings can access a store of reserve energy unknown to them. And this psychophysical brinksmanship can have remarkable results.

J. G. Bennett recounts his own experience of Gurdjieff's bullying treatment during his brief time at the Prieuré. Bennett had returned to London from Constantinople and had attended Ouspensky's lectures.

Unlike Orage, Bennett was a weekend worker, making the journey to Fontainebleau when his work in London allowed. Yet he was compelled to go, because of an "absolute need to break out of the spiritual prison" into which he had fallen.[13] In *Witness*, his autobiography, Bennett tells of how, when suffering dysentery, he forced himself to attempt a series of new and extremely difficult "movements."[14] They were of an "incredible complexity," and as he forced himself to master them, and not collapse from fever, he watched as the other students, even those long used to these dances, dropped out until only he and a few others were left. He felt Gurdjieff's attention on him and believed that he had made an "unspoken demand" that he carry on, even if it killed him. Bennett did, and suddenly he was "filled with the influx of an immense power." His body seemed to have "turned into light" and he felt a "bliss beyond anything" he had known. He had entered some timeless zone. The dysentery had left him and he went into the garden. Finding a shovel, he began to dig at great speed, for more than an hour, enjoying it as had Orage. His thoughts achieved a new clarity and he saw the "eternal pattern" of everything around him.

When he went into the forest, Bennett came upon Gurdjieff, who spoke of what he called the Great Accumulator, a kind of reservoir of vital force, and how some people connected with it can transfer reserves of the higher emotional energy needed for self-transformation to others. Gurdjieff undoubtedly was one of these people, as more than one account makes clear.*

Yet Bennett had tapped his own "accumulator," just as Orage had, by pushing himself past the "degrees of fatigue," which, as William James said, "we have come only from habit to obey"—an insight with which Gurdjieff would have wholeheartedly agreed. In fact it forms the basis of one of Gurdjieff's trademark teaching strategies, what he

---

*See Fritz Peters's account of how Gurdjieff cured him of nervous exhaustion in postwar Paris in *Gurdjieff Remembered*, collected in *My Journey with a Mystic*, 251.

called "super-effort," purposefully pushing yourself beyond your limits. If you've already walked ten miles and are exhausted, walk another two before resting; that should give you the idea. The many who came to Fontainebleau that year would become well acquainted with the practice. Curiously, Nicoll does not seem to have had a "second wind" experience while at the Prieuré, as Orage and Bennett did, although his "degrees of fatigue" were pushed just as much as theirs were. Or if he did have such an experience, he doesn't seem to have left any record of it.*

One who came to Fontainebleau who wasn't subjected to the bullying treatment or asked to make super-efforts, was the New Zealand writer Katherine Mansfield, most known for the short story collection *In a German Pension* (1911). She had been a discovery and mistress of Orage. They had gone separate ways—she had become something of a satellite of the Bloomsbury set, becoming friends with Virginia Woolf— but she had been drawn back to him because of a crisis in her life. She had been diagnosed with tuberculosis, and the prognosis wasn't good. The prospect of imminent death had "woken" her to the fact that she had been leading a meaningless life, a tried-and-true existential alarm clock that both Gurdjieff and the philosopher Martin Heidegger agreed was one sure way of shaking us out of our "forgetfulness of being." She felt that her work was worthless—there wasn't a single one of her stories that she felt she could show God—but she had had glimpses of *another way* of living that would not be meaningless.[15]

Orage commiserated and shared his own sense of failure and decision to cash in his chips. But there was one hope. He mentioned the names Gurdjieff and Ouspensky. Not long after that, smart, fashionable, tubercular Katherine Mansfield made her way to the dull, somewhat drab interior of 38 Warwick Gardens where she heard about the

---

*He does mention, in notes taken at the time, that Gurdjieff's method is "to tire people beyond the first accumulator. Then when at two or three a.m. when he stops no one seems to want to go to bed." But he doesn't describe this effect on himself. Pogson, *Maurice Nicoll*, 91.

"psychology of man's possible evolution." She attended a few lectures, then asked for a private audience. Ouspensky agreed.

When she came to Gwendyr Road she told Ouspensky that she was heading to Paris to receive a new treatment for tuberculosis that involved treating the spleen with X-rays. Ouspensky had his own ideas about doctors, but he could offer her no assurances about this last hope. Her real reason for visiting him, though, was to secure an invitation to the Prieuré. Like Orage, like James Young, and like Nicoll, Mansfield was ready to bank everything on the possibility that Gurdjieff could do *something*. But exactly what? Ouspensky had no illusions about her chances of recovery. She was, he felt, already "halfway to death," and was aware of it.[16] No doubt Ouspensky would have felt the same about Mansfield's stories as he did about other works of modern literature, and most likely she would not have otherwise struck him as a potential candidate for waking up. Yet her crisis had disturbed her profoundly, and an unusual honesty and urgency had risen to the surface. Ouspensky was impressed by "the striving in her to make the best use even of these last days, to find the truth whose presence she clearly felt but which she was unable to touch."[17] Accordingly he put her in touch with people in Paris who could get her to Fontainebleau.

James Young was dispatched to meet her *en route* and to subject her to a rigorous physical examination. She was already carrying a letter from the doctor she had seen in Paris, asking Gurdjieff to decline her request for admission to the Prieuré, on the grounds of her deteriorating health. But she was determined to live her last days as consciously as she could, and Gurdjieff must have recognized in her the same desire as Ouspensky had. He granted her request.

She arrived on October 17; ten weeks later, on the evening of January 9, 1923, she was dead, suffering a violent seizure and hemorrhage as she was returning to her room after watching a performance of the "The Initiation of the Priestess," one of Gurdjieff's sacred dances and one to which Mansfield felt a powerful connection. She had spent her last days inhaling the breath of cows from the loft space devised for her by Gurdjieff and decorated in Persian fashion by the stage designer and lighting expert Alexandre de Salzmann, who had joined Gurdjieff's band when they were camped in Tiflis. Mansfield reclined on a divan covered in a Persian carpet, while the cow's exhalation—which Gurdjieff believed had a curative effect—helped in whatever way it could. It did not save her life, but from her last letters one gets the impression that the little she had left of it was lived more intensely than it had ever been before.*

Ouspensky himself saw her for the last time there, during one of the several visits he made to the Prieuré. Gurdjieff had kept an open invitation to him to take part in the work he was carrying out, but Ouspensky declined, preferring to stay on the sidelines and help in whatever way he could from a distance. Yet he had seen "very interesting and animated work" going on, and felt that the "atmosphere on the whole was very right" and that it left "a strong impression." Impressions change, however, and over time Ouspensky's did.

Ouspensky arrived at the Prieuré on November 10, just short of a week after the Nicolls had, but there doesn't seem to be any record of any conversation between them. Nevertheless, *Sonnez fort!* the sign said. So they did.

As mentioned Nicoll showed up in Fontainebleau that November 4 with his wife, their child, her nanny, two goats, and a considerable amount of luggage. They were convinced that they would be staying for some time, hence the excess baggage. It, and the fact that they were putting their newborn daughter into an environment about which they knew practically nothing, suggests the strength of their conviction and

---

*During a visit to the Prieuré Des Basse Logges in 1983, I saw the plaque commemorating Katherine Mansfield's time with the Forest Philosophers, the name given to Gurdjieff's students by the press. There was no mention of Gurdjieff.

the trust they put in a man they had seen only briefly and about whom they knew even less. As recounted by Ouspensky, Gurdjieff had traveled in the East for many years and had acquired much knowledge unknown to modern science. He was the agent of the Inner Circle of Humanity, the esoteric center from which C influences radiate out into the world. He was remarkable; this they had seen for themselves when he had appeared in London. But more than that they did not know.

Catherine's sister had gone on ahead to scout things out and prepare for the family's arrival. Difficulties to overcome were certainly in store for the apostate Jungian, but already *en route* he had encountered one not purposefully devised by the master into whose hands he was about to commend his fate. Baby Jane was prescribed goat's milk and someone had the sense to realize it might be difficult to secure a supply once they had passed through the Prieuré's gates. The only way to obtain a steady source was to bring along a goat, and the only place where Nicoll could purchase one—two in fact—was the zoo. Gurdjieff's teaching strategies often involve situations and "difficulties" that resemble live action Zen *koans*, with the student being put in some uncomfortable position with little room to wriggle out of it, in order to bring the need to "self-remember" into sharp focus. The image of Nicoll bargaining with a Parisian zookeeper over the price of two goats while on his way to get his psyche synthesized by Gurdjieff has a Marx Brothers absurdity to it that hits the appropriate note.

When Nicoll arrived, the "animated work" that Ouspensky had mentioned was in full swing, the main objective being to raise what was known as the Study House. This was a huge hall, where the movements were performed, erected using the frame of a decommissioned aircraft hangar left over from the war. Gurdjieff was nothing if not resourceful. Yet Ouspensky, ever the soul of tact, was understating things. The "animation" more likely resembled a productive chaos, with groups of students hammering, sawing, digging, chopping, and attacking the long-neglected grounds and buildings—including an orangerie and fountain—with solemn intent, or tending to the farm animals, while doing their best to "remember" themselves, to observe their "centers" (moving, intellectual, emotional) to refrain from expressing "negative emotions" (practically an impossibility given the conflicts that Gurdjieff engineered) and to keep an eye on their ever-changing "I's." On top of this was a medley of different mental exercises carried on while performing the physical work.

Things were made more difficult because of a lack of proper tools, so improvisation was in order. As an example, consider the English ladies given the task of digging out the roots of felled trees with table-spoons, all the while memorizing Tibetan words.[18] Depending on when they arrived, who they were, and who had responded to the bell, new inmates were thrown headfirst into the deep end, left to their own devices, or treated like royalty, before falling in with the rest of the crew.

Work, work. Super-effort. Dig the hole. Fill it in. According to one account, the Prieuré had "the atmosphere of a savage boarding-house," where the residents lived "under permanent siege," subjected to "bully-ing threats" and "persuasive eloquence" by a "demented if genial head-master," the enemy within the gates, Gurdjieff himself.[19] By another account it was a place where "habits are changed, fixed ideas are broken up, mechanical routines do not exist, and adaptability to ever-changing forms and modes of life is practised."[20] Change was the order of the day: sudden, unexpected, and "shocking"—a technical term in the Work. Had Nicoll passed into the "outer court of one of those old Mystery Schools" over whose gates was the challenging dictum, Know thyself? Or was another motto, emblazoned over the entrance to another place of difficulties, more appropriate: Abandon all hope, ye who enter here. . . .

The Prieuré was indeed a place of suffering—of the intentional kind—and more than one of its inhabitants would wonder if the mus-tachioed overseer who directed its affairs had more than a slighting resemblance to the devil.

Because they were traveling with a child, the Nicolls were sent to the Paradou, the midrange accommodation at the institute. This was a small house in the garden, where families stayed and the children would be cared for by a communal mother, a different one each week. The best rooms in the house were on the second floor and known collectively as the Ritz. These were occupied by Gurdjieff and his wife, Madame Ostrowsky, a former lady-in-waiting at the Russian court. Any important dignitaries—such as financial investors—who visited stayed in the Ritz as guests, not students, and were given the royal treatment, wined and dined in a way unheard of among the troops. Others, the rank and file, were housed in the Monk's Corridor on the third floor, or in what were the servants' quarters in another wing. The few hours of sleep they were allowed were taken on a mattress, sometimes four to a room. But they were not there for a rest cure, and sleep was at a premium. Nicoll had by this time stopped recording his dreams, under advice by Ouspensky that Gurdjieff would second. They were not helpful for awakening, he was told, which was just as well, as he would hardly have had the time to write them down, or even to have had them in the first place.

Nicoll had sold his Harley Street practice and borrowed heavily against expectations of his inheritance in order to secure a place at the Prieuré. When Ouspensky remarked that some of his students were too eager to throw everything over and head to Fontainebleau, he may have had Nicoll in mind. Ouspensky knew of Nicoll's wavering allegiance to Jung, and now Nicoll was leaving Ouspensky for Gurdjieff. Was that not a bit precipitate—if not to say fickle? But Nicoll was desperate to escape the burden of Chester Terrace and to jettison all pretense of normal life, and Gurdjieff's institute was waiting for him to do just that. It afforded an outlet for that "tremendous momentary impulse toward a life other than conventional life," that was always in the back of his mind. He was not going to pass it up.

Nicoll learned the doctrine of super-effort the hard way. Soon after his arrival, he was appointed kitchen boy, the lowest man on the institute's totem pole. As mentioned, this required him to wake at 5:00 a.m. in order to light the boilers so breakfast—meager though it was— could be prepared for as many as sixty people. At the other end of the cycle, Nicoll had to wash stacks of greasy dishes and cups, without hot water or soap—a practice that, according to some accounts, he continued in later life. Although in her article about her stay at Prieuré published in the *New York Times* Maud Hoffman says that one was kitchen boy for only a short while, Nicoll was stuck with the position for some months, an endurance test comparable to Mesopotamia, where he at least had *Jane Eyre* to distract him. Bennett, who served as kitchen boy as well, seems to have got off easy by comparison. The worst that he had to contend with was mopping the kitchen floor and witnessing the avarice of his malnourished fellow workers, when he saw them take more than their share of the lunch food.[21]

Catherine too, labored like a scullery maid, toiling over huge cauldrons of soup, and her sister had the honor of cleaning out the bathrooms in the Ritz. (An account by Fritz Peters who had the task of cleaning up after Gurdjieff shows how onerous this could be.) Although we can assume a good measure of resentment and stupefaction over their decision to come, we can also assume that they, like Orage and Bennett, came to positively enjoy the work. This isn't surprising. Most of Gurdjieff's students were well-off and used to servants doing chores for them; as kitchen boy Bennett was amazed to discover one could soak up dirty water with a towel.[22] Being forced to do it themselves put them in touch with parts of their being that were dormant—asleep. Their accumulators kicked in. A similar if more disturbing shock was administered when Gurdjieff had students who had never slaughtered an animal put in charge of killing pigs and turkeys when it came to the Christmas feasts, which were lavish affairs. If his students were used to doing housework, hard labor, and working on a farm, it might not have had the same effect.

Gurdjieff didn't lecture regularly, and when he did it was a big affair; one lecture consisted of Gurdjieff sitting before his students in silence for an hour, at the end of which he told them that "Patience is the mother of will. If you do not have a mother, how can you be born," and walked out. For most of his time there, Nicoll didn't see him. Yet the master's presence was everywhere, overseeing every activity, shouting at people to work quicker, suddenly changing plans, upsetting everyone. Undoubtedly the most upsetting practice was the "stop" exercise, when everyone had to freeze in whatever position they were in, rather like the old children's game of statues, and remain that way until Gurdjieff allowed them to move. The idea was to catch oneself in transit from one habitual posture to another, another form of "shock." One student had just taken a drag of a cigarette when Gurdjieff gave the command and could not exhale until the master nodded.

There are also many accounts of Gurdjieff stepping in to avert disaster. Stories abound about his superhuman capacities. Katherine Mansfield tells how a fire that had already burnt through two of the rooms in the Prieuré was stopped by Gurdjieff appearing in the midst of the smoke and flames with a sledgehammer, knocking the burning wall down. During work on the Study House, one exhausted student working on the roof fell asleep between two beams. Gurdjieff, lithe as a cat, scrambled up and brought him down, like a kitten caught up a tree. When a boiler had burst Gurdjieff saved it from ruin by pelting the hole with lumps of clay. These, and demonstrations more dramatic, were among the seemingly daily wonders that the students of the Fourth Way witnessed that winter of 1922–23. Nicoll later told his students that it was soon clear to him that everyone there was expected to "be able to do everything."[23] Gurdjieff apparently could, so there were no excuses.

A usual day would start early with a light breakfast (it would start even earlier for Nicoll). Then whatever physical work was required: clearing paths, tending vegetable patches, tending animals, mowing lawns—a major operation for Fritz Peters, who, as a boy, was asked to mow the Prieuré's extensive lawns in a single day, a task that usually took four.[24] Along with the Study House another big project was the building of a Turkish bath. The limestone needed for the bath was quarried at the Prieuré itself; Bennett tells the story of how Gurdjieff knew exactly where to strike a huge, immovable block of it, so that it could be split up and carted away.[25] A light lunch and dinner would interrupt the physical work, and the students would have a brief time to rest before the real work began, that of mastering the movements, instruction in which would continue until past midnight, with piano accompaniment by the composer Thomas de Hartmann.

For the movements, the Nicolls were assigned Olgivanna Hinzenburg as their teacher. She was a society lady, another who had joined Gurdjieff's troupe in Tiflis. Now, along with teaching the movements, she labored consciously cleaning out the Prieuré's pigsties. She would later marry the architect Frank Lloyd Wright, another master with whom Gurdjieff carried on a kind of friendly rivalry. If laboring all day at difficult, unfamiliar tasks while on a meager diet was not super-effort enough, performing the complicated twists and turns of the movements while going through some equally difficult mental exercise surely required superhuman effort.

Gurdjieff had a curious relationship with Nicoll. He seemed to hold him responsible for every mishap that occurred since his arrival. He became the scapegoat. When anything went wrong, and it often did, Gurdjieff would call out "Nicoll!" and gesture in mock despair.[26] This was a teaching strategy, no doubt, part of the individual education that formed the second stage of Gurdjieff's approach. The first stage was the collective work: the demanding regimen, the physical labor, the personality clashes, the friction needed to produce the heat to "hatch eggs," as he told Nicoll. The institute was a kind of psychological incubator, providing the required heat and turning the eggs over, not necessarily gently. But the egg must want to hatch. The "chicken inside must try to break shell, then help and individual teaching possible," Gurdjieff told Nicoll.[27] He must work on himself.

Gurdjieff had some idea of what was waiting to hatch inside Nicoll's shell, and he happily provided the heat. Neither did he treat Catherine with kid gloves. Once, when she arrived late for a lesson because she needed a bath, he punished her by making her hold out her arms until they ached.* Cleanliness may be next to godliness, but at the Prieuré it took a back seat to work. When Bennett's partner Mrs. Beaumont came to visit, she was appalled at the number of flies that swarmed in the kitchen, and at the apparent all-around lack of hygiene. Bennett remarks that students thought the flies were a "test" of some sort, but Gurdjieff praised Mrs. Beaumont's good sense when she "overcame" a difficulty by putting up flypaper.[28] If it was a test, she seemed to be the only one who passed.

Exactly what was a test and what wasn't became a question on practically everyone's mind—except for those who decided that yes, *everything* was a test, arranged by the magus. This created a strange atmosphere, a kind of esoteric gaslighting, which pits one's desire to change against one's common sense or even self-esteem. But who was gaslighting whom? Nicoll wondered if the difficulties Gurdjieff created were as effective as the ones he wasn't responsible for—or was he?[29] With Ouspensky everything was up front. There were ideas and exercises one could practice and see if one got results. If you didn't understand you could ask a question. The answer might be abrupt but at least you could ask it. It was a science, or a discipline, like mathematics or learning how to play a musical instrument. A competent teacher and an industrious student were all that were needed.

But here? Here one really had no idea what was going on, and

---

*This was a practice noted by more than one person. Webb recounts one witness to a student forced to stand with arms outstretched for several minutes whose "anger at the director of this torture chamber burst into a smouldering rage." *The Harmonious Circle,* 244. Aleister Crowley, who visited the Prieuré when it was past its prime, heard about this form of punishment from Frank Pinder, but considered it "childish and morally valueless." John Symonds, *The Great Beast* (St. Albans, UK: Mayflower, 1973), 304.

asking others what they thought was no help. When a fellow student approached Nicoll and asked for help in understanding exactly what they were doing, Nicoll put him off. "How can I help you?" he replied. "Don't you know I need to help myself?"[30] But exactly how was one to do that?

Thoughtful students, like Nicoll, recognized the double bind. If one preferred not to perform some unpleasant duty or one that clearly was absurd, was it the better part of waking up to go against one's own will and just do it—to like what "it," that is, the "you" that you have come to the Prieuré to change, doesn't like? Or was your revulsion a sign of your essence perking up and an opportunity to stand on your own feet and not seek guidance from the guru in everything? In the early days, Gurdjieff tried to get Ouspensky to drink a glass of milk, which he disliked. But he refused. Did he pass the test? Did he fail? Was it a test? Do you put up with the flies in the kitchen, or do you do something about them? Or do you ask the master? Or none of the above?

Gurdjieff certainly had no qualms about forcing the issue. According to Bennett, he "seemed to invite and yet to detest a kind of stupid adoration which made his every word and gesture into symbols of eternal truth," a tendency among some of Gurdjieff devotees that unfortunately carries on today.[31] One poor woman was made to serve as an example. Gurdjieff found her fawning wearisome and wanted to get rid of her. While eating ice cream made fresh from the milk of the Prieuré's cows, he informed her that the best way to get the most out of it was to have it with mustard. The woman dutifully went to the kitchen to retrieve the mustard pot. When she returned Gurdjieff roared so all could hear: "You see what is round idiot. She all time idiot. Why you here?" The woman broke out in tears and left the next day. Who could blame her?

Madame Blavatsky, with whom Gurdjieff had much in common—although he went out of his way to dismiss her—did not suffer fools gladly either, and did not hesitate to let them know. She too could fly into rages at the drop of a hat, as Gurdjieff did, and then appear perfectly civil a moment later. Yet there is a slight flavor of malice in some of Gurdjieff's abrasive tactics that suggests that he invited "stupid adoration" because he enjoyed showing it up. He told C. S. Nott that he needed "rats" for his experiments, and in the ill-considered and quickly rescinded bizarre work, *Herald of Coming Good*—which Ouspensky thought the creation of an unbalanced mind—he called his students his "trained and freely moving Guinea pigs." When the writer Denis Saurat, a friend of Orage and director of the *Institut Français* in London, visited the Prieuré, he detected an atmosphere of anxiety. He asked Gurdjieff if he knew that some of his students were "close to despair." Gurdjieff said yes, he did, and remarked on a necessary "sinister" character to what was going on.[32] If they were close to despair it meant the method was working.

Bennett remarks on the "extraordinary state of tension," in which people were stripped of their "psychological protections" and says that "some went mad" and that there were "even suicides," although he does not provide any details.[33] (Years later, the psychiatrist Anthony Storr remarked that he treated some of Bennett's own students because of the "dire effects" of the instruction they received from him.[34]) Gurdjieff said it was better to die waking up than to sleep peacefully. He was the "arch disturber of sleep," and from his perspective anyone who felt troubled at Fontainebleau was being done a favor.

Yet not only annoying idiots were affected by the atmosphere. James Young left the Prieuré about a year after he arrived, because of an argument with Gurdjieff over his diagnosis of a sick student. The student vomited blood, and Young diagnosed an intestinal ulcer and advised an operation. Gurdjieff disagreed. Yet the student did have the operation and Young's diagnosis had been proved correct. When Young pointed this out Gurdjieff said he was of little faith. When he spoke about it with Orage, he was told that the whole affair was another test. Flies or flypaper? Young left after that. Orage would later say that Gurdjieff had made it easy for him to go, by putting himself in a bad light. Nicoll noted that after Young left, Gurdjieff lectured on the need to remember that each of them had come to him with a specific object in view, using Young's departure as an example of someone having lost sight of this.[35]

Perhaps, and the misdiagnosis of the ill student may have been a test after all; of what, I guess, is the question. Yet such a sensibility effectively puts the teacher beyond criticism, rather as Freud sidestepped any second thoughts about his approach by relegating any hesitation about his theories to the neuroses of his followers.

Yet the misdiagnosis was only the last straw. Young had begun to wonder if he and his fellow inmates were suffering from a kind of mass "transference," imbuing Gurdjieff with all the "power that accrues to a man once he has been invested with the magical attributes of the 'all powerful father' or has had the 'magician' archetype projected onto him, as Jung would say."[36] An example of this was the aura that surrounded the otherwise banal event of purchasing an automobile. Gurdjieff bought one, which isn't surprising: he was keen on machines and contraptions—an interest he shared with Nicoll, and that came out when they worked together in the carpentry shop—and at one point spent a considerable sum on buying bicycles for everyone and making them learn how to ride. He wanted to get to Paris easily, where he was carrying on several businesses and where he could get away from his flock when needed.

Young said that it was believed by many that Gurdjieff would not have to learn how to drive as anyone else would, but would do so by "inspiration." When the gears grinded and the engine stalled, this was not evidence of Gurdjieff's inspiration but a test of the faithful. But he was an appalling driver, as the many accounts of journeys with him show, and the real test of faith was getting in the car with him. Nicoll was privy to one mad motor trip, on a breakneck journey to Switzerland, so Gurdjieff could sleep at a high altitude. They ate roast goat by the roadside along the way, and after three hours at the hotel, turned around and headed back.

From one perspective the entire notion of the institute was a test. By any standards the Study House was a remarkable achievement, a fantastic, magical structure erected in record time by people for the most part without any skill in construction, who labored twelve or more hours a day, with little sustenance, all the while practicing difficult psychological exercises. It was a hundred feet long and forty wide, with a stage, a gallery, and a space where the students sat on cushions on the floor. It had fountains in the corners, a draped box from which Madame Ostrowsky observed the movements, and the windows were painted in a way to resemble stained glass. The enneagram, a nine-pointed symbol central to the Work, adorned the ceiling, and aphorisms lined the walls: "Like what 'it' does not like," "Remember yourself always and everywhere," "We can only strive to be able to be Christians"—a maxim that appealed to Nicoll—"Remember you came here having already understood the necessity of struggling with yourself," "I love him who loves work," were among the many sayings that students struggling with themselves and the movements saw each evening.

Bennett said it reminded him of a dervish *tekke*, with Persian carpets hanging on the walls. Yet Bennett, who had seen the first efforts to raise it and returned months later when it was done, recognized that the building "had an impromptu air about it—more like a stage set than a permanent structure."[37] It was a piece of theatre. It was not made to last.

"This is only temporary," Gurdjieff told a surprised Nicoll, regarding the building they had labored at consciously. "In a very short time everything will be different. Everyone will be elsewhere. Nothing can be built permanent at this moment."[38] The Work, he told Nicoll, "would have no permanent home." Yet, if this was so, why the urgency to get the institute up and running? Why, too, did Gurdjieff tell Bennett about the plans he had to erect an observatory on a clearing overlooking the Prieuré, where he could use special means he had developed to make the planets appear larger, if indeed "nothing permanent" could be built and "everyone will be elsewhere," which as it turned out would indeed be the case? Flies or flypaper? Institute or no institute?

Gurdjieff made extraordinary claims about his work there. A prospectus for the institute claimed, among other things, that it had an extensive and elaborate medical department, where hydrotherapy, electrotherapy, magnetotherapy, something called "phototherapy" and other health-bestowing practices would be available.[39] None of this was the case. He had made similar claims about his earlier attempts at the institute, including the less than truthful remark that it had offices in the major capitals of the world. Test? False advertising? Others wondered if the speed with which Gurdjieff worked resulted in anything more than jerry-rigged projects that didn't withstand close scrutiny, a situation Nicoll would find himself in years later, when his own construction work was subjected to an official inspection and Nicoll had to apply some Fourth Way charm to get approval. Speed in working might be a sign of "inner harmony," as Gurdjieff had passed on to Nicoll.[40] But haste makes waste, and it doesn't always get the job done.[41] And inner harmony can arrive by the opposite means: by *slowing down* instead of rushing ahead. Hence the virtue of any number of meditative practices.

Other esoteric teachers, such as Rudolf Steiner, did build to last, as visitors to his monumental Goetheanum in Dornach, Switzerland, know. Gurdjieff was not interested in putting up something that would last or that even displayed craftsmanship. He wanted to get it up "quick and dirty" as the field hospitals in Mesopotamia had been. That is, the buildings were needed for a specific purpose at a specific time and a specific place. Once that was accomplished, there was no need for them. The speed, the effort, the focus, the friction were what mattered, not the end result. As Nicoll said, nothing that happened at the Prieuré mattered, only the *effect* it had on him.[42] Dig the hole. Fill it in. Remember yourself. The Work took place where and when it could, not at a particular location. This was something that Nicoll would have to tell his own students, when circumstances demanded they give up their associations with a place they had come to love.

Giving up "associations" was something Gurdjieff impressed upon Nicoll. We see the world through our associations; that is, we never see *it* but only the associations—memories, ideas—that whatever we are looking at stimulate in us. Because of this we never see things as they *are*, but only as symbols, abstract generalities: "tree," "cloud," "flower," not the specific thing *itself.* Gurdjieff impressed upon Nicoll the need to focus our attention so that we see the reality and not our *idea* of the world.[43] The effect of doing so would be the same as if we were seeing in essence: everything more vivid. This is rather like the sudden clarity of vision that comes in the Zen moment, which is another discipline aimed at "waking up" and which shares more than a little with Gurdjieff's method, the *koans* serving as cognitive "shocks" to our system (and we are familiar with the often crazy antics of some of the old Zen masters).

Perceiving the world in this way, we then see the kind of *difference* among things that Ouspensky spoke of in *Tertium Organum*, rather than the bland sameness that we now perceive.[44] For us now "a rose is a rose is a rose," as Gertrude Stein said. Seeing *differences* we can understand how William Blake could speak of seeing "a world in a grain of sand" and "heaven in a wild flower." That Ouspensky himself saw the *differences* that Gurdjieff labored to get his students to see, suggests that he already had an idea of what "waking up" would be like, before Gurdjieff had pulled him into his work.

IN APRIL 1923 NICOLL GOT WORD that his father was ill. His health had been worsening for several months; as early as January there were signs that it had taken a bad turn. Now it seemed that there was little hope of a recovery, and Nicoll had been told that he should return to London. He arrived just in time, and was at his father's bedside on

May 4 when he died, at the family home in Hampstead. He was seventy years old. Catherine arrived for the funeral, but returned to the Prieuré soon after, eager to get back to Jane, who had been left with the nanny. Nicoll remained in London for three months, settling his father's affairs.

What words may have passed between father and son isn't known, but Nicoll was thankful that he was able to be with his father at the end. He knew that he had never approved of or even understood the decision to abandon the lucrative and prestigious practice he had built up on Harley Street, to which his father had contributed much support, in order to bring his wife and child to what appeared to be a very dubious chateau in France and to place himself under the tutelage of an enigmatic guru. What he would have thought about his son becoming a teacher of an esoteric philosophy must be left to the imagination. But as Jung believed, it is only after the father passes away, that the son can fully become his own person.

Jung may have felt something of this himself. In that same April Nicoll wrote his "Dear Carl" letter to his ex-teacher, hoping to explain why he had abandoned analytical psychology for Gurdjieff's system. Although Gurdjieff had told Nicoll to forget his dreams, he nevertheless told Jung of one he had, about finding himself at a kind of "fire festival," which turned out to be the top floor of the department store Selfridge's—a London landmark—going up in flames. The symbolism seemed apt. Nicoll's central complaint about Jung's approach was that it lacked something "outside" the self, a "supreme orientating principle," or "crown," an image perhaps harkening to Kether, the highest *sephiroth* or "vessel" on the Kabbalistic Tree of Life, known as the Crown. He also told Jung of other dreams, in which he was visited by a schoolmaster of his youth, a man of strong physical presence. Nicoll told Jung that when he met Gurdjieff, he realized that he was the schoolmaster.

Yet apart from any lack he may have found in Jung's approach, what comes across most in Nicoll's letter is his own admission of weakness. He lacked the "force" needed to work on himself. Gurdjieff told him that he wasted energy thinking about the different ways he *could* change; he also told him that he was too fat. "The inertia of my body is very great," he told Jung. In a nutshell: Nicoll has left Jung because he is too lazy to do anything himself, and needs someone to *make him* work.[45] Jung did reply to Nicoll, but sadly that letter is lost. Yet it doesn't take much to imagine what he might have said. When James Young had written to Jung about his own departure from the Prieuré, Jung wrote back to congratulate him on his escape.

When Nicoll returned to Fontainebleau, Gurdjieff's remarks about everything being temporary seemed to be coming true. It was soon after his return to the Prieuré in August that James Young pulled up stakes and left. There was a shift in the atmosphere, a sense of things coming to an end. Nicoll's delight in being back among his fellow workers soon turned into a sense of anxiety, a mood swing that Gurdjieff observed. When he saw Nicoll again, he spoke with him. "When you return to institute two men—one happy to meet friends, old associates, etc. The other does not begin to be felt until you arrive. Suddenly you begin to fear. He thinks of all the difficulties to be faced. He thinks seriously."[46]

What Nicoll himself said about his return was that it gave him resolution. He had experienced the unique life at the Prieuré, and knowing what to expect, he returned. A glutton for punishment? Or a convert fully on the road of his new faith? How long his new resolution would have lasted, we do not know. For all intents and purposes, within three months of Nicoll's return the Institute for the Harmonious Development of Man of G. I. Gurdjieff closed up shop, never to operate again. Gurdjieff would remain at the Prieuré for a number of years, but as a going concern, the institute was no more. Gurdjieff was right. Nothing was permanent. In the time remaining Gurdjieff was getting rid of dead wood, chucking out the students he found useless, and gearing up his energies for a new production: the conquest of America. A shock? A test? Or just a change of plans? Were new rats needed for new experiments?

While Nicoll had been away, there had been public performances of the movements in the Study House. These were a kind of dry run for the next phase of Gurdjieff's trajectory. He planned to bring his troupe of dancers to the States. The performances in the Study House had attracted attention, and Gurdjieff was eager to get across the Atlantic. He was sending Orage on ahead to pave the way. Would Nicoll like to accompany him?

Was it a test? Nicoll was not fond of Orage, and the thought of being a kind of lieutenant to him as he proselytized for the Work in a foreign land most likely did not appeal. Perhaps the few months he had spent in London were enough to remind him that there were some benefits to living in comfort. (Can we imagine an orgy of reading while back home?) He declined the offer, saying that he would rather teach the work in Scotland, when he was ready to. We don't know Gurdjieff's reply, but we can assume he wasn't concerned. He was sizing up Bennett as well, and talked with him about his future in the Work, and suggested that he, too, accompany him to America. Bennett too demurred, and Gurdjieff had no further use for him; when Bennett was leaving the Prieuré and wanted to say goodbye to his teacher, he was nowhere to be found. Bennett wouldn't see Gurdjieff again for another twenty-five years when, after the death of Ouspensky, he sought out his old teacher.

We don't know if the Nicolls had a chance to say goodbye, but by all accounts, after they left the Prieuré, in October 1923, they never saw Gurdjieff again.

9

"Go Away—and Teach the System!"

O ne of the first people Nicoll ran into when he had returned to London was Kenneth Walker. As Walker tells it in his book, *Venture with Ideas*—one of the more balanced and readable accounts of a life in the Work—they literally did run into each other, on the corner of Weymouth and Harley Streets, in fashionable Marylebone.[1] Walker, himself a physician with a particular focus on human sexuality, had a practice in the neighborhood and was on his way to catch the Underground at Oxford Circus when he bumped into Nicoll.* We can assume some hearty greetings and warm exchanges passed between them. But the subject on Nicoll's mind was a children's book of Walker's that had just been published, *The Log of the Ark*.[2] Like Nicoll, Walker combined a medical practice with authorship, producing over his long career some twenty-odd popular works on medical topics, philosophy, religion, and more than one memoir; *Venture with Ideas* is an updated version of an earlier autobiographical work, *I Talk of Dreams*. But Nicoll

---

*See, for example, his *The Physiology of Sex* (Harmondsworth, UK: Penguin Books, 1946).

wasn't interested in the book itself so much as in its subject, the ark. We know that in his consulting room in Golders Green at the beginning of his career, Nicoll had a frieze of the animals from Noah's ark painted on the walls. But the ark he had in mind now wasn't for children or animals.

When Nicoll asked Walker why he had written the book, his friend replied that it simply seemed like a good idea. But why, Walker wondered, was Nicoll so interested in it? Nicoll's answer surprised him. "The ark is a symbol for a refuge in a time of trouble," he said. "Noah," Nicoll informed his bemused friend, "was warned of the disasters ahead; we also will require an ark in the time to come, and there is a small group of people now in London that has started building one."[3]

Before Walker could express his bafflement, Nicoll continued. Great disasters were on their way, Nicoll informed his friend, and it was incumbent upon them to prepare for them. "There will be wars, political unrest, revolutions and all on such a scale that everything that humanity has managed to build up may well fall into ruins."[4] When Walker expressed some hesitation in accepting this bleak forecast, suggesting that the League of Nations would ensure that war was a thing of the past, an excited Nicoll interrupted him again, gripping his arm to get his attention. "It won't work," he assured his friend. In a few years, he insisted, the League of Nations wouldn't exist. But more to the point, the problem wasn't with leagues or plans or politics, but with people. "All these treaties and high-sounding words mean nothing, absolutely nothing," Nicoll told Walker. "So long as men remain as they are everything will continue as it has always been. . . . You don't believe me, but what I am telling you is the truth."

Walker wasn't convinced, but he was impressed by Nicoll's conviction. He was used to Nicoll's "dramatic pronouncements," and refused to believe that the world was as mad as Nicoll apparently thought it was. But the "tone of authority" with which Nicoll spoke, led Walker to wonder if he was privy to some inside information. At Oxford

Street he asked Nicoll exactly who had predicted these catastrophes?

Nicoll answered "Gurdjieff."

Walker took some liberties in his account, and for dramatic effect made out that he had heard this name on only "one or two previous occasions," and each time it was Nicoll who spoke it. He neglected to remark that a year and a half earlier, Nicoll had sought his help in getting the Home Office to allow Gurdjieff to settle in England, commandeering him on that impromptu and unsuccessful diplomatic mission. But aside from that, Walker had never met Gurdjieff or Ouspensky. He did, of course, know that Nicoll had just returned from a year spent at Gurdjieff's institute in France. Like everyone else who knew Nicoll, Walker was stunned to hear that his friend had thrown up everything, his medical practice and home on Chester Terrace, to go to Fontainebleau and put himself and his wife under the supervision of— well, exactly *who* was this Gurdjieff? Walker wouldn't know himself, until many years later, when, following the death of Ouspensky, like Bennett, he would find a way to Gurdjieff's door in postwar Paris. At the moment, all he had to go on were Nicoll's remarks.

According to Nicoll, Gurdjieff was "a man possessed of immense knowledge and of unusual powers," and whose method of teaching involved "irritation and exhaustion"—that is, the bullying treatment.[5] He must have made a powerful impression on Nicoll, because Walker could detect a note of "unusual respect" when Nicoll mentioned his name. Walker's other source of information about Gurdjieff was an article about "The Forest Philosophers" that he had read in a newspaper.

When Walker asked Nicoll if Gurdjieff was in London, Nicoll replied that no, he was in France. But Ouspensky was in London. Would Walker like to go to one of his meetings, possibly even to join one of his groups?

Visions of Madame Blavatsky and a coterie of devoted followers, mostly women, receiving instruction from mahatmas in Tibet danced before Walker's eyes. He knew of such a group that practiced "spiritual healing under the inspired guidance of bus-conductor and an ex-postman," and the thought repelled him—suggesting, perhaps, a bit of snobbery on Walker's part. Walker would not have known it then, but Ouspensky himself said that "members of esoteric schools" often belong "even to the uncultured classes" and may be "engaged in insignificant and perhaps . . . even vulgar professions."[6] This, however, did not prevent Ouspensky, and Nicoll, from exhibiting a certain degree of what we might call "esoteric snobbery," eliciting their students mostly from well-heeled backgrounds and looking askance at applicants from less conventional or successful ones. Hence the irony of both of them being picked up by the counterculture of the 1960s.

Walker had heard of Ouspensky, but mostly as the author of a best-selling book. He'd be happy to meet him, personally, but not as a "seeker" or anything like that; Walker had none of the spiritual crises that so tormented Nicoll, something that in fact he would later try to get across to Ouspensky.[7] He was about to decline Nicoll's offer when he suddenly changed his mind. If Gurdjieff's and Ouspensky's ideas were meaningful enough to Nicoll that he would abandon his career and, with wife and child, put himself under their tutelage for a year, maybe there was something to them? After all, his friend had made such an impression on Jung that the Swiss psychoanalyst saw him as his lieutenant in Britain. Perhaps he should check out Ouspensky after all? Walker accepted Nicoll's invitation and attended a meeting. He would do so for the next twenty-four years.

NICOLL JUMPED BACK INTO his place at Warwick Gardens almost immediately on his return to London, bringing Walker with him, but the impact of his months at Fontainebleau was just beginning to sink in. He told Beryl Pogson that nothing that happened at the Prieuré mattered, only its effect on him. One of those effects was exhaustion. The bullying treatment he had been subjected to caught up with him; that, and the emotions raised by the death of his father and the demanding business of settling his affairs, had taken their toll. There was also the break with Jung. Another factor to consider was finding somewhere to live. They had cut their ties to Chester Terrace, and the Nicolls were, in effect, homeless. The answer to the question of where they would spend the winter months lay north. They left London and headed to the Old Manse, where Nicoll recuperated from his "intentional suffering" and "conscious labor" by randomly reading through his grandfather's library, which consisted mostly of theological works.

A curious convalescence, we might think. But then God and Nicoll's relation to him was never far from Nicoll's mind. Snow came early that year, and we can imagine Nicoll, curled up before a fire, after an ample meal, luxuriating in the quiet, the space, and the lack of dishes to wash. One result of his recuperation was a return to writing for the *Strand*, where Nicoll managed to publish a few stories.

In the spring, they moved back again to Frognal, changing places with Nicoll's stepmother, who, following the death of her husband, was leaving Hampstead and retiring to the manse. Nicoll was ready to start up his practice again when a bout of scarlet fever hit. This required an operation and he was in bed for three months. The inactivity led to what is known in monastic literature as *acedia*, an utter lack of interest in anything, a boredom that is not too distant from clinical depression. Although the prompt for this lack of motivation was his illness, as we've seen, Nicoll had a tendency toward something along these lines, and he usually required some external stimulant to get him going again. In this case it was some good news. A legacy left to him by his mother had finally arrived; it had been held by his father and now that he had passed away it came into Nicoll's hands.

If evidence is needed to show that the mind has remarkable curative powers, the good news that Nicoll had received in the mail should serve admirably. Nothing the doctors had done had any effect. But the realization that his financial problems were solved—at least for the time being— did the trick. The day the news came he got out of bed. It may have been the fever that had landed him there or he may have been suffering from a kind of existential hangover, triggered by his return to "normal" life after his months leading an "other than conventional" one. Either way, the knowledge that he had money in the bank was a tonic.

One of the first things Nicoll did with his new wealth was to buy a car—two, in fact, one for himself and one for Catherine (we remember the kick he got out of his first car back in his student days). It was also decided that Bay Tree Lodge was too big for them, and they arranged to share it with a Mr. and Mrs. Healey, an apt name for a couple sharing a house with a doctor. With this Nicoll was ready to resume his practice on Harley Street, where he would introduce insights and techniques picked up at Fontainebleau in his dealings with neurotics and other troubled individuals.

Nicoll was also able to return to Ouspensky's meetings, which he and Catherine attended three times a week, and where he began to take on more responsibilities, something Bennett started doing as well. He started the meetings by taking questions, fielding the less serious ones and generally acting as Ouspensky's aide-de-camp. Yet even this privilege was no sign that Nicoll was out of the fire. On the first occasion when Nicoll was scheduled to open a meeting, he devoted much time the previous week to figuring out exactly how he would go about it, no doubt wanting to get it right and win Ouspensky's approval. But when the time came, at the last minute Ouspensky pulled a Gurdjieff, and told Nicoll his services would not be needed.[8] Nicoll rolled with the punch, his sangfroid more than likely a sign to Ouspensky that he was making progress.

Kenneth Walker has provided an account of what these meetings were like. After having difficulty finding the location, Walker entered into a small hall, where he found a Russian lady who ticked off his name from a list. This was most likely Madame Kadloubovsky, who would later translate a revised edition of *Tertium Organum*. Some remark of hers assured Walker that she had a sense of humor. If so, this would be about the only glimpse of one he would get. Although the early Ouspensky could crack a smile—his story "The Inventor," one of his *Talks with the Devil*, includes a comic send up of a Black Mass— the Ouspensky who reached London had jettisoned his earlier "weaknesses," and now was about as humorous and imperturbable as a stone. Walker doubted if "even an explosion" would shake him.[9]

There was an oppressive air about the place. When Walker reached the lecture hall, he saw that the "austere and rather dreary room" was sparsely furnished.[10] There were a number of small—and uncomfortable—chairs, facing a blackboard and a table, on which rested a jug of water, a glass, an ashtray, some chalk, and an eraser. An indistinct painting adorned one wall, and on the windowsill Walker saw a vase with some artificial flowers. People entered in small groups. Most everyone sat in silence, and Walker couldn't help but be reminded of "a Scottish congregation awaiting the arrival of the minister;" like Nicoll, Walker had been brought up in a repressive Presbyterianism, although his response to it differed from his friend's. In this case, the minister took his time in arriving, a "let them wait" tactic that proved as successful in esoteric contexts as it does in show business.

When Walker observed the "builders of the ark," he wondered what had brought them there? He concluded that "disillusionment" was the prompt, a disability he tells us that he did not share. As Walker tried to make clear to Ouspensky during his visit to Gwendyr Road, he was a "confirmed optimist" who found life "more and more satisfactory," an outlook shared by those whom William James called the "once-born," who come into the world with a bottle or two of champagne to their credit, an inapt metaphor for Walker, who was teetotal, but it makes the point.* He

---

*There is an entry in Nicoll's diary in which he misunderstands James's distinction between the "once" and "twice-born." The "once-born" are optimists; James's example is Walt Whitman. The "twice-born" live closer to the "pain threshold" than the "once-born" and are acutely aware of the world's suffering. Dostoyevsky and Nietzsche would fall into this category. Nicoll interprets James's "twice-born" as referring to the spiritual rebirth, the birth in spirit, that he sought.

came to Ouspensky's meetings because he was interested in his ideas, not out of the self-torment that his friend, Nicoll, whom he refers to as "M" in the book, suffered. This does not mean that Walker was shallow and insensitive; his thoughtful books suggest the opposite. It merely means that not everyone became interested in the Work because they were disappointed in life, or felt that it was something to escape.

Disillusionment could account for the number of middle-aged people, of both sexes, that made up the majority of those present; and we have seen already that the Fourth Way presents itself as the last resort to people who had already tried their hand at other ways. Life had not turned out quite as these people had expected, or they were disappointed in themselves. Walker recognized that at an earlier time these "seekers" might have found some answer in the church. But the skeptical tone of our secular age—even more secular a century on—diminished the efficacy of this solace, and more often it was to the psychiatrist and not the vicar that people feeling a loss of *meaning* in their life went for guidance. Jung himself would say that practically all of his cases involving people past middle age centered on this sense of a loss of meaning. But the half dozen or so young people who filled some seats would not have lived long enough to reach the disillusionment that was the usual overture to joining the Work. Walker pondered their reasons for being there when a door behind him opened and the minister walked in. Ouspensky had arrived.

The Ouspensky of the mid 1920s was, at least according to Walker, a "very solid man of medium height, with closely cropped grey hair." He made his way to the front of the room without regarding the audience, drew his notes out of his pocket, held them inches from his face and peered at them over the tops of his pebbled pince-nez. Walker had come expecting a mystic. Everything he had heard about *Tertium Organum* had suggested this. Instead he found himself looking at someone who seemed more of a scientist or lawyer than any kind of guru; indeed, Ouspensky was described by one biographer as an "earnest metropolitan bourgeois."[11]

Ouspensky dove headfirst into his talk, speaking English with a Russian accent so strong that Walker thought he was listening to some strange, unknown language. Ouspensky had by this time perfected his "take it or leave" delivery, stating his conclusions with no attempt to persuade or explain. If his audience didn't like what he had to say, they were free to go. From Walker's account one gets the impression that Ouspensky would have delivered his talk in the same flat, matter-of-fact style if he had a hundred people before him or just one. He was not there to convince. If his audience understood what he had to say, their own observations would do that themselves.

What did Ouspensky have to say? His brief hadn't changed since his first appearance at Lady Rothermere's soirees. We have no permanent "I" but are a bundle of conflicting "I's," each ruling the roost until it is dislodged by the next. To illustrate this point, Ouspensky drew a large circle on the blackboard, which he then filled in with a kind of crosshatching. In each little section formed by the pattern he wrote "I." "This is a picture of man," he told his audience. "He has innumerable 'I's' that are always changing. One 'I' is there at one moment and at the next it is replaced by another."[12] And with variations on that, the talk was more or less over, and Ouspensky asked for questions.

There were many. How long does an "I" last? Are our "I's" connected in some way? Why do we *feel* we have a permanent "I" if indeed we don't? Ouspensky answered these briefly and without hesitation. "I's" exist for various durations, but they are always changing. One "I" decides to go on a diet. The next day, another "I" forgets all about that, and has a large breakfast. They are all connected in some way, but we are unaware of these connections. And the fact that we have a body and a name accounts for our sense of a permanent self. Our body changes too slowly for us to be aware of the changes, and we are called by our name throughout our life and so identify with it. This creates in us the illusion of "unity and permanence," both of which we lack. Putting aside the question of who the "we" is that lacks this permanence, what

Ouspensky is saying here—by way of Walker—is something that the Buddha proposed millennia ago, and which contemporary neuroscience advocates now: the illusory nature of the self.

We possessed other illusions as well, at least according to Ouspensky. We believe we are conscious, that we possess free will, that we can "do." But all this is false. A little self-observation reveals how little consciousness we possess, and that our capacity for free will and ability to "do" are equally paltry. Our interior world follows its own weather patterns. And just as "it" rains, snows, is hot or cold, so too the "it" in us is angry, sad, happy, and so on. "We are machines set in motion by external influences, by impressions reaching us from the outside world."[13] Nothing more. When one woman asked if this was true of great artists, of Leonardo, Michelangelo, and others, Ouspensky replied that yes, it was. They were merely very good machines, but machines nonetheless.

This cheery outlook was not very different from the behaviorism of John Watson, then the dominant force in academic psychology. Behaviorism had no truck with consciousness, subjectivity, an "inner world," or anything like that. All that interested it was how people behaved, that is, what was *observable* about them. Behaviorism, too, saw human beings as machines, or as we would say today, computers waiting to be programmed. As Watson famously said, if he was given a child and his own environment in which to bring him up, he could produce whatever the parents wanted: a doctor, lawyer, artist, even a beggar man or thief. The conditioning is all that mattered; everything depended on nurture; nature had nothing to do with it. We are blank slates, *tabulae rasae*, waiting to be written upon by experience, a view that goes back to the philosopher John Locke and that Gurdjieff shared. "A man is born like an empty cupboard or storehouse," he told his students.[14] This, incidentally, is precisely the view of the psyche that Jung argued against, with his positing of the "archetypes," which are what we might call preinstalled software that enable us to have any experience in the first place.

Walker was well up on the latest psychology, and he recognized the similarity between Watson's behaviorism and what he was hearing. But Ouspensky had an addendum to this dour view. We are machines—but we can learn how to be less mechanical, and, with much work, to be truly conscious and possessed of will. Walker also recognized that what Ouspensky said about our lack of a permanent "I" was not far different from the philosopher David Hume's remark that when he looked inside himself, he could find no "self," merely a shifting procession of thoughts, feelings, memories, sensations, impressions. Yet one question Hume didn't ask was, exactly *who* was doing the looking?

At this point, all Ouspensky asked of his audience was that they observe themselves. This did not mean introspection, or analysis, or brooding, but an objective, impartial, unbiased observation of their daily life. He suggested that the French verb *constater* described what he meant, which would be helpful if you knew French, which Ouspensky was fluent in. It means to "register everything," to take note of what is taking place. It is through this that we can get a glimpse of our mechanicalness, what T. S. Eliot, perhaps influenced by his attendance at Ouspensky's early lectures, called the "partial observation of one's own automatism."[15] Perhaps an easy way to grasp what Ouspensky meant is to try to see oneself as others see you, from the "outside"—a not always easy or pleasant challenge. He also insisted that no one take anything on faith. Everything must be tested. To accept on trust is simply laziness. His audience must find out for themselves if what he says is true. And with that he was done.

At the end of the meeting, Walker was surprised to see the woman who had let him in chide a few of the attendees who had stopped on their way out and were chatting outside the door. If they wanted to talk, she said, could they do it elsewhere? "You know that he"—Ouspensky—"doesn't want attention drawn to these meetings."[16] Why Ouspensky would want to keep these meetings secret baffled Walker, who was already puzzled by the strange cloak-and-dagger air that surrounded them. When he asked if there would be another meeting at the same time next week, he was told that, perhaps there would be, perhaps not. "We can never be sure," a "keep them guessing" ploy that Ouspensky had been subjected to during his first months with Gurdjieff. The idea was to keep the attendees on their toes, and also to make attending the meetings themselves difficult, so that people would value them more. People undervalue what comes to them easily, Gurdjieff told Ouspensky, and so his followers in Moscow and St. Petersburg would often not know until the last minute if there would be a meeting that evening or not—and in an age without mobile phones or the Internet, even letting people know that there would be a meeting provided its own challenges.

When Walker asked Nicoll about all the secrecy, wondering why he was obliged to park his car in another street and sneak into Warwick Gardens as though he were "a conspirator or burglar," Nicoll laughed.[17] "It is not always easy to disentangle the teacher from the Russian in Ouspensky," he told his friend. Yes, Ouspensky was "unnecessarily scared about the police." This was an unfortunate hangover from his days in czarist and Bolshevik Russia. Ouspensky, we know, held the Bolsheviks in contempt, but he had no love for the old regime either; his sister was arrested during the failed 1905 revolution and died in prison. (And although he was an outspoken critic of the Communists, during the 1930s Ouspensky was under observation by the Home Office as a potential Russian agent.) But there were other, psychological reasons for the secretive air. One of our most mechanical activities is talking. Being obliged not to talk about the system with people outside of it installs an "alarm clock," that helps us to "remember ourselves." We begin to chatter and then remember and are "woken up" for a moment. The other rules help to secure a sense that this is "special," different from our ordinary affairs, which is essentially the purpose of ritual. They generate a tension that can be directed at the work at hand. As Ouspensky wrote, "keeping secrets is connected in esotericism with the idea of conserving energy. Silence, secrecy, create a closed circuit, that is, an "accumulator."[18]

AS WE MIGHT EXPECT, Walker and Nicoll spoke a great deal about the Work, Gurdjieff, and Ouspensky. One conversation took place at the "full-bodied Café Royal of former days," not the "anaemic" version of post–World War II Britain, the time of Walker's writing. This was a spot where Nicoll would later meet with his own students in the early days of his ministry.[19] Nicoll had chosen the dinner. Walker, a teetotaler, declined brandy with his coffee. Nicoll questioned him on his abstinence but rejected Walker's reply. "The true explanation of your distaste for alcohol," Nicoll told his friend, "is that you and I were brought up in a gloomy Presbyterian atmosphere and, unlike me, you've never recovered from it."[20] The degree to which Nicoll recovered from his upbringing is debatable, as what we've seen of his diary suggests, yet at that dinner he was expansive. "You make a great mistake," he told Walker, although in exactly what way he didn't make clear. Gesturing to the other diners, Nicoll said "Either live like these people," whom we must assume he considered a cross section of "sleeping humanity," or else "live in accordance with the principles of the work." "Get what you can out of life," he told Walker, something for which Nicoll, by his own admission, was not constitutionally suited, "or turn your back on it and seek the Kingdom of God," a principality that more and more occupied his thoughts.

Walker was not in sympathy with Nicoll's Manichean separation of humanity into "these people" and those who seek the Kingdom of Heaven, a typology that will increasingly inform Nicoll's views. But he did want to hear more about the system. "Where did it come from? What is its source?" questions still asked by Fourth Way devotees today.

Nicoll didn't know. He wasn't quite sure about Gurdjieff. He is a "strange man," Nicoll told Walker, "different from anyone you have ever met." He was a "wonderful actor" and one could never be sure when he was "romancing" or telling the truth, something Bennett admitted to as well.[21] He was also the polar opposite of Ouspensky, and wouldn't give a damn what the police or anyone else thought about him or his meetings. Nicoll repeated what he had heard about Gurdjieff's early travels in search of lost knowledge, an account of which Gurdjieff would provide in the allegory-rich pages of *Meetings with Remarkable Men*. Nicoll made a point of mentioning Gurdjieff's use of some scientific terms, most likely referring to the strange "table of hydrogens" that chart the transformations of energy in man, from very raw crude forms to much finer ones, energies needed in order to "work on oneself."[22] Nicoll would tell his students that Gurdjieff gave him the task of bringing together the ideas of the system with those of modern science, and he remarked to Walker that he saw the Work as a "bridge that links up Eastern and Western learning." What made it unique, and convinced Nicoll of its importance, he told his friend, was that it "establishes a connection between esoteric knowledge and modern science."[23]

At the words "esoteric knowledge," Walker demurred, the thought of that theosophical bus conductor and ex-postman possibly passing through his mind. But Nicoll insisted. For centuries before the earliest religious scriptures were written, he said, there was an oral tradition, the roots of which may lay somewhere in the East or, perhaps, even in Atlantis. And even when the teachings were committed to writing, there were different levels of reading, providing an exoteric, literal meaning and an esoteric, symbolic one, a distinction that would occupy Nicoll more and more.

Not everyone could grasp this deeper meaning, only the initiate, "a man who has reached a certain level of understanding and who is judged fit to receive more knowledge."[24] Not "the ordinary knowledge to be found in books written by ordinary men," but the "esoteric knowledge coming to us from some ancient and conscious source."[25] That is, C influences coming from the inner circle of humanity. It was there, around us, in the architecture of the Gothic cathedrals, in the obscure writings of the alchemists, even in the scriptures themselves. We only had to look for it. And that is what Nicoll did.

In one of his talks at the Prieuré, Gurdjieff made some remarks about Christianity that Nicoll took very much to heart. The aim of his institute, he said, could be expressed very simply. It was "to help one to be able to be a Christian."[26] Indeed, one of the aphorisms adorning the walls of the Study House said precisely this. This process must begin with the *wish* to become a Christian; a big wish, Gurdjieff said, is a great thing. But most of the people at the Prieuré believed they were Christian already, just as they believed they had free will and consciousness. But they were all really only "Christians in quotation marks," that is, what Gurdjieff would call a "so to say" Christian, one in name only, a criticism we've seen Nicoll make himself. To be a real Christian is the most difficult thing. Who among them could love others as Christ instructs us to love them? None of them. If we have had our coffee we love them; if we haven't, we don't. But it is true that one must be able to love. How does one gain this ability? And it doesn't matter what name we give to whatever religion it is that people may profess. It made no difference. It was all Christianity, but a Christianity, as we've seen, that went back much further than historical Christianity, and had its roots in ancient Egypt and perhaps even earlier. "There were Christians," Gurdjieff said, "long before the advent of Christianity."[27]

But in the past, not all men were Christian, or, more precisely, all were not Christian to the same degree. There were non-Christians, pre-Christians, and Christians, suggesting the kind of triadic typology familiar to the early days of Christianity, such as the Gnostic distinction among the "hylic," "psychic," and "pneumatic" souls, and the "heathen," "believer," and "gnostic" of Clement of Alexandria. We can understand the differences among these types as being characterized by a more literal or more symbolic understanding of Christianity and the Gospels, a distinction that will inform Nicoll's own efforts to arrive at an esoteric reading of scripture.

On his return to his groups, one of the tasks Nicoll was engaged in was helping Ouspensky prepare material for what would become *A New Model of the Universe*. Ouspensky had been working on the book when he was ensnared by Gurdjieff. We should remember that Ouspensky did not "go to" Gurdjieff, either because of a personal crisis—as Nicoll did— or because of interest in his ideas, as Walker was drawn to Ouspensky, but was "entangled" by him because Gurdjieff wanted to make use of him. Claude Bragdon's Manas Press edition of *Tertium Organum* adver- tises the forthcoming book with its original title, *The Wisdom of the Gods*, which is what the term theosophy means, and Ouspensky men- tions it in what would become *In Search of the Miraculous*, the account of his time with Gurdjieff that he would tinker with until his death, and which would be published, against his wishes, posthumously.

A New Model of the Universe is a remarkable a book, one, as Colin Wilson comments, that "guarantees [Ouspensky] a place as one of the most important thinkers of the twentieth century."[28] It is a collection of independent essays, most begun before World War I or the revo- lution, loosely tied together with the ribbon of "esotericism" or what Ouspensky calls "the psychological method."[29] This is fundamentally the symbolic, rather than the literal way of looking at the world, a her- meneutic that Ouspensky and his main students, Nicoll, Bennett, and Rodney Collin, would apply to the study of history, in search of traces of "esoteric schools."[30] Among the book's many chapters, dealing with dreams, "experimental mysticism," time, and "eternal recurrence"—an idea that Nicoll would explore—the Laws of Manu, the fourth dimen- sion, the Superman, and esotericism itself, is one in which Ouspensky, like Gurdjieff, speaks of "esoteric Christianity." Their approaches, how- ever, differed considerably. Gurdjieff was happy to simply state what he had to say. Ouspensky, the scholar, was somewhat more thorough.

On a visit to Gwendyr Road, Nicoll got a look at Ouspensky in action in his pursuit of esoteric Christianity. He recounts how Ouspensky had "the New Testament in German, French, Russian, and English" translations, and how when referring to a verse "he looks at the translation in each of them and in the Greek version."[31] A number of dictionaries found space on his bookshelves, and the fact that Ouspensky was "fond of pencils sharpened to a very fine point" may suggest something about his character, a penchant for precision. Nicoll also mentioned the old photographs and prints that covered Ouspensky's mantelpiece, and the uncomfortable chair, much like the ones at Warwick Gardens, that he sat on.

How did Ouspensky see the New Testament? "The four Gospels," he tells us, "are written for the few, the very few, for the pupils of esoteric schools."[32] To understand them requires "*special* indications" and "*special* esoteric knowledge."[33] This idea of a knowledge unlike any we can find or acquire in the ordinary ways in life, runs throughout the book and throughout Ouspensky's teaching as a whole. It is a knowledge that "surpasses all ordinary human knowledge," and is "inaccessible to ordinary people," but which "permeates the whole history of the thought of mankind from the most remote period."[34] It is a product of what Ouspensky calls "higher mind," that is the "conscious" men and women making up the "inner circle of humanity."

The New Testament is not a "simple book," intelligible to the "simple and humble," or at least its true, inner meaning is not accessible to them.[35] Christ's message, Ouspensky assures us, is not sentimental, egalitarian, or concerned with social reform, as some forms of "liberation theology" Christianity see it today. The "Kingdom of Heaven," Ouspensky tells us, whatever these words may mean, "*belongs to the few*," not the many, and certainly not to the people making up the congregation from which the young Nicoll felt alienated.[36] This exclusivity, however, which is so contrary to the usual idea of Christianity as a religion of solace for the weak and suffering, is not based on merit or social standing or a pharisaical adherence to the "letter of the law." It is determined by one's efforts to "wake up," one's desire for consciousness, and by one's understanding that this is what the Gospels are about. What separates the few from the many is what Bernard Shaw in *Don Juan in Hell*—which presents an oddly Swedenborgian idea of heaven—calls the "great gulf of taste." Nothing prevents anyone from attempting to wake up, except their own lack of desire to do so.

How does Ouspensky's reading of the Gospels as works "written consciously for a definite purpose by men who knew more than they wrote," stand up to scholarly scrutiny? Most likely not very well, but he would be the first to point out that if the "psychological method" is not applied, then this is not surprising. That method recognizes that "perceptions change according to the powers and properties of the perceiving apparatus." That is, one's state of consciousness informs what one will find. The knower delimits the known. A literal mind will only see things literally. As Nicoll will later point out, to understand the parables in the Gospel, another kind of mind is required.

NICOLL DID MORE THAN SHARE with Ouspensky a desire to unpack the esoteric meaning of the parables. There developed between them a warmth and friendship that in many ways has its parallel in the relationship that developed between Gurdjieff and Orage, whom the master "loved as brother," and with whom he would joke and, in so far as it was possible for Gurdjieff to do, unwind. Kenneth Walker, who remained Ouspensky's student following that first meeting until his teacher's death in 1947, never achieved anything like the intimacy that his friend M reached with him. "As human being and human being," Walker wrote, "we two had never met." Walker compares his relation to his teacher with the relationship he had with his father, which does not sound altogether that different from the relationship Nicoll had with his father. "As I had always respected, but never really known, my father, so had I always respected, but never really known, Ouspensky."[37]

Yes, in later years, Walker had seen Ouspensky loosen up a bit after a few glasses of Montrachet, an upmarket Chardonnay that Ouspensky favored, and which on more than one occasion became an item in Nicoll's bag of teaching tricks. "But the next day, the old relationship was always resumed." Walker and Ouspensky had "never met on any footing other than that of master and pupil."[38] And Ouspensky's relations with J. G. Bennett, also his student at this time, were never very good. At one point Ouspensky took legal action against Bennett, saying he had "stolen" his ideas and was unauthorized to teach the system, in the same way that Gurdjieff had made this accusation against him. Bennett, however, was the most unlikely candidate to provide Ouspensky with some congenial company.

Bennett was an esoteric masochist. At one point he had progressed with the exercise of repeating the "Jesus Prayer" inwardly—a meditation coming from the Russian Orthodox Church—so far that he was saying it in his mind several hundred times a day, simultaneously in Greek, Latin, Russian, and German. On another occasion, he spent a three-day weekend in reading aloud nonstop Gurdjieff's jawbreaking magnum opus *Beelzebub's Tales to His Grandson*, a one-thousand-plus-page work, rife with neologisms, dependent clauses, and a syntax and grammar that makes *Finnegan's Wake* seem a model of clarity and brevity. Long before the end Bennett had to drink ice water to prevent his teeth from slicing his swollen tongue. His idea of working on himself, he admitted, was "merely to make life as unpleasant and exhausting for myself as I could," a gloss on Bernard Shaw's quip that an Englishman believes he is being moral when he is merely being uncomfortable.[39] "There is something so revolting and humiliating in one's enjoyment of pleasant things," Bennett noted, a remark that would not be out of place in Nicoll's diaries.[40] And although Bennett tried unsuccessfully to talk with Ouspensky about his experience in Fontainebleau—as he was in trying to talk about it to any of the people there—he seems somehow to have failed to grasp its import, given that his examples of "super-effort" and attempts to push through to the Great Accumulator, only led to exhaustion, despair, and doubt about the system.[41]

It was different with Nicoll. Exactly why he and Ouspensky hit it off isn't immediately clear, except perhaps for the fact that Nicoll was perpetually in search of a father figure, something one doesn't sense about Walker, and that Ouspensky was a lonely man. Ouspensky was a Pisces and Nicoll a Cancer, two water signs that are practically designed to get along—the law of fate—so maybe it was written in the stars. Nicoll's love of wine and food and song certainly had something to do with it. The Ouspensky that Nicoll knew tended to be quiet; years later, the journalist Rom Landau would remark regarding Ouspensky's taciturn character that it was "the outcome of an inner command not to talk," and that it was difficult to "carry on a conversation with a man who made no concessions to . . . social conventions."[42] That is, who avoided chitchat. Yet this iron resolve to refrain from small talk had its drawbacks. Count Hermann Keyserling, author of the bestselling *Travel Diary of a Philosopher* (1919), and founder of the School of Wisdom in Darmstadt—which Jung attended on more than one occasion—said that Ouspensky was the most self-controlled individual he had ever met, but that he had too strong a grip on himself.*

Landau and the Count would have been surprised to have met the pre-Gurdjieff Ouspensky, who had the "smells of the tavern" in his blood, who knew the local police and hotel porters, and who was often called on at the Stray Dog Café in St. Petersburg to break up fights and calm his fellow bohemians down. This life-affirming Ouspensky, the Peter in his soul, had been routed by the bullying of his master; it was part of the weakness he had jettisoned *en route* from

---

*According to James Webb, noting some similarities in their work, Keyserling once asked Jung if he and Gurdjieff had ever met. Jung said no.

Russia to London. Now the Demian in him was dominant, the ascetic pessimist who knew *what life was like.* Yet on occasion in the company of Nicoll, Peter emerged briefly and life was good again.

This happened most often at Alley Cottage, at Sidlesham, by the sea.

IN 1926 THE NICOLLS, accompanied by Catherine's sister, moved into a flat in Netherhall Gardens, not far from Maresfield Gardens, in Hampstead, where in 1938 Freud would spend the last year of his life, exiled from a Nazified Austria. The next year they rented the cottage in Sidlesham, and would do so for the following seven. The cottage was surrounded on three sides by marshland and the sea; at high tide the water would reach the garden wall. Every other weekend Ouspensky would accompany Nicoll as they headed to Sidlesham through the night in Nicoll's Buick—Catherine, Jane, and her new nanny having gone on ahead. Here the iron man Ouspensky could relax. Nicoll did the cooking, roughing it on oil stoves, and the rooms were lit by candle-light. There was lobster, borscht—a bid to give Ouspensky some taste of home (he would never see Russia again)—and wine. In a sense it was a replay of the evenings with Jung at Aylesbury, although the guest of honor on these occasions was more introverted and not, as Jung had been, the life of the party.

Ouspensky enjoyed walking by the sea. He usually carried a num-ber of cameras and binoculars with him, and would often look through them at some distant object, without saying a word. Ouspensky said that he slept better at the cottage than in London; it was the sea air that made the difference. He told Nicoll that "One could almost feel the world turning here," a remark that suggests that in Sidlesham he truly managed to relax, not an easy task for a man engaged in a "war against sleep."[43] He enjoyed playing with Nicoll's dog Pushti, and dur-ing his visits made friends with a number of animals, including a mouse and a swan. He would sometimes bring his cat Vashka, who played with Pushti. Ouspensky had a strange relationship with the cat; his hands were often covered in scratches. He complained that Vashka would jump on his bed in the morning and disturb him while he was enjoying his "waking dreams," the hypnagogic visions he wrote about in the chapter "On the Study of Dreams and Hypnotism" in *A New Model of the Universe*. Ouspensky did not care much for the interpretation of dreams à la either Freud or Jung, but he was fascinated with dream states and how they come about and had trained himself to watch his dreams form as he fell asleep.

Ouspensky would often spend an entire day not saying a word, reading a novel, his mind usually on something else. A Russian song Nicoll played for him on his guitar elicited little response, as did an oil portrait Nicoll did of him from a photograph. He did enjoy their visits to the Crab and Lobster, the local pub, where Ouspensky sat and listened to the fishermen sing along to a concertina. On occasion Madame Ouspensky would join him. Along with practically all of his students, she had been exiled by Gurdjieff from Fontainebleau and returned to living with her husband; in 1924, Ouspensky had broken off all relations with Gurdjieff, and indeed suspected that he had gone mad.[44] As accounts from students make clear, Madame O, as she was called, was a kind of female Gurdjieff, lashing out at students' "false personalities" and deflating their pretentious egos with well-placed assessments, an aggressive teaching tactic that the more gentle Ouspensky generally avoided. As the years went by, Madame O would become more and more the real "teacher" in Ouspensky's groups—coming to prominence at Lyne Place, Ouspensky's version of the Prieurè—her more philosophical husband retreating into solitary study and late-night binge sessions.

Ouspensky had a lot to say about diet. He said the English eat far too much meat; he himself ate only a little, and was for the most part vegetarian. One "obvious absurdity" that struck him was when he witnessed Nicoll squeezing juice out of an orange; rather than squeeze six oranges to fill a glass, why not simply eat the orange itself? Another was the ridiculous English habit of eating at strict times rather than when one was hungry. That did more damage than anything else. Accounts of these visits sound very much like what we would expect most people away for a long weekend by the sea would do. The Nicolls and Ouspenskys visited local sites, ate crab and lobster and drank Chablis at different seaside restaurants, took in coastal towns, and engaged in casual small talk (Why had an ocean liner *en route* to Southampton dropped anchor in the water near the Crab and Lobster? Why were so many inns named "The White Hart"?) with even the reticent Ouspensky joining in, adding an occasional esoteric interpretation or aside.

One topic of conversation, at least for Ouspensky, on which he would become expansive, were his reminiscences of old Russia, a theme that would dominate his later years and inform his late-night drinking sessions. On one occasion, Ouspensky told the story of Ouspensky Mountain in the Caucasus, named after one of his ancestors. One of Ouspensky's favorite books was Lermontov's *A Hero of Our Time*, a tale of adventure and mystery set in the Caucasus, and from Nicoll's account of Ouspensky's reminiscences, the nostalgia for his lost homeland that would increasingly burden him was already firmly in place. Gurdjieff was not the only one to travel to remote places in search of knowledge and experience. Ouspensky told Nicoll of his encounters with Circassian chiefs, and how he repaid them for their often-ruinous hospitality by making them presents of revolvers he carried with him. He described in detail the distinctive dress of each tribe and how they were able to drink several bottles of a thick red wine that was almost too powerful for him. "No one realises how big Russia is," he told Nicoll. "There are twenty Switzerlands in the Caucasus" alone.

One odd reference to Ouspensky's motherland Nicoll might not have caught. Nicoll described to Ouspensky the nail-biting motor ride he had had with Gurdjieff, when they went to Switzerland and ate roast goat by the roadside. Ouspensky laughed and said "The Suicide Club." This was the title of a story by Robert Louis Stevenson, an author Ouspensky liked and to whose fable "The Song of the Morrow," he would refer as an example of a work of literature dealing with his favorite theme, "eternal recurrence." But in the St. Petersburg and Moscow that Ouspensky had long left behind, cities filled with the febrile, feverish expectations of the *fin de siècle*, "suicide clubs" were popular. One very fashionable one was named The Black Swan and was presided over by the art collector Nicolai Riabushinsky, and Ouspensky had once given a lecture on Mikhail Artzybasheff's nihilist novel *The Breaking Point*, in which practically all the characters wind up killing themselves.

As Nicoll gradually assumed more responsibility at Ouspensky's meetings, he seemed to gather to himself individuals purposefully sent to him for his help. It may have been their magnetic centers at work, although for one individual the connecting link was nothing more fateful than a referral from a colleague. One new face was that of J. H. Reyner, who later went on to write a slim book about Ouspensky, and other titles related to the Work. Reyner's *Diary of a Modern Alchemist* is an account of his time as Ouspensky's student, and provides a few pictures of Nicoll from this period, although his remark that Nicoll studied with Jung in Vienna suggests that we might take his observations with a grain of salt.[45] Nicoll interpreted some of Reyner's dreams, and suggested that he saw things "upside down." Reyner recalls Nicoll's comments about the "dumb blonde" in our mental office, who was "continually putting incoming calls through to the wrong department," a metaphor that might receive some flak in our oversensitive age. He advised Reyner to go to sleep each night with "a rose on our hearts," wiping the slate clean of the events of the day, a practice advocated by the thirteenth-century Rhineland mystic Meister Eckhart, whom Nicoll read. Another remark Reyner remembers being made by Nicoll was to the effect that "to be eaten by an angel was a moment of bliss," an expression, perhaps, of Gurdjieff's belief that different levels of being provide sustenance for each other but which also seems slightly suggestive of the erotic element that Nicoll seems to have associated with "spiritual experiences."[46]

More important for Nicoll was his meeting with H. Fulford Bush, a lawyer who had spent many years in China, and who in 1926 had been sent to Nicoll on advice by Kenneth Walker. Bush visited Nicoll's surgery on Harley Street for a neurological complaint. Practically from the moment he entered his office he became, in succession, Nicoll's "most responsive patient," his "most loyal supporter," and "most devoted disciple."[47] Although it was Bush who sought out Nicoll for help, the encounter would prove mutually beneficial. Bush speaks of the effect meeting Nicoll had on him, in the hagiographic terms common to those close to Nicoll. Nicoll, he wrote years after the meeting, which was for both parties "momentous," had that mystical something called "presence," "that indefinable quality one so rarely encounters and which is so unmistakable." Like Gurdjieff, H. Fulford Bush had met many "remarkable men" in his travels in the East. They all had "presence" to some degree—that "inner poise" and "dignity born of self-command." But none to the extent that Nicoll possessed it.

At the time of their meeting, Nicoll was of "middle height" and possessed of a "classically shaped head," with "clear-cut features" and "light blues eyes" that saw through you and made evasion impossible, rather as Gurdjieff's piercing eyes were said to do. He had "artistic" and "capable" hands and a voice of an "infinite range of expression." Such was the effect the bedside manner of Dr. Maurice Nicoll had on Mr. Bush.[48]

What was ailing Mr. Bush, Nicoll made him see, was that he lacked "psychological force," the kind of force that Nicoll had gone to Fontainebleau to obtain. Like most people, he believed he possessed what was necessary to carry out his will, but when the time came to do it, something happened, and it was nowhere to be found. What force he had he wasted on unimportant things, one of which was his insistence that other people see things the way he did. Apparently this was something Bush, an old-school Englishman of the time of the Empire, was used to doing, and it took some work to get him to see that there was *another way* to achieve what he wanted. For one thing, he needed to learn how to relax. If he relaxed, so would others around him. Nicoll appealed to Bush's knowledge of the East and spoke in terms of a kind of psychological jiu-jitsu.

Whatever Nicoll said to Bush, it did the trick. Some months after starting his analysis with Nicoll, Bush told him he wanted to give up his legal practice and take up physical education; that is, he wanted to open a gym. Nicoll thought it was an excellent idea, one much more in keeping with Bush's real character, what Nicoll would have called his "essence." Nicoll even advised Bush on how best to go about it. One thing he should incorporate is Gurdjieff's "quick change" tactic; that is, he should break up someone's training routine before it becomes a habit. Another thing was to focus on developing nerve rather than muscle strength; Nicoll insisted that the nerves give out long before the muscles do. He spoke with Bush about psychosomatic illness, something still relatively new and yet to be accepted by the medical establishment.

The most important bit of advice Nicoll had, according to Beryl Pogson, was that "increased use of the mind for new thinking" had immense health benefits, as it put people in contact with a source of energy they were unaware of. Ouspensky's call in *New Model of the Universe* to "think in new categories" most likely never had such an incongruent context as the gym Bush established in his house in

Redcliffe Gardens. Bush was also interested in the esoteric character of Christianity, and through Nicoll he came to a new understanding of the parables and of some aspects of the work of Plato.

If H. Fulford Bush was sent to Nicoll by Kenneth Walker, Frances Ney, from Buffalo, New York, arrived at his doorstep in 1927 by her own volition. She had read *Dream Psychology* and some works of Jung and had traveled across the Atlantic to seek out Dr. Nicoll's insights. As it happened, Nicoll at the time was in need of a secretary. His work was expanding, and his private study was too. Nicoll had taken to spending any free time he had at the Reading Room of the British Museum, a much-hallowed space that had given refuge to a number of famous names: Karl Marx, John Ruskin, H. G. Wells, Bernard Shaw among them. Nicoll was collecting material for an essay he had planned on the Scottish Rosicrucian, Robert Fludd. The Fludd project never saw light—yet another work that Nicoll didn't finish—but Nicoll had given Neys an interesting challenge: to find the source of a quotation about "two streams of knowledge."

This was Nicoll's hint about "esoteric schools," and the traces they left in the construction of the Gothic cathedrals and the works of "wandering scholars." Neys could not find the exact quotation, but she did come upon the curious work known as *The Canon*, which was published anonymously in 1896—we since know the author was William Stirling—and has come to be seen as a source for what is known as "sacred geometry," the proportions and measurements used in the construction of sacred sites, and the "objective art" that Gurdjieff spoke of with Ouspensky. The material that Nicoll read in those afternoons in the Reading Room, works on Greek philosophy, Neoplatonism, the Hermetic writings, Christian mysticism, and Swedenborg, would later find its way into his book *Living Time*, his meditation on the mysteries of eternity, that would, however, not see print until shortly before his death.

Was Ouspensky aware of these developments in his best and closest student's life? He may have been, we don't know for sure. But one thing is certain. After ten years of teaching him, in September, 1931, Ouspensky gave Nicoll what must have been one of his biggest shocks yet. He told Nicoll to "go away." Dramatic pause. Hushed breath. Anxious Nicoll. "Go away, Nicoll," Ouspensky said. "And teach the system."

10

Working at Home

Ouspensky's injunction to Nicoll to leave the Warwick Gardens nest was part of a decision he had made to expand his own work. He had spent the 1920s relatively quietly, having his meetings, working on the manuscript of what would eventually be published as *In Search of the Miraculous*, keeping an eye on what Gurdjieff was up to, and preparing *A New Model of the Universe* for publication. He had been in contact with the system for some fifteen years, the last seven—an important number in Fourth Way cosmology—being spent operating on his own. During that time Gurdjieff's fortunes had taken a roller-coaster ride. His relations with Orage were about to rupture, his finances were minimal—he would soon have to leave the Prieuré for good—his reputation was at a low, he had put on weight, and his health was not at its best. He had cast off many of his closest followers, like the de Hartmanns. The Wall Street Crash had not helped. Although Gurdjieff had completed his eccentric masterpiece *Beelzebub's Tales to His Grandson*, it could not find a publisher, and would not find one until after his death. According to one of his biographers, Gurdjieff "had a positive relish for living from hand to mouth."[1] If so, it seemed that this taste for life "on the edge" was sorely tried at this time.

Ouspensky on the other hand was in a secure position. But the time had come, he felt, to move on to a new "octave," an important term in the Work, referring to the process by which events come about following the "law of seven." He could carry on behind the scenes as it were, or he could go public. He decided on this second option. In the fall of 1930, Ouspensky gave a series of public lectures on "The Search for Objective Consciousness," the highest rung on the ladder of our "possible evolution," and something he had reported on from experience in perhaps his single most important piece of writing, the essay on "Experimental Mysticism" in *A New Model of the Universe*. The aim of the lectures was to attract more people to his meetings. As early as 1926 he had told Rosamund Sharp—wife of the editor Clifford Sharp and one of his closest students—that "the system is waiting for workers." Now apparently he believed it was time to draw them in.

One who was brought back into the fold was Bennett, who had been in Ouspensky's bad books for some time and who would now, with the departure of Nicoll, play a more important role in his groups. When Ouspensky met with his prodigal student, he told Bennett that he had waited many years "to see what Gurdjieff would do." Ouspensky assured Bennett that "there is a Great Source from which our system comes," and that Gurdjieff had had contact with this. But it was not a "complete contact." Something, he believed, was missing. He wasn't sure if Gurdjieff had found it—he was, in fact, certain that he hadn't—and if they could not find what was missing through him, their only hope was to find "a direct contact with the source," with, that is, the Inner Circle itself. But they had no chance of finding this contact on their own (although years later, Bennett would indeed make the effort), so they had to do their best to attract attention to themselves, in the hope that "the source will seek us out." "If those who have the real knowledge," Ouspensky told Bennett, "see that we are useful to them, they may send someone."[2]

It would be this idée fixe concerning the Inner Circle, combined with Ouspensky's innate pessimism and romanticism, that would eventually kill him, through what can be seen as a slow process of drinking himself to death. He had taken to heart Gurdjieff's austere dictum that a man alone can *do absolutely nothing*, and had given up all efforts to achieve anything on his own, in effect castrating his own creativity. After leaving one teacher and setting up for himself, his only hope of any future, after all his struggle, it seems, was to find yet another teacher, yet another emissary of the Inner Circle. He was still in search of the miraculous although, as we've seen, he had encountered it once or twice already. One might have pointed him in the direction of *Tertium Organum*, and the exhilarating optimism it had generated in its readers, and which its author clearly felt, writing its inspired pages. Yet all Ouspensky could think of in that regard was that it was his "weakness." Yet it was a weakness that he might have looked to in order to find some strength.

Along with the lecture series, the publication of *A New Model of the Universe* was designed to send signals out to a readership intelligent and interested enough to recognize that it was peppered with hints and slightly camouflaged clues relating to a special teaching that Ouspensky only alluded to and never spoke of openly. These hints would draw in suitable students, and would also send a message to the Inner Circle— assuming, of course, that it existed and that its agents had bought a copy of the book. Whether they did or not is unclear; as I mention in my book about Ouspensky, he seems never to have considered the possibility that emissaries from the Great Source might have come to his lectures and read his book and decided *not* to get in touch. Certainly others in the Work were not impressed by *A New Model of the Universe*, Orage's quip about it being a "new muddle of the universe" expressing the general assessment. But by this time the Gurdjieff vs. Ouspensky schism had opened, the "struggle of the magicians" had begun, and the long, convoluted and often petty history of the animosity felt by either side for the other was underway.

Orage might not have cared for the book, but others certainly did.

Perhaps the biggest high-profile name among its readers was that of the novelist and playwright J. B. Priestley.

Priestley, like Ouspensky, was a "time-haunted man," and in the playbill for *I Have Been Here Before*, his play about "eternal recurrence" that debuted on September 22, 1937, he made clear his debt to Ouspensky and his "astonishing book."[3] Priestley would ponder questions of time and eternal recurrence throughout his career, and address the idea specifically in his classic work *Man and Time*, where he also looks at Nicoll's work *Living Time*.* Priestley tried repeatedly to meet Ouspensky, but Ouspensky's pessimism and paranoia—he would accuse Priestley of "stealing" his ideas—prevented this. Ouspensky failed to recognize that having someone like Priestley discussing his ideas— a popular writer who would soon become a household name during the coming war because of his radio broadcasts—would be an excellent means of bringing in the workers needed for the system.† Gurdjieff would have reeled Priestley in forthwith, or at least would have tried to ensnare him. Ouspensky kept his distance.‡

As DID NICOLL, at least from Ouspensky. Becoming a teacher of the Work in his own right meant that Nicoll had to cut ties with his own

---

*Some of Priestley's most important reflections on Ouspensky's work and on time in general can be found in his autobiographical books *Midnight on the Desert* (1937) and *Rain upon Godshill* (1939).

†Other writers who spoke highly of *A New Model of the Universe* or were influenced by it include Aldous Huxley, Jorge Luis Borges, and Malcolm Lowry. Ouspensky's reclusiveness did not prevent him from hosting a visit by Huxley and his guru, Gerald Heard, to Lyne Place, the large mansion in Virginia Water, outside of London, that Ouspensky decamped to in the mid-1930s. Ouspensky knew enough of Huxley's reputation to know that if he wrote about his work, it would reach a large number of intelligent readers. Why he failed to see this about Priestley remains unclear, especially given their shared character as "time-haunted men."

‡Oddly enough, Priestley became a great reader of Jung around the same time; the two would meet in 1946. See Vincent Brome, *J. B. Priestley*, 288.

teacher, and become absolutely independent. By some accounts, the parting between the two was not as amicable or dramatic as Nicoll told it, and may have been much more abrupt.[4] Other reports suggest a show of humor on Ouspensky's part, or a manifestation of what Jung would have called "inflation." When asked why he had commanded his right-hand man to leave and set up shop on his own, Ouspensky is said to have replied "Well, God gave his only begotten son."[5] As we have no diary from this time, we don't have a clear idea of what Nicoll might have felt. Later though, in his diaries from the late 1940s, there is evidence that Nicoll felt guilty in some way about his relationship with Ouspensky, just as letters written to Jung during this time—after long years of silence—show a similar sense of regret. In the Fourth Way there is a tradition of harsh, if not actually cruel partings between teacher and student, and Nicoll may have thought better about this tactic down the line.*

Nicoll's inaugural meeting as a fully fledged instructor in the Fourth Way was held on September 9, 1931, at the studio of his "first lieutenant," Fulford Bush, in Redcliffe Gardens.[6] Exactly how many people attended is unclear; Samuel Copley suggests no more than twenty to twenty-five people were in the group.[7] Catherine remained Ouspensky's student until his death in 1947, but one imagines she was on hand. A few others from the Warwick Gardens group joined Nicoll's offshoot, but most of the small group was made up of people Nicoll had met and spoken with. Copley tells us that he brought in a rugby player who showed promise.[8] Fulford Bush brought in his two sisters, at whose home in Kensington some later meetings were held; Harley Street, too, was similarly commandeered into service. Bush also brought in his secretary, and some of the people who frequented his gym. Bush became indispensable to Nicoll. He organized the meetings, was the

*See, for example, the story of Gurdjieff refusing to see his longtime student Alexandre de Salzman in his last days. Webb, *The Harmonious Circle,* 435.

group's treasurer, provided the space, and in general took care of all the practical business involved, leaving Nicoll free to concentrate on communicating the ideas.

Nicoll continued seeing patients in Harley Street, and one who became a member of his group has left an account of how she found herself seeking him out for help. In a state of despair she heard the name "Maurice Nicoll" pop into her head and stay there.[9] She didn't know who he was or why his name should have come to her. Finally she remembered that she had heard it from a friend, who had gone to Nicoll for help. She needed help too and decided to track him down. In a phone box she looked up the name; there were two Maurice Nicolls and she rang the number with a Harley Street address. An appointment was made. After seeing Nicoll a few times, he asked if she would like to attend a meeting of a group he was leading. She did, and soon found herself walking into the gym at Redcliffe Gardens.

Although he had cut his esoteric apron strings, in the early days of Nicoll's group the scene was much as it had been at Warwick Gardens. Four rows of straight-backed chairs faced a small table, a chair, and a blackboard. When she entered the room, Nicoll's anonymous student was told to sit wherever she liked. But Nicoll had already instructed her to sit in the front row, so she did, apparently passing her first "test." After some time, Nicoll entered, paying no attention to his audience. He sat before them, his eyes "lowered," remaining silent. The tension began to mount given that, as at Warwick Gardens, no one made a sound. Finally, someone plucked up the courage to ask a question. After speaking around that question for an hour or so, Nicoll simply said "Well, we'll stop now," and left, as unconcernedly as he had entered.

The apple doesn't fall far from the tree, and in the early days of his group Nicoll maintained the "cloak of secrecy" that had annoyed Kenneth Walker on his first visit to Warwick Gardens. People were not to speak about what they had heard at the meetings, except to people who might possibly be candidates for membership. Of these there turned out to be not many. Members of the group were surprised to realize how few of their acquaintances would possibly be open to the idea of building an ark, and how pointless it would be to talk to them about the teaching they were exploring. Any who did show an interest were asked to attend a certain number of meetings before they decided to continue or not. If they decided that the system wasn't for them, they had to consent to not speaking about it to anyone else, accepting a kind of gag order or nondisclosure agreement. As at Warwick Gardens, cars were to be parked a few streets away, people entered and left only in ones and twos, never *en masse*, and no one was to linger about after the meeting. Once again, these security measures were chalked up to Ouspensky's Russianness—or paranoia, depending on how one saw it— and suggest that the atmosphere of Warwick Gardens reached out to the new workplace, at least in its early days.

This could been seen in the stringently formal tone of the meetings, at least the early ones. "In the middle thirties," Copley writes, "we were more formal than in the post war years."[10] People were addressed as Mr., Mrs., or Miss So-and-So, never by their Christian or, as they came to be known, "essence" name. Copley was once taken to task for using a shortened version of someone's Christian name. His Australian good nature was to blame. "Damned colonials," one of Nicoll's more proper students remarked, "always trying to establish a low level of equality and intimacy from the word go."[11] (What, one wonders, would he have thought of an American?) Why being friendly, as one assumes Copley was, should generate a "low level of equality and intimacy" is not immediately clear. What does come across is the stuffiness and snootiness of some of Nicoll's followers, a character trait that could be found in Ouspensky's students as well, and, sad to say, often in Ouspensky and Nicoll too. One also wonders if anyone took Copley's critic to task for expressing some very negative emotions or for failing to generate enough "external considering" to give him the benefit of the doubt.

This formal character informed the dress and speech code at the meetings. Nicoll "did not approve of slovenly dress or speech," seeing in the notion of dressing up and being "well-spoken" a measure of discipline and a show of respect for the Work, rather as one put on one's Sunday best to head to church.[12] It made the women more "womanly" and the men more "manly," distinctions that would raise an eyebrow or two today. As Copley explains it, the idea was more or less to maintain a certain dignity and not "go native." Nicoll, he writes, had "some sympathy for those pre-war Britons in outposts of Empire who dressed for dinner in the jungle and maintained standards of social convention," which sounds rather like an appreciation of the Raj and an esoteric "white man's burden," with "sleeping humanity" the indigenous people. Perhaps even more suggestive is Copley's comparison of the group's formal requirements to those inmates of a "prisoner of war camp" who "kept themselves and their camps clean, shaved, dressed as well as they could, had regular exercise, Church parades and so on," and who because of this "had a better chance of coming through with a good morale and psychologically undamaged" than those who didn't.

This is undoubtedly true—it is good to keep a clean house and run a tight ship—and Copley's metaphor of a prison camp reminds us that Gurdjieff believed we were all in a similar situation, although one remembers Bennett's remarks about the filth and lack of hygiene at the Prieuré, and the masterstroke of Mrs. Beaumont's flypaper. Discipline certainly helps to dispel laziness. Yet a certain air of elitism and superiority, of belonging to a better class of people than the scruffy hoi polloi, does seem to be present here. One recognizes that for all his desire to satisfy that burning hunger for a "more than conventional life," that cast him out of Chester Terrace, Nicoll certainly embraced many of the conventions of his class and upbringing. And again we are reminded of the irony that many hippie households and their scruffy inhabitants had copies of Gurdjieff, Ouspensky, and Nicoll on their untidy bookshelves.

One also wonders what part Nicoll's own psychology played in his penchant for dressing up and not succumbing to sloth and slovenliness. Hester Lord, who joined the group around this time, notes that she believed Nicoll "positively enjoyed cleanliness," and that one of her "cherished recollections" is of Nicoll "in white shirt and flannels, Panama hat on head, pipe in mouth, hands in pockets, snow white pumps on feet," walking across a field or across "the kitchen floor I had just washed."[13] "Nicoll nearly always looked immaculate," Lord writes, and photographs of Nicoll do give the impression of an Englishman properly dressed for his holiday; he would not seem out of place in an episode of *Poirot*. Yet when we recall Nicoll's self-torture over his "unclean thoughts," we can't help but wonder if this penchant for being well pressed and tidy can be understood as a form of compensation, a fetish to keep at bay the fantasies that, although we have no evidence for this being so at this time, we have every reason to assume he continued to pursue.

WHAT DID NICOLL TELL HIS GROUP in the first meeting? Beryl Pogson was not there—she would not join Nicoll's group until 1935—but she does give us a general idea of what Nicoll spoke about.[14] He told them about the Fourth Way, whose followers remain in life—they do not retire to caves or ashrams—but are not "of" it, a status associated with Jesus but also with the Sufis. The teaching of the Fourth Way is guarded from those who would distort it (as Ouspensky increasingly believed happened with Gurdjieff, and which Gurdjieff accused Ouspensky and practically everyone else of doing), yet it could be said to be hidden in plain sight. The teaching of the Fourth Way is not locked away in safes or vaults or hidden chambers, but can be found encoded in many monuments and artifacts of the past: in the Gothic cathedrals, in the strange writings of the medieval alchemists, in fairy tales, and in one of Nicoll's additions, the art of chivalry.* As noted, they were not to speak about this to people outside the group. The teaching they were receiving had been handed down through the ages, solely to those who could understand it. It came from a higher source. They were receiving instructions in how to "walk on the waters of life," as Christ did, an ability, it seems, sought by Eastern yogis as well.[15] Although to the plebeian— we might even say pedestrian—mind, this was a miracle, a work of magic, and to the sceptical one it was impossible, to Nicoll it symbolized the detachment from "life" and its meaninglessness and the entry into something *other*, that he had craved practically all his conscious life.

Some notes of Nicoll's "first instructions to his group" fill out Pogson's outline.[16] At the start, we might say, of his ministry, Nicoll impressed on his first gathering the importance of one's personal attitude toward the Work. One had to see that when the Work spoke of "sleep" and "mechanicalness," that it applied to *you*. *You* are asleep. *You* are mechanical. Not that person over there, although undoubtedly he or she is asleep too. That was the beginning of the self-knowledge they sought. The ideas had to have this emotional impact or they would stimulate interest for a time, but soon lose their potency. Nicoll's experience as a psychologist would help here; the first step in overcoming a neurosis is recognizing you have one. At Ouspensky's meetings Nicoll was always able to relate the ideas Ouspensky was presenting to his own immediate—we might say existential—experience, to unpack their emotional force, and to translate to others the true significance of what they were attempting, which was nothing less than a change of *being*, a work

---

*This linkage of a hidden teaching to the medieval knightly system was shared, although not in the context of the Work, with at least two important figures in twentieth-century esotericism, the Italian esoteric philosopher Julius Evola, and the French maverick Egyptologist and alchemist, René Schwaller de Lubicz, both of whom embraced radical far-right political ideals. See my *Politics and the Occult* (Wheaton, Il: Quest Books, 2008), 183–93 and 212–20.

of self-transformation. He was the only one, Ouspensky said, "who would really speak to him emotionally about what he had said at a meeting."[17]

Yet this work is not for everyone. It is a teaching for "widows and orphans." It is for those who feel "lost inside," who have no idea about the meaning of their lives—which suggests that it should not have suited someone like Kenneth Walker, whom we know made a point of expressing his satisfaction with life. It is certainly not for those who accept the laws of heredity and Darwinian evolution, nor the second law of thermodynamics. If we believe that we live in a "dying universe," which the second law of thermodynamics—or, as it is also known, entropy—tells us we do, we can't possibly "remember ourselves." Entropy tells us that the energy of the universe is running down, and will sooner or later eventuate in a lukewarm, featureless cosmic soup. The Fourth Way says that the universe is alive and intelligent and is growing through what it calls the "ray of creation," a nod, perhaps, to the "seven rays" of Theosophical cosmology.

Darwin tells us that we have descended from the apes. The Fourth Way tells us that we are creatures created for a specific cosmic purpose, to transmit energies that facilitate the universe's growth. Nicoll will later say that our essence "comes down from the stars," not from our parents, and that all our work is to "lead us back to where we have originally come from." This Hermetic trope is one of the several extracurricular ideas that Nicoll brought into the Work. As we've seen, in the Hermetic tradition, we descend from the stars through the seven ancient planets, acquiring limitations on our being along the way.[18] The Hermetic work is aimed at freeing ourselves of these limitations, and making our return ascent to our source, through a "journey through the planets," which is very much like the Fourth Way motif of rising on the "ray of creation" and becoming subject to fewer and fewer "laws." Certain energies are needed to make this ascent, and in his first meeting Nicoll introduced his group to the "food diagram" that charts the transformation of lower foods into higher energies.

We consume three kinds of food: the usual food we eat; the air we breathe; and another nutrient, our *impressions*, our perceptions of the world. Through certain efforts we can transform these foods into the energies needed for working on ourselves.

We have already seen the importance Gurdjieff placed on seeing "without associations," that is, freshly, without our preconceptions getting in the way. When asked what being conscious in essence would be like, he replied "Everything more vivid." Gurdjieff insisted that, although a man could live for a certain amount of time without food, and could go without breathing for at least a few minutes, without impressions, he would die in seconds. This seems to suggest again that Gurdjieff held the "blank slate" view of the mind: without stimulus from the outer world, we are like puppets without strings. Experiments in sensory deprivation chambers and the challenge of the "black room" seem to corroborate Gurdjieff's belief.[19] Placed in a pitch dark, soundless, scentless room, most people soon go to pieces, the lack of sensory input leaving them open to attack by their own neuroses and fears. One aim of the Work is to eliminate those fears through a war of attrition, starving them by not allowing oneself to express "negative emotions."

ALTHOUGH SCHOOLED IN THE STYLE of Ouspensky, Nicoll's approach differed considerably from his master's. In fact, Nicoll told Copley that he considered himself a "subtype" of Gurdjieff, meaning, one assumes, that he modeled his Work persona on him.[20] Copley assures us that Nicoll didn't "suffer from the 'Heir Apparent' syndrome" that infected others who had encountered Gurdjieff, yet one might wonder what Gurdjieff would have thought of the kitchen boy who was now taking him as his model. Nicoll would have been the first to recognize the "transference" that was taking place. And although subject to the same phenomenon himself—both as a therapist and as a teacher—it is true, as Copley remarks, that very few people "do not identify with the teacher of the Work."[21] What this meant in Nicoll's case was that where Ouspensky was "definite," Gurdjieff was "vague," and that he, Nicoll, fell more in the vague camp than the definite one, something that should not surprise us.

Ouspensky's writings are clarity themselves, and a look at the records of his meetings show that he always strove to make his point as unambiguously as possible, and dismissed all questions of a general nature. Gurdjieff left a great deal for the student to discover for himself, and often was so general that no two students could agree on what he had said, something Bennett noted in his account.[22] Where Ouspensky would patiently—sometimes not so—spell out step-by-step some aspect of the Work with the rigor one might expect in a mathematics teacher, Nicoll would often resort to a kind of pantomime, to gesture and metaphor to get his message across, hoping the student would "catch" it.[23] Not all did, but those who were able to, experienced an emotional connection that, as we've seen, was a rare event with Ouspensky.

Yet Nicoll's being Gurdjieff's "subtype" did not prevent him from unbuttoning about the master on occasion. Gurdjieff was undoubtedly a "conscious man," but not, Nicoll told Copley, all the time.[24] Like Homer, even Gurdjieff nodded. As mentioned, not everything that happened at the Prieuré was planned, and the inconveniences that arose were not always of Gurdjieff's making. And some of his behavior Nicoll found positively repugnant; exactly what, he didn't say, but we can imagine. But even with these reservations, Gurdjieff's position was unassailable. He was a "round man who could not be judged or criticised on any one particular point on his circumference, but only taken as a whole."[25]

MEETINGS CONTINUED AT BUSH'S GYM for some time, supplemented by occasional gatherings at Harley Street—where Nicoll often met students one-on-one—and at Bush's sisters' flat. But eventually, as the group grew, it became clear that a proper hall dedicated to the meetings was needed, something like Warwick Gardens. Ouspensky, whose own groups swelled after the publication of *A New Model of the Universe*, would himself soon move to his new London location of Colet House, Baron's Court, where the Study Society, based on his work, continues today.[26] Suitable locations for the group's new meeting place were investigated, and in the end a large studio in a dancing school in Finchley Road, North London, not far from Frognal, where Nicoll grew up, was chosen.* Whether the fact that Gurdjieff was known as a "dance instructor," and that his movements were the central part of his teaching, had anything to do with the choice is unknown, but one can't deny a certain symbolic element here.

The lectures at the new location were based for the most part on the material that would be published posthumously in 1954 as Ouspensky's *The Psychology of Man's Possible Evolution,* the last thing he wrote, and passages from what would become *In Search of the Miraculous.* Students were allowed to take notes and to copy the diagrams on the blackboard, with the proviso that these could be confiscated at any time and possibly destroyed, another hangover from Ouspensky's paranoia.

Copley was brought into the group by a friend from a swimming club, and early on he was subjected to the kind of psychological stress that was par for this course.[27] As at Warwick Gardens, some members were often asked to start the meetings by taking questions, getting the group going, as it were, rather as an opening act warms up the audience for the main show. Nicoll's "sub-Gurdjieff" style included something like a kind of pantomime, with a male student sitting alongside him at the table, and acting out a Work lesson, hoping the group would "catch" it. On one occasion, Copley was asked to start a meeting, after

---

*I have not been able to discover exactly which dancing school this was, but I suspect it may have been the Aida Forster Theatre School, which opened on Finchley Road, Golders Greene, in 1929 and closed in 1970. We remember that Nicoll's first surgery was in Golders Greene.

which Nicoll would take it up after ten minutes. Copley agreed, but when he arrived at the meeting he was surprised to see the members of his swimming club filling the seats. These were the "cheerful, beer-drinking, water polo players and singers of bawdy songs" that he had met with in many pubs.[28] Now he was supposed to introduce them to ideas about esoteric knowledge and having descended from the stars. Copley thought he could get through the ten minutes he had agreed to, but Nicoll never appeared. He continued for an hour and with still no sign of Nicoll, he closed the meeting. Needless to say, none of his fellow swimmers surfaced at the meetings again.

On another occasion Nicoll handed Copley some questions from the group that he said were stupid. He wanted Copley to ask them, "for the benefit of someone else." Copley agreed, but as the meeting drew to a close, he had yet to ask the first question. He caught Nicoll's eye and realized whose benefit he really had in mind. It was a lesson in pride and ego, spelling out to Copley how afraid he was to look foolish.

Yet Nicoll himself was not so afraid. He had already assured Copley that he knew what it was like to "play the sacrificial fool," and if acting silly could help someone "catch" what he was tossing at them—or scare them away, as the case may be—he was all for it. At one meeting, Nicoll picked up the table in front of him and tried to walk through the doorway with it. When he couldn't he complained that builders always make the doorways too narrow. When one of Nicoll's "stooges" said "But why not put the table down?" he received the indignant reply "What table? This is I, Dr. Nicoll." The point of the pantomime was to show that our essence is "blocked" by all the hard edges of our personality, which bangs up against everything and makes difficulties. If we can divest ourselves of some of it—lose a leg or two—we will see how much more easily we can pass through situations. At later meetings, members would engage in a variation of "musical chairs," carrying their chairs (personalities) around the room, and bumping into one another.

Copley remarks on something that would become a larger part of

Nicoll's practice some years later. When he began attending meetings, Copley lived with his mother. He stuck to the "oath of secrecy," so when she asked where he was going every Thursday evening and what he was doing, he was evasive. This led his mother to worry. He didn't want to cause her concern, but he also wanted to stick to the rules. Eventually he spoke with Nicoll about it. He suggested that he tell his mother that he was attending lectures that dealt with ideas along the lines of the New Thought philosophy of Ralph Waldo Trine and Henry Drummond, authors of the "mental science" classics *In Tune with the Infinite* (1910) and *Natural Law in the Spiritual World* (1884). Copley was surprised that Nicoll knew his mother read this kind of literature, but Nicoll told him it was fairly common among women of her generation.

Trine, Drummond, Ernest Holmes, and other New Thought authors do not immediately suggest themselves as "gateway" sages to the Work. Generally their writings would be considered to fall within a very watered-down version of C influences, of a homeopathic potency, that is, diluted to the extreme. Yet during World War II, when many of Nicoll's students were either involved in the fighting, or were in London during the Blitz, Nicoll and others engaged in exercises in "visualization," picturing those in danger being safe. Such "visualizing" is the key to New Thought, which takes as its maxim that "thoughts are things" and can be projected into the world with real effect, something we've seen Nicoll knew of and may have practiced himself. This is a far cry from Gurdjieff's maxim that man "cannot do." Nicoll's link to New Thought seems acknowledged by the homage paid to him by a later "mental science" teacher, Neville Goddard, who was fond of what we can see as a mantra of sorts of Nicoll's, "your level of being attracts your life," which Neville quotes in several of his books.

Copley remarks that at one point in the early thirties, Nicoll's group attended a meeting of Ouspensky's at Warwick Gardens, at which Nicoll resumed his old position of lieutenant. The general impression was of the "cold formality" of Ouspensky's meetings, compared to the rather more unbuttoned gatherings at the dance hall. Copley recalls a few of these meetings, which suggest that Nicoll had not cut his ties with his teacher as completely as one might have suspected. Indeed, James Webb states that on at least two later occasions, Nicoll visited Ouspensky, once at Hayes House in Gadsden, Kent, and on another "special celebration" at Lyne Place. "On both occasions," Webb writes, "a large quantity of drink was consumed," and Nicoll "became highly critical."[29] He is said to have told his ex-teacher that he had "gone soft," and had come too much under his wife's—the formidable Madame O's—influence.

Sadly, by all accounts, this was true. As Ouspensky retreated more and more from his students and any outer, non-Work activities, into the life of a country gentlemen and his late-night boozing, Madame O became the real teacher. Kenneth Walker and Bennett, among others, have left accounts of her teaching style, which consisted of the deft puncturing of inflated egos and puffed up false personalities, with her own husband's numbering among them. We get an idea of what being around Ouspensky's common-law wife—there is doubt they were ever legally married—was like, from a remark of Walker's. He comments about how "dumbfounded" his friends would be, if they were transported to one of Madame O's soirees, to find him, and other "reasonably intelligent people," sitting "at the feet of a woman who seemingly did nothing but insult us."[30] Gurdjieff we know pulled no punches, but the exercise can easily backfire. Mrs. Beaumont was cold-shouldered by Ouspensky's group, and the demands Bennett made on their relationship because of his increasing involvement in the Work led to her making a suicide attempt, by taking an overdose of sleeping pills, a perhaps symbolic method of eliminating herself.

We know alcohol plays a large part in the Work. Gurdjieff's "toasts to the idiots" are legendary, and even Ouspensky's boozing was seen by some as a teaching strategy, "an acid test whereby those weaker members who had fallen by the wayside through over-indulgence . . . lived to regret it."[31] Perhaps. Bennett recounts one all-night session during which he enjoyed an "out of the body experience," after finishing off several bottles of wine with his teacher. But not all were so rewarded for their perseverance and fortitude. Robert S. de Ropp, whose early work *Drugs and the Mind* (1957) made him something of a psychedelic authority in the 1960s, began attending Ouspensky's groups at Lyne Place in the late 1930s. In his autobiography, *Warrior's Way* (1980), de Ropp remarks about the number of times he "sat up with Ouspensky . . . drinking far more than was good for me, losing sleep in vain waiting for him to let fall some pearls of wisdom. But the pearls rarely fell."[32] What de Ropp was treated to were Ouspensky's memories of Russia, of pre-Bolshevik St. Petersburg, the Stray Dog Café and the life that Ouspensky had long ago left behind. Yet on one topic, Ouspensky did deliver. When de Ropp hazarded a guess that, when all was said and done, Gurdjieff must have been a "strange man," Ouspensky came to attention. "Strange?" he asked de Ropp. "He was extraordinary! You cannot possibly imagine how extraordinary Gurdjieff was."

Nicoll, too, would sometimes use alcohol as an aid in performing some Work duty that he would otherwise find impossible. Hester Lord tells us that although Nicoll would on occasion feign drunkenness, or at least being tipsy, to "shock" one of his group, more than once she saw him truly in his cups. Nicoll told Lord that "he had to drink in order to be able to tell people what he had to tell them, or to give them a jolt out of their self-complacency," which by today's health-conscious standards, sounds awfully like dependency.[33] As his later diaries tell us, more than once Nicoll had to put himself temporarily on the wagon, or at least had to seriously monitor his intake. Unlike Ouspensky, who positively disliked it, Nicoll took up Gurdjieff's tactic of "acting," although, with him too, it was often difficult to know what was an act and what wasn't. On one occasion Catherine warned Lord that they were "going to have a bad time" that evening. One of the group was bringing along a woman he intended to marry, and according to Mr. and Mrs. Nicoll, "she won't do at all."[34] They planned to "put her off," and succeeded, by having a "drunk and lewd evening," one of the worst Lord could remember—which suggests that such evenings were not that uncommon. The woman never returned, although the fellow they saved from a fate worse than death—or so it must have seemed to them—continued attending for some years afterward.

Without knowing the people involved, it is hard to judge whether this was a kind of divine intervention—something any group of friends who truly believed one of them was making a big mistake might do—or esoteric busy-bodying, the kind of control exerted over their followers that the leaders of some cults enjoy. We know that Gurdjieff disapproved of Jesse Dwight. But then she and Orage were both more strong-minded than Nicoll's student and potential wife evidently were. Ouspensky was always delighted when two of his group got together and married and made it a cause for celebration. There are no reports—at least I haven't come across any—that show he interfered with any of his students' marriage plans.

Beryl Pogson, too, was brought into the group through friends. She had recently divorced her husband and moved to Hampstead, and over dinner with her new neighbors heard about the lectures they were attending and which they thought she might find of interest.[35] She was not undergoing a crisis; she makes a point of saying that she knew nothing of psychology and agreed to go to the lectures sheerly out of curiosity. Newly divorced and out to make new friends, it seems a perfectly natural thing to do. She had no idea that this decision would change her life. At that meeting she didn't feel any of the tension that others reported. What struck her was Nicoll's "fine quality of mind," and the "quiet way" in which he answered questions.[36] There was no immediate sense of "this is it," of the kind that Nicoll experienced that evening at the Quest Society back in 1921. In fact, she found the lectures a bit confusing, the material discussed one week was not followed up the next, which left her unsure how it all fit together—this, we remember, was the piecemeal way that Gurdjieff had taught. When she heard a section of what would become *In Search of the Miraculous* read to the group, she was disappointed to learn that there was no printed copy that she could study. The teaching, she was told, was entirely oral.

Her friends did suggest reading *A New Model of the Universe*, and this did the trick. The chapter on "Christianity and the New Testament" impressed her forcefully. It was a moment in which she had the distinct knowledge that what she was reading here was something she knew long ago but *had forgotten*. Plato had said that all knowledge is remembering, and Pogson now saw the truth of that insight. The Work, too, was all about remembering. If the ideas that she was hearing at the meetings she was attending were part of what Ouspensky called "esoteric Christianity," then she was determined to continue and to make them the center of her life. She was so taken with *A New Model* that after finishing it she went on to *Tertium Organum*.

Pogson has left us an account of what a one-on-one meeting with Dr. Nicoll was like. She had received instruction to report to Harley Street. When she arrived, she found Nicoll sitting, not at his desk, but near the fire. She was a bit in awe of the surroundings—Harley Street is as upmarket as it comes, so one imagines Nicoll's consulting rooms were well-appointed—and had to submit to some "stern words" that shook her "out of her self-pity."[37] Then they had a chat, during which Nicoll "read" her psychologically. This was something Nicoll would do with Copley and other members of the group when they retired of an evening to the Café Royal and Nicoll, Sherlock Holmes–like, would inform his group of Watsons about the secret life of the other habitués.[38]

As with his secretary Frances Ney, Nicoll gave Pogson some research work to do, a therapy to help focus her mind and introduce her to the history of some of the ideas she was hearing about at the meetings. He suggested that she compile an anthology of writings about death. This was a project he had intended to do himself, but had never got around to. She agreed eagerly and she tells us that the work became a "great solace" to her, although what became of the anthology itself is unclear.[39] Nevertheless the project allowed her to become reacquainted with works she had read years ago—Plato, Plutarch, Herodotus, Epictetus, Marcus Aurelius—but now she could detect something of the Work in them. She came to see that "many of the psychological truths" they were studying "had been expressed long ago in Greece and Rome."[40] Pogson even records a synchronicity, one of Jung's "meaningful coincidences," around her reading. One evening she felt urged to take Plato's *Republic* off the shelf, were it had been collecting dust. She read it all that day, and was surprised to hear Nicoll suggest at the meeting that evening that everyone read Plato's *Republic*. Pogson was surprised to find that she had been "in tune" with the group beforehand, thinking in advance along the lines they would be discussing. Nicoll often suggested to his students that they read the *Republic* as a work of psychology, and not only politics. Copley found it "fascinating" to wonder what part of his own being corresponded to Plato's ideal state, when philosophers would be king, and what part the tyrants, the oligarchs, the *demos* or crowd of "I's," each clamoring for attention, while the myth of the cave was a clear variant on the idea of "sleep."[41]

Copley, too, gives us some insights into meeting with Nicoll one-on-one. Copley did not meet with Nicoll at Harley Street often, but the few occasions when he did, his visits were of "inestimable value." Copley enjoyed the freedom to speak and the opportunity to "sweep away" a lot of "useless junk." It was an unusual experience to feel that someone was actually listening to what he had to say. At the same time, he felt unusually able to *hear* what was said to him. He also had an opportunity to see Nicoll a bit more unbuttoned than at the evening meetings. Like many Fourth Way students, Copley was doing his best not to act mechanically, and when he caught himself absentmindedly rubbing the edge of Nicoll's desk with his finger, he abruptly stopped. Nicoll noticed this and told him not to. "Give the dog a bone," Nicoll said. "It is more important to keep the train of thought alive than to stop this action which keeps Moving Centre happy and does not use much force."[42]

So some mechanical behavior—habits—are not that bad. Copley records that Nicoll himself exhibited them—or was he "acting"? Copley writes that Nicoll had a habit of overstuffing his pipe with tobacco, so much that it tumbled down his waistcoat, then trying to light it with a match, that often went out before it reached the bowl. He did this repeatedly throughout their conversation. Was he sleeping? Or was he giving Copley an opportunity to "see" him, and so abort a "transference"? Copley records that these early talks with Nicoll helped him through a difficult time with his father, and with overcoming certain traits in his behavior—a certain stinginess—that had accumulated over time and become automatic.

NOT LONG AFTER NICOLL HAD RECEIVED Ouspensky's blessing to go away and teach the system, he and Catherine began to spend time with Miss C. M. Lydall, who had been at the Prieuré. Miss Lydall had a house at Rayne, near Braintree in Essex, northeast of London, called Lake Farms. The house was surrounded by a "sea of mud," yet once this was safely crossed, one found an attractive old gabled structure, bordered by flowers and fruit trees, with a veranda in the back and some livestock—pigs, hens, sheep, and rabbits. The Nicolls began to spend weekends there and gradually invited select students to join them. Catherine would cook, and the place began to take on the character of ceaseless activity that had been the case at Fontainebleau, although downsized to just two people. The two were "tremendously active," Catherine with cooking and gardening, Nicoll with his writing or with working in his woodshop, an encore of the Prieuré and a pastime that will become more and more part of his routine.

Two early visitors, Selene Moxon and Sunday Wilshin, who joined the group in 1932, wound up buying a cottage named Wymers—the British have an odd penchant for naming houses—in nearby Little

Sailing. Nicoll took to visiting them when he was at Lake Farms alone and to having his dinner there. He also started what became something of a tradition, staying up into the wee hours with Moxon and Wilshin, and talking. On the early occasions of these all-nighters, Nicoll was fortified by something less substantial than Ouspensky's Chardonnay. Apparently he was fond of "biscuits attractively spread with cream cheese or patum peperium" an anchovy paste, and ate these "absent-mindedly but with evident appreciation." A bone he gave his dog, a "test," or simply late-night munchies?

Another tradition that started at this time were the Christmas and Boxing Day—the day after Christmas—dinners that would be held at Lake Farms and at Wymers. The Nicolls were fond of having Christmas in the country, but in 1932, Catherine had to tend to her ailing mother, so Nicoll asked Moxon and Wilshin if they would do Christmas dinner for the group. Although the idea of cooking for twenty or so people was daunting, the two took it as a test, and apparently they passed with flying colors. The "party" atmosphere that would inform much of Nicoll's teaching in the years to come had taken hold—the festivities went on for three days—and would remain firmly in place.

In 1934, C. M. Lydall died, leaving Lake Farms to the Nicolls' daughter, Jane. Almost immediately, Nicoll began to think of building on the property. Already students were coming to Lake Farms on the weekend, where they could engage in more physical work than they could in London. Their numbers were growing, and even now there was little space for them. Nicoll envisioned a large structure, with studios and workrooms on the ground floor, and sleeping quarters above. By this time Ouspensky had found a large Victorian mansion in Gadsden, Kent, on the Great West Road out of London. Hays House came with seven acres, and it was here that Ouspensky made his first attempt at setting up his own institute, although the real impetus behind acquiring the place most likely came from Mrs. O—Sophie Grigorievna—than anyone else. She had spent more time at the Prieuré than her husband

and, as we've seen, had come to teach the Work in her own formidable manner. Even with his new mansion, Ouspensky spent most of his time in London, in his studio with his cat.

Nicoll had cut his ties, but he was aware of what his former teacher was doing. It would take some time, but he was determined to build. Perhaps not an ark, or at least not literally. But something would go up. It was the onset of "institute-itis." Would it last any longer than what he had labored at in Fontainebleau? Who could tell? What was important now was that they got to work.

11

"You Are Not Building for Posterity!"

Across a ditch from Lake Farms was a field called Tyeponds—the English apparently naming not only their houses. The name came from a weed that grew in a pond in the field. It seemed the perfect spot on which to build. One of the members of the group, a Miss Wadham, donated the money to buy the field, and according to a diary entry by Mr. Cassell—the husband of the couple who had introduced Pogson to Nicoll—work on the new structure began on May 18, 1935, when he and Nicoll put together a plank bridge across the ditch.[1] The first structure to be built was a workshop, which went up fairly quickly. Plans for the larger building were drawn up by George Kadleigh, the son of Mme. Kadloubovsky, Ouspensky's secretary, which again suggests that there may have been more contact between Nicoll and his ex-teacher than we assume.[2] George Kadleigh later became a prestigious architect under the name Sergei Kadleigh; it seems that he retained the Anglicized version of his last name and reverted to the original Russian version of his "essence" name. His own involvement in the Work is unclear, but in this instance at least, we find one person who did build to last.*

At first only a few students were allowed to visit Lake Farms. The privilege no doubt had to be earned, but in any case in the early days there wasn't space to house many guests, hence the need for the new building. Those who did come would have to drive there in their own cars, or arrange a lift from someone who was going. Most would arrive early Saturday afternoon, stay that night, and head back to London late Sunday evening. Hester Lord was lucky in that her companion, Winifred Park, who had brought her into the group, had discovered the "invaluable Hicks Brothers Bus," which left for Rayne on Friday evenings from Gower Street—in London's Bloomsbury—arriving there two hours later.[3] They would often be there when Nicoll and Catherine would arrive early on Saturday, with the Nicolls' dog Pushti in tow, in order to do the shopping for the weekend in Rayne. Lord tells us that her request to visit was accepted only because she said she would bring a tent. Others were more enterprising. Fulford Bush had a hut, as did a Miss Corcoran. Others who came stayed in rooms at the local pub. Some were committed enough to buy a cottage, as Sunday Wilshin and Selene Moxon had done, and so could take in some guests. Others even had a house built in the area—by professionals.[4] Those without these options made do as they could. In the summer, when work on the new building had started, this was not so demanding. But as the season turned, the need for proper shelter was clear, and a workforce was in place to erect it.

By September the outline of the house was complete, again according to Mr. Cassel.[5] The foundations were dug, Nicoll and Co. putting their backs into it, and the part of the building facing Lake Farms was

---

*Sergei Kadleigh was a lecturer at the Royal College of Art, and is most remembered today for his ambitious plans for a huge residential structure to be built over London's Paddington Station, and for his part in the "Kadleigh plan" for redeveloping the Barbican, another modernist apartment complex in London's City. "The Kadleigh Plan for the Barbican Area," barbicanliving.co.uk.

already covered in lathing. This was a skill Nicoll had picked up at the Prieuré and that he put to good use here and had passed on to his flock. The rest of the structure, however, was still bare beams. One early near catastrophe almost brought the building down before it was finished. Cassel records that he and his wife had spent their holiday at a cottage near Lake Farms that belonged to another couple in the group, and that each day they went to do some work on the new building. One evening there was a fierce wind, and when they arrived the next morning, they saw that the gales had pushed the back half of the building out of alignment, leaving it tilting precariously at a seventy-five-degree angle, rather like the leaning tower of Pisa.

Here was an inconvenience for which no one had planned. Yet when Nicoll arrived, he was up to it, and soon overcame the difficulty.[6] He got some strong rope, and a sturdy stake. He hammered the stake deep into the slope opposite the building, and attached one end of the rope to it and the other to the top corner of the structure. He did this twice, so two lines of rope ran parallel to each other. Then he got a thick iron bar and put it between the twin lines of rope. Then he got several of the men to turn the bar end over end, thereby twisting the rope. It took some effort, but eventually the structure was righted, and the group got busy putting struts and supports in place. The next day and for successive weekends they hurriedly hammered in the lathing. It was a successful expression of Nicoll's "sub-Gurdjieff" style.

Nicoll had spent some time prior to erecting the new building in preparing himself for the task—or rather, preparing himself to get the building up as quickly as possible. Pogson records that in the days before construction started, Nicoll would set himself a time limit in which to make something; for example, he'd aim to "knock up" a chair in half an hour.[7] The idea, drilled into him at the Prieuré, that one should "work for quick results rather than for durability," made good Fourth Way sense. But one wonders if professional builders make allowances for the kind of surprises Nicoll encountered with the brisk September wind?

(Or what the chair was like that he "knocked up?") Pogson tells us that while building Nicoll was "in his element," and that "all he had learned from Gurdjieff about building was put into practice." Under his guidance, the group felt that "nothing was impossible."[8]

Yet some things Nicoll did realize were beyond them. When it came to thatching the roof, they called in a local thatcher. When they needed to locate the best spot for a well, they called in a dowser, although when it came to it, the spot he chose was too far from the house. Nicoll asked one of the group where he thought the well should be. When he pointed to a spot just outside the kitchen, Nicoll said to do it—one of his "typical" quick decisions—and a team was brought in to dig. And later, when it became clear that still more space was needed and they decided to build an extension to Tyeponds, Nicoll decided to call in the professionals. Yet even here, he requested that they work as quickly as possible. Regrettably, like any sensible builder, they did not work on weekends.

Understandably the extension, though sturdier than the structure it was attached to, never felt quite right to those who had worked on Tyeponds. As Pogson put it, a part of themselves had gone into the building; she was particularly attached to a bit of plastering she had done. Whether or not they would ever put anything together again, the work Nicoll's group did on Tyeponds built something in themselves: a sense of community, of belonging, and of being stretched to their limits. Just as Nicoll's time at Fontainebleau stayed with him for the rest of his life—so much that he tried to recreate it at Lake Farms—so too for the group who worked on Tyeponds: it was an experience they would never forget. For people who were not craftsmen and builders, their work was a remarkable achievement, on a par, in its way, with the Prieuré's Study House. Yet, in fact, when events demanded it, Nicoll told them that they would absolutely have to forget it.[9] They had not, he reminded them, built for posterity

That Nicoll wanted to recreate his time at Fontainebleau—but as a participant somewhat less humble than the kitchen boy—seems clear from remarks he made to Pogson. At dinners over wine, while the group relaxed from their labors, he remarked on how he wanted to have his own institute.[10] The atmosphere during the construction was like that at Fontainebleau, one of constant, hectic activity, with Nicoll overseeing everything and hurrying the group on as he had been hurried by Gurdjieff and, inevitably, creating difficulties, just as Gurdjieff had done. Nicoll had aphorisms from the Study House written on the walls, reminding people that they had come to work on themselves, and he even had a goldfish pond put in, like the one at the Prieuré. It was again a chance at pursuing a "more than conventional life." Only this time, Nicoll was making life rather unconventional for others too.

Hester Lord's account gives us an idea what that life was like. She arrived at Lake Farms for the first time just shortly after work on the new building had begun. She had been asked to bring her "weaving things"—she and her companion Winifred had long practiced the craft, and Nicoll was interested in practically any "hands-on" work that he could incorporate into the group.[11] Soon weaving, knitting, stitching, rug making, and other similar handiwork found a place in it. Nicoll believed that "everyone should be in touch with the earth"—apparently this was why he wore thin-soled shoes—and he believed they would be by performing these activities, although Nicoll himself never took to gardening, which is about as close to the earth as one can get.[12] Lord arrived a bit frightened, not knowing what to expect, and already in awe of the Nicolls. She was relieved to discover that Catherine was not as aloof as she had thought, just shy and withdrawn. She would never get over a certain fear of Nicoll though, whom she believed could see right through her and knew her better than she knew herself, the often clichéd effect of gurus on their chelas. She found his presence intimidating; he was, she said, in certain respects "a very impatient man."[13]

One target of Nicoll's impatience, Lord records, were women who didn't try to "develop their intellect."[14] Another was Lord's habit of having to explain her actions. This, she came to see, was because she was "identified" with them. Whenever Nicoll called attention to something she was doing, she would launch into a long explanation to which Nicoll responded with a pained expression, or something less subtle. He could, she said, be "unpredictable and fiercely spoken," even violent.[15]

Yet on other occasions he was patience incarnate. When asked to lay bricks for the work shed, Lord, like many there, was eager to acquit herself well. She took pains to do so, using a spirit level to ensure that each brick was perfectly in place. Yet the kind of accuracy she aimed at took time, and when Nicoll returned a half hour after leaving her, only five bricks were in place. At such a pace, he explained, the shed would be a long time coming, not to mention the house. He then showed her how to do it "quick and dirty," and work carried on apace. Lord also mentions that whenever she saw Nicoll, he always had a very worried expression. Then she realized that he was "mirroring" her, reflecting back her unconscious fretting. Lord mentions another mirror, the one in the kitchen, which the women used in order to "make beauty," that is, put on their face for dinner.

The work that went on was coed. "Men and women fetched and carried, mixed cement and later plaster, sawed and hammered alike, and worked together in, as far as I can remember, harmony and fellowship," Lord tells us.[16] This sounds very much like most attempts at a commune, or a self-sufficient community "off the grid," which is what the experiment at Tyeponds reminds us of today. If nothing else, the people involved certainly received a crash course in DIY living. And like at Fontainebleau, they were also subject to sudden "scurries," when Nicoll decided that some project needed an all-out effort, and, Gurdjieff-style, everyone was press-ganged into intense, constant "super-effort," from morning to night. As Nicoll told Copley, with echoes of the Prieuré, "Come on. Get it up! You are not building for posterity!"[17]

Lord was present when Nicoll, once again evoking his "sub-Gurdjieff type," plied the county surveyor with sherry, before taking him through the building for inspection.[18] By this time most of the ground floor was in place, room divisions were up, ceilings put in, and the general shape of the structure secure, if not the structure itself. If Nicoll hadn't taken the precaution of a few glasses of cheer before the inspection, the building most likely would not have passed; its foundations, Lord said, were in places rather shaky. As it was, the surveyor told Nicoll that the second floor was suitable for storage only. Nicoll agreed, but when the time came what was stored there were bodies, the sleeping ones of his flock.

Nicoll was lucky. Had the surveyor come another time, he might have witnessed the foot and leg that appeared in an unfinished ceiling when someone upstairs stepped on a plasterboard instead of a beam.[19] Such incidents evoke an atmosphere of humor and lightheartedness, characteristics we already associate with Nicoll. If he was intent on recreating the Prieuré, it was a recreation somewhat less grim than the original. The incident of the soap powder in the white sauce suggests as much.

Lord recounts one occasion when a member, known to be a good cook—not all were—was given the task of preparing lunch for the group. It was a particularly cold day—the house had no heating—and the group was eagerly expecting a hot meal: lamb with white sauce and haricot beans, to be exact. (The cooking was done on oil stoves.) They sat down and at the first bite everyone lowered their forks and knives. Nicoll was extrapolating on something and hadn't yet tried his lunch. When he did he "ejaculated something . . . unprintable" and demanded to know who had put soap powder in the sauce?[20]

It was a mistake, an inconvenience not planned on—in the hustle and bustle going on something like it was practically inevitable—and Lord was thankful that it was not a "test" and that they would not be forced to eat their lunch. Had it happened at the Prieuré would they have? Almost certainly some people there would have thought so and made themselves sick; we remember the unfortunate woman and the ice cream and mustard. Here it sounds like a scene in a comedy. One collateral benefit was that henceforth the cook involved tested each dish she prepared before serving it.

Another incident with comic potential involved peacocks that an eccentric member of the group donated to the farm, to add to the menagerie of hens, rabbits, sheep, and other livestock. The peacocks were allowed to roam free, and would often wander onto the nearby railway line. The stationmaster would then call and demand that someone come and collect the peacocks.[21] This was an inconvenience that profited no one, except possibly the peacocks, and they soon left the farm.

Copley, who came into the group some time after Hester Lord, remarks that work parties often had "sergeant majors" appointed for the day, whose job it seemed was geared more to creating friction than to improving results. Those with specialized knowledge often had to follow the directions of the less informed, which more times than not provided ample opportunity to "contend with oneself," as one of the Prieuré aphorisms advised. The aim, again, was not to achieve lasting results, but to observe oneself in the process of working, and to be aware of the "dark side" of oneself, reflected in the mirrors of your workmates. Copley himself became such a mirror for several of his coworkers when, in the midst of hectic work on the roof during a "scurry," Nicoll insisted that he down tools and take his fiancée for a walk, in full view of his sweating workmates.[22] Like Gurdjieff, Nicoll was becoming adept at arranging situations that would create misunderstanding.

There was no electricity, so the place was lit by oil lamps and candles. Bathing facilities were at a minimum—only much later was a proper bathroom installed—as were toilets. Portable toilets—known as Elsans—were set up at a distance from the house. Two young men brought into the group were given the task of putting together a kind of hut, to shelter the toilets. At the first rain it was discovered that they had put the weather proofing on incorrectly, so that the water dripped inside.[23] An inconvenience indeed.

Some humor, though, was intentional. One Christmas, which was always a big formal affair, Nicoll gave all the women thermometers, saying that they didn't know how to keep a room at a decent temperature, but roasted everyone. Oddly, like Gurdjieff and Jung, Nicoll gathered around himself a coterie of adoring females, a fan base the austere Ouspensky lacked, any candidates most likely shooed away by Madame O. And although Gurdjieff had lectured Nicoll on the virtues of little sleep—the biological kind—on one occasion he insisted that Lord had exhausted herself and that she spend the weekend in bed. Nicoll himself would on occasion drive from London late on a Friday and sleep in late on Saturday, having exhausted himself with work—he was at this point still seeing clients at Harley Street—and with the four group meetings he was holding each week.*

Yet there were many evenings when, after the day's work had been done, and the evening meal over, Nicoll would speak informally to the group for hours; proper meetings would not take place at Lake Farms until the extension to Tyeponds was built. At dinner, Nicoll would launch an attack on the "vanity" and "false personalities" of some of those present, taking a feather from Madame O's cap, and giving his students a roasting of his own, in full view of the others.[24] But when these caustic sessions were over, Nicoll turned reflective and would share his thoughts with the group. These unbuttoned soliloquies would often go on until the wee hours, with his listeners standing; seating, like everything else in the early days, was at a minimum. Here Nicoll continued the practice he had established with his neighbors Moxon and Wilshin, of late-night conversation.

Nicoll's penchant for talking rather than writing found a perfect forum and a captive audience. Nicoll would speak about his plans for the group, his desire to establish his own institute, the books he was reading, or about the mysteries of time, recurrence, and the other ideas they

---

*We can get an idea of what Nicoll taught at these meetings from *Notes Taken at Meetings with Maurice Nicoll, January 18, 1934, to April 18, 1934* (Utrecht, Netherlands: Eureka Editions, 1995).

were trying to bring into their lives. Nicoll would also remind them of the practical necessities of what they were doing. Copley recalls that initially Nicoll was hesitant to ask for contributions from his group, but that with the work on Tyeponds, this was inevitable.[25] This may have been a part of Nicoll's personality he needed to work on; generosity came to him naturally. Gurdjieff had no trouble demanding from his students that they provide the funds necessary for him to properly deal with what he called "the material question." It was his incessant demands for money that eventually drove Orage away. Ouspensky, it seems, never had this problem; his well-heeled students were always ready to fund his work.

MUSIC PLAYED A LARGE PART in Nicoll's groups. Learning to play an instrument—in this case guitar—became part of the work routine, along with acquiring skill in other arts and crafts, like painting, carving, and later, sculpting, although, again, the aim was not to achieve proficiency but to observe oneself while so engaged. Nicoll himself would often end an evening by playing guitar and singing. He had a liking for Spanish songs, tunes like "Hasta Mañana," "Juanita," and "She Is a Flower." Nicoll had a good voice—he had been in the choir at St. Albans—and another trigger for his impatience were students who wouldn't or couldn't sing.[26] (Was this a "test," or simply irritation at others who didn't want to "play"?) Later, evenings full of song, dance, and other gaiety would make up a great part of Nicoll's approach to the Work.

By 1936 another kind of music, from another part of the world, began to be incorporated into the group's activities. That summer, Nicoll began to try to recall the music Gurdjieff and Thomas de Hartmann had devised to accompany the movements.[27] More than a decade had passed since he had heard it, but Nicoll had a good ear, and he could still hum a few of the tunes. He met with a pianist in the group, and while he hummed the melodies, she picked them out on the piano. Eventually they had the score for three pieces, "The

Obligatories," "The March," and the "Counting Exercise."

Around the same time, C. S. Nott, who had been in Orage's group in New York, met with Nicoll.

After the death of Orage, Nott, whose wife had been a close friend of the Nicolls, returned to London. (The Gurdjieff-Ouspensky feud meant that as students of rival teachers, Nott and the Nicolls had lost touch with each other.) Nott had spent time at the Prieuré and had been in contact with Gurdjieff, who by this time was living in Paris. In 1934, Thomas and Olga de Hartmann had visited Nott, and during a visit to Hayes House, Ouspensky's mansion in Kent, they mentioned Nott to Ouspensky, saying that he was anxious to make contact with anyone with whom he could talk about the Work. Nott in fact had tried to make contact with Ouspensky years earlier, but had no luck. Now Ouspensky told the de Hartmanns that he would be happy to see Nott. He was interested in acquiring students who already had some background in the Work, and Nott fit the bill. But no doubt Ouspensky was also curious to hear about Orage's activities, and those of Gurdjieff as well.

Nott visited Hayes House, and was surprised to discover Ouspensky to be a much warmer personality than the cold intellectual he had expected to meet.[28] Yet on his first visit he was subjected to the Madame O treatment, who put him through the ropes, with a barrage of questions, trying to determine his level of "understanding." Nott did not rise to the bait, but Ouspensky recognized that at least on this occasion, he should step in. He talked with Nott about the Work, and in the course of the conversation, Nott mentioned that Gurdjieff had abandoned terms like "self-remembering" and "self-observation," which Ouspensky still used, as did Nicoll. Gurdjieff was using a completely new terminology stemming from his book, *Beelzebub's Tales to His Grandson*. Neither Ouspensky or Madame O had heard of this. It was, Nott told them, the bible of the Work.[29] And as coincidence would have it, he happened to have a typescript copy of it with him; it was one of a hundred that Orage had sold at ten dollars apiece. (Given that in book form the work runs to some twelve-hundred-plus pages, the typescript must have been enormous.) Ouspensky asked if he could borrow it. In return he offered Nott a place at his meetings.

By the time Tyeponds was up, Ouspensky had moved his base to the even larger Lyne Place, where Nott continued to visit him. Nott had attended some of Ouspensky's London meetings, with the proviso that he ask no questions, and didn't mention Gurdjieff or *Beelzebub's Tales*. Like the members of Nicoll's group who had attended these meetings, Nott found Ouspensky's group to be rather dry and rigid, altogether too stiff compared to Gurdjieff, or even Orage, who had brought his own panache and flair to the Work. Yet Nott and Ouspensky got on, even though they disagreed completely in their assessment of Gurdjieff. Like Bennett, De Ropp, and others, for a time Nott joined Ouspensky for conversation over a bottle of wine. Nott was probably not the most intellectually stimulating companion, but the increasingly isolated Ouspensky was glad of the contact. But with Nott the topic of discussion was not the lost Silver Age of Russia, but Gurdjieff.

Ouspensky believed that after his motor accident in 1924—which some believe he had purposefully arranged—Gurdjieff's mind had come "unhinged."* One sign of this, Ouspensky believed, was the only piece

---

*In July, 1924, returning to Fontainebleau from Paris, Gurdjieff left the road at high speed and drove his Citroën into a tree. Gurdjieff was found unconscious—he would remain so for five days—and he had sustained serious injuries. When found he was lying near the wreck, with his head on a cushion. How he came to be in that position in the condition he was in, has never been explained. Other unusual circumstances surround the crash: Gurdjieff had had the car thoroughly checked, especially the steering, and he had asked Olga de Hartmann, who usually drove back with him, to instead take the train. He had also signed over to her his power of attorney. At the time of the accident, Olga de Hartmann, in Paris waiting for the train, heard Gurdjieff's voice calling to her. See Webb, *The Harmonious Circle*, 228–99, and James Moore, *Gurdjieff: The Anatomy of a Myth*, 206–24. Ouspensky believed that Gurdjieff had somehow aroused forces against himself by his "getting off the path." Others suggest that Gurdjieff was always an appalling driver. Yet his actions before the crash suggest that he anticipated something of the sort and may actually have planned it. It was after the crash that the Prieuré more or less permanently closed—although Gurdjieff resided there for several years after—and that he devoted his efforts to capturing his ideas in words, that is, *Beelzebub's Tales*.

of Gurdjieff's writing to be published in his lifetime, the bizarre *Herald of Coming Good* (1933). Ouspensky was convinced that its outrageous and megalomaniacal claims were the work of a "paranoiac." Nott, who had published the book—he was in the trade—politely disagreed. Yet he could sense that Ouspensky was looking for *something*. He too must have recognized that the spirit, if not the letter, was no longer infusing his classes. Kenneth Walker had grasped the problem when he remarked that too many of the people showing up at Warwick Gardens had their "meeting faces" on. It was rather as if the effort to be less mechanical had created some mechanical habits of its own. Yet when Nott suggested that Ouspensky allow him to read *Beelzebub's Tales* to a small group of selected students, Ouspensky said no.

When Nott asked why, Ouspensky demurred, and when pressed, admitted that he had yet to read the book. He told the astonished Nott that "it sticks in my throat."[30] Most likely it produced in the logical and fastidious Ouspensky the same faint sense of insanity that had been aroused by the *Herald*. And it is no surprise that Ouspensky would not want it read to any member of his groups. He had already confiscated all the copies of the *Herald* that Gurdjieff had sent to his groups—each person had got one—and destroyed them. Ouspensky certainly would not want to give his ex-teacher another opportunity to siphon off some of his students. (Gurdjieff too soon recalled the *Herald*, realizing it was a major miscalculation, a tacit concession to Ouspensky.)

Ouspensky made repeated overtures to Nott to join one of his groups and to work at Lyne Place. Here much practical work went on. There was a farm with livestock, a garden, and Madame O had students growing their own wheat, milling the flour, and baking their own bread, much as was starting up at Tyeponds. There was a printing press, and Nott could work on that; they were looking to self-publish, a considerably more difficult venture than it is today. Yet Nott could make no emotional contact with Ouspensky's students, and he felt that working with Ouspensky after Gurdjieff would be like having earned a degree, and then returning to grammar school. Yet when Nott suggested that he and his wife teach some of the movements to some of Ouspensky's students, Ouspensky agreed, although Ouspensky himself never made them a part of his work.

It was around this time that Nott paid a visit to Nicoll. He was "impressed with the quality" of Nicoll's group, and remarked that Nicoll was an "unusual man." But he added that it was "a great pity that he had cut himself off from Gurdjieff after only a four month stay at the Prieuré in 1922."[31] Nott's muted appreciation of Nicoll's tenure with Gurdjieff—which differs from Nicoll's own account—seems to suggest that he believed Nicoll hadn't the qualification to teach the Fourth Way. It also smacks ever so faintly of the superior distinction supposedly conferred on those who had spent greater and more intimate time with the master, as Nott had, something of the "heir apparent" effect that Copley mentioned. Nott's patronizing remark that Nicoll was nevertheless able to "attract good people, good material, for whom Gurdjieff's ideas, and even Ouspensky's, were then too strong," seems to confirm this.[32] His suggestion seems to be that Nicoll was good at attracting "material" that Gurdjieff, even Ouspensky could have put to good use, but which was left in a somewhat half-baked state in his own groups.

Nevertheless, as he had with Ouspensky's students, Nott agreed to teach some of the movements to some of Nicoll's group. Actually it was Nott's wife, Rosemary, and Jessmin Howarth, who had been at Fontainebleau and with Orage in New York, who taught them; Howarth had been one of the students at the Dalcroze Institute in Hellerau who had joined Gurdjieff's troupe when he tried to set up camp in Germany. At first the lessons were given in the basement of a house on Finchley Road where meetings were held.[33] (It's unclear if this is the same as the dance studio.) It wasn't the best location but at the time it was all they had. Eventually the musicians in the group picked up the tunes and the movements slowly became part of Nicoll's teaching.

When the extension to Tyeponds had been complete, work on

the movements took place there. The ground floor was large enough to accommodate this comfortably, and it was also used for other purposes, including dancing, theatre, and larger group meetings. On the floor above were bedrooms, and a music room. Pogson points out that each room in the extension had a radiator, a distinct improvement on Tyeponds, whatever personal feelings one may have had about it. (She also remarked on how the floors were much better than the rough wood in Tyeponds, which suggests Nicoll didn't bother to varnish the floors there.)

The movement exercises could be quite intense. Hester Lord recalls that the classes seemed to go on for hours; one performance of "The Dervish Prayer" that went on for twenty minutes produced, she said, an "enormous force."[34] Yet Copley remarks that Rosemary Nott and Jessmin Howarth soon stopped teaching the movements once they saw that people were making notes of the music and positions. This was strictly *verboten*, and the transmission stopped. Copley, who became involved with the Gurdjieff Society after Nicoll's death, was later told that he and his fellows had learned the movements incorrectly. The idea, he was informed, was not to master them, that is, to be able to perform them easily, as ballet dancers can perform a difficult pirouette. They would become useless as a means of "work on oneself" then. The important point was to observe oneself as one made unusual and uncharacteristic movements.

We can also see that if, as I suggest, the movements were a way of inducing "second wind," then it is precisely their difficulty that makes this possible. Second wind kicks in when we are brought to the point of exhaustion and frustration, that is, to our "habitual"—not actual—limits. If we then make one last effort, the "accumulator" opens up, and we are filled with fresh energy. If the movements no longer bring one to this point because one has got the hang of them, then the switch to the extra fuel tank won't happen. Copley records that, while Nicoll had some exposure to the movements in the Prieuré, they never became a central part of his teaching, just as they didn't for Ouspensky. Copley regrets this, and suggests that they, Nicoll's group, would have "profited enormously," if they had had a "gifted movements teacher."[35]

If the movements were given but quickly taken away, other physical pastimes took up the slack. One of the extra activities that went on in the new extension was something novel at the time. A Parsee friend of Fulford Bush, a Mr. Pagose, was a jiu-jitsu instructor to the police, and Nicoll asked him if he would come to Lake Farms and instruct the group. Pogson remembers her surprise at how easily the "thin, lithe instructor" with minimal force was able to throw Bush, who she suspected must have weighed twenty stone (280 lbs.), rather much for a gymnastics teacher.[36] Nicoll adapted the principal of jiu-jitsu, that of using one's opponent's own force against him, to psychological use. "It is not by resisting but by recognising that one conquers," Nicoll remarked, after the demonstration. "Freedom from certain desires," he said, "is obtained not by fighting against them so much as by observing them, by expressing in words the peculiar antics they induced—thereby losing their grip on one."[37] These are sound principles, and they suggest to some degree Jung's "active imagination," or even Freud's "talking cure," which both succeed by making inner obsessions concrete and objective. How much Nicoll was able to apply his own psychological jiu-jitsu to his own "certain desires" may become clear when we take a look at his later diaries.

AROUND THIS TIME, circa 1937, Nicoll asked Pogson if she would type up some short stories of his that he wanted to give to his literary agent to see if he could get them published. The law of fate must have got the message, because Pogson's future position as Nicoll's secretary was thereby secured. She retyped some pages, corrected others, and then took on what had until then seemed an impossible task: deciphering Nicoll's handwriting, which, she says, struck her as curiously familiar. The difficulties involved in decoding a doctor's handwriting are the stuff of comedy; we all know jokes about reading a prescription. Apparently Nicoll was one of the worst offenders. Frances Ney, his American secretary, only worked from dictation. Why Pogson was able to crack the secret of Nicoll's hieratic script is unclear, unless we accept, as she did, that it was fated. The stories did not find a home—although they displayed, according to Pogson, "startling originality"—and to my knowledge remain unpublished; the taste for *Strand*-like light reading had changed. Soon Pogson was given other material to type. Nicoll got into the habit of meeting with her at a restaurant before they would attend one of the evening meetings in London, to discuss ideas he had for new stories.

One idea involved Ouspensky's strange belief that one could reincarnate into the past, with the aim of changing it, to prevent future evil—that is, an evil of the present the source of which is in the past. By now, dozens of films, like *Terminator* and *Twelve Monkeys*, have inured us to this notion, which nevertheless remains difficult to grasp, involving logical perplexities and unwieldy concepts such as "time loops" that bedevil any attempt to present a coherent notion of "time travel."[38] Nevertheless, the situation in Europe had been darkening for some time. The rise of fascism in Italy, National Socialism in Germany, and Franco's attack on the Republicans in Spain suggested that, as Nicoll had predicted, Kenneth Walker's sanguine belief in the ability of the League of Nations to put an end to war was misguided. The "history of crime" was moving on. An ark was still needed. But if Ouspensky was right and one *could* return to an earlier time and prevent some action from taking place and so *alter the future*, wouldn't preventing a second world war from erupting warrant such an intervention? This was the theme of Nicoll's aborted novel *Pelican Hotel*, aborted because the evil its protagonist, Gregory Dixon—Nicoll's alter ego—sets out to prevent had become a *fait accompli* well before Nicoll could finish it.

Nicoll wanted to recapture the flavor of the time leading up to

World War One, so he had Pogson at the British Museum, researching what was happening in 1913, just as she had researched for the collection of writings on death. Back then, Nicoll was as eager as practically everyone else to have a chance to "smash the blighters," Kaiser Wilhelm and "the Huns." But now, his attitude toward war had changed, and his novel would be about Gregory Dixon's finding himself cast back from 1939 to 1913, with full knowledge of what would happen in Sarajevo in June 1914, and with the hope that he could use that knowledge to prevent the start of the First World War. Because if there was a single cause for the rise of Hitler and the catastrophe of the Second World War, which Nicoll saw looming, it was the crushing reparations that Germany had to pay to France, which left a smoldering resentment in the Germans that Hitler was able to blow into a flame. And these reparations themselves were so severe because of France's humiliating defeat in the Franco-Prussian war of 1870. In this way the "history of crime" perpetuates itself. But if one could go *back*, could one, if not stop this history, at least slow it down?

The logical problems involved in ever *knowing* if some event in the past was altered in such a way that the future that came after it was altered too are considerable. For our sense of the past strikes us with an immediacy that is indubitable, but what is to prevent our sense of the past from being altered in the same way that the past event presumably was? So we may find ourselves with a sense of the past in which the events that have been altered appear to us to have "always been that way," although, until the past event has been altered, we were absolutely sure that they had "always been" another way.* This would mean that, for us, with our

---

*Readers who know the film *Dark City* (1997) will remember that the characters in it live in a simulated world, the features of which and their *own identities* change each night. One goes to sleep as a banker, and wakes up as a policeman, with a full memory of *always* having been the policeman. Again, scriptwriters can play around with "wormholes" and "time loops," but logic seems a more effective "time travel preventative" than anything quantum physics can muster.

altered sense of the past, the past would in no way seem to have been altered. We simply would not know that it had been. Nicoll, however, would not have to find a way around this sort of hurdle, because while he was contemplating a jump back in time, the future caught up with him.

Nicoll was on holiday in France when rumors of war became news reports. He was in Normandy with Catherine, Jane, her fiancé, Mme. Kadloubovsky, and some others, when word broke out. He had planned a rest and was looking forward to some time at cafés, and to doing a bit of painting. All that changed when one of the group received a telegram from her husband, a colonel in the armed forces, urging her and the party to return home immediately. Nicoll sent messages to the group, telling everyone to head to Lake Farms. Even before he arrived there, Colonel Maffett, one of his closest students and an old gunner, and some others had started digging a trench. Nicoll and his troupe arrived shortly after they did, getting out of France and onto the last ferry across the Channel just as the borders closed. It seemed that the flood of violence and barbarism that years ago he had told Kenneth Walker was on its way had arrived. They would soon see how seaworthy their ark was.

NICOLL TOLD ALL WHO WISHED to that they should come to Tyeponds. Everyone expected London to be bombed immediately, and by September 3, when Chamberlain announced to the nation that a state of war existed between Great Britain and Germany, that expectation mounted considerably. Many came to Lake Farms. Some with children, some with their pets, some alone. Some people arrived with as much of their belongings as they could carry. Others turned up with practically nothing. As Pogson points out, as soon as war broke out, there was no need for Nicoll or anyone else to "create difficulties." The little corporal across the Channel was doing that for them.

Pogson recalls that they soon initiated two-hour watches, so they would be aware of any enemy planes approaching. She tells of one night when it was her turn to watch, when she and her fellow sentry felt an actual eagerness, an excited expectation, as they scanned the night sky, "almost wishing that something would happen."[39] On one occasion, there was an early morning air-raid warning. The sentries went to work, ringing bells, banging on doors, getting everyone to the trench. Pogson recalls that "it was very strange in the crowded trench." Everyone felt they were in danger, and "expected the bombers to arrive at any moment."[40] It turned out to be a false alarm—the planes overhead were British. What is interesting is that Pogson remarks on how, when the all-clear signal was given, they came out "into the early morning sunshine and had a wonderful breakfast in the open air of coffee and hot bacon sandwiches." She speaks of remembering particularly "the freshness of that morning."

I would say that what Pogson experienced was a milder version of what J. G. Bennett had at Fontainebleau when he forced himself to do the movements in spite of his dysentery, and tapped into the "Great Accumulator." The urgency and sense of crisis had "galvanized" Pogson to such an extent that she was actually *looking forward* to spotting enemy plans, something her everyday rational mind would have found less appealing. In *Beelzebub's Tales* Gurdjieff remarks that the one sure way to overcome the soporific effects of the "organ Kundabuffer"— implanted in humans millennia ago in order to prevent them from upsetting the cosmic balance and not serving their purpose as "food for the moon"—was to have a vivid sense of the *reality* of one's inevitable death. Crouching in the trench, expecting bombs to fall at any moment, produced in Pogson—and one suspects others—precisely the same effect. It had woken her up, and she was seeing "everything more vivid," as Gurdjieff had said about seeing in "essence."

One collateral benefit of war being declared was that Frances Ney, Nicoll's American secretary, had to return to the States. This left Nicoll without a secretary. Pogson was ready to fill the gap. She had already been working with Nicoll for some time and now he made it official.

Soon evacuees from London were arriving at Lake Farms, and Nicoll found himself with enough unplanned inconveniences to keep even him busy. The place was crowded enough already, with the members and their children who had fled London. To this number were added many evacuees, mothers, and children, to whom Nicoll opened Tyeponds' doors. If not an ark, it was certainly turning out to be a place of refuge. The music room became sleeping quarters for seven school children. The carpentry shop was, like the Paradour at the Prieuré, given over to expectant mothers and mothers with infants. Nicoll greeted the newcomers warmly, and provided all he could for the mothers, buying baby carriages, oil stoves, and other necessities. He got to work digging another trench; the first was already too crowded, although in the end neither one was ever needed.

The flurry of unexpected inconvenience, however—Pogson describes the various chores in detail, mostly cooking, washing, and taking care of the children—did not last that long. After a few weeks, the mothers in the carpentry shop grew tired of the inconveniences they had to face. For one thing, the shop had no floor, so they were sleeping in camp beds on the bare ground. For another, these young city mothers felt completely isolated stuck in the country, away from any shops. The older children found country life dull as well, and also asked to be moved. Their request to be rehoused elsewhere was granted, and Nicoll was secretly glad the expectant mothers had moved on before he was called upon in his capacity as a doctor.

As the threat of London being bombed receded—it would of course return in full force during the Blitz—and with most of the evacuees moving elsewhere, Tyeponds returned to something of its normal activity, in so far as we can say that what went on there was "normal." Nicoll and Catherine stayed at Lake Farms, with Nicoll beginning to shuttle into London for meetings. Only a few people remained in residence at Tyeponds—Pogson was one of them—but on the weekends people would come and there would be meetings, talks, dinners, and movement classes, followed by more talks or music, a routine that would carry on for most of the rest of Nicoll's ministry. Routine may seem an inappropriate term for activities designed to overcome mechanicalness, but a pattern was emerging, and Nicoll would pretty much stick to it.

Occasionally new elements were brought in. Sunday Wilshin—an actress who had appeared in several films—taught drama and mime. Pogson recounts a time when they were learning Morse code, and expresses regret that it was dropped from the curriculum just as she was getting good at it. But the basic pattern of the rest of Nicoll's life was coming into shape. Aside from occasional "retreats" that he spent alone, Nicoll would live in what was more or less a commune, established in different places, for his remaining years. There was rarely a time when he was not surrounded by people, all of whom were engaged in the teachings that he was transmitting to them. Copley remarks that the environment Nicoll created "provided special conditions in which we might glimpse the possibilities of another way of being." But he goes on to say that were the group to remain in those conditions, it's members might "resemble long, weak hothouse plants with little chance of survival . . . in the harsh conditions of the outside world."[41]

We remember that the Fourth Way is to be followed in the conditions of life in which we find ourselves, and that it is precisely those conditions that are the best for us in which to work. Yet, certainly by the time the war had broken out, Nicoll was less and less in any "usual" conditions of life, and more and more in the "special conditions" that he had created for his students. Ouspensky was in the same situation, increasingly isolated at Lyne Place, which he would soon leave for the United States, where he established himself in another set of "special conditions," Franklin Farms, in Mendham, New Jersey.* Here he would become even more isolated.

Nicoll never retreated into the kind of self-imposed internal exile that Ouspensky had. He was always available to his students, although

---

*In the winter of 1985 I visited Franklin Farms in the company of two of Ouspensky's students who were with him there until Ouspensky's return to England in 1947, shortly before his death.

as his groups grew, there was less and less individual personal contact. Yet it is difficult not to feel that Nicoll had succeeded in creating, if not a cult or a sect, a kind of extended family, or perhaps congregation, in which he felt at home and out of whose warm atmosphere he did not like to stray, much as any pastor might. It is also difficult not to recognize that more and more Nicoll was making the Work the whole of his life, something that had also happened to Ouspensky. In fact, in his case, the Work had become something of a job. As Ouspensky told one of his closest students, by the time he had reached America, it had become a "profession."[42]

Yet years ago Gurdjieff had told Ouspensky that the system could not be an end in itself, but only a means by which a man could achieve his aims.[43] Having an "aim" was a very important thing, Gurdjieff said. But the system itself could not be one's aim. Again, it was a means, not an end. Certainly after he stopped writing—which, until he met Gurdjieff, was his "aim"—Ouspensky had turned the system into an end in itself. Nicoll did not follow Ouspensky, but there is a sense in which the same caution could apply to him as it did to his ex-teacher.

THE REDUCED ACTIVITY following the departure of the evacuees meant that Nicoll also had time to return to writing, and it was around this time that he began to work on ideas that would later find their way into his books *The New Man* and *The Mark*, his forays into uncovering the esoteric meaning of the Gospels.[44] Catherine had already suggested that the group begin to look at the New Testament from the Work point of view, and this aligned nicely with Nicoll's attempts to spell out what Ouspensky had suggested in *A New Model of the Universe*, that the Gospels were the work of "conscious man," aimed at awakening the consciousness of those who were able to grasp their true meaning.

By the early spring of 1940, the "real war" had yet to begin. In France people spoke of the "phony war;" six months after it had been declared, there had been little combat and no bombs had been dropped. This allowed Britain to prepare for what was to come. The French, however, grew overconfident, and when the German surge came they were not prepared. Yet on the Nicoll home front, celebrations were in order. On May 26, Jane and her fiancé, John Mounsey, an artist who had already become part of the household, were married in the Rayne Parish Church. The weather was glorious, and the entire group attended the wedding and the celebrations afterward. A photograph of the group was taken in front of the garden at Lake Farms. It was the last time they would all be together for some years.

After the newlyweds headed off on their honeymoon, Nicoll and the group gathered to discuss some news that Colonel Butler had conveyed to him. It had been Butler who had sent the telegram to his wife, who had been on holiday with the Nicolls, telling them war was imminent and that they should immediately return. Now he had more bad news. Lake Farms, Tyeponds, and the surrounding area had been designated a militarized zone; it was considered in the path of a possible German invasion. The building they had labored at and had put their souls into was being requisitioned by the army. They had twenty-four hours in which to pack and vacate the premises. Nicoll had been right. They had not built for posterity.

12

The Home Front

If Nicoll had ever felt that his group needed a "scurry," they certainly got one when they received word that they would have to abandon Tyeponds and Lake Farms. The next day, everyone was up early, packing everything they could carry. That turned out to be quite a bit, even though they had to leave much behind, not knowing if they would ever see it, or the building they had worked on, again. As it turned out, they wouldn't, although Nicoll and Pogson would make separate visits after the war, and Nicoll would be entangled in protracted negotiations with the War Office over compensation. Food, silverware, cutlery, and other necessities were thrown into heaps and bundled up in sheets and blankets. Catherine suggested they take as much bedding as possible for the others, now scattered, who would join them later at their new encampment. Luckily a van was secured, and the bundles and whatever else could fit were packed away. It set off for London, where people would spend the night, put up at friends, before setting out for the new location the next day.

It was the kind of abrupt adventure that the de Hartmanns and others had experienced with Gurdjieff while on the run from the Russian Civil War, and once again war was the prompt. Across the country, people were abandoning their homes for fear of air raids, or sending their children off away from the city, to be rehoused somewhere safer. Others, unable to relocate, endured the Blitz as best they could. If ever there were inconveniences unplanned for, they had arrived, and Nicoll's training in Fontainebleau and the previous war was put to good use.

The Nicolls themselves had retreated to London to do their own packing. Pogson's description of them arriving in Birdlip, a village in the Cotswolds, Gloucestershire, about one hundred miles north-west of London, with their car as jam-packed as the van, again brings Gurdjieff's manic motor adventures to mind, when as many people as possible crammed into his Citroen and away they went.[1] Gurdjieff himself did little driving then, gasoline rationing in occupied France being rather severe. Having rejected attempts by his students to sequester him somewhere safer during the occupation, Gurdjieff remained in Paris, in his little flat on the rue des Colonels-Renard, where he carried on teaching and managed to live fairly well and to provide for others under Nazi rule. He was, as we said, a born survivor.[*]

The place Nicoll had chosen to relocate was called the Knapp, a late-Victorian house with gables, set off from the road at the steepest part of Birdlip Hill, with a sweeping view of the vale of Gloucester, and a hillside garden. Compared to the Zen-like austerity of Tyeponds, whose rooms were for the most part empty, it was like moving into an antique-furniture storehouse. Pogson tells of how Mrs. Wadham, as the elder member of the group, was given a large drawing room for her use. But it was so full of furniture that getting around in it was rather like walking through a maze; she was later relocated to a smaller but more comfortable space.[2] For a time the new occupants had to tiptoe across the floor for fear that one of the bronze Burmese cranes that adorned the walls would come crashing down—an exercise Gurdjieff himself might have devised. This happened so often that the birds were eventu-

---

[*]An idea of the Paris Gurdjieff lived in under the occupation can be found in William Patrick Paterson's interesting work, *Voices in the Dark: Esoteric, Occult and Secular Voices in Nazi-Occupied Paris, 1940–44* (Fairfax, CA: Arete Communications, 2000).

ally locked away, and after a time an arrangement was made with the owners to move as much of the unused furniture throughout the house into an empty spare room. Nicoll chose a ground floor dining room with a private entrance for his space, the fact that he could exit the building unobserved when needed no doubt influencing his choice.

At first Pogson and the Nicolls were the only occupants, but soon others gravitated toward the new center for the Work. It would be temporary, of course, as the ones that followed it would be. The followers of the Fourth Way were nomads, transients, always on the move. The Work was not fixed at a certain place or time or housed in a temple or church, but must, as they were now doing, accommodate itself to the everchanging "turn of events." That turn had brought them here, and they would remain there for the duration of the war.

Gradually a nucleus would form at the Knapp, with Nicoll at the center, and a cluster of female followers around him; large group activities were reserved for weekends. As Pogson commented, for the time being "it seemed that we had become a family rather than a group," yet one made up mostly of aunts, with a token patriarch.[3] If Gurdjieff had "the Rope," a group of lesbian writers that gathered around him in Paris, and Jung his *Jungfrauen* and "Valkyries," Nicoll had his own feminine circle, which deserves its own nickname.[4] (I suggest "the Kitchen," as this is where most of their interaction took place.) When the dust had settled, and his housemates had settled in, Nicoll was sharing the Knapp with Catherine, Jane, and Mrs. Butler, who brought along her poodle, chow, butler, and housemaid; Miss Wadham and Miss Corcoran, who was sadly bitten by an adder; Mrs. Hodder, who had been crammed into the Nicoll's car, along with an ironing board and oil drum; a Mrs. Currie; and Pogson. No wonder Nicoll wanted a handy means of exit.

He was the leader of his flock no doubt, but the women around him kept an eye on things, and at times had to correct the doctor surreptitiously. Pogson recounts that Nicoll would insist on doing the dishes after breakfast, a reenactment of his kitchen-boy routine in

Fontainebleau. It was perhaps because there was no opportunity now to recreate the Prieuré as there had been at Tyeponds, that he did the washing up as he had in Fontainebleau, using no soap or detergent of any kind—claiming, as a rationale, the fact that the soapy remnants cause indigestion. No doubt the women nodded their heads in approval before, Mrs. Beaumont–like, washing the dishes properly when Nicoll's back was turned.[5]

As the Knapp filled up, Nicoll rented out the King's Head, a former inn turned boardinghouse, across from the Royal George, a pub that would become a place of work for Nicoll, as the cafés of Paris and New York were for Gurdjieff. Mothers in the group would come to stay with their children at the King's Head. As Copley, who visited the Knapp only a few times—military service keeping him away—remarks, Nicoll felt that he had to be the father for these children, in the sense of providing them with some idea of authority and structure, and no doubt at times playing the villain when a necessary punishment was called for that the exhausted mothers could not mete out.[6] Nicoll accepted the position seriously—perhaps having so much feminine "energy" around him he was happy to exert some masculine force in return—and there is a sense that the war produced a kind of permanent "scurry" in him, at least a heightened sense of what was at stake. Wives whose husbands were in the service came to him for courage if not comfort. If they could not get to Birdlip he wrote to them, as he wrote to all the others, eager to maintain contact.

As Pogson remarks, all Nicoll's thoughts were "for his scattered people," and the hint of a "diaspora" here should not be missed.[7] Yet having his "people in his thoughts," was true for Nicoll in more than a sentimental sense. As mentioned, throughout the war, Nicoll put time aside to visualize those of his "scattered people" who were in harm's way and to picture their safe return. In this he was engaging in the kind of "creative visualization" that Dion Fortune, one of the most influential "magicians" of the last century and, like Nicoll, originally a psychotherapist, was pursuing at the same time. Throughout the Battle of Britain, from the headquarters of her mystical society the Fraternity of Light at 3 Queensborough Terrace, Bayswater, London, Fortune visualized "angelic presences" protecting sacred Albion from Nazi *Messerschmitts* and keeping her precious waters safe from U-boats.[8]

It was the kind of thing that Ouspensky would have frowned upon as a wasteful form of imagination, yet Gurdjieff himself would teach J. G. Bennett a similar practice after the war.[9] Bennett visited Gurdjieff in his flat in Paris in the rue des Colonels-Renard, and Gurdjieff began to ask Bennett about his mother, when she had died, and how he felt about her. He then told Bennett that his mother needed help, that she could not find her way in the afterlife. Gurdjieff's mother had passed away years before, and he remarked to Bennett that she, his mother, could help Bennett's mother. In order to do this, Bennett would, as it were, have to introduce them. Gurdjieff told him to take two chairs and to visualize his mother and Gurdjieff's mother sitting in them. It took a terrific effort, but over time, Bennett was able to visualize them enough to feel their presence. At that point contact between the two was made, and Bennett felt an enormous relief. So not only did Gurdjieff believe in the power of "creative visualization," it also worked in the afterlife.

I should point out that although official Work doctrine has it that we do not possess souls that, as it were, enter the afterlife automatically after death, but must create these through "friction" in life, Gurdjieff clearly accepted that Bennett's mother, who did not "work on herself," had in some form survived bodily death.[10] Similar contradictions suggest that Gurdjieff's "system" was not as airtight and self-sufficient as Ouspensky believed and that Gurdjieff bent the rules whenever it seemed appropriate.

Mention of the afterlife reminds us that it was around this time that Nicoll's reading of Swedenborg began in earnest—at least it is relatively safe to say that by this time he was reading him regularly. Copley tells us that on one of his few visits to the Knapp, he was *en route* to his next port of call as a sailor in the navy. Before he left, Nicoll handed him a "pleasantly bound copy of Swedenborg's *Divine Love and Wisdom*."[11] It was not a book that Copley could absorb more than a few pages of at a time, finding Swedenborg's dry Latin, when translated into an equally dry English, difficult to digest, an experience many who are interested in the ideas of the Scandinavian sage share. (Swedenborg's sober matter-of-fact accounts of heaven and hell are the furthest thing from Gurdjieff's dizzying report on a particular devil, Beelzebub.) Yet according to Copley, Nicoll quoted from the book and others of Swedenborg's frequently, which suggests a familiarity.

Swedenborg too, of course, wanted to reveal the true meaning of Scripture, just as Nicoll did, a task given him by the Lord Jesus himself.[12] Swedenborg's efforts in this pursuit produced the twelve volumes of his *Arcana Coelistia,* the "secrets of heaven." The twelve volumes cover only Genesis and Exodus; sufficient for Swedenborg's purposes and including the rest of the Bible would most likely have taxed even Swedenborg's considerable powers. But out of this the whole of Swedenborg's unique theology emerges, as well as the vignettes of the afterlife that make up his most well known work, *Heaven and Hell.*

As Jefferey Adams suggests, Nicoll was a deep and highly sensitive reader of Swedenborg, and textual evidence may suggest that this reading began earlier than previously thought. We have also remarked that Nicoll's pursuit of "sacred sexuality" had a parallel in Swedenborg's similar interest. Among the many items Pogson scurried to get into the van that last morning at Tyeponds were considerably portions of Nicoll's library. She mentions "every version of the Bible . . . the Hermetica, Plato" and "all the volumes of Swedenborg," works that went into writing the still-unpublished *Living Time* and that an unphilosophical fellow internal refugee would have considered an unconscionable luxury to lug to a temporary shelter.[13] Nevertheless, they soon found a home in Nicoll's new lodgings. As Adams points out, references in Nicoll's diaries, which start up again soon after the move to Birdlip, suggest that just as Swedenborg's books found a place within the Edwardian décor of Nicoll's new rooms, his ideas were finding a similar place alongside Jung, Gurdjieff, and Ouspensky in Nicoll's mind.

IF ONE DIDN'T KNOW THAT NICOLL was the leader of a group of followers of the Fourth Way, accounts of the period at the Knapp perhaps not seem very different from those of others at the time, forced together by circumstances and making the best of it. Having to relocate at practically a moment's notice, Nicoll had chosen well. Although Birdlip was near Cheltenham, a relatively large town, and an aerodrome, what the group saw of the bombing was mostly at a distance. Larger cities like Bristol took most of the damage, although one explosion near the Knapp did smash a drawing room window. The sound of airplanes overhead and gunfire was common and, as it did with many others, it drove the group into the air-raid shelters. Like everyone at the time they put up with privations, shortages of everyday staples, but also of beer, wine, and tobacco—necessities that Nicoll and Co. would feel the lack of. One "tragedy" that Nicoll recounts was the bombing of a wine warehouse in Cheltenham, which prompted reflections on the role of wine in civilization.[14] Closer to home, at least to the "family," a birdseed factory that Copley owned was hit in London, but the worse damage was that it was looted by some members of the auxiliary fire service, who tried to steal his typewriters.[15] Along with the relative safety, there was little risk of them being asked to leave the Knapp, although the military was in the neighborhood, and the sight of tanks making their way up Birdlip Hill became familiar. Their ark, as it were, had found a mooring, at least for the time being.

Although there was no construction work to act as a focus, as there was at Tyeponds, and no space for movements, the group soon fell into a routine, a way of life dealing with inconveniences not of their own making. Mrs. Wadham, with any luck relocated in her new room, started up art lessons. Painting was very important for Nicoll at this point. He had abandoned *Pelican Hotel*, his "speculations about the possibility of preventing war" being "cut short by the shock of reality."[16] He found it increasingly difficult to write, admitting to a "tiredness and lack of inclination to muster mental effort," much as he had felt during the worst days in Mesopotamia.[17] Super-efforts were out of the question; or, conversely, were being made all the time simply to deal with everyday things.

Mrs. Butler and Catherine did the household shopping. Mrs. Currie oversaw the lodgers at the King's Head. Pogson, who was in charge of the ration books, would go into Cheltenham, famous for its spa, with Miss Corcoran. While Miss Corcoran secured food for Nicoll's dog Pushti, Pogson would head to the libraries and snatch up half a dozen books of detective stories for Nicoll to read. Like Jung, who was a big fan of detective fiction—Simenon's Maigret and Agatha Christie were favorites—Nicoll relaxed in the evening with a whodunit. Conan Doyle's Sherlock Holmes was Nicoll's favorite, and Nicoll "identified" with Holmes—something to watch out for in the Work—so much that when they played charades, he took to acting out Holmes with his pipe and deerstalker cap, an accoutrement not found in the stories but added by Sidney Paget in his illustrations to them in the *Strand*.[18] Charades took up many evenings. On one occasion, Kenneth Walker, who remained in London, came to the Knapp for a weekend, and organized a "charade operation," in which Mrs. Butler was subjected to a butcher's knife, with the others making up the audience in the operating theater.[19]

There were parties, much merriment, the guitar came out in the evening, and the Spanish songs were sung; Nicoll had some particular ideas about the guitar and was not keen on Segovia.[20] These musical evenings became so regular that Nicoll referred to them as the "Knapp Cabaret."[21] Breakfast was a "family meal," with Nicoll reading letters from other members, stuck in London or somewhere further afield. He would talk to the others about what he had read or share with them his thoughts about the war that, as it did for many others, weighed heavily on his mind.

As Pogson remarked, the "gay evenings" had by all at the Knapp were necessary to expend energy built up during the group meetings. Yet they were necessary for another reason too. Nicoll recounts one evening when they had a "lovely, mad night" when they all went to bed late "not knowing whether there had been planes overhead or not."[22] Such a mad night happened more than once. Nicoll and Co. were not alone in savoring a few hours of blissful oblivion. All across Britain people sought out ways in which to *forget*, not remember, themselves, and to give way to the wisdom of eating, drinking, and being merry. The "merry parties" Nicoll and his group enjoyed were a safety mechanism, a means of blotting out, if only briefly, the nagging awareness of the reality they were in. The tension of living under the ever-present threat of death, combined with the reports of Hitler's seemingly unstoppable advance, had introduced a kind of background radiation of despair. The history of crime was rolling on, and taking most of Europe with it. As Nicoll himself confessed, the only thing to do, "the one thing," was to "enjoy yourself," as difficult as that may be.[23]

ENJOYING HIMSELF MAY HAVE been work, but Nicoll took to it. Never one to look askance at a pint, as mentioned, he took to spending time at the local pub, the Royal George. In fact, as his diaries show, Nicoll's beer intake became a matter of concern, and more than once he put himself on the wagon. On one of his first visits he met some seamen who had been evacuated from Dunkirk. They were part of the more than 300,000 servicemen—Belgians, French, and British—who had to be saved after being cut off by the Germans. It was an enormous operation and even small, local craft had to be used. This was the "miracle of Dunkirk" that inspired Churchill's famous "We shall fight on the beaches" speech. The seamen were " a strong-looking lot," who drank little, and seemed to share "a common strong brotherhood of feeling." They didn't complain and "all talked very sensibly and gravely."[24]

It was after meeting these sailors that Nicoll began to keep a "war diary," which he maintained until 1943. Compared to his dream diaries, Nicoll's war notes are a model of clarity and should be read by anyone interested in accounts of the war from the home front. They are a clear record of what life was like at a certain place during the Battle of Britain. They are of historical and sociological importance, rather in the way that Ouspensky's *Letters from Russia* are, albeit Nicoll's jottings are more rambling and less polemic. Nicoll is a keen observer, and it is not surprising that he enjoyed painting; scattered throughout the diary are descriptions of landscapes, gardens, flowers, trees, birds, and other wildlife.

As his personal diaries show, Nicoll suffered a kind of protracted writer's block during this time. Increasingly he felt unable to put down in words his insights and intuitions about the esoteric meaning of the Gospels. An effect of the war, no doubt, but we have already seen that Nicoll had difficulty focusing on writing. An indolence and disinclination to make efforts assailed him, the acedia he had felt before. It must have been a relief for him to write *something*, even if, as many entries are, it was merely his account of his daily activities, his concerns about losing weight, his thoughts about what he has been reading, or his reflections and observations on the natural world around him and the local people he was meeting.

Understandably, much of Nicoll's diary is taken up with his gloomy reflections about the war, which he saw as a kind of "disease of nations," or even as a kind of collective demonic possession, something Jung himself had suggested when he spoke of Nazism as an awakening of the ancient archetype of the god Wotan.[25] All fighting is "anti-Christian," Nicoll observes, yet the Christianity Nicoll had in mind wasn't the sentimental kind that he associated with Dickens and the Pre-Raphaelite painter Holman Hunt, who popularized the image of Jesus "meek and mild."[26] His Christianity, the Christianity he was struggling to put into words, contained "the most terrible, most harsh, and most aristocratic teaching ever given to man."[27] Nicoll criticized Nietzsche's depiction of Christianity as a "slave religion" as insane. Yet the kind of Christianity he envisions is not that far distant from the "higher morality" of Nietzsche's *Übermensch*.

In Nicoll's description of the kind of Christianity he envisioned, the word "aristocratic" stands out, rather as it might in one of Jung's early "word association tests," and will appear more than few times in Nicoll's notes. We remember Nicoll's penchant for formal dress and manners. While the kind of "spiritual aristocracy" Nicoll had in mind wasn't the same as the kind that populated the upper classes of his day, the two are not that far apart, at least not as much as Nicoll imagines them to be. Although the true Christian or "new man" Nicoll was struggling to realize, those "born of the spirit," would not be like anything seen before—he would be so strange, Nicoll believed, that people would not be able to endure him—he would also, presumably, be among that group of people who were "a little more expert in manners and address," that made up Nicoll's "good aristocracy."[28]

These "higher types" appear in every nation—something Ouspensky said as well—and recognize each other, and Nicoll ponders what kind of world it will be when such "possibilities of mutual regard and relation" disappear.[29] Yet when one remembers that it was precisely the well-bred who were shocked at Christ's consorting with prostitutes and other riffraff, one is left considering a "new man" "born of the spirit" who would show up in formal wear and know his etiquette. The contrast with Gurdjieff, who was not known to confine himself to social niceties, could not be greater.

Nicoll's reflections on aristocracy emerge from his recognition of the "need for society."[30] What Nicoll means by society is some sort of hierarchical social structure, an ordering of merit of some kind. Not exactly a caste system, although some, in our hyper-egalitarian time, might see it as such. This was in clear opposition to the movement to level social distinctions that Nicoll saw in the culture around him, and which today, at least in the "progressive" West, is taken for granted as a recognized and unquestioned good. Like those today concerned about the influence of "cultural Marxism" in the academies, Nicoll was troubled by the apparent insertion of communist ideas into science textbooks.[31] The calls for "equality" that echo in today's culture wars, were being made back in Nicoll's day. "Equal in what?" Nicoll asks, like any sensible person, there being no "equality" in itself. And while science today is under fire from many critics because of its insistence on the objective truths of biology—arguing, against much current sentiment, that there are clear differences between men and women that cannot be "identified" away—for Nicoll, it seemed that the science of his time was busily arguing the opposite. And this resulted, he believed, in a "general diminution of sex-feeling and the rise of homosexuality."[32] By "sex-feeling" Nicoll means recognition of the differences between men and women.

Many today may feel that this is a development all for the good, if indeed it is the case, but Nicoll had his reservations. We may find his insistence on men being "manly" and women "womanly" a bit stuffy and archaic. Yet it is difficult to argue against his remark that heterosexuality is "based on the power of seeing *differences* or wishing for what is different from oneself."[33] And we remember the importance Gurdjieff and Ouspensky placed on the ability to see *differences*, and not the bland sameness we usually do. What Nicoll was concerned was happening was that the science of his time was promoting a gradual elimination of difference and the institution of a kind of "sameness" as a natural fact.

Science, which "rides the heavens with meaningless gestures," was responsible for the loss of hierarchy in society that Nicoll was witnessing—evident in everything from the BBC's flippant attitude to

Christmas carols to the glorifying of the criminal in popular fiction—but it was also responsible for the war.[34] Science—materialist, reductive science—had awakened the Titans, the ancient destructive forces that the gods had sent to Tartarus, and they were again "tearing up everything sacred and holy."[35] "Hatred seems abroad today," Nicoll noted, not unlike in our own time. Gurdjieff had said that wars were caused by planetary tensions. When two planets passed too closely to each other, the result was war, revolution, mass migration—an expression of the idea, common in Russia at the time Gurdjieff met Ouspensky, that cosmic forces determine events on earth.* Swedenborg had said that it was only on earth that the habit of engaging in mutual destruction had developed, a reflection not far from Gurdjieff's, and one which Nicoll noted down.[36]

Reading of the siege of Saragossa during the Napoleonic wars, Nicoll caught sight of Ouspensky's eternal recurrence. It was "the same old thing," nothing was "new." "Man revolves in the circle of his own nature and comes always back to the same point of horror and carnage."[37] This led Nicoll to a sobering if discouraging insight. "History," he wrote, "is *man as he is*—and nothing else."[38] As we are, we attract what is called history. That is to say, that the history we know, the "history of crime," as Ouspensky called it, is an expression of our nature. And that nature, according to Gurdjieff, was one of being asleep, mechanical, robotic, caught up in dreams and fantasies and oblivious to the true state of things.

---

*This idea was part of a general view of human life called "Cosmism" that saw it in its relation to the wider cosmos. It was most associated with Nikolai Federov, Konstantin Tsiolkovsky, and Vladimir Vernadsky. Vernadsky's work, *The Biosphere* (1926) was translated into English by the philosopher Jacob Needleman and the physicist David Langmuir, both of whom were involved in the Work, from a manuscript in the possession of a student of Nicoll's. Vernadsky's book was used as a blueprint for Biosphere 2. See Anthony Blake, ed., *Biosphere 2: The Human Experiment* (New York: Viking Penguin, 1991), 103. For more on Cosmism and Vernadsky see my *Dark Star Rising: Magick and Power in the Age of Trump*, and *The Return of Holy Russia*.

"How long will man remain asleep to others, so dead in feeling?"[39] Nicoll asks. If "each man in each bomber had sufficient development of consciousness to be able to think what each bomb would do to others," war would be impossible.[40]

That would be the millennium, indeed, yet more than likely there were some individuals, on either side, who felt a pang of reality, realizing—in a flash of empathic imagination—that people would die because of their actions. These sensitive souls would have been placed in an unenviable position of having to follow either their orders or their conscience, and suffering the consequences thereof. Worse were the madmen behind it all, the dictators—Hitler, Mussolini, Stalin (Nicoll even includes Churchill, his father's friend, in this group)—who all suffered from and caused suffering by their "terrible desire to be first," and their dangerous powers of inflicting this fantasy on their nations.[41] These characters were the types Gurdjieff called "hasnamuss," whose main objective in life is to cause enormous suffering for others.[42]

Yet, even on the Allies' side confusion reigned. Along with detective stories, Nicoll spent his evenings reading memoirs of statesmen, accounts of previous wars, and war diaries, much like his own, but written by some of the men "in charge." Yet, what Nicoll came to see, was that these men—some of whom, such as Lloyd George, had known his father—had barely a better grasp of things than the layman. He came to the same conclusion that he had years ago, in school, when he realized that the headmaster knew nothing—at least, nothing important. There was no "mastermind" collating all the intelligence, plotting out strategies and anticipating events, steering the war effort to victory. The men on the war cabinet each had a limited view of events, and each kept what he knew to himself as much as possible. Rivalries between departments led to as many problems as the Germans themselves were providing. Nicoll's memories of his own experience of official inefficiency in the previous war no doubt helped to encourage the view that we should rid ourselves of the "illusion that 'they' exist—a race of supermen who know everything," and into whose hands we can safely put our trust.[43]

When applied to the people responsible for the war, this was no doubt a salutary perspective. But didn't Ouspensky, now in America and, while safe from the war, subject to other dangers, still pin his hopes on making contact with such a race, or something close to it, the Inner Circle? And didn't Nicoll spend a memorable several months with a superman of sorts in Fontainebleau? But these are not the supermen Nicoll has in mind. What his teachers taught was something different. "If men would make war on themselves"—the kind of "spiritual warfare" that George Fox, founder of the Quakers, promoted—"the world might improve."[44] If men took life "as a training for spiritual development," they might begin to "transform it."[45] But in order to do this, one must stand apart from life and the forces at work in it. "Is it not clear," Nicoll asks, "that to develop anything in oneself one must isolate oneself from collective influences," just as they had done at Tyeponds and would continue to do at their new port of call?[46] The Work they were trying to carry on aimed at such transformation, and with a world once again at war, the need for it was more obvious than ever.

YET WHILE THESE DARK THOUGHTS about the war, and other, more personal ones that he confined to his other diaries, oppressed Nicoll, he still found time to notice the occasional odd experience that suggests that the materialist view of the universe, as a lifeless, mindless machine powered by inescapable cause and effect is perhaps not as unassailable as its proponents believe. Nicoll belonged to that peculiar society known as the "collectors of coincidences," a name coined by the French scientist Camille Flammarion, who wrote extensively on astronomy but who was also a keen student of the paranormal, at a time when such interests were not disparaged by men of science. Flammarion collected accounts of remarkable coincidences and was subject to them himself. For example, Flammarion was working on a book about meteorology when a gust of wind blew his pages out the window. Before he could retrieve them, it started to rain. He assumed they would be ruined so he let the pages go. A few days later, when the proof pages of the book arrived from his printer for his review, he was astonished to find the missing pages among them. The porter carrying the pages to the printer had seen the missing ones on the ground and assumed he had dropped them; he picked them up and brought them to the printer. What had Flammarion been writing about? The wind.

Such odd coincidences were subsequently christened "synchron-icities" by Jung, who had been collecting them himself for decades, although he only spoke openly about synchronicity in his later years. Synchronicity and coincidence are related but not the same, the differ-ence being that in a synchronicity the element of meaning is central: the coincidence concerns something *meaningful* to you. Whether there was any personal meaning in Flammarion's coincidence involving the wind is unclear; yet it remains a remarkable coincidence nonetheless, and in his books Flammarion gathered many others.

Jung provides an example of synchronicity that by this time is well known.[47] One of his patients was an infuriatingly rationalistic woman whose staunch intellectualism made therapy tough going. As she told Jung of a dream she had about a golden scarab, Jung heard a knocking at his window. He opened it and a golden-green scarab beetle flew in. They were rare to begin with in his part of Switzerland and not taken to knocking on windows. Jung's patient was stunned at the coincidence; her rationalism cracked, and Jung was able to get on with the job.

In Jung's case, the scarab beetle knocking at his window at the same time his patient related her dream—the two events were synchronous— was a coincidence chock-full of meaning that was specifically related to her. It had an emotional impact that other coincidences, bizarre as they may be, do not necessarily carry.

The coincidences Nicoll records are noteworthy, even if they don't qualify as synchronicities, at least by my reading. So he notes that after talking about Spoonerisms, when one reverses the initial or first syllable of two or more words ("half-warmed fish" for "half-formed wish"), he noticed that the young son of one of the members was busy on the floor playing a game of his own devising with spoons.[48] Some other coincidences seem the work of what Arthur Koestler, himself a great collector of coincidences, called "the Library Angel."[49] This is a most helpful spirit who puts into one's hand exactly what one is looking for, or something very much along the lines of what one has been thinking about. So when Nicoll was writing about the miracle of turning "water into wine," an important metaphor for the rebirth he sought, he randomly opened a copy of *Chamber's Journal* to an article about the miracle at Cana.[50] And later that evening, in a detective novel Pogson had found for him, he came across a drawing of two glasses, labeled "water" and "wine."[51] The Library Angel, somehow hearing that he was interested in this, generously provided some samples. Another time, after a conversation at the pub about the difference between a butterfly and a moth, back home Nicoll randomly opened a copy of *Country Life*, again to an article on precisely this.[52]

Some of Nicoll's other coincidences qualify as what the twentieth-century Austrian biologist Paul Kammerer called "clusters," an effect of a phenomenon he christened "seriality," a "law of nature" that brings like things together.[53] Nicoll noted that "on one of those special days in which normal accidents are as it were concentrated in one place," he witnessed a "cluster" indeed.[54] He noted a "vast army lorry lying across the hill with two petrol tankers," "a car on fire, a motorcycle smashed, a car in a ditch" and a little girl who sprained her leg, all "within a short distance on the hill, just by our house." Nicoll reflected that something similar happens when "we meet an old friend of years ago and lo, another one comes into view." Or it may be that an odd word, that one has rarely come across, suddenly turns up in a successive "book, paper, talk."

Nicoll gives as an example a cluster that Kammerer would have envied, of losing several items on succession in the same day. While washing, the soap popped out of his hands and he searched high and low for it, only finding it when he looked into a jug it had miraculously entered. He dropped his keys and practically took his car apart looking for them, only to discover that they had landed in his trouser cuff. A pen may just as well have entered a black hole, until it turned up in a book he had been reading.

We can't say if any of these inconveniences held any special meaning for Nicoll, but we can say that they do suggest some odd tendency of "like to attract like," which may be the source of the old adage that "things happen in threes." It was not something Gurdjieff or Ouspensky ever spoke of, and was decidedly more in Jung's line of work. Nicoll himself accounts for the phenomenon biblically, reminding his readers that, "there is a time for everything."[55]

And this was true too of the Work, which was available for only a limited time to a limited number of people depending on circumstances and events. As things seemed then, it looked like the opportunities for getting on with it were quickly diminishing.

Yet even amid the chaos and rubble, opportunities could still be found.

FULFORD BUSH HAD REMAINED in London, braving the bombing, to serve at his post as a fire warden. After a time he wrote to Nicoll, asking if it was all right for him to start holding meetings in London, for people who could not get out to the Knapp. Nicoll agreed, and after nearly a decade, Redcliffe Gardens was once again one of the outposts of the Work. Anyone who could manage it came to Bush's house in Earl's Court on Saturdays, when the meetings were held. The discussions were lively and it was out of these that the work that Nicoll is most known for today, his *Psychological Commentaries on the Teachings of Gurdjieff and Ouspensky*, arose. Questions that came up during these meetings were sent to Nicoll through Bush, and Nicoll responded to them in some detail. It was through this exchange that the *Commentaries* came into being.

Pogson began to make copies of these letters—a tedious business in the years before emails or even Xerox machines, and at a time when the postal service must have been reduced—and they were sent out to other workmates further afield, who could not get to London or Birdlip. Nicoll's people may have been scattered, but this method linked them all together. In a sense, Nicoll was providing Fourth Way sermons by post. Each week he would write his letter—generally on a Friday evening—and it would be sent out that weekend. He kept up this practise until his death. He gave his last talk two weeks before he died; his last letter was left unfinished, Nicoll having fallen into a coma before he was able to complete it. Although the *Commentaries* wouldn't see print until shortly before Nicoll died—their content deemed top secret until Gurdjieff's death lifted the ban on the publication of any Work literature—they circulated in typescript for many years.

Nicoll always insisted that the distinction between the *Commentaries* and the Work-teaching proper should be kept clear. "The teaching of the work-ideas is permanent," he told his groups, although, as we've seen, Gurdjieff had by then abandoned practically all of the "system" that he had taught to Ouspensky, and which Nicoll was passing on, and more than one biographer of Gurdjieff has suggested that the "teaching" was experimental in the extreme, and not an immutable sacred knowledge.[56] However this may be, Nicoll's *Commentaries* were not permanent, and were subject to circumstances. And at the time he started recording them, they were subject to rather demanding circumstances indeed. The commentaries were in the nature of subjective "suggestions, amplifications, explanations," designed to get his audience to "think for themselves," at least about and in relation to the Work.[57] Their aim was to get their audience to grasp the importance of the ideas in relation to their own lives, to see them, as it were, in action. Yet they were not the Work itself. "The teaching of the work-ideas is one thing," Nicoll wrote. "The commentaries are another."[58]

The responsibility of a teacher of the Work, Nicoll said, is to pass it on in its purest form. "The work ideas as originally taught must be handed on just as they were taught," Nicoll told his flock.[59] The sacred texts must suffer no revision. Scripture is sacrosanct, every jot and tittle must be accounted for, as Scripture itself tells us. We get an idea of how Nicoll did this in the various notes taken by his followers, which were subsequently published after his death.* In them we see the vocabulary, diagrams, and other items of the Work apparatus, as originally transmitted to Ouspensky and which he taught to Nicoll, and which, of course, turn up in the *Commentaries*.

In this sense, once you have read one book spelling out the "system," you have read them all, in the same way that a book about basic mathematics should not differ greatly from another, nor a manual giving instructions in how to operate a particular machine, nor a guide in strict Marxism, for that matter. In none of these cases is there any room for variation or addition. That is what makes a system a system.

This idea of keeping the teaching "pure" haunts the psychohistory of the Work. Gurdjieff complained that practically all his students who set out to teach the Work—or "his ideas"; the distinction is important but often muddled or overlooked—got it wrong. We've seen how he undermined Ouspensky's authority. Even Orage, whom Gurdjieff "loved as a brother," went off the rails so much, according to the master, that he was forced to sign a document declaring that

---

*See, for example, the *Informal Work Talks and Teachings 1940–1950* (Eureka Editions, 1998), compiled by Lewis Creed.

he would have nothing to do with himself.* Gurdjieff also gave precise instructions as to the sequence and number of times his writings should be read.[60] Ouspensky believed the essence of the Work couldn't be communicated in words; it was against his wishes that *In Search of the Miraculous*, the foundation text of the "system," saw print.

Even so, when Ouspensky left England for America, shortly before Nicoll and Co. descended on Birdlip, he gave instructions that "all in London should make sure to avoid the smallest departure from the letter of the System as contained in the writings I have left." With an ocean between him and his students, he took no chances with the risk of revisionism.

We may not agree with Colin Wilson, who suggests that in his last years, Ouspensky had ironically turned the system into a kind of esoteric Marxism, at least in the sense that he maintained it as a kind of "science" that was self-sufficient and capable of explaining all situations and answering all questions, an adamantine dogma, and that any deviation from this was *verboten*. Yet, except for the starry-eyed true believer,

---

*There seems a tradition in the Fourth Way for one teacher of it to declare that the other teachers of it don't know what they are talking about. Some years ago, I attended a talk by William Patrick Paterson, considered one of the most important contemporary practitioners of the Work, here in London. I had read a few of his books and had reviewed *The Struggle of the Magicians* (Fairfax, CA: Arete Communications, 1996), his look at the Gurdjieff/Ouspensky relationship, for Gnosis magazine. During his talk—as well as in the book—Paterson made clear that Ouspensky didn't "get" what Gurdjieff was trying to teach him, nor did Orage, Bennett, or anyone else, if I remember correctly. One assumes that Paterson believed he did, otherwise how could he conclude that the others didn't? At the end of the talk, I asked Paterson if the fact that not one of his frontline students understood what he was teaching didn't suggest that Gurdjieff was a bad teacher, given that none of his top students passed the course with flying colors. He did not reply. On an earlier occasion, I met James Moore, Gurdjieff's biographer, and a controversial figure in the Work. He had been a student of Kenneth Walker who, according to Moore, didn't understand what Gurdjieff was about either. I declined Moore's offer to become his student. Some time later, when my publisher sent him a proof copy of my book on Ouspensky, seeking endorsements, Moore replied with a scathing, highly critical letter. Most writers unwilling to provide an endorsement simply ignore the request. Moore went out of his way to say how bad he thought the book was.

it is difficult not to see that Ouspensky's adherence to "the system and nothing but the system," led to a dead end. In America he was more isolated than he had been in Lyne Place, with Madame O effectively in charge. His drinking increased, as did the feeling that something had gone wrong and that he had lost his way. Following a system that was as infallible as he believed it was—or at least that offered the only hope of any kind of self-transformation—shouldn't he have arrived at a different destination?

This is perhaps an unanswerable question, or one that Ouspensky himself may resolve in his next—or current—recurrence. What a reader of the *Commentaries* soon grasps is that Nicoll is doing the system an inestimable favor by clothing its bare bones with something warm and approachable. Ouspensky's fastidiousness prevented him from relaxing and making any unbuttoned comments about the work they were doing, except perhaps when in his cups. And there was never a time when Gurdjieff wasn't Gurdjieff, and when what he said could be taken without considerable helpings of salt. And Orage's "Commentaries on *Beelzebub*"—collected in C. S. Nott's *Teachings of Gurdjieff*—as helpful as they are, require a familiarity with that most difficult of texts, which, as Colin Wilson remarks, will always have fewer readers than Hegel's *Logic*, another famously impenetrable work.[61] Nicoll's hortatory commentaries are not far from Fourth Way pep talks, encouraging his audience to take what they are doing seriously. In them he comes across not as the inscrutable master or the stern logician, but as a friendly, if firm, local vicar, reminding his flock that religion is not only a matter for Sunday, but must be practiced throughout the week.

NICOLL'S COMMENTARIES WENT ON to fill five volumes, to which a sixth, an index, was added after his death. This brought their total number of pages to just under two thousand, rivaling in bulk Swedenborg's *Arcana Coelistia*, and outstripping Gurdjieff's compendious *Beelzebub's*

Tales. In terms of readability, for all their unavoidable repetition and oratorical style, the *Commentaries* leave both far behind, Swedenborg's dry rhetoric and Gurdjieff's neologisms and boa constrictor syntax presenting insurmountable barriers for most readers.

In the *Commentaries*, a follower of the Fourth Way can find Nicoll's take on all aspects of the Work, as it was taught to him by Ouspensky. And, as noted, a perceptive reader can also find hints of and allusions to some ideas of Jung and Swedenborg. A look through the contents pages of the published version of the *Commentaries* shows sections devoted to "self-observation," "A, B, and C influences," "self-remembering," "centers," the "laws of three and seven," "negative emotions," "internal and external considering," the "ray of creation," Gurdjieff's bizarre "table of hydrogens," "the doctrine of 'I's," "the Enneagram," and everything else Ouspensky put into *In Search of the Miraculous*. We can as well find Ouspensky's own ideas about time, scale, and recurrence, which are not part of Work doctrine, but which Nicoll included in his transmission of it.

As this is a book about Nicoll and not the Work—although by now the two are practically inseparable—what strikes me as important is to spell out the direction Nicoll would take in the *Commentaries*, and, possibly, his motivations in doing so. We know that what attracted Nicoll to the Work and the aspect of it that he would communicate to his groups was what we've called "esoteric Christianity." What did Nicoll mean by that?

Nicoll would labor at this question, and after much effort and close to the end of his life, produce *The New Man* and the unfinished *The Mark* in answer to it. What Nicoll presents in a very distilled form in these short but fairly dense works is the essence of the ideas and reflections that inform the *Commentaries*. *The New Man* and *The Mark* present Nicoll's "esoteric Christianity" without the scaffolding of the system. In the *Commentaries*, Nicoll's "aristocratic" Christianity is presented under the auspices of the Work. Readers interested in what

Nicoll understands as "esoteric Christianity" but not interested in the
Work, can find what he has to say about it in *The New Man*, which
makes no reference to the Work, or to Swedenborg, or to any source
whatever for his interpretation of the Gospels. Nicoll makes no argument nor informs the reader how he came to his conclusions. He just
presents them, and we can accept them, or not.

Although the *Commentaries* proper begin with Nicoll's letter of
May 4, 1941, in which he explains that the "Fourth Way must always
be related to the varying circumstances of life and can never become
fixed and habitual"—in other words, that people should not feel nos-
talgic about Tyeponds and want to somehow get it back—the general
outlook or forecast for the Work as Nicoll saw it can be found in his
replies to Bush's original letters.[62] It is here that Nicoll spells out what
will be a recurring theme in the *Commentaries* and what strikes me as
that aspect of the Work that Nicoll felt most personally. This is the
relation between "essence" and "personality," and which we can also see
as the distinction Nicoll makes between the "vertical" and "horizontal" aspects of our "being," a change in which is the system's central
preoccupation.

This change Nicoll came to refer to as *metanoia*, although the
Greek for "change of mind" means something more than it does in
English. This is also a theme that informs *Living Time*, with its contrast
between the "tick tock" time of everyday life, made up of "one damned
thing after another"—the horizontal—and those strange unforgettable
moments "out of time," which, like moments of "self-remembering,"
lift us out of the stream of events and awaken us to something like
eternity: the vertical. These "intersections of the timeless with time," as
T. S. Eliot speaks of them in the *Four Quartets*—influenced, perhaps,
by attending Ouspensky's lectures—make up the essence of "mystical
experiences."

Nicoll makes his distinction between the horizontal and the vertical
aspects of human existence by pointing out the fallacy in the modern

notion of progress, a reflection that by the mid-twentieth century had become something of a cliché. "If we look at history," Nicoll told Bush, "we find that man has not really developed."[63] With bombs dropping on London and totalitarian regimes overrunning Europe, Nicoll could with some confidence say that, "if we look at the present day we cannot boast that man has reached any real further stage of development."[64] War, violence, destruction—the history of crime—which we take to be "exceptional" are really the norm. It has always been such and we have no reason to suspect it will be any different in the future. Men think that time itself will bring about change, but this is a fantasy.

Vanitas vanitatum, et omnia vanitas, "vanity of vanities, all is vanity," as Ecclesiastes pointed out millennia ago. As Nicoll saw while reading of the siege of Saragossa, men, people, as they are, attract history—the history of crime—because their nature, or, as he will more often say, their *being* doesn't change. It remains the same. Any chance of escaping the history of crime depends on a change in our *being*. As long as we remain as we are, the same cycle of destruction and chaos will repeat. "The level of being of a man attracts his life," Nicoll said, at times like a mantra, and the same applies to humanity in general.[65] "History repeats itself because man remains at the same level of being."[66] And so he attracts "the same circumstances, feels the same things, says the same things, hopes the same things."[67] Yet he fails to see that unless he *changes*, nothing else will. He believes that simply by time passing, by "now" becoming "then," all will be different.

This is what Gurdjieff called the "disease of tomorrow," which is the habit of putting off until tomorrow what you should do today; an aphorism to that effect adorned the wall of the Study House in Fontainebleau. At one of their earliest meetings, one of Gurdjieff's students told Ouspensky that the Work was a way of making sure that tomorrow would not be a mere repetition of today. But, in the words of an old Italian song, "tomorrow never comes," and can be put off indefinitely.[68] So, why work today?

Yet if time, human effort, technology, and all the good intentions in the world won't bring about a change, what will? This is where the Work and "esoteric Christianity" come in. It is through them that the needed "change of being" can come about.

We remember that Gurdjieff spoke to Nicoll about esotericism being a kind of "rope," that one could climb and so escape the stream of events, that is, "life," whose turbulent currents Nicoll wanted very much to avoid. Here Nicoll changes the metaphor and speaks of a "ladder," the rungs of which stand for different levels of being.[69] What do we mean by "being"? If we think for a moment of "freedom," rather than "being," it may be easier to see what Nicoll means.

A stone seems to possess no freedom. It is inert and subject to the environment. It will remain where it is unless someone kicks it. A plant doesn't seem particularly free, but in comparison to the stone it has advantages. It absorbs nutrients from the environment and grows; that is to say, it takes advantage of its situation, makes use of it; it is not entirely passive. An animal does this even more. It can move. Unlike the plant, which it eats, it can seek out its food and is not solely dependent on the soil in which it is planted. Humans have even more freedom. We inhabit a mental world, as well as the physical one. We have language, thought, art, culture, civilization, and so on.

We can think of each shift from one level of freedom to the next as a qualitative break with the level below. There is a distinct change in kind, not merely in degree. The modern view wants to say that this ascent, as it were, reaches its peak with humankind, *as we are*, and that any change in our world will be one on the horizontal level, that is, only a *quantitative* change, a different distribution of what already exists. What Nicoll wants to tell us is that there is the possibility of a *qualitative* change, one that will bring us something *new* and not merely more of the same, a way of taking a step up on the ladder of being, which is at the same time a ladder of freedom.

How do we do this? By moving our sense of "I" from our personality, which is the horizontal aspect of our being, to our essence, which is the vertical, from what he calls "tick tock" time to "living time." But for this change to happen, something different than what is available to us on the horizontal level is needed. That is where esotericism comes in.

We remember that essence is what we are born with. Nicoll, adding a Hermetic touch, says that "essence comes from the stars," which he equates with the note *la* on the Ray of Creation.[70] Passing through the intermediary zones of the sun and the planets, it reaches earth and enters us at our conception. "We are not born merely of our parents," who only provide the "apparatus" for essence to be received.[71] Our true home is among the stars, and the aim of the Work, according to Nicoll, is to "lead us back to where we have originally come from."[72] This is not standard Work doctrine, but it captures the idea that we have "fallen" from a higher state to a lower one, which, we know, is the central theme of Christianity.

Essence grows until about the age of five. Then it hits a stage of arrested development. What begins to form around essence is personality, which we are not born with but which we acquire from the world around us. We see things, hear things, imitate people, take role models, and begin to adopt certain habits and behavior and ideas and opinions that we gradually come to think of as "ourselves," but that are really a kind of protective coloring we adopt in order to get on in life. Jung calls this the "persona," likening it to the masks worn by actors in ancient theater.[73] What Jung means by "personality" is rather different from how the Work uses the term, but one can see a similarity in his use of "Self" and what Nicoll means by essence.* People with weak personas or

---

*"Personality is the supreme realization of the innate idiosyncrasy of a living being. It is an act of high courage flung in the face of life, the absolute affirmation of all that constitutes the individual, the most successful adaptation to the universal conditions of existence coupled with the greatest possible freedom for self-determination." Quoted in Anthony Storr, ed., *The Essential Jung,* 195. The Self for Jung comprises the whole psyche, conscious and unconscious, not only the ego, whose dominance obscures the self, just as "personality," in the Work sense, obscures essence. We can see here that Jung had a somewhat higher regard for personality than Nicoll had.

none at all we call "simple"; those with strong personas we call "sophis-ticated." The persona is, as Eliot says, the face we prepare "to meet the faces that we meet."[74] Our true selves are too easily bruised, so we create a kind of "false self" as a defense. The problem is that this "false self," whether we call it "personality" or "persona," begins to take over. The mask becomes the face, the persona the person, and we lose touch with who we really are.

When this happens we may begin to feel a sense of meaningless-ness in our lives. "A point comes in a man's development," Nicoll writes, "when he feels empty."[75] "Some of you who have done your duty in life," he writes, may wonder "what the meaning of it all is." "Have you felt in some way that life does not quite give you what you expected," Nicoll asks.[76] Do the things that used to hold interest for you no longer move you? Jung said that practically all of his clients over middle age, suc-cessful, accomplished people, came to him precisely because they felt an odd lack of meaning in their lives. His suggestion was that they try to reconnect with what gave them that sense of meaning in the past, and with the lost self who felt it, through paying attention to their dreams and fantasies, that is, to their unconscious. Nicoll's remedy was esoteric Christianity.

The sense of meaning can be recaptured, Nicoll believed, but not through any further development on the horizontal plane, not, that is, through an increase in personality, or what goes with it: success, money, power, and so on, all the attractions of "life." It can only be regained through moving a step up on the vertical level, on, that is, the ladder of being. If we change our being, *meaning* will return. As it is, our being is stuck at the level of our personality, that is, on the horizontal plane. How can we move it up a rung? By helping essence to grow.

In what Nicoll calls the "third stage of development," essence begins to grow, at the *expense* of personality. This starts when we recognize that the person we have been is not our real self, which suggests a certain unhappiness with ourself to begin with. "We" have to separate our-selves from "him" or "her." Then we begin to dismantle this false self, by making personality "passive."[77] Fundamentally, this means humbling personality, in the sense of giving up all the accretions that have gath-ered around essence, all the habits and mechanical behavior acquired over years. It is a process of emptying ourselves out, what, in the lan-guage of the parables, is meant by the rich man giving up his riches.[78] But personality can be tenacious, and it is easy for us to think that we are going against it when we are merely carrying on as usual. We cannot trust ourselves. To make personality passive requires special measures. It requires the Work.

In his letters to Bush, Nicoll speaks of the Work in evangelical tones. "This work, this system of teaching, these ideas we are study-ing, are the most beautiful things you can possibly imagine . . . far more lovely and beautiful."[79] Does this not sound like glad tidings? Beauty is in the eye of the beholder, perhaps. But the system as beauti-ful? Whether or not we accept them, Gurdjieff and Ouspensky's ideas are striking, worthy of study, and, in my experience, offer fascinating insights into human psychology. But I would not call them beautiful. Why does Nicoll? Because they "hold no conviction of sin."[80]

We know that Nicoll grew up with a huge conviction of sin, and that this fed his fear of and obsession with his "unclean thoughts." His sense of sin prevented him from feeling a part of the church con-gregation, that he was unworthy of it, and that he would not want to go to heaven in their company. Sin was also a preoccupation of his father. But now, here was a teaching that did not mention sin, which, in his study of the Gospels, he came to see did not mean what he was brought up to believe it meant, but merely "missing the mark," not hitting the target (*harmatia*), hence the title of his unfinished book. We are not sinners, but sleepers, and there is a way to wake up. Nicoll had finally found the congregation he could belong to. In fact, he was leading it.

He had also found a way out of "life," which was going nowhere. At best it was "nothing but a field for working on oneself, so that one can return from whence one came."[81] "Each one of us is down here on this dark planet because he or she has some special thing in themselves, some special factor, some"—in the Work vocabulary—"*chief feature* to see . . . and to begin to dislike and so to work against," which seems to suggest that the whole cosmos is so arranged for us to "work on ourselves."[82] Anyway, life was disappointing, not delivering on what it promised. Life in itself was not an end, and any of its ordinary rewards—so coveted by personality—were nothing. They were to be discarded. The rope of esotericism could pull him out of it.

This seems to hit the note of Gnostic world-rejection that we don't find in Kenneth Walker. And however much he wanted to forget it, it sounds not too distant from the religion of Nicoll's childhood. Like predestination in Presbyterianism, the "the most terrible, most harsh, and most aristocratic teaching ever given to man," is very exclusive, and those who do not make the grade—the seeds that fall on stony ground—are chaff to be burned, or, as Gurdjieff has it, "food for the moon." Only the "good aristocrats" would escape this fate. There was no salvation outside the Work, and it was his task to spread the word.

And he did so once a week, generally on Fridays, in the form of his *Commentaries.*

13
Working against Time

The years at the Knapp were not a good time for Nicoll.* There was, of course, the war. It seemed that the flood of barbarism that he had warned his good friend Walker about twenty years earlier had reached a crest and was poised to come crashing down on plucky Britain. A wave of evil was on its way from the Continent; this was the esoteric reading of the biblical flood, and another, it seemed, was approaching. Noah, according to Nicoll's reading, was not a man to whom God had given advance warning of a coming physical deluge, the forty days and nights of rain. "Noah" was the name of an esoteric school at that time, and its "ark" served the same function that Nicoll's own was designed to perform: to preserve the teaching during a time of trouble.[1]

Throughout history others had done the same. Ouspensky had said that this was the purpose of the Gothic cathedrals, to preserve in their sacred geometry the esoteric knowledge that had become lost in the dark ages.[2] Now it seemed to Nicoll that those ages had returned. It was clear to him that the "age of the good men" was over, and that the rise of "bad men"

---

*We remember that Hester Lord remarked that Nicoll was "sometimes violent" at the Knapp. Copley, *Portrait of a Vertical Man*, 44. During this time it seems that Nicoll had to ask some of his group to leave, and was even forced to call the police to eject someone who "is back and a nuisance." Earlier, at Birdlip, he had similar trouble with a member appropriately named Moon, a source of many problems in the Work. It appears things were not always well in the ark.

had begun. "Violence and evil were on the ascendant and everything to do with truth and good was being lost sight of."[3] The floodwaters were rising. Their ark had been rocked by the waves of the flood, but for the time being it looked like its mooring was secure. He was thankful for that. But there were no guarantees. Gurdjieff had said long ago that everything was temporary, and that soon everything would be different—and he was right.

For Nicoll to be depressed over the war and the prospects for the future seems perfectly understandable, even if he was doing all he could to keep the teaching safe and above the floodwaters, just as Christ had walked on them. He would not have been the only one to have gloomy thoughts over what seemed like a very bleak situation. But there were other sources for the depression and *acedia* that came over Nicoll in Birdlip and that remained with him throughout the war years and beyond. The inertia that prevented him from working on what would become *The New Man* and that may have contributed to his decline in health that began at this time was rooted, it seems, in something else.

The diaries recovered by John Willmett from Samuel Copley's daughter start up again in the spring of 1941 and continue until 1948, five years before Nicoll's death and when he knew that his last days were approaching. He would even inform his groups of that fact. They are the "dream diaries" that Pogson occasionally refers to and that Nicoll continued during the years of his "war diaries." The war diaries themselves stop in 1943, evidence perhaps that Nicoll no longer had the energy or incentive to continue them. They served, perhaps, to battle his writer's block.* But now, at least for a time, as many entries in his diaries show, the lethargy that came over him was total. The two last years of the war brought Nicoll "much weariness of soul," Pogson tells us, and she was right.[4] It was a weariness that lingered.

Covering so many years, the later diaries contain a great deal, much

---

*Writer's block, when words simply do not flow and the page remains blank, usually indicates something wrong with the original idea, or that there is some dissonance between what you think you want to say and what you really feel; in Gurdjieffean terms, between your essence and your personality.

of it not immediately accessible, and interested readers will have to wait until they are fully edited and annotated to get a real idea of their contents. Here I can only touch on a small selection of Nicoll's entries, but even this limited amount gives us an idea of what, in addition to the war, was on Nicoll's mind during this time. And one thing that was on his mind was sex.

Along with his declining health, his concern about his weight and growing portliness, his drinking, and his inability to get to grips with the work that would eventually become *The New Man*, many of the entries in Nicoll's later diaries concern either what seems his continued devotions—the Greek letter μ makes repeated appearances, as does some of his other cryptic notation—or his dreams. These frequently revolve around sex. It would be quite easy for a hostile critic to pick a handful of dreams at random from the hundreds Nicoll recorded to show that sex was on his mind practically all the time. One could even turn to practically any page in the diaries to make this point. But a hostile critic isn't needed to arrive at such a conclusion. Nicoll tells us this himself. In an entry for March 13, 1945, he admits that if it weren't for the Work, his whole life could have been devoted to sex.[5] This was something that caused Nicoll a great deal of conflict and, as we've seen, was with him from an early age.

But a reader of his diaries might scratch his head at Nicoll's remark about the Work preventing him from devoting his life to sex, because at least in his imaginative life, it seems that Nicoll did devote himself to it. For apparently that is the medium in which Nicoll continued to prefer to conduct his sexual activities. From his diary entries, it becomes clear that his moments of greatest satisfaction and value, moments even, it may be, of mystical insight, were achieved in this way. Yet, as in the early diary, in the later one there is no mention of his sexual relations with "real" women, if, in fact, he had any.

I am not suggesting Nicoll didn't, although it seems highly unlikely, merely that there is no evidence for any affairs or of any brief liaisons with any of the women with whom he lived. And we remember that from about Tyeponds on, he was practically surrounded by them. (His dreams though are a different matter.) We also remember that his wife was a woman who, at least at the start of their relationship, had a "horror of physical sex." More than one diary entry concerns dreams in which Catherine has left him, or wants a divorce, or in some way is not with him, or has sex with someone else, while in more than one he has had erotic relations with Mme. Kadloubovsky, Ouspensky's secretary, which may suggest a desire to take his teacher's place. Many later entries concern Nicoll's remorse over what he refers to as his "slandering" of Ouspensky, but what he means by this is not exactly clear.

It is true that by this time Nicoll was entering his sixties, an age when it is not unusual for a man's sexual urges to lessen; although of course the opposite is also true, and randy sexagenarians are not uncommon. So it may not be unusual for him not to be hopping into bed with lovers, or even his wife, and to be turning to other means for sexual relief. Yet, from what I can tell from my reading of the diaries, practically *all* of Nicoll's sexual experience took place in his mind, and the only thing to inhibit his devotions, as far as I can tell, was his decline in health. In the later years of the diary, Nicoll even begins to refer to something that seems to have served as a kind of fetish for his self-sex devotions, something he calls the "model," which he fashioned, Pygmalion-like, in his workshop.[6] Exactly what this was is unclear; he seems at one point to have destroyed it in an attempt to free himself of the habit. But Nicoll devotes many entries to it and it even preoccupies him in his dreams. Whatever it may have been, it seemed to have offered Nicoll access to the kind of eroto-mystical experiences he sought.

Yet more times than not, Nicoll paid for these ecstasies, which at times seem to have reached a level of spiritual vision, with something of a moral, or at least a psychological hangover. In several entries we find Nicoll, whose self-esteem was never very high, repeatedly reminding himself of his nothingness and insignificance, echoing Gurdjieff and agreeing that "man can do nothing," and berating himself over his "broken promises."[7]

This struggle, this "friction between 'yes' and 'no'" as Gurdjieff would have said, between his sexual obsessions and his guilt over them, produced in Nicoll much pain and occasionally some ecstasy, as some of his entries show.* Yet, what these diaries also show is that, although he wanted to, Nicoll was never able to fully integrate the two central passions of his life, sex and religion, and the dissonance between them threw him into fits of self-torture and recrimination. At least it strikes me that this was so. These crises would sometimes pass into a spirited justification of his actions but never into a calm acceptance of them. Or into what seems most desirable, a mature recognition of the need to *outgrow* the habit, although there are a few entries in which he seems to resolve to do so.

Even from the tenets of the Work this would be obvious, and one equally obvious question that comes to mind is how qualified Nicoll was at this point to teach the Work, given that a great deal of his time away from it seems to have been spent in his solitary practices?† (One

---

*Ouspensky, *In Search of the Miraculous*, 32. They should also have led to a stronger feeling of "real I," the friction having "crystallized" this in him. Yet from the diaries we can see that more times than not, Nicoll's struggles ended in yes, rather than no.

†A comparison can be made with Nicoll's contemporary Paul Tillich, the Lutheran Protestant theologian and existentialist. Nine years after Tillich's death in 1965, his widow Hannah published an account of their life, *From Time to Time* (New York: Stein and Day, 1974), that revealed Tillich to be as obsessed with sex as Nicoll, although he satisfied his urges through affairs and pornography, which he would often ogle concealed inside a Bible. When caught, Tillich would deny it, often erupting into tantrums, although his pastimes were well known among his colleagues and students, some of whom he seduced. Commenting on Tillich, Colin Wilson remarks that Tillich "kept his religious beliefs and his sexual obsessions in separate compartments. . . . There was no real attempt at individuation, at growing up, because he found the two-compartment system pleasant and convenient." As to how Tillich's obsessions affected his authenticity as a spiritual teacher, Wilson asks "Is it not inevitable that a man who cannot keep his hands off his female students will emphasize human helplessness and man's inability to resist sin, and throw the whole burden of salvation on 'Jesus the Christ'?" Similar questions can be raised about Nicoll's own obsessions and his increasing emphasis on human "nothingness" and the need for anyone entering the Work to feel a sense of shame. Wilson, *The Misfits*, 214–15.

could have asked the same question of Ouspensky, when he was drinking heavily, and he recognized that the Work had become for him "a profession."*) There was no question that he knew it and had faith in it and that many who came to him profited from this, although as the forties went on, he moved more and more in a Swedenborgian direction. But, at least in this matter, was he actually *doing* the Work? Was Nicoll allowing what Gurdjieff called "buffers," psychological shock absorbers that prevent us from feeling the truth about ourselves, to blind him to what he was doing?[8] And it need not be solely a matter of the Work. It would behove *any* teacher of any spiritual discipline aimed at overcoming our habitual behavior and our "vanity" and "self-love," two of Nicoll's favorite targets in the *Commentaries*, to explain how he could present himself as an exemplar—he must be, if he is teaching the discipline—when he continued a practice that, for many psychotherapists today, would appear obsessive, if not an addiction.[9] This was something that, at least in his dreams, Nicoll himself seems to have recognized.[10]

Should not the physician heal himself before he heals others? What would Jung have said to him? In a diary entry for June 14, 1946, Nicoll writes that "A man must be quite open to himself and without deception."[11] Was Nicoll "open to himself," not to mention anyone else? Was he free of deception? Did his wife know what was going on? Did anyone else in their commune? Was Nicoll being dishonest—he, for whom a change in *being* was all-important? It strikes me that, with all the goodwill in the world, no serious writer can avoid asking these questions.

Gurdjieff said that when one continues to do something that one has recognized is wrong, it is a difficult sin to forgive; Nicoll would

---

*One who did ask it was Robert S. De Ropp, who was with Ouspensky in Mendham, New Jersey. Recognizing Ouspensky's decline into increasing boozing and nostalgia, De Ropp remarks that Ouspensky was "no longer a teacher. He had lost his power and had wrecked his health. . . . The only honest thing for him to do . . . was to face his own weakness [and] send all his disciples packing." De Ropp, *Warrior's Way*, 171.

have seen the aphorism to this effect adorning the Study House in Fontainebleau.[12] Perhaps more to the point, in *Beelzebub*, Gurdjieff talks about a "sacred substance which is the final result of the evolving transformations of every kind of being-food formed in the presence of every being without distinction of brain system"—which, if nothing else, gives the reader a slight taste of Gurdjieff's tortuous syntax.[13] This substance Gurdjieff calls "exioëhary," which, on planet Earth—and in English—is known as "sperm." This substance is nature's way of perpetuating the species, but it is also useful in other ways. One is that in "three-brained beings," that is, humans, it "may be consciously transformed" into a kind of "coating" necessary for the creation of our "highest being-bodies."[14] These are the other bodies—"astral," "mental," and "causal"—that Gurdjieff told Ouspensky man needs to create through his own efforts, in order to survive the death of the physical body.[15] (This immortal body Gurdjieff called the "kesdjan body," and we have seen earlier, in the case of Bennett's mother, that occasionally Gurdjieff made exceptions to this rule.)

"Exioëhary" or sperm can be used to create this higher body, if one resists the urge to "remove" it from the physical body through indulgence in "pleasure."[16] This means not ejaculating for purposes other than procreation, or at least with that being the end result, a bad habit human males picked up in the course of our wholly misdirected evolution, according to Gurdjieff.* (How women, who do not produce sperm, create their higher bodies is another story.)

According to Gurdjieff's eccentric view of the history of the human race, men who did not reserve their "exioëhary" for actual sex—which

---

*The notion that the retention of sperm is an aid in spiritual development can be found in a variety of esoteric practices, from Taoist alchemy to Tantra, in which sexual intercourse is permitted but without ejaculation. The general idea, found in kundalini yoga, is to reverse the flow of the sexual energy so that it moves upward, toward the *sahasrāra* chakra, the "crown" that is located above the scalp. According to the research of Marsha Keith Schuchard, Swedenborg aimed at achieving "perpetual virile potency" through practices taught him by the Rabbi Jacob Chayim Falk.

could result in procreation—or retained it in order to use it to coat their "higher being bodies," resorted to dodges to have the pleasure of getting rid of it, without the consequences, namely pederasty and onanism. One result of these "anti-natural means" was that one lacked the material out of which to fashion one's immortality. (The number of illegitimate offspring Gurdjieff left behind suggests that he succumbed to neither of these temptations, nor made much use of contraceptives.)

Whatever we want to make of this, according to Gurdjieff, Nicoll may have been throwing away the very thing that could enable him to "return to where we have come from," given that the body that survives physical death is "composed of the material of the *starry world*," and comes from a very high place in the Ray of Creation.[17] It is unclear if Nicoll read *Beelzebub*, or if he did if he got to this section, but he was aware of Gurdjieff's teaching concerning the "second body." In his diaries he remarks that Ouspensky said that "a man must be saturated with sex for 2nd body," and that "for Second Body, sex must concentrate. Yes. But it must be the imaginative sex it seems."[18] We've seen how important "imaginative sex" was for Nicoll, and what its results could be.

In our ultra-tolerant times one does, of course, hesitate to judge. Someone's sex life is their own business, even if it often seems these days that they are of public, even political importance. In his war diaries, Nicoll wrote that "a country is free when it follows its usual traditions, but allows a 'secret life' at home."[19] Nicoll certainly seemed to have followed this dictum. But as more than one of his dreams show, maintaining a "secret life" when living with a group of followers was not always easy. Talk about overcoming difficulties. He even consulted the *I Ching*, the ancient Chinese oracle about it.[20] The strain on him must have been enormous, and as several entries in his diaries show, it was. He may as well have been trying to keep a drug addiction secret, and in some entries Nicoll admits to an urge to "come out of the closet," or wherever it was that he carried out his devotions, and admit to them. So a generous view may be to turn a blind eye to what is ultimately a relatively harmless habit and eccentricity. After all, Nicoll did much good, and if not for the curiosity of academics ferreting out research material, these matters may never have come to light.

But then Nicoll himself judged the majority of human beings, those unable or unwilling to do the Work, as "sleeping humanity," and their lives as meaningless and heading nowhere, unlike his and those of his followers, who were heading to the stars. "I hate the common man and avoid them," he notes at one point.[21] We have seen throughout this book that for all his desire to lead a "more than conventional life," Nicoll retained much of the snobbery and values of his class, and judged a great deal that fell afoul of it, from matters of dress to one's choice in marriage. Perhaps more to the point, Nicoll himself was never one to pull punches, even if at times he needed a pint or two to get in the mood. One of the odder rituals those who followed him were put through, was to be given some "valuable information" about oneself, generally critical, "at the cost of some pain," as a birthday present.[22] Another was to be subject to an "endless" review of one's "shortcomings" in a pub, as Copley was, "loud enough for all the locals to hear."[23] We remember what Madame O was like, and although not as abrasive as she was, Nicoll could be equally forthright.

If these dressing downs were beneficial to his students, should we not treat Nicoll in the same uncompromising way he treated them? Following the public rundown of his shortcomings, Nicoll told Copley that it was "permissible to 'hit' people provided that at the moment of hitting you love that person more than you hate him."[24] I neither love nor hate Nicoll, but my remarks here arise from that same place of concern. What would he have said to one of his group who came to him with his dilemma? Knowing of his obsession, one can only wonder if the energy that leaked out of him because of it was one source of the writer's block Nicoll endured for several years? Or if the guilt he felt over his devotions informed his increasing emphasis on the dangers of "vanity" and "self-love" and the need for all who came to the

Work to approach it with a sense of shame, something it seems that did not occur to Kenneth Walker?[25] Or if the low self-esteem Nicoll felt throughout his life was diminished even more by his apparent inability to give up what seems to have been a debilitating practice? Or indeed if that practice and the tensions and downright self-loathing that came of it contributed to the decline in health that seems to have begun around the mid-1940s, when Nicoll would have entered his sixties?

A follower of the Fourth Way might not concern himself with these questions, and it is clear that Nicoll's hagiographers did not, although it seems unlikely that they were completely unaware of what Nicoll was going through and the source of it. But if one wants to get an idea of the outline of Nicoll's time-body, they are unavoidable.

ONE THING NICOLL'S TIME-BODY was about to experience was another change in location. Toward the end of 1944, when the tide of the war had turned in the Allies' favor, the Nicolls began to look for another home for themselves and the Work. They would find it the next year in a place called Ugley, and their stay there would be short. But before they left the Knapp, a very important octave for Nicoll was started, a "*do*" was struck, the reverberations of which would echo throughout the following years, although more often than not they dwindled to almost nothing. Pogson tells us that the idea for what would become *The New Man* began when she had the notion of collecting everything said about Saint Peter in the Gospels and arranging it in chronological order.[26] Nicoll had already written about the Lord's Prayer, material that would eventually find its way into the unfinished *The Mark*, and he was taken with Pogson's suggestion that he write about the part played by Peter in the Gospels.

According to Pogson, Nicoll wrote the chapter of *The New Man*, "Simon Peter and the Gospels," with "the utmost rapidity," and it later went into the book unedited. If so, it would have been one of the few times when Nicoll wrote anything with the "utmost rapidity"; as we've seen he always had difficulty writing. That difficulty continued throughout the 1940s. Nicoll's research for *The New Man*, Pogson tells us, ended in 1943, the same year that he stopped his war diaries. As late as January 1948, Nicoll is noting in his diary that he "can't work on Gospels."[27] By September of that year, eight months later, he is praying "to be able to work," although by this time the cancer that he will be diagnosed with a few years later may well have started.[28]

In the years leading up to this, in many entries in his diaries, Nicoll notes a dizziness or giddiness, a pain on his left side, a feeling of "emptiness," only relieved by a few pints of beer. By 1945 he is taking a variety of patent medicines, one of which, Pulmo Bailly, a cough suppressant, contained codeine, an opiate. Later he will take kaolin, a clay thought to have medicinal properties (used mostly for diarrhea), and Chlorodyne, a patent medicine containing laudanum (opium mixed with alcohol), cannabis, and chloroform.[29] This was a painkiller, but also used for diarrhea.

Cancer is an illness often linked to frustration, disappointment, depression, and general low vitality, and also with a tendency to supress anger.[30] In the *Commentaries*, Nicoll remarks that "depression is not due only to loss of hope and belief in the future," something many going through the war may have felt, but that it "can arise simply from making no efforts of any kind."[31] Nicoll also rightly points out that a depression can be lifted even by doing "just ordinary small necessary things."[32] He also points out that "depression often happens to people who like to think that they are always bright, cheerful, and happy."[33] People, perhaps, who do their utmost not to express "negative emotions," and who have a penchant for "gaiety" and "merriment"?

Throughout his diaries, Nicoll frequently notes that he finds it difficult to make any efforts, specifically at working on what would eventually appear as *The New Man*. Did Nicoll's illness prevent him from making efforts, or did something in him stop him from making efforts, and provide his illness with a grab hold? Whatever may have been at the root of Nicoll's procrastination, it was practically a miracle itself that *The New Man* didn't join the ranks of other projects that Nicoll started but was unable to complete.*

One such task was the project Gurdjieff had entrusted Nicoll with years earlier, to find a way to synthesize esoteric knowledge with science. This too was something Nicoll began to work on in their last days at the Knapp, but would not be able to complete. It was, however, one project that, had Nicoll been alive to know of it, he would have been surprised to see science itself seemingly reaching out to help make possible.

Around this time, Nicoll read the physicist Erwin Schrödinger's book *What Is Life?* in which he argues that life—biological life—is a force that *goes against* the second law of thermodynamics. This is the entropy, or "increase of disorder," that, according to science, will eventually turn the universe into a featureless cosmic soup. Whatever was behind life—Schrödinger speaks of "God" and "consciousness"—it feeds on what he called "negative entropy," or in other words, order. Life is a force that injects order into a universe that is otherwise running down.†

---

*Pogson comments that regarding the role of Judas in the Gospel, "Gurdjieff and Ouspensky and Dr. Nicoll were all in agreement." *Maurice Nicoll,* 201. This refers to the idea in the Work that the Crucifixion was a kind of mystery drama, enacted in real life, and that Judas had the difficult role of consciously playing the traitor, so that Jesus could fulfill his part. This is a view more recently put forth by commentators on the Gnostic Gospel of Judas, discovered in the 1970s but not made public until 2006. See Elaine Pagels and Karen L. King, *Reading Judas* (London: Allen Lane, 2007). Yet in *A New Model of the Universe,* in the chapter on "Superman," Ouspensky offers a different view, and even denies that Judas "sacrificed himself . . . in order that the miracle of redemption should be accomplished." Instead, he argues that Judas was actually "a small man who found himself in the wrong place . . . an ordinary man . . . who understood nothing of what Jesus said to his disciples" and "that he feared to be exposed," and so betrayed Christ (117).
†Nicoll also read a paper by the biologist C. H. Waddington, "Canalization of Development and the Inheritance of Acquired Characteristics," in which he tries to make room for the Lamarckian notion of "purpose" in nature within the framework of neo-Darwinism. Nicoll, Later Diary, March 31, 1943.

It was not quite Gurdjieff—for him, the universe is growing—but it was a start. And it was also a rather different view of "life" than the one Nicoll usually held. Throughout his diaries and the *Commentaries*, Nicoll invariably portrays "life" as something out to get him, or at least to take him away from what is really important. It is a "pain factory," it "drains us," it "eats us," and is even a burglar that "will break in on you and steal everything."[34] We remember that for him, esotericism was a "rope" with which he could climb up out of life. This pessimistic, almost paranoid view of "life"—everyday life, not the kind Schrödinger wrote about—must have informed the low spirits that depressed Nicoll in these and later years.

Nicoll may have been trying to recapture some of the interests of his early years. He began to give lectures on various sciences, introductory talks in biology, chemistry, physics, physiology, and to write introductory accounts of these for his students. He learned the lesson that many writers have learned: that the best way to learn about something is to write a book about it. We've seen that Nicoll thought the science textbooks of his time were infected with communism, so it is no surprise that he decided he would have to write his own. His students enjoyed his lectures, and some biology even made it into some Work routines. Copley recalls a "dance of the chromosomes" in which participants had to act out the process of mitosis and meiosis.[35] But the lectures that seemed to have made the strongest impression on Nicoll's groups were his talks about the brain.

We remember that Nicoll was always impressed by the work of the surgeon Wilfred Trotter, and now he recalled Trotter's high regard for the brain, which he believed was an organ very different from the rest of the body. Nicoll became fascinated with the findings of recent research into the electrical activity of the brain and its attendant "brain waves." When the brain is in neutral, when we are not thinking about or attending to anything in particular, it generates what is known as an alpha rhythm. But this changes to beta or gamma as soon as we focus our attention, rather as an open palm turns into a fist when we grab hold of something. Nicoll recognized that this focusing, which is something we do, was the factor that changed the rhythm, not any input from the senses. He concluded that there was some "deep part" of the brain that was in control of our attention, and that this was "the beginning of consciousness." Nicoll also observed that there were "silent areas" of the brain, that he speculated may represent "latent possibilities," perhaps the "higher centers" that Gurdjieff said are already present in human beings and that we are unaware of only because of our mechanicalness.

Nicoll was also taken with the work of the nineteenth-century neurologist Hughlings Jackson. Jackson spoke of the body as structured hierarchically, something that appealed to Nicoll, and he made the interesting observation that the more organized an organ, the more mechanical it is. And the obverse was true: less organization but more complexity allowed for greater freedom, and the brain, Jackson saw, was the most complex thing we knew. He was also one of the earliest to recognize something that we now take for granted and to which a great deal of attention and speculation has been directed: the differences between our cerebral hemispheres.

Jackson's famous one-liner—"Expression on the left, recognition on the right"—sums up the general division of labor between our left and right brains, with the left oriented to language and the right to images. One of the striking things that Gurdjieff said years ago during his thunderbolt appearance in London was that "essence and personality" are "in different parts of the brain."[36] Split brain research was on no one's agenda then, and it isn't clear if Nicoll remembered Gurdjieff's remark twenty years later when he began to give his lectures.* But if we recall the distinc-

---

*We've seen that Gurdjieff called human beings "three brained beings." This may be a remarkable anticipation of the work of the neuroscientist Paul MacLean, who proposed the idea that man has three brains: the reptilian, the mammalian, and our distinctly human cortex. See Arthur Koestler, *The Ghost in the Machine*, 277–85. It may also seem to refer to our two cerebral hemispheres and the cerebellum, which lies below them. See Pogson, *Maurice Nicoll*, 25. Or it may refer to the right and left brain and the mass of fibers, the *corpus callosum*, linking them, which is severed in split brain surgery in order to prevent epileptic attacks from passing from one hemisphere to the other.

tion between the two, with essence being what we are born with, and personality what we acquire, we can see that they line up quite nicely with what we know of the differences between the right and left brain.

To risk oversimplifying, the right brain presents the world in its immediacy, providing a total but slightly vague picture of things as they are. It is trusting and innocent. (Essence, Gurdjieff said, "has no critical mind.") Aesthetic, poetic, and mystical experiences are associated with the right brain. When Gurdjieff spoke of "seeing without associations," he meant seeing with the right brain, which is how we saw the world when we were children. This is why when asked what it would be like to see with essence, he replied that everything would be more vivid.*

The left brain's business is to unpack this picture, to register the details, and create a re-presentation of it in order to deal with it. It is practical, suspicious, and goal-oriented. Science, logic, and technology are products of the left brain. We can say that the right brain is concerned with "isness," the left with business. What has happened, from Gurdjieff's perspective, is that "personality" has taken over, obscuring "essence." And according to more than one investigator into the relations between our brains, something similar has happened in our heads, with the left brain getting the upper hand and suppressing the input from the right.[37]

It is unclear how much Nicoll understood of split-brain psychology—there wasn't a great deal of material on it available at the time—but some remarks Nicoll makes in the *Commentaries* about the esoteric meaning of right and left, suggest at least an intuitive understanding of it. For some reason that no one yet understands, the right side of the body is controlled by the left brain, and the left side by the right. With this in mind, consider Nicoll's remarks:

---

*Wordsworth captures this in the opening of "Intimations of Immortality": "There was a time when meadow, grove, and stream / The earth, and every common sight, / To me did seem / Apparelled in celestial light, / The glory and the freshness of a dream. / It is not now as it hath been of yore;— / Turn whereso'er I may, / By night or day, / The things which I have seen I now can see no more."

The right hand is ordinarily the more conscious. [That is the one connected to the left brain.] The more conscious side of a man is the external man, the side he makes use of most: the less conscious side is the inner, deeper man. The outer man is formed by contact with outer life, to adapt to life. . . . A man with only an outer side developed toward life is a *half-man*—a one-sided man in the sense of a man cut longitudinally in half. He has one leg and arm and half a brain. There are two sides to a man, a right and left, an outer and inner. They have to be joined together to form the entire man.[38]

Whatever Nicoll knew of split-brain psychology, his reading here seems pretty accurate. Whatever we want to make of it, it seems that esotericism was aware of something that neuroscience is just learning about.

Mention of an "inner" and "outer" man tells us that Nicoll's reading of Swedenborg was informing his language. Swedenborg, too, knew of the division of labor between our brains, delegating the rational to the left side and the "affections or things of the will" to the right. Swedenborg, we know, wrote a great deal about the brain, and Nicoll seems to have read it. One area of the brain they were both interested in was the cerebellum, the "little brain" that is located in the back of the skull below the more evolutionarily recent cerebral cortex. Swedenborg believed that it was through the cerebellum that the "divine influx" reached us; this was why in heaven, angels do not stand behind one another, so as not to block the flow.

In a diary entry for May 27, 1944, Nicoll notes that Swedenborg said the brain "has changed," that is, evolved, and that when the cerebrum took over from the cerebellum, which was the source of "higher dreams," direct contact with the divine was lost, and now had to be achieved through the intellect.[39] This is in keeping with Swedenborg's belief that long ago, humankind was closer to the divine, and could perceive its presence directly, unlike we, who are separated from it by our limited rationality.

Swedenborg also believed that in earlier times people could understand the language of parables, or, as he called it, "correspondences," but with the rise of the cerebrum, which he equates with the Fall, this understanding was lost.[40] We know that Swedenborg too was interested in dreams and their symbolic language and that they too arise from an area of the psyche beyond the rational ego.

Oddly, some confirmation of Swedenborg's ideas about the cerebellum may be found in the work of the psychologist Stan Gooch and his researches into Neanderthal man. Gooch believed that the cerebellum is the seat of paranormal and mystical experiences, and he argued that Neanderthal possessed a much larger cerebellum than Cro-Magnon man, our direct ancestor. Neanderthal was something of a mystic, and would be superseded by his more practical rival, who possessed a larger cerebrum. Gooch believed that modern *Homo sapiens* were the product of crossbreeding between Neanderthal and Cro-Magnon, and that individuals who exhibited paranormal phenomena would have larger than average cerebella. Oddly enough, having reached this conclusion he came across a reference to someone who reported "actual conscious experience of the cerebellum . . . during paranormal activity."[41] It was Swedenborg.*

---

*On November 29, 1944, Nicoll noted that he had read Ouspensky's chapter "Experimental Mysticism" in *A New Model of the Universe* and had found similar observations about the plurality of ideas that came to Ouspensky under the influence of nitrous oxide with how Swedenborg speaks of "how many things are in a single expression of the Word," shown to him "by the opening of the mind." In my book on Swedenborg I draw the same comparisons, and also relate Swedenborg's notions of the complexity of angelic language to William James's experience of nitrous oxide, which inspired Ouspensky's. As far as I knew, I was the first to make this connection, but I am pleased to see Nicoll had recognized it too. See my *Swedenborg: An Introduction to His Life and Ideas,* 130–35.

No one liked Quaremead, the house in Ugley, on the borders of Hertfordshire and Essex, about forty-five miles north of London, that Nicoll and his group moved to in the spring of 1945.* According to Copley, it did not suit Nicoll's being, which, as his diaries tell us, was not doing that well as it was.[42] For Pogson, they "never quite fitted harmoniously into that house," although it had its good points.[43] They must not have been many, for their time there was short, a little more than a year and a half, and when they left, they would not be sorry to go. Copley felt particularly "out of step with what went on there," which seems a curious way to phrase it, as what went on there was the same as had gone on at their previous two encampments.[44] Did he have something else in mind? And what could that have been? Perhaps the fact that it was in Ugley that Copley endured the lengthy litany of his failings at the local pub, within earshot of everyone, that made him feel out of sorts in the new location. In any event, he had just been demobilized, and was moving into a new home himself, so he and his wife did not visit that often.

Copley even wondered if Nicoll had made a mistake this time.[45] There is a time for everything, Ecclesiastes tells us, and perhaps this time Nicoll's usual nose for the propitious moment was somehow off? This is one of the few occasions when one of Nicoll's followers voiced the slightest doubt about their teacher's decisions, which, as we've seen, were usually made quickly and without much deliberation. (Pogson never breathes a word of it.) How had Nicoll come to settle on a place in which no one felt comfortable, not even himself, although that possibility itself was becoming increasingly rare? Had it anything to do

---

*Nicoll stayed behind at the King's Head for a time before joining the others at Quaremead. During at least one ten-day stay in January 1945, he "starved" himself in an attempt to lose weight. It was not successful; by March he records that he weighs "15 stone," or 210 pounds. For a "tall short man," as Nicoll called himself, this was an unhealthy size. He also "cut back" on his beer and wine intake on several occasions, going "dry" on at least one. In several dreams during this time Nicoll is concerned about his appearance. He also records that walking is not a reliable way of reducing weight.

with him? Were his own inner contradictions reaching out beyond his psyche into the outer world? We know that Nicoll believed in the power of thought to affect reality, an idea that informed the "visualization" he continued to practice, and the synchronicities he continued to collect argued for some open participation between our inner and outer worlds.[46] Swedenborg believed that the world we experience is an "outpicturing" of our inner one. Was Nicoll somehow creating difficulties but was unaware that he was? The Work, of course, is about overcoming difficulties, not pining over the past, and embraces considerable "muddle and friction," turning them to its profit. Yet at Quaremead it seemed the group was simply not able to adjust and that whatever the reason, the place just wasn't right. Perhaps there are some difficulties you simply can't overcome.

Some problems were obvious. The house was big, set back from the main road to Newmarket, where Nicoll used to frequent the races while at Cambridge. Built around the turn of the century, it had a large garden, a summerhouse, orchard, and eight acres of land. This was good, as the group acquired livestock, as they had before, pigs, ducks, and chickens. But because the rooms were large they were difficult to heat, and the electricity was unreliable. The electric fires would short and the lamps would dim. The one warm room was the kitchen, and, as at most parties, everyone gravitated there.

It was also awkward for the mothers who still remained at the King's Head in Birdlip. When they finally joined the rest of the group, they too felt out of sorts. From being in the center of town, where they could visit shops and get a bus somewhere if they liked, they were now isolated in the countryside, with no public transportation.[47] But for the short time they would be there, this was it. Nicoll had plans for the place, even if it didn't feel right. The household staff would soon be let go and the mothers who remained would take over the housekeeping. Memories of Fontainebleau and the work they had abandoned at Tyeponds came to him. He had a relapse of "institute-itis" and intended to turn Quaremead into a proper Work environment. It was time to get organized.

Things followed a routine that must have been fairly familiar by now. People arrived, responsibilities were divvied up—who would cook, who would clean—meetings were held, late-night chats followed, that week's commentary was worked out and sent to everyone, and so on. Rooms were apportioned. Nicoll once again chose a ground floor room with its own entrance, this one opening onto a veranda, where he would often see woodpeckers. Although, aside from sleeping and working he apparently did not spend much time here. Why is not quite clear, but he quickly spotted another location where he could often be found.

The White Hart, the local pub, was near the gate to the drive to Quaremead, and Nicoll found his way there regularly, becoming a real habitué. It was here that Copley received his dressing down. It was a well-stocked village pub, the kind one expects to find in an Agatha Christie story, and Nicoll and the group often gathered there. Nicoll would get to know the owners quite well, and at one point, when he began to include toy making in the sort of handiwork that had become a great part of his teaching, he made a model of the White Hart. For a time Nicoll seemed to have returned again to the interests of his youth, and he started devising little contraptions and bringing them to life with electricity, as he had years ago at Bay Tree Lodge. He produced a merry-go-round that played music, an organ grinder, a hansom cab, and he electrified a miniature caravan that one of his group had made.[48] Nicoll was also keen on discovering the secret of making snowballs— not the ones used in a fight, but the glass balls containing a winter scene that when shaken produce the effect of a blizzard. This began to occupy quite a lot of his time, and the group no doubt enjoyed it.

But for all that it may have helped him and his group to remember themselves, in his diaries Nicoll did have some second thoughts about devoting so much of his time to making toys. On March 7, 1946, near the end of their first year at Quaremead, Nicoll recorded a dream that he thought suggested that he was wasting "force making toys."[49] If he was wasting force making snowballs and merry-go-rounds, what should he have been directing it at? As Nicoll himself knew, he should have been working on what would eventually become *The New Man*, as his many diary entries to this effect make clear. Yet try as he may, he couldn't.

Nicoll was nevertheless busy, and events seemed to be speeding up. With the war winding down—it would be over by August—travel was possible, and Nicoll began to make trips to London. Soon it was arranged for him to give lectures there as the interest in his work seemed to be growing, as if his aim to turn Quaremead into an institute had somehow alerted people who would be attracted to this. Perhaps it was their magnetic centers. Or perhaps, as Nicoll began to formulate it now, the universe operated on a principle of "response to request." If the request was formulated correctly, the universe would respond in kind. As far as I know this is not part of Fourth Way philosophy, but it is rather like the "mental science" that Nicoll suggested Copley speak to his mother about years before, when she asked what he was doing on his Thursday evenings. It was also rather a different attitude from the one that saw "life" as something out to get him. It suggested instead that it meant well by us and would respond to a serious request for help.

Whether it was the universe or his magnetic center, one person who responded to Nicoll's request was Vincent Stuart, a publisher of spiritual literature who would later add Nicoll to his list, along with other Fourth Way authors, like Rodney Collin and the French poet René Daumal, a student of Gurdjieff's during the occupation. He attended Nicoll's London lectures and then took a trip to Quaremead, where he experienced something of "shock."[50] It must have been beneficial, for Stuart would spend his subsequent weekends there, and at the group's next port of call, in contact with Nicoll until his death. One loss to the group was Miss Corcoran, who died during this time. She had been with the group almost from the start and of course was missed. She was not the only one who fell ill. In September 1945 Catherine went into the hospital for an operation. What the operation was for is not clear. Nicoll notes in his diary that she was "all right" after it, but doesn't mention why she had it, although it may have been for the breast cancer that would return a few years later. Whatever the reason, it was successful, and Catherine had returned to Quaremead to see out the winter.

But by this time the need to find a larger, more suitable location closer to London had become apparent, at least to Catherine, who voiced this opinion practically on her return. More people were coming on the weekends, and it was not easy to get to Ugley from London, where most of the new recruits were from. In any case, they had never felt that they had "really belonged to Quaremead," and perhaps after a stay away from it, even at a hospital, this became apparent to Catherine. Perhaps she voiced what everyone else felt, but were too conscious of not expressing a negative emotion to admit.[51] In any event, a request was sent out. It took a bit of time, but the response, when it came, seemed accurate.

By the spring of 1946, a year after they had found themselves at Quaremead, a new mooring for the ark had been found. Six months later, at the start of September, its occupants arrived to settle in. The place was Great Amwell House, about twenty miles north of London. And it was there that, according to some reports, the Work acquired a "perceptible Nicoll character."[52]

14

The End of an Octave

It may have been Catherine's idea to pull up stakes and move to yet another homestead, but the thought may very well have been on Nicoll's mind too. His "institute-itis" had started up again—if it had ever really left him—and he was eager to get back to where he was before the war intervened and forced him to put his plans on hold. This urgency to get the Work as he was teaching it back on its proper track is understandable. With the war ending, he was not the only person who was looking forward to picking up their lives where they had left them before "the history of crime" had rudely interrupted and brought everything to a halt. But it may have been more than expectations about getting back to his proper business that occupied Nicoll. A look at his diary entries from this time tells us that quite a few other things were on his mind.

His inability to get to grips with what would become *The New Man* troubled him deeply. "Must get to Gospels," he notes on December 8, 1944.[1] A few days later he is lamenting that he is "over 60" but "has nothing."[2] Eight months later, in August the next year, not long before Catherine announced the need to move, he is still not getting on with "the Gospel book," although a dream he records may, he believes, be a sign of encouragement.[3] At the end of January 1945 he is taking a "ten day retreat" at the King's Head—one of the few times when he wasn't surrounded by people—where he is "eating nothing after lunch" and "going to bed at 4 P.M. and rising at 11 A.M." This means that he was sleeping almost twenty hours a day, something a physician like Nicoll would have recognized as not a good sign.[4]

In February the term *puer aeternus* begins to turn up in the diaries. We've had occasion to mention it before. The *puer aeternus* is the "eternal child" first mentioned by Ovid in his *Metamorphoses.* In Jungian psychology it stands for a personality whose emotional life has not matured beyond adolescence and who is reluctant to enter into "real life" and take up the responsibilities and obligations thereof. We have seen that this was something that Nicoll was not happy about doing. Today this is popularly known as the "Peter Pan syndrome," the name taken, oddly enough, from the creation of Nicoll's father's friend, James Barrie. In at least one dream Nicoll made the connection between these two perpetual adolescents.[5]

The *puer aeternus* became an important symbol for Nicoll—it was, as Jung would say, an archetype—and he even owned a statuette of the "eternal youth" from the Roman period. Nicoll saw the *puer aeternus* as a kind of intermediary between ourselves, limited to our everyday ordinary personality, and the selves we could be, if we were in touch with the higher centers Gurdjieff spoke of, and which may have been located in the "silent places" Nicoll detected in the brain.[6] In this way, the *puer aeternus* acts rather like the Greek god Hermes, who is a messenger, and who is also known to be a trickster. Yet it doesn't seem to have occurred to Nicoll to consider the eternal youth in his negative aspect, that of the eternal adolescent. As the Jungian psychologist Anthony Stevens remarks, "The fear that initiation into manhood will turn one into a zombie is the classic complaint of the *puer aeternus* and the commonest justification he gives for 'dropping out of the rat race' and declining to be 'incorporated' into the social structure."[7]

Nicoll may not have called people who did not embrace the Work "zombies," but he certainly thought they were "dead."[8] And being a machine and acting mechanically, which you presumably are if you are not doing the Work, is a fair approximation to a zombie-like state. And we have also seen how distasteful Nicoll found the life of his father and his successful friends, and his efforts and failures to finally feel "a man among men."* And living in communes, self-sustaining and, as we say today, "off the grid," is one alternative to being "incorporated" into the social structure.

I'm sure many who value Nicoll's work would disagree, but with all the "gaiety" and "merriment," the singing and dancing, the charades and making toys, and many parties, in many ways he does strike me as embodying aspects of the eternal youth that most of us see the need to outgrow or at least to assimilate into a more serious attitude to life. And if Freud was right in believing that a satisfactory sexual relationship with another person—preferably of the opposite sex—was the *sine qua non* of psychological and emotional maturity, then Nicoll's continued self-sex devotions may have presented an obstacle to that achievement.

By March 1945, Nicoll is still sleeping most of the day, retiring "at tea-time," which is usually around 6:00 p.m. He notes that he can read only "pleasant interesting things that do not strain the thought," and he comments on a certain "giddiness" that comes over him.[9] Giddiness or dizziness is a symptom of a number of ailments—low blood pressure, problems with the inner ear, clogged arteries, stress and anxiety—and at this point it is difficult to determine what was causing it in Nicoll, who starts noting the sensation in his diaries around this time. We know that he will be diagnosed with cancer in 1951, but we don't know when the disease started, although he may have had an intuition of it in 1948, when he told his group that he did not have long to live.

---

*In many ways the negative aspect of the *puer aeternus* is very similar to the type of individual Gurdjieff called a "tramp." "I call 'tramps' all the so-called 'intelligentsia,' artists, poets, any kind of 'bohemian' in general." Ouspensky, *In Search of the Miraculous,* 363.

Yet it was also around this time, the spring of 1945, that Nicoll seems to have had some sort of mystical experience, although exactly what this was is difficult to determine from his entry about it in his diaries, something true of similar entries. Nicoll writes that he woke from a dream in which he saw "Christ in Enneagram," a nine-pointed symbol central to the Work.[10] He slipped back into sleep but the vision continued. He felt as if it was coming down to him as "a pipe of meaning, flowing in through the top of the head."[11] We recall Swedenborg's teaching that the "divine influx" reaches us via the cerebellum. But this sounds like something more along the lines of the *sahasrāra* or crown chakra, located above the top of the skull.

Yet a day later he sounds as if he is reconfirming his faith in the Work. "To live the Work," he writes on March 9. "The beginning of a new will—to do the Work—to bring the knowledge of it into action and to believe it," which may suggest a certain lack of belief of late.[12] A few days later, among much else, he notes a dream in which Ouspensky appears as Christ.[13] Not long after this, he dreams of Christ appearing as a seal, which in some traditions, he explains, is seen as a sacrificial animal.[14] This, he is told by his inner voice—which appears in the later diaries as it does in the earlier ones—is the attitude he needs to take.

A little later, his voice is again berating him for his laziness, and his pride in thinking that he *is* the Work, rather than a vehicle for it.[15] Then there is a dream about the Holy Grail.[16] And around the time that Catherine returned from her operation and decided to pull up stakes and move house, Nicoll records several dreams in which his authority as a teacher of the Work is questioned or simply ignored.[17] He also records a type of dream that will recur often in later entries in the diary: one in which he finds a "small room" somewhere, away from everything, where he could pursue his devotions undisturbed and not have to teach the Work.[18] Other dreams, about "choked up lavatories" and other such blockages suggest a very graphic representation of Nicoll's costiveness, as least regarding what will eventually become *The New Man*.[19]

What conclusion, if any, can we draw from this small sampling of Nicoll's dream life from this time? Clearly analyzing someone's dreams, even under the best conditions, is always risky, and doing so from a fragmentary, at times indecipherable account, such as Nicoll's diaries present, decades after the dreams were recorded, is fraught with hazard. Nevertheless, if nothing else, this representative selection suggests to me that his psyche remained as turbulent and self-divided as ever. Again, I have merely touched on only some of the entries from this period. Yet I think it is safe to say that although Catherine made the need to move official, she wasn't alone in feeling that it was time for a change.

NICOLL'S DECISION TO TAKE the large Georgian house of cold, gray stone but "noble proportions" was characteristically swift. A friend had told Catherine of an advertisement she had seen for a house near Ware, and the next day she had driven over to have a look. When she returned she announced that the place was exactly what they needed. Nicoll immediately set off with a few of the group to see for himself. The huge impersonal courtyard at first seemed forbidding. But when they reached the other side of the house, their initial uncertainty instantly dissolved. A long terrace peppered with crocuses sloped down to an expanse of lawn that stretched to some woods in the distance. Nicoll's inspection of the property was done at a clip. He "raced" through the house, his Inverness cloak flapping behind him, followed by a panting owner and Nicoll's entourage. He then raced through the grounds, taking in the handsome wrought-iron gates that led to a walled vegetable garden. That seemed sufficient. Half an hour later, Nicoll said he wanted to take the place and instructed one of the group to make an offer.

As had become tradition during these negotiations, Nicoll and the others found their way to the local pub. The George IV was just down the hill—which suggests it was easier to get to than to return from— and Nicoll soon made friends with the proprietor. As at the White

Hart in Ugley, he soon became a regular. Nicoll could often be found sitting in his favorite seat, by the window, on Saturdays, where he could observe students approach and judge their "state" before speaking with them, performing the Sherlock Holmes act he put on years before at the Café Royal. One does not haggle for the pearl of great price, nor for the new location of the Work. An equitable figure was swiftly agreed on, a deal struck, and a deposit paid. In September 1946, Nicoll and his group moved into Great Amwell House, about a mile beyond Ware.

As Pogson noted, it was the start of Nicoll's last "seven year cycle."[20] This was a way of measuring one's life that was quite popular in astrological circles and remains so today. Nicoll had an interest in astrology, but in the Work the idea took on the character of an "octave." This musical term carried peculiar significance in the Fourth Way, being an emblem of the "law of seven," the cosmic blueprint for any process, starting with the Ray of Creation itself. Nicoll believed that after the age of five, his life could be divided into these cycles, with assorted fallow patches in between. There was his early childhood, his years at school, and those at Cambridge. These made up his first three octaves. His fourth octave was centered on his meeting with Jung, the fifth on his meeting with Ouspensky and his break with Jung, and the sixth on his return from Fontainebleau and his decision to become a teacher of the Work. Now he was entering his seventh and final octave. Oddly enough, Nicoll would die practically seven years to the day that the group officially took over Great Amwell House. Was it destiny? Pogson believed so and evidently so did Nicoll.

Although their spirits were high, the move was something of an ordeal, with rain pelting down as they carried in their belongings. The next morning they woke to discover a curious peculiarity of the house. The locks on the doors wouldn't open—there was a strange system of double locking—and that morning it seemed they were prisoners in their new home, an inconvenience no one had planned for. (Or was it a sign that Nicoll would not leave?) Another peculiarity was the kitchen table, which was "colossal in size" and "oblong in shape."[21] It was much higher off the floor than most tables, and some of the more petite members of the group found that when sitting at it their chins were level with it, which must have made dining difficult. (As a "tall short man" Nicoll may have experienced this himself.) Eventually the legs were shortened but the image of Nicoll holding court, commenting on whatever he had read in the *Evening Standard*—his favorite newspaper—that day to his followers, some of whom would have seemed to have needed a highchair, has comic appeal.

Again the ritual of assigning rooms was performed. Nicoll first chose a room on the first floor, with large bay windows that opened out onto the garden.* From this perch, he could watch over the activities that started up soon after their arrival. Nicoll seemed intent on getting the Work routines going as soon as possible. Everything he needed seemed at hand. Catherine had already got the group to pick fruit that they would then make into jam. The wide lawns needed to be cut with motorized mowers, unlike the huge lawns at Fontainebleau that were shorn by an adolescent Fritz Peters with a manual one, all in one day.

A studio was set up in the stable, there was a carpenter's shed, a space set aside for modeling, and space set aside for toy making. When the move from Quaremead to Great Amwell House began, the wooden huts they had erected there had to be dismantled. This caused Nicoll some distress. On August 19, 1946, he noted in his diary that, "since the big shed has been dismantled I have been bored, not being able to make toys. I should do my book. Yes—but I have to talk to all those people—and drink beer to do so."[22]

The fact that he is bored because he cannot make toys yet also cannot face writing is instructive. Nicoll's remark about drinking beer in order to "talk to all those people," referred to a dream in which he is

---

*In England, the first floor is not the ground floor, as it is in the U.S., but the floor above.

told that he "must work." He is also told that he must drink in order to do so. This seems more of a warning than an encouragement, as increasingly Nicoll records that he needs the inspiration of a few pints of beer or a bottle of claret to get in the mood to teach, something he seems to have shared with other teachers of the Fourth Way.

Something else he seems to have shared with them was the boredom that required a stimulant to escape from it. When C. S. Nott visited Ouspensky and, as was customary, drank with him, Ouspensky admitted that the strong concoctions he was imbibing were the only thing that relieved the boredom and depression that came over him. As Colin Wilson points out, for someone like Ouspensky, who was really a "gentle romantic" and not the "scientific guru" he tried to turn himself into, the best remedy for boredom and depression was some creative work. In Ouspensky's case this meant writing, but Ouspensky had abandoned that years earlier.[23]

The same, I believe, was true of Nicoll, and this may be why the two got on together. Like Ouspensky, Nicoll started out as a writer, but had put that side of his character into storage to become a teacher of the Work. (He had given up his psychological practice in 1939 at the start of the war.) At the end of 1945 he is recording in his diary what seem to me regrets about abandoning his fictional work, and of not honoring his muse.[24] Yet even his esoteric writing was not forthcoming. Why had a teaching aimed at awakening consciousness and transforming being resulted in the loss of creativity in two of its most dedicated practitioners?

In any event, the erection of the Quaremead huts on their new turf provided Nicoll with a reason to call a "scurry," something he hadn't had an opportunity to do since Tyeponds. It must have seemed like old times, although according to Copley, some of the older members didn't think so. They thought the newcomers had it soft. Although there was "an ample supply of young and able bodies in the growing Group to cope with physical tasks," conditions were not as primitive as at

Tyeponds, and erecting a hut was not the same as putting up a building from scratch.[25] There seemed a shortage of inconvenience and a dearth of difficulties. Although there was plenty of housework and gardening, conditions at Great Amwell House were simply not as demanding as at Lake Farms, and this may account for the increased emphasis on arts and crafts. One manifestation of this was the "guitar orchestra" that was formed, composed of thirty highly amateur guitarists, fortified with a few mandolins.

Yet it seemed that many in the group had not yet learned the lesson that Nicoll tried to get across to them when they had to leave Tyeponds for the Knapp. They continued to pine for the days "when work was work, lighting was by paraffin lamps and the Elsan closets [outdoor toilets] needed daily attention."[26] Those days, as Copley remarks, may have been over, and it was now "time for something other." Yet one can't help but wonder if Nicoll himself did not have the old days in mind as he looked out upon his new estate with the thought of carrying on with the project he had to abandon five years earlier.

COPLEY REMARKS THAT MOST members came to Great Amwell House for the weekend. Some came only for a day and some only for a meeting, which on Sundays were held in the afternoon, an awkward time, yet necessary for people who could not stay over until Monday. With the war over, many people were searching for a new meaning and direction in their life, just as had happened after the First World War, when people like Nicoll, Orage, and others were drawn to Ouspensky's lectures. These seekers had heard about Nicoll's group, and the number of new recruits swelled. Newcomers usually first joined a subgroup, such as the one Copley led in London, and only after a probationary period, when their commitment to the Work was determined, would they receive an invitation to a weekend gathering.

There was, however, a cluster of permanent residents at Great

Amwell House, about fifteen in all, counting Nicoll and Catherine. A usual weekend would begin on Friday, with people calling to ask if they could attend. A list was made of those coming, rooms given to the non-residents, chores assigned, and other activities settled. Fridays were the most hectic and stressful. As he had done before, at the meetings Nicoll sat in a chair with an assistant next to him, and questions were based on that week's commentary. Getting that done was something of a gamble. Nicoll did not prepare his commentary until the last minute and would often change his mind midway and have to start again.

Nicoll seemed intent on having as much activity as possible going on during the weekends, as if he wanted to establish a permanent scurry. Along with woodcutting, fruit picking, gardening, guitar lessons, tending to the ducks, geese, and hens, and other busy work, the movements were reintroduced. There were even productions of Gilbert and Sullivan operettas. Yet one was not supposed to perform them too well, or, it seems, even well at all. Copley records an evening when a "strong professional soprano voice" was among those rehearsing for one performance. When Nicoll heard this, he "stormed in from his room" and stopped the singing immediately. "No. It is not about this!" he bellowed and stormed out, leaving them guessing what he meant by "this."[27]

"This" apparently meant singing well. It seems that any sign of mastery or even natural talent was to be suppressed. "No activity was regarded as an end in itself," Copley comments. The singing was "not intended to make the adept more adept," but was supposed to be done in the "quick and dirty" methods of the Work. Singing, and the other artistic endeavors, were intended to "open new ground which otherwise would lie fallow in people who would perhaps have neglected the experience, say, of making music or painting for the remainder of their lives." "If real talent were discovered," Copley remarks, "the individual could pursue it elsewhere."[28]

He or she certainly could not pursue it at Great Amwell House, where it would be subsumed beneath the general admonition not to take any credit for oneself, to avoid "self-love" and "vanity" at all costs, and not to allow anything to distract you from the Work, even your own creativity.* Yet if the idea was to "open new ground" in oneself, to have that new ground declared off limits if it seemed too "well done," seems, to me at least, contradictory and self-defeating. One wonders how anyone in Nicoll's group with some natural talent felt when they were told not to exhibit it nor to feel any pride or confidence in oneself for having it? This may have been a means of making "personality" passive, but then perhaps it was "essence" that broke out in song, having its first opportunity to do so?

NOT LONG AFTER THE MOVE, Nicoll decided to relocate from his room on the first floor to the room below. Why he did not choose this room initially is unclear, given that it had what he always required, that is, a separate entrance. Perhaps he enjoyed the view from the room above, where he could oversee the action on the weekends. But once business started picking up, he realized the room below was more practical. He did a complete makeover, having the walls painted with images of the solar system, "the Universe as vibrations"—a key idea in the Work—and the table of elements, rather as he had had the animals from Noah's ark painted on the walls of his surgery in Golders Greene.[29] He later added an image from a curious alchemical work, the *Mutus Liber*, or "silent book," a work composed entirely of pictures. This was the picture of a man lying asleep on the ground, with a ladder rising up to the heavens above him, on which are angels, blowing their trumpets, trying to awaken him, which Nicoll refers to in his letters to Bush that started the *Commentaries*.[30]

Nicoll would work in this room, and have selected students visit

*Yet this instruction not to show "talent" seems contradicted by the admonition to be "more than adequate," that Copley records. "I was told 'Try to do what you do with a degree of flair. You cannot afford to be average.'" *Portrait of a Vertical Man*, 74.

him for a talk. It was also here that he read. Along with detective stories and biographies, Nicoll kept up with his former mentor's work, reading Jolande Jacobi's *The Psychology of C. G. Jung* (1942), a sturdy and still very readable exposition of Jung's basic ideas, and Jung's own *Psychology and Religion* (1940). He even secured transcripts of some of Jung's lectures from mutual acquaintances. He also read more diverting fare, like the thrilling *Man-Eaters of Kumaon* (1944) by the hunter Jim Corbett, famous for his accounts of tracking man-eating tigers. Nicoll wrote Corbett a fan letter, suggesting he write another book. Another book that seems to have engaged Nicoll's imagination powerfully was William Seabrook's *Jungle Ways* (1931).

Seabrook was an American writer and journalist with an interest in the occult and other exotic practices, such as cannibalism, which he wrote about in *Jungle Ways* and other books. He was a friend of the dark magician Aleister Crowley—and a participant in some of his sex magic rituals—and attended Gurdjieff's performances of the movements in New York in January 1924, which he wrote about in *Witchcraft: Its Power in the World Today* (1940).* Seabrook noted the "brilliant, automaton-like, inhuman, almost incredible docility and robot-like obedience of the disciples," who struck him as a group of "perfectly trained zombies."[31] It was Seabrook who invited the behaviorist John Watson, and the journalists Lincoln Steffens and George Seldes, to a reading of *Beelzebub* that left them singularly unimpressed but delighted with Gurdjieff's cooking. Seabrook was also an alcoholic and a sadomasochist with a taste for bondage; in September 1945 he committed suicide, taking an overdose of barbiturates.

---

*It is interesting to recognize that all during the years in which Nicoll pursued and struggled with his "self-sex" devotions, Crowley made masturbation a central part of his magical arsenal, resorting to it most times when he was without a partner, female or male. The VIII degree workings of his Ordo Templi Orientis rituals involves masturbation and visualization, much along the same lines as Nicoll's devotions, although Crowley was up front about his practice and did not hide it. The IX degree involves heterosexual intercourse; the XI, homosexual unions. See Lachman, *Aleister Crowley,* 178.

Jungle Ways is an account of Seabrook's fascination with voodoo; he is said to have popularized the term "zombie." The book had a powerful effect on Nicoll, leading him to accept that the "black magic" it depicted was real, and closely linked to the more "white" form of magic Nicoll practiced in his "visualization."* Copley admits that this belief of Nicoll's made him "uncomfortable," but it was something that Nicoll confessed to in his diary, writing that the practices depicted in the book show that the Haitians Seabrook wrote about "had knowledge."[32] A dream Nicoll recorded while reading the book showed two virile blacks possessing great sexual power: a symbol of the "black magic" that impressed him, but also perhaps of the "primitive" creative energies that remained in the hands of his "shadow," and which he was unable to draw on to finish "the Gospel book."

Nicoll's favorite book, Boswell's *Life of Samuel Johnson*, suggests one reason why Nicoll had such difficulty trying to write. Pogson remarks that Nicoll enjoyed Boswell's biography because it captured what would have otherwise been lost to posterity: Johnson's conversation. Nicoll loved the book because "he was fond of good talk and Dr. Johnson has fittingly been described as 'incomparably the best talker of whom the world knows anything.'"[33] Nicoll identified with Johnson; like him, he too "could hold his company spellbound for hours," or at least some of them. Pogson notes that at Great Amwell House Nicoll "liked to settle down and talk well through the night," something, we know, he also did at Lake Farms, fortified by biscuits and anchovy paste. But apparently not everyone had the stamina to stay up late and listen to him. Nothing "irritated" Nicoll more, Pogson admits, "than if one of his companions said he must go, thereby perhaps breaking the octave."[34]

---

*Pogson records that at one point, Nicoll invited a conjuror—stage magician—he had met at the pub to the house to perform. "Eric's" performance was "memorable," and convinced Nicoll and Catherine of his power to "control matter." "He could change cards in mid-air. We could see them in the process of changing." *Maurice Nicoll*, 247.

Staying up late with the teacher seemed de rigueur within the Ouspensky line of the Work. Students who went the limit with Ouspensky did so with the hope of catching an occasional esoteric pearl, dropped amid the nostalgia for lost Russia. In Nicoll's case, it seemed the wisdom may have poured forth in quantities that some could not absorb. Was it a test, as some considered Ouspensky's boozing to be? Or did Nicoll simply like to talk, and was annoyed if not everyone liked to listen?*

Holding court and keeping one's audience captive—sometimes in a more than metaphorical sense—is a common practice among many gurus.[35] Yet more to the point, the famous "talkers" of literature, like Dr. Johnson, tend to write comparatively little. It is a truism of any instruction in writing that one can "talk a good book" so well, that when it comes time to write it, it has dissipated, expressed already in conversation. Another thing that the great talkers have is an audience, and the instant gratification of impressing them with a well-rounded period, something a writer, on his own in a room, lacks. Nicoll's pleasure in "folding his legs and having out his talk," as Dr. Johnson did, may have left him with nothing to start with, and no audience to give approval, when he faced the difficulty of putting his ideas about the meaning of the parables down in words.

JUST BEFORE NICOLL AND Co. had moved into Great Amwell House, another octave, which had intertwined with Nicoll's, was drawing to its close. In the summer of 1946, in the Grand Ballroom of Steinway

---

*Something else that seemed to annoy Nicoll was if a student was not as interested in something as he was. Copley records that when Nicoll was reading through the Captain Hornblower novels by C. S. Forester, he asked Copley what he knew of "barques and barquentines, brigs and brigantines," assuming his brief career in the navy during the war would have provided him with such knowledge. When Copley confessed to relative ignorance, Nicoll chided him for passing too "many faeces without assimilating much that you could extract from this rich source of the food of impressions." *Portrait of a Vertical Man,* 74.

Hall in New York, an ill and increasingly disillusioned P. D. Ouspensky told his stunned students that he was leaving America and returning to England. Madame O was remaining at Franklin Farms, the estate she ruled with an iron hand, in Mendham, New Jersey, not far from Manhattan, where she would carry on the Work. But his time in the New World was over. He was heading to the only place to which he could return. It was not home, but it did contain something that Ouspensky increasingly prized: memories.

Accounts of Ouspensky's decision to return to London differ, as do accounts of the conditions at Franklin Farms that he was leaving behind. Some paint a picture of an old, ill, tired, and broken man, held captive by his own students, and desperate to escape. Others suggest that his departure was something Ouspensky had planned well in advance and was part of a vision of a new stage in the Work. We may never know the truth. What we do know is that when Ouspensky arrived at the Southampton Docks in January 1947, he was a man upon whom "Death had already set its mark," as Kenneth Walker, his longtime student, saw when he greeted him there.[36] Ouspensky's work in England had more or less ground to a halt when he left London for New York six years earlier. His students, Walker among them, feared that if he did not return and reestablish his operation, the Work as they knew it would die. Walker does not mention what he and Ouspensky's other students knew or thought of Nicoll's activities, but it is clear that they weren't considered an immediate successor to Ouspensky's project. And at this point Walker believed that Gurdjieff—whom he had not yet met—though still alive and active in Paris, would be too old to "safeguard the future of his own teaching."

Yet when Ouspensky did return, it was clear that whatever future he had in mind for the Work, he would not be around to see it. It would be even more accurate to say that it was unclear *if* Ouspensky believed there was a future for the Work. For one thing, it was not "the Ouspensky of old" who was wheeled off the ocean liner and driven to

Lyne Place, where he retired to his former room, speaking to hardly anyone, preoccupied with his thoughts and the pain of his malfunctioning body. Whatever he may have had in mind, it was obvious to Walker that he did not have "sufficient strength to carry this plan through."[37] Ouspensky declined to receive medical help, so the exact nature of his illness remains unclear, but it was most likely liver failure exacerbated by the marathon drinking sessions he had held over the years.

Even the England Ouspensky was returning to seemed against him. Long ago, Gurdjieff had told him that the earth was in a "very bad place" in the universe, being almost the bottom planet on the Ray of Creation. In the winter of 1947, one of the worst places to be in this very bad place was England. Unlike America, it had felt the war at firsthand. Its economy was gutted, much of London was in ruins, food, electricity, and fuel were rationed, even radio broadcasts and the newer television were severely limited as was book, newspaper, and magazine publication. And to top it off, the winter of 1947 was one of the coldest on record, with snow covering much of the country for weeks on end. If Ouspensky had learned the lesson of super-efforts, he would certainly put it into practice now.

The super-effort the dying Ouspensky made resulted in his students in England receiving the shock of their lives. In a series of meetings held at Colet House between February and June Ouspensky stunned a bewildered and baffled three-hundred-strong audience by informing them, among other things, that such things as self-remembering, "real I," being mechanical, asleep, and other such terminology of the Work were unknown to him. What teaching did they refer to? he asked his puzzled students. He had never taught them anything. Who had said that they were asleep, that they were mechanical? And, perhaps more important, why did they believe him?

More questions received similar replies. What is harmony? A musical term. What is the aim of an esoteric school? That is a very big thing—or maybe not. What is reality? Nothing, probably. I want to escape from sleep. Probably impossible. Ouspensky seemed intent on ignoring or rejecting anything to do with the Work. But his remarks were not all negative. He encouraged his audience—they were no longer his students—that if they wanted anything out of life, they needed to begin with what they knew. They had to start from what they wanted, and knowing what you want is a very big thing. They had to start from themselves, with something that truly mattered to them, some everyday aim they wished to accomplish. And they had to work alone.[38] From a man who had told them for many years that *nothing* could be accomplished on one's own, this was indeed something new.

A silence much like the one from the Warwick Gardens days settled over the audience in the long spaces between these staccato deadpan replies. Communication was not good. Ouspensky's English was almost indecipherable, he seemed to lose interest easily, and the secretary he had brought from Mendham, whom no one knew, was not that adept at interpreting his gnomic remarks. Student after student found their questions given either brusque unsatisfying replies or simply ignored. Finally, Kenneth Walker summoned the consciousness to ask the question no one else seemed able to, something of a super-effort itself. "Do you mean, Mr. Ouspensky, that you have abandoned the System," Walker asked. To which Ouspensky replied: "There is no System."

Not even Gurdjieff was that shocking.

At the end of his last lecture, given on June 18, Ouspensky needed an injection to make it out of the hall and into his car. Four months later, he was dead. He left one recurrence for his next at dawn on October 2, 1947, amid circumstances that were, to say the least, unusual.

NICOLL DID NOT VISIT his old teacher, although a few months after Ouspensky returned, he sent a picture of Sidlesham—where Ouspensky had felt "the world turning"—along with a letter to him at Lyne Place via a student. What he said in the letter is unclear. He did not attend the extraordinary last talks in which Ouspensky had apparently rejected the system he had spent twenty-six years teaching—the system that he had sent Nicoll away to teach many years ago and that now was facing something of a crisis, at the very least an enormous inconvenience that was totally unplanned for. His diary entries on hearing of Ouspensky's return are brief, merely noting the fact.[39]

Kenneth Walker, who had seen and spoken with Ouspensky, visited Nicoll toward the end of May and spoke with him about their teacher. Walker said that Ouspensky had shrunk—reports say that he had aged twenty years in his time in America—and moved only very slowly. He answered very few questions, and the answers he did give were not particularly enlightening. He avoided Work terminology and referred to a "system that does not give results."[40] Other reports were equally distressing. They spoke of Ouspensky's "shuffling" step, of his needing to be helped with everything, of his sitting all day in silence, looking out a window, of his suffering from advanced arteriosclerosis, of his incontinence, and of his speaking only with great difficulty.[41]

One report seemed incomprehensible. Ouspensky had even decided against publishing his account of his time with Gurdjieff, the masterpiece that would appear as *In Search of Miraculous*—not his title—against his wishes and after his death.* The book he was intent on seeing published was his revised early novel *Kinedrama*, about eternal recurrence, which he had now entitled *Strange Life of Ivan Osokin*. He had written it well before a certain meeting he had had with a mysterious individual long ago in a Moscow café.

What Nicoll seemed to be unaware of—or if he was aware of them, made no mention of it—are the extraordinary events that allegedly took

---

*Ouspensky had tentatively entitled the work *Fragments of an Unknown Teaching*, but eventually decided against it because his friend G. R. S. Mead had already published *Fragments of a Faith Forgotten*, his study of Gnosticism, in 1900. "In Search of the Miraculous" is the title of a chapter in *New Model of the Universe*, as well as that of a series of lectures Ouspensky gave in Russia about his "journey to the East."

place around Ouspensky in the months following his last talks and leading up to his death. One thing that Ouspensky did impress upon his
audience during his last lectures was the need to develop their memory.
Not the memory that Orage had played with and devised exercises for,
as presented in his *Psychological Exercises and Essays*, and which made up
part of his approach to the Work. The memory Ouspensky had in mind
was the kind that could help in one's next recurrence. Ouspensky "advised
people to go back into their pasts and to try to recall . . . those cross-roads
at which it might have been possible to take a different turning."[42]

In Ouspensky's six-dimensional view of time, each moment contains possibilities left un-actualized by the choices we make. But those
possibilities nevertheless still exist, and if next time we can *remember*,
we might actualize a different one. With this in mind, Walker said,
Ouspensky had "insisted on being driven to all the places that had been
the scene of his life since he had first arrived in England."[43]

Had he been able to, he may very well have gone back to Russia,
but he had to make do with what he had. Ouspensky seemed intent on
impressing on his consciousness places in his life so that when he next
encountered them *he would remember*. Why? Because "if a man could
recollect and also had will, he would be able to alter the whole course of
his life," an idea Nicoll tried to put into fictional form in the abandoned
Pelican Hotel.[44]

What did Ouspensky want to alter? With his rejection of the system
and his entreaties to his ex-students that it was only by themselves that
they could make any efforts toward any "possible evolution," one suspects
that what he wanted to alter was his meeting with Gurdjieff. One can
only imagine what the consequences would be if he had managed to do
that. For one thing, I might not be here writing this book. Perhaps in
some corner of six-dimensional time, Ouspensky did not meet Gurdjieff
and I am not.

Someone who seemed intent on helping Ouspensky remember and
so die as consciously as possible was Rodney Collin. Collin and his wife

attended some lectures by Nicoll in 1935, but were not persuaded by them to join his group.[45] In 1936 they met Ouspensky and became his most devoted students. Like Ouspensky, they had made the journey to the West in 1941, eventually living at Franklin Farms. And now Collin was at Ouspensky's side, aiding him in his efforts to recapture his past. Or so one side of the story has it. Another suggests that "dying consciously" was more Collin's idea than Ouspensky's, and that a sick man was driven around England against his wishes. Joyce Collin-Smith, Collin's sister-in-law and a student of the Work, believed that Ouspensky suffered from Alzheimer's disease and was not accountable for his actions.[46] Part of these excursions included Ouspensky spending one night in the car, surrounded by cats— whom he believed possessed astral bodies—with a steadfast female pupil standing outside at salute. (Had Ouspensky not been ill, he would have certainly told the woman not to do anything so silly.)

Collin's relationship with Ouspensky was by many accounts one-sided, with Ouspensky often making super-efforts to endure Collin's too-earnest devotion.* Unlike Walker, who told Nicoll that he believed Ouspensky had no plan for the future, and had truly abandoned the Work—jumped ship off the ark, we might say—Collin believed that Ouspensky's ostensible rejection of his life's work was part of a great mystery play, along the lines of the Crucifixion. Like his apparent estrangement from Gurdjieff—à la Judas's betrayal of Christ—it was part of the psychohistory of the Work, a stop exercise on a grand scale.†

---

*Yet Collin and his wife were major financial investors in Ouspensky's work, something of which, according to some reports, Ouspensky took advantage. See Lachman, *In Search of P. D. Ouspensky,* 2006, 255–56.

†Ouspensky may have had such a "shock" in mind when, on September 4, a month before his death, he announced that he was returning to America. Passage was booked, luggage secured, and just as Ouspensky and his group were about to board, he announced that, "I am not going to America this time," and returned to Lyne. Had he gone back to America in his last recurrence? Was he taking a different step at this crossroads? Or was it the vagary of a dying man, having lost all sense of direction? For Collin such questions were like Zen *koans,* aimed at upsetting the logical—formatory— mind. For others they raise sad reflections on their teacher's illness and mental capacity.

And just as miracles took place around that tremendous event millennia ago, the miraculous arrived at Lyne Place, with Ouspensky, Collin believed, as its source.

Collin's account of Ouspensky's last days in *The Theory of Conscious Harmony* and other works brims over with fantastic events and phenomena. It is full of reports of telepathy, visionary experiences, incursions of supernatural powers, angels, and a "Christlike being" that suggested the Catholic orientation that Collin's magnetic center would pull him toward for his own few remaining years.[47] Following Ouspensky's conscious death—which, according to Collin, had transformed Ouspensky into a spiritual being, achieving the miraculous he had searched for—Collin locked himself in Ouspensky's room for a week, taking no food, neither bathing nor shaving, and only unlocking the door after his wife arrived from Mendham. (He had earlier pushed away a ladder propped up against the window when other Ouspenskians tried to gain access to the room.)

Collin told his wife that he had been in telepathic contact with Ouspensky the entire time, and he assured her that this time, he had finally escaped recurrence. It was now up to him to help the Work enter its next phase, which, like Nicoll's—and eventually Bennett's too—was more Christocentric than anything Ouspensky had ever envisioned. In the 1950s Collin established Work groups in Mexico and South America, at the same time converting to Roman Catholicism, something Bennett would do as well.[48] In 1956 in Cuzco, Peru, Collin fell to his death from a cathedral tower under mysterious circumstances. Some reports suggest that the position of his body upon impact was like that of the Crucifixion, and that he had sacrificed himself in order to cure a young crippled peasant boy.[49]

WE CAN ONLY SPECULATE on why Nicoll, the only one of Ouspensky's students who ever made contact with him as a human being and as a friend, decided not to see his old teacher before he died. He did not attend any of Ouspensky's last lectures, nor did he see him at Lyne Place, relying on Walker for any information about the man who had answered his prayers many years ago. We know that Nicoll wrote to Ouspensky, but it is doubtful he received a reply; if he did it could only have come from Miss Quinn, Ouspensky's American secretary, Ouspensky himself being too ill to answer any letters. Bennett, the other of Ouspensky's students to branch out on his own, had become persona non grata. Bennett had been excommunicated, and Ouspensky's students had been instructed to have nothing to do with him. When Bennett heard that Ouspensky had returned, and that he was ill, he wrote to him, and asked to see him, but received no reply. Bennett did meet with Janet Collin-Smith, Rodney Collin's wife, who told him of Ouspensky's last days, although she herself only knew of them secondhand. In his autobiography, Bennett remarked that "a great cycle of my own life which had lasted nearly twenty-seven years had closed." He felt "love and gratitude" toward Ouspensky, but like Kenneth Walker, he "felt no nearer to him than I had before."[50]

Nicoll seems not to have made a public statement about the death of his teacher and friend. Pogson records that when Nicoll heard of his teacher's passing, he simply said "Ouspensky has died." She remarks that "There was no more to say." Nicoll was prepared for it—he knew Ouspensky was very ill—but it was clear he was nonetheless moved.[51] Catherine was more shaken. Ouspensky had remained her teacher, even though she herself led groups. Like the others in Ouspensky's groups, she was now left adrift. As far as I know neither of them attended the requiem service for Ouspensky, held at the Russian Church in Pimlico, London. Kenneth Walker was among those who did.

Nicoll himself was ill, or at least not in the best health, so perhaps that may account for him not making an effort—let alone a super one—to see Ouspensky before his death. Yet around this time, in his diary he records a party at which he danced until 2:00 a.m.[52] Other parties are also reported, so illness could not have been the problem (unless Nicoll reserved his super-efforts for these exertions.) As we have seen there is also the strange tradition in the Fourth Way of speaking ill of the dead, and of not seeing them out kindly. This was something that Bennett called the "way of blame," a means, apparently, of hastening the departed on to their new adventures, as speaking well of them may cause them to linger in this world.

Yet this doesn't seem to be case here, as Nicoll did not speak ill of Ouspensky after his death. If anything, he spoke ill of himself, and the self-recriminations over the "slander" and other misdemeanors against Ouspensky that Nicoll believed he committed began, oddly enough, exactly a year before Ouspensky's death. On October 2, 1946, Nicoll records a dream in which, among other things, he recognizes that, in the words of his inner voice, "you slander people if you think they do not esteem you." To which he replies, "Yes—as I did O."[53]

It is curious that Nicoll berates himself for "slandering" people who do not "esteem" him, when one of the problems Nicoll faced throughout his life was his low self-esteem. It is often the case that people with a weak grasp on their own self-worth, "project" this insecurity onto others, as Jung would say, seeing it in them rather than in themselves, a manifestation of what Jung would call their "shadow." They do not esteem themselves and so they believe that others do not, and they hold that against them.* This is an expression of what Gurdjieff called "inner considering," when we believe that others do not recognize our worth, and do not treat us in the way befitting our opinion of ourselves—something, of course, that rarely happens. We know how central exhortations to avoid "self-love" and "vanity" were to Nicoll's approach to the Work. In what way Ouspensky should have esteemed Nicoll is unclear, but his remorse for his "slander" against his teacher for not doing so is the subject of more than a few diary entries in the time leading up to and following his death.

---

*This is a theme Nicoll takes up quite often in the *Commentaries*, although he doesn't use the Jungian term "shadow."

THE IMMEDIATE EFFECT OF THE DEATH of Ouspensky on his groups was a sense of disorientation. That their teacher had died was difficult enough to face. That he had apparently abandoned the system he had taught them presented unique problems of its own. For some this meant the end of the system, and they moved on to something else. Others followed their own path, or put their spiritual striving aside. But for many the question, "What do we do now?" loomed very large. Catherine knew many of the people from Ouspensky's groups, and when they had recovered from the initial shock of his death, many of these came to her and were welcomed into the Nicoll fold. Some of the older Ouspensky students found themselves in one of Copley's subgroups, or one of the many others that were forming.

As the numbers at Great Amwell House grew, the need for greater "external organization" became evident. In the early days, students could count on personal contact with Nicoll or Catherine, and the older members of the group had become used to this. As Pogson had said, they were often more a family than a group. But now with their numbers swelling, this intimacy was less available, and people who had had direct contact with their teachers for many years now had to withdraw to allow newer recruits that access.

This is a law of any kind of group, whether an esoteric or political one. In its early days there is a strong sense of camaraderie and common purpose among its few members. But as the group grows, unavoidably this dissipates, and things become more impersonal. Copley remarks that "once our Group reached a certain size and the form of their work became formalised and crystallised, even widely accepted as religion, the esoteric content would become clouded over with the exoteric." The "real Work" would have to find "other forms of expression," although he suggests that "there might remain a core of serious people . . . who remembered their aim and kept something alive."[54]

This is a curious statement. It suggests that Copley, and possibly Nicoll, believed that the teaching they were following could become

"widely accepted as religion." This goes against one of the central tenets
of esotericism, and one that Nicoll made clear from the start, namely that
it is for the *few*. But it also suggests that Nicoll, or at least Copley, saw
their work as a religion. Or at least he saw that it had the potential to
turn into something like a religion. Copley even alludes to Christianity,
which in its early days, he suggests, was "probably one of the most pure
forms of esotericism," something we know that Nicoll and Ouspensky
believed. Yet it succumbed to the hardening and fracturing into different
sects that had men torturing and murdering each other in the name of
Christ's love, an example of what Ouspensky called the "law of Opposite
Aims and Results."[55] This is a particular expression of the law of seven in
which something turns into its opposite. Ouspensky had firsthand experience of this when he saw the revolution that promised his fellow Russians
equality and prosperity turn into the "dictatorship of the criminal element." Yet even with this, all the "distortions, mistranslations and changing of meaning of words"—which Nicoll, we know, argued had happened
to the Gospels—Copley insisted that "something could still be found in
the Gospels of esoteric truth," something, we know, Nicoll had been trying to fix onto the page for several years now. Did Copley mean that at
some point in the future, when the Work has been "widely accepted as
religion," people like Nicoll will labor over its scriptures, which will have
hardened into literalized dogmas, seeking the kernel of esoteric truth,
much as Nicoll had been doing with the Gospels?

In any event, although some of Ouspensky's people found their way
into Nicoll's groups, many did not. When news of his renegade student's demise reached Gurdjieff, the master was said to have remarked
that had he returned to him as a student, he need not have "perished
like a dog."[56] To perish like a dog is the fate of those who do not work
on themselves, and according to Gurdjieff, at least on this occasion,
Ouspensky did not. But Gurdjieff was magnanimous, and soon after he
learned of Ouspensky's death he sent a telegram to Lyne Place. "You are
sheep without a shepherd," it read. "Come to me."

Sheep, guinea pigs, rats, even "worms in shit": Gurdjieff had a suggestive way of alluding to his pupils.* Copley remarks that it is the aim of the Work that its students should "more and more stand on [their] own feet and bear [their] own weight."[57] Yet when circumstances pushed Ouspensky's chicks out of their nest, most of them immediately looked for another to occupy.

Ouspensky's ex-students certainly faced an inconvenience. Ouspensky had told them years ago that in his opinion Gurdjieff had gone mad, jumped the esoteric rails and had become dangerous. What they had seen of *Herald of Coming Good* should have told them as much. They should have nothing to do with him or with any of his students. Now their teacher was dead, having abjured the system, and Ouspensky's dark genius was inviting them to Paris. Even Madame O saw there was only one option. When the faithful at Lyne Place asked her what they should do, she made it clear. Go to Gurdjieff, she said.

Nicoll was somehow left outside of all this. Or at least it seems that he felt that he was, going by some remarks in his diaries. On November 13, just a few weeks after Ouspensky's death, his old secretary, Madame Kadloubovsky, visited Nicoll and told him of Madame Ouspensky's plans to stay in America and not to follow her husband and return to England. She also told him that Jeanne de Salzmann, an increasingly important figure in Gurdjieff's line of the Work, would be going to Franklin Farms to see her. In his diaries, Nicoll wonders if Gurdjieff would join her.

He notes that he "felt some sarcasm and bitterness" about this, but does not say why, although there is the sense that important events are moving around him but that he is not a part of them. A dream suggests that he did not "show good feeling or talk" about Ouspensky when Madame Kadloubovsky visited, and that the dream means that Ouspensky has "rejected" him. This was shortly after Nicoll had a dream

---

*This was how Gurdjieff spoke of Robert S. De Ropp when he attempted learning the movements.

in which Madame O invites him into her bed. In another dream from around this time, Rodney Collin gate-crashes one of Nicoll's meetings, and "sneers" at his "Christianity." In another dream not long after this, Nicoll wonders why he feels "inferior" to the "London people," which one assumes means the people from Lyne Place, Ouspensky's crowd.[58]

Nicoll's dream life was rather turbulent around this time, as might be expected. A few weeks before his death, Ouspensky appeared to Nicoll in a dream and warned him of the dangers of alcohol.[59] Not long after Ouspensky's death, Nicoll has a dream in which his left hand is amputated; he also dreams that his scissors have only one blade. Both images are suggestive: one half of himself is missing.[60] When we recall Nicoll's association of the left hand—controlled, we remember, by the right brain—with the "inner man," the possible interpretation of the dream widens. Was Nicoll's unconscious telling him that he had lost the esoteric connection? Was it saying, in the punning way in which dreams often communicate, that Nicoll couldn't "cut it"?

Soon after this he has a conversation with his inner voice over the meaning of Ouspensky's death. He is told that Ouspensky "took on himself to swallow your excreta," a rather graphic description of what I assume to mean Ouspensky's putting up with Nicoll's mechanical behavior, or what Gurdjieff called "the unpleasant manifestations of others."[61] Yet in an earlier dream, Nicoll tells Ouspensky that he "overdid" the idea that man is a machine, something many readers of Ouspensky might agree with. In the same dream, he contemplates moving to Brighton—a seaside town—and setting himself up in practice, advertising himself as "Dr N of Harley Street."[62] This too becomes a theme that is repeated, the idea that he might go back into practice.

Yet many of his dreams revolve around his self-sex eroto-mysticism, and his inability to come to some terms with himself about it. He makes several resolutions to put this aside and to finish *The New Man*. But each resolution is broken. He chides himself over his "broken promises"— basically not giving up his devotions—and for slandering Ouspensky and for being disloyal to him. (Nicoll notes "O in the America business," which suggests he was unhappy about Ouspensky decamping to the states.[63]) He is even told that the more time and attention he devotes to his "model," which one can only assume is some kind of fetish Nicoll has made and that aids him in his devotions, the less "force" he has for Catherine, whom he notes is at this point "weak and upset . . . invalid."[64] On April 12, 1947, he seems to come to some conclusion. "I suppose last night I ceased to have childish thoughts about myself," he writes. "I must give up Algerian wine"—of which he was drinking quite a bit—"and models." "Life," he notes, "was closing in and things had to be done." Yet at the end of the entry he asks, "Are you really growing up?"[65]

For a *puer aeternus* that is a difficult prospect. A few days after this entry he records "an intense moment of feeling free with brief model."[66] Exactly what this means is not clear, but it was apparently very significant for Nicoll, for he records again soon after that "the model is so intense." He later records that he is "deeply occupied with faith work and sex." A few days before Ouspensky dies, Nicoll records that he is thinking of making a golf course and makes a note of a "dart party" he had recently, some light fare for a change. A month after Ouspensky's death, Nicoll records that he feels "so alive these last days with model," yet he wonders what it means and if it is a "contradiction."[67] And amidst all this he is still not able to get to work on the Gospels.

ONE OF OUSPENSKY'S OLD GUARD who did follow Madame O's advice and go to Gurdjieff was Kenneth Walker. Walker had yet to meet the man whom his friend Nicoll had insisted he help secure a visa decades earlier. A year after Ouspensky's death he did, going to Paris for that express purpose on October 1, 1948. Nicoll, who had met this remarkable man and whose teaching he had devoted his life to disseminating, declined the invitation to visit the master. Or rather, it is unclear if he received one, given that Nicoll was not one of Ouspensky's flock.

Walker paints a colorful picture of his first encounter with Gurdjieff at the rue des Colonels-Renard, which he compares to sitting down to coffee with Harun ar-Rashid of the *Arabian Nights*. His depiction of Gurdjieff's small flat, overflowing with people, food, kitschy bric-a-brac, tobacco fumes, and alcohol, makes it sound like a combination delicatessen, Aladdin's cave, and the stateroom scene from the Marx Brothers film *A Night at the Opera*. The "haphazard arrangement of the flat's content," Walker writes, "gave it the appearance of a junk-shop."[68] The aroma of Gurdjieff's spices filled the place with the scent of "Eastern bazaars." Furniture crammed every space, much as it had at the Knapp, the curtains were perpetually drawn and the electric lights on. Walker sat through a reading of *Beelzebub,* but when Gurdjieff entered the room his magnetic center turned dead on him.

Reports of Gurdjieff's age differ; several dates for his birth have been offered, but as Gurdjieff went out of his way to erase any traces of his past, how old he may have been when Walker visited him remains open. Walker himself said he was eighty-three. What we can say is that if it was not the Ouspensky of old who arrived at the Southampton Docks, it was not the Gurdjieff of old whom Walker met that remarkable afternoon. He was short, stout, and his once black moustache was now gray. But his eyes remained as Walker had imagined them to be, still piercing, but suggesting a sense of humor. This impression was strengthened when the master rubbed his "rather prominent abdomen" and announced that, "Le Patron is demanding instant attention."[69] This meant that Gurdjieff was hungry and that lunch was served. Gurdjieff was the chef, and anything up to fifty people would "scurry" to find a place for themselves at his table.

For someone limited to the meager portions afforded in Britain during postwar rationing, the huge offerings at Gurdjieff's table were as sumptuous as they were exotic. One salad alone contained "cucumber, pickles, red-pepper, onions, fragments of bread . . . various kinds of preserves, pieces of dried fish and . . . large spoonfuls of sour cream."[70] As

Nicoll would "read" people at the pub, Gurdjieff did so over lunch, and later at dinner, which if anything would be even more sumptuous. When Walker could not keep up with the cornucopia, Gurdjieff asked why he didn't eat more. He explained that he had just arrived from England.

But if the food was too much for Walker, for a teetotaler like him, the famous "toasts to the Idiots" proved something of an ordeal—which, of course, was the idea. By the time Walker and his wife, also teetotal, had hoisted a few glasses of various kinds of vodka, Walker had to remind himself that he really wasn't in Baghdad being entertained by Harun ar-Rashid. Or that Mr. Gurdjieff was not really "behaving . . . just as the gas-jet in my old nursery used to behave whenever I was kept in bed with a temperature." Gurdjieff seemed to "recede to an immense distance away," then suddenly "come rushing forwards to meet me," becoming so large that he filled the room.[71] (Was this just the effect of strong potions on a nondrinker, or some mesmerism of Gurdjieff's?) Walker came away impressed, as did his wife. Gurdjieff was "the most astonishing man" she had ever met. Then she corrected herself. He was not a man, "but a magician." A black magician or a white one? She wasn't sure. Probably a bit of both. But of one thing she was certain. He was "utterly ruthless."[72]

On April 21, 1949, six months after his first visit to rue des Colonels-Renards, Walker gave a report to Nicoll's group about his meetings with this remarkable man. He had found a way to keep up with the food and to surreptitiously abstain from the toasts.[73] He had seen Gurdjieff earlier that month, as one of a group of old Ouspenskians who had taken Madame O's advice to make contact with the master. Nicoll's group were understandably curious about Gurdjieff's plans. Walker explained what the teaching was like at Gurdjieff's table, about the feasts, the toasts, the moving music Gurdjieff would play on his accordion, the readings of *Beelzebub*, the plans for its publication—and that for *In Search of the Miraculous*, which Gurdjieff had seen and given his imprimatur—and Gurdjieff's need for money. But perhaps what was most on the group's, and Nicoll's, mind, was Gurdjieff's attitude toward them.

Walker explained that he had not come to gather Nicoll's flock into Gurdjieff's fold, and he made it clear that Gurdjieff had not mentioned any plans for this. He had no "commission to gather in flocks that had already got a shepherd."[74] Gurdjieff's interest in them, if any, he admitted, would depend on their capacity to generate money he could use to spread the teaching. Although he did not know it then, Walker was right when he had assumed that Gurdjieff wouldn't be able to "safeguard the future of his own teaching," and would have to find candidates to carry it on. Walker notes that Gurdjieff "hopes to live a long time, beyond the century," as the characters in Nicoll's novel *The Blue Germ* almost do.[75] But then Gurdjieff once announced to some of his followers that he, Gurdjieff, "*not* will die."[76]

Walker, a doctor, had a different opinion. It "required no expert medical knowledge to see that in spite of his good spirits and unflagging vigour his health was deteriorating."[77] Gurdjieff's breathing was labored, and a blue tinge around his lips had developed. Walker could tell that fluid was accumulating in his abdomen and that he was a very ill man. When Walker gave Gurdjieff his professional opinion regarding his health, Gurdjieff nodded and said that he was awaiting a new drug being flown in from America. Walker advised him not to wait too long and to go into hospital to have his abdomen drained.

And what did Gurdjieff have to say about Dr. Nicoll? Nothing very flattering, only "uncomplimentary innuendo," along the lines that the good doctor and his now-deceased teacher had "stolen his teaching."[78] It was not likely that there would be contact. Walker had come to speak with them about his meetings with Gurdjieff to see what Nicoll's response would be. Walker felt that there was something to be got out of going to Gurdjieff. Gurdjieff was an "astonishing man, a man of conscious power . . . and considerable knowledge." But he was also a "dangerous man," a man "not to be trusted," and one needed to constantly be on "the lookout."[79] Still, Walker felt there was much to be gained by being in touch with this dangerous man.

Nicoll did not agree. According to James Moore "the good doctor (no longer young nor in perfect health) could count on a welcome in Paris but felt it improper to 're-enter his mother's womb.'"[80] As Walker reported, "Dr N thinks there is nothing further to be got from him," meaning Gurdjieff.[81] He was not alone. Rodney Collin did not make the pilgrimage to rue des Colonels-Renards. Nor did Francis Roles, who took over proceedings at Colet House—and whose eardrum Collin once shattered, believing he was following a teaching strategy, after an irate Ouspensky had slapped his face. Bennett did go to Gurdjieff, renewing a contact he had for a short time twenty-five years earlier, and went on to establish his own institute.*

One who did go to Gurdjieff but didn't stay was Robert S. De Ropp. Disgusted with what he had seen at Franklin Farms and disillusioned with Ouspensky, De Ropp met one of Gurdjieff's American students who pointed him in the master's direction. Following Orage's tub-thumping, Gurdjieff had made several journeys to the States, and it was on his last, a year before his death, that De Ropp met him. Gurdjieff was clearly "the most extraordinary human being" De Ropp had ever met. But De Ropp was fond of wholesome living and nature, and he found the atmosphere around Gurdjieff—the crowded, smoky hotel rooms, the eager disciples, the readings and endless feasts and toasts—oppressive. He had already seen too much alcohol around Ouspensky. Gurdjieff seemed old and sad to De Ropp, and his remarks about guinea pigs recalled to mind his own experiments with the creatures whom, all told, were pretty stupid. After a few meetings he did not return.

---

*This was Coombe Springs, in Kingston upon Thames, just outside of London, which was Bennett's version of the Prieuré and Lyne Place. In 1965, Idries Shah, the writer on Sufism, convinced Bennett that he was an emissary of the "Master of Wisdom," another name for the Inner Circle of Humanity. Sure of his authenticity, Bennett decided to put Coombe Springs entirely at Shah's disposal. As soon as he acquired ownership of the extensive estate, he sold it to developers. Shah may not have been one of the Inner Circle, but he certainly seems to have behaved as Gurdjieff would.

So there is precedent for Nicoll not "returning to his mother's womb." Yet, one can't help but wonder if one reason Nicoll did not cross the Channel to meet Gurdjieff was that the master might "see" him, "read" him in the way that he did his own students at the pub. Could it be that there was something Nicoll did not want the dangerous Mr. G to see?

We will never know. Not long after Walker's last visit to Gurdjieff, news had come that the master was in the American Hospital in Paris, having the fluid drained from his abdomen, as Walker had insisted, as well as other treatment. Several telephone calls followed in quick succession. His condition had improved but then something had gone wrong. He worsened. And then the unthinkable: Gurdjieff was dead. The banquets and toasts had, it seemed, taken their toll. The doctor treating him is said to have remarked that he should have died long before, going by the condition of his internal organs. It seemed the master had indeed willed himself to stay alive. But even Gurdjieff nodded. On October 29, 1949, Gurdjieff died, surviving Ouspensky by two years and twenty-seven days. The octave had ended.

15

Last Days

There is one possible reason why Nicoll decided not to see his old teachers that I haven't mentioned. It may have been that, although he continued to teach the Work, his own spiritual orientation, his magnetic center as it were, had in recent years turned away from Gurdjieff and Ouspensky and moved more toward Swedenborg and other sources of insight—and, one has to say, comfort.* As early as January 1946, he writes of a dream that in it he was in "the spiritual world." Why did he think this? Because in the dream he asks the time and receives no answer. Why was this? "Because it is the spiritual world, and there is no time there."[1]

Swedenborg believed that our dreams formed the frontiers of the spiritual worlds, and that in the spiritual worlds, time and space as we know them do not exist.[2] In the next entry in his diary Nicoll asks "Does nature imitate the spiritual world? Does everything look up and seek to follow what it can see above it?"[3] This seems a way of speaking about Swedenborg's notion of "correspondences," the idea

---

*For example, a reading of Gurdjieff's *Herald of Coming Good* left him wondering about his teacher's "vanity" and if it was "conscious bluff." It had "aroused conflict" in him. Nicoll, Later Diary, September 24, 1946.

that everything in the sensory world has a spiritual counterpart, a non-physical original without which it would not exist.* A few months later, Nicoll forgets the details of a dream, but notes that it was "good." He then asks "Why do I say dream? Is it not being in the spiritual world?" To which he answers "Yes—a thousand times."[4] Not long after this he records a dream in which he blesses people around him with his blood.[5]

Dreams such as these seem to have led Nicoll to turn to Swedenborg rather than the Work or Jung for some guidance. He also records some unusual experiences associated with his devotions. Although he continues to struggle with his penchant for "self-sex," he never comes to any resolution about it, and still argues with his inner voice over it. So in early February 1947, he records that "you said self sex seemed something necessary," although it is unclear who "you" is, whether it is Nicoll himself or his inner voice. Either way, he remarks that, "such affirmation seems to be better than dark thoughts and apprehension."[6] Yet, as we've seen, whatever positive effect such common sense may have had, it did not last.

On July 18, 1947, Nicoll records "moments of adoration" that leave him with "little sense of time." He notes that "God made all things and all comes from Him. We are nothing in ourselves," which is another Swedenborgian trope.[7] At the beginning of 1948, he has a dream in which he sees God.[8] Later that year, in a dream, Christ visits him in a room in a "rather foreign" quarter. This strikes me as somewhat reminiscent of Swedenborg's visitation by Jesus in a room in London's East End, at the start of his conversion from scientist to religious visionary.[9] In the room is an "apparatus" that represents his "model," the fetish Nicoll uses in his devotions; in some way that Nicoll doesn't understand, he associates Christ with this "apparatus." In his exchange with his voice about the dream, Nicoll notes that in it he has a room of his

---

*For a brief introduction to Swedenborg's notion of correspondences see my *Introducing Swedenborg: Correspondences* (London: Swedenborg Society, 2021).

own, is content, his "people"—meaning his groups—don't "have his number," so can't contact him and don't know where he is.

As mentioned, in several entries in his later diaries, Nicoll records either a dream about or a wish for a room of his own, away from Catherine and his groups, where he could "wander"—a word that turns up often in this context—and "model" as he pleases.* For example, in one dream he has an argument with Catherine and Jane and ends up declaring that "I won't go on. I'll get rid of the house, plans, work, everybody . . ."[10] Such sentiments drift through the diaries at this time. But the general direction is toward the divine. On August 17, 1948, he notes that one must be continually aware of God's "infinite mercy," otherwise one is sunk in life.[11]

Nicoll's reading has also changed, and has moved in an Eastern direction. One such text he refers to is the *Lankavatara Sutra,* a classic of Mahayana Buddhism and one of the founding works of Zen Buddhism.[12] Another was *The Gospel of Sri Ramakrishna*, an account of the Hindu holy man's conversations with his disciples recorded by Swami Nikhilananda, and published in an English translation in 1942. Nicoll notes that Ramakrishna's teaching comes down to the basic formula that "all is God," an experience of which Ramakrishna speaks of as entering an "ocean of consciousness." Nicoll is so taken with Ramakrishna's mysticism, that in a dream Jung and Ouspensky—two father figures—tell him that they are asking Ramakrishna for "aid and advice," a development that pleases him.[13] Again, he notes that Ramakrishna "sees God everywhere"; as one commentator remarked, Ramakrishna was "drunk with God."

---

*These rooms are often in foreign cities, such as Paris. Yet Nicoll often dreams of being in Camden Town, a part of London just down the hill from Frognal, where he grew up. In recent times it is a part of town associated with youth culture, with many bars, clubs, cafés, clothes shops, tattoo parlors, and so on. In Nicoll's time it would have been an even more raffish neighborhood, associated with low dives, the working class, and a criminal element.

Yet Nicoll admits that he does not share this vision, at least not at the moment. A "heaviness" and "guilt" prevent him from having it. He wonders if "this dissolving into God did not make loss of force and that feeling I was the reverse" a succinct expression of the difference between mysticism and what Gurdjieff had in mind.[14] Oddly, in the same entry he remarks on a "temptation to 'grow up'" and "face life" and its "weight of responsibility," something the *puer aeternus* in him has so far resisted. Dissolving into God seems something rather different from this.

Other entries in the diaries suggest that as he entered his last years, Nicoll's personal spiritual orientation was less along the lines of the system he continued to teach and more in keeping with a kind of religious mysticism, heavily slanted toward Swedenborg, but also informed by the kind of negative theology associated with Meister Eckhart and *The Cloud of Unknowing*. This is the *via negativa* that proceeds through the process of *kenosis*, an "inner emptying" that has much in common with the idea of making personality "passive." The rich man, who has many things (a "rich" personality) must become poor—divest himself of false ideas about himself—in order to enter the "kingdom of heaven," the change in being that Nicoll believed was the object of esoteric Christianity. With this in mind, could some sense of disloyalty to the Work, coupled with an acute awareness of his own inner conflict, have prevented Nicoll from seeing in their last days the two people who put him on the road to his destiny?

In any event, that destiny was drawing to a close, and Nicoll's time-body was reaching its limit. Nicoll would soon have to tie up as many loose ends as he could. Between the death of Ouspensky and that of Gurdjieff, Nicoll came to understand that whatever time was left to him, he had to make the best possible use of it. Opportunities were not endless, and their availability was limited, and now both seemed close to running out. It became clear to Nicoll that he only had a short period left in order to, in his own words, "hit the mark."

SOMETIME IN THE AUTUMN of 1948—more or less midway between
the deaths of Ouspensky and Gurdjieff—Nicoll announced to his
groups that he thought he did not have long to live.[15] What reason he
gave for this premonition—or what was more likely his own considered
professional opinion—is unclear, yet the people who were around him
the past few years could not have been unaware of the decline in his
health. Most likely his announcement caused a shock—and some of his
students may have seen it as aiming at precisely that—but to some it
may not have been a surprise. At sixty-four, Nicoll was not young, yet
the "lawful infirmities of age," as Gurdjieff referred to the effects of
aging, should still have been some years off. But we've seen in his diaries that as early as 1945, Nicoll's health began to suffer. What effect
his inner conflict over his self-sex devotions, his inability to finish "the
Gospel book," his remorse about "slandering" his teacher Ouspensky,
the demands of carrying on the teaching, and the claims of individual
students on his time and energies had on his health is debatable. The
punch line however was clear: time was running out.

Nicoll made clear that Catherine would carry on the teaching after
his death. In fact, she soon started a new group in London—bringing along many from the old Ouspensky group—although she herself
did not have long to live, something neither of them knew at the time.
What was important now was that those closest to Nicoll were able to
continue what he had started. As Gurdjieff had handed on the teaching to Ouspensky—putting aside those times when he accused him of
stealing it—and Ouspensky had passed it on to Nicoll, now Nicoll had
to pass the esoteric baton on to those of his students able to carry on
the race.

I may be pushing an analogy too far, but remembering that Nicoll
had a band of faithful followers, is it too extravagant to suggest an echo
here of Christ and his disciples, who were enjoined to spread the glad
tidings of the Gospels after Christ's Crucifixion and Resurrection?
We've seen that in some of the dreams Nicoll recorded around this

time, he seems to have identified with Christ. Nicoll may not have consciously done so, but we know that he believed that the teaching he had dedicated his life to was the same that Christ had taught. It was, we remember, what Christianity was *really* about, while what went on in the churches was a very watered-down and distorted substitute. And as the apostles went out into the world to spread the good word, Nicoll hoped that the able among his students would do the same.

One person galvanized by Nicoll's announcement was Fulford Bush. He proposed something that most likely had been on Nicoll's mind, and that of his students, for some time. Bush suggested that the group privately publish the commentaries Nicoll had been writing since 1941. By now their number had grown considerably. Bush estimated that a collection of the commentaries would probably exceed 500,000 words, a hefty number. So what they had in mind would require a substantial effort. Given the difficulties Nicoll faced trying to complete *The New Man*, I don't think it is too off the mark to suggest that if it wasn't for Bush's urging, the commentaries may never have reached the printer.

Different ideas about how to go about the publication and the number of copies involved were discussed. In the end, Nicoll, Pogson, and Bush settled on an edition of two hundred copies in three volumes, printed on high-quality paper. These would be sold at £9 9s. (shillings) each, which in today's money would be roughly £335 or $450, a considerable sum, although the advance copy of *Beelzebub's Tales* that Nicoll bought around this time cost him a £100.[16] As usual, Nicoll made his decisions swiftly, laying out what needed to be done in "five minutes." Aside from choosing the paper, Nicoll had little to do with the publication. There would be no editing. Bush insisted that the commentaries "would be printed as they were written."[17] This may have been to preserve their spoken character, and also to get the preparation done as quickly as possible without getting bogged down in making any changes to the text. The actual production of the books was carried out, in Pogson's words, with "the usual speed of anything done at Dr Nicoll's wish," and the person most involved was Bush.[18]

The urgency with which Bush applied himself to the task may have been informed with something more than Nicoll's announcement about the limited time left to him. The state of Bush's health around this time isn't known—at least I haven't seen mention of it—so his own death, almost immediately after the first copies of volume 1 of the *Commentaries* appeared, may or may not have been a shock. They received the first copies in late June 1949; soon after that, Bush died. All Pogson tells us is that "the sense of urgency which prompted him to ensure that the publication of the *Commentaries* went forward at all possible speed was a true intuition," which suggests that he too had some sense that his own end was near.[19] Bush had been with Nicoll for nearly two decades, from the early days in Redcliffe Gardens and before, and once again had proved indispensable. Getting the *Commentaries* in print was his last act of service to the man who had changed his life many years ago. Readers today who profit from the *Commentaries* may not know it, but they have Bush to thank for making them available.

Someone else galvanized by Nicoll's announcement was Vincent Stuart. If Fulford Bush is the man responsible for seeing the *Commentaries* to print, then we have Vincent Stuart to thank for finally securing the same service for *The New Man*. Just before the first copies of the *Commentaries* arrived at Great Amwell House, in the spring of 1949, Stuart wrote to Nicoll and asked if he "might publish his Gospel Chapters."[20] This suggests that these were more or less done and that Nicoll intended to add further material in order to complete the book—presumably the material that was posthumously published as *The Mark*. Pogson sent Stuart the chapters, and on May 5 Stuart wrote to Nicoll, saying that he found them "particularly clear and valuable," adding that "as they are they will make an excellent book."[21]

It's unclear if Stuart knew of the difficulty Nicoll had with the work, but if he did, the emphasis on the excellence of what he had read and of publishing it as it was may have been informed by something more than his good editorial sense. He may have had an intuition that if he had suggested any changes, Nicoll's difficulty in finishing an extended piece of writing may have kept the material from ever getting back to him. (Something similar may have been on Bush's mind as well.) Nicoll's own "humble amazement" at having the chapters published may be an expression of his lack of vanity, although one might be excused for feeling that this almost saintly response comes across as a bit too pat.[22] But it may also have been an honest surprise at the fact that he had a book ready to go but didn't know it. One could also be excused for wondering if that very lack of vanity undermined the self-confidence that may have allowed Nicoll to recognize when he did good work.

IF THERE WAS AN ANNUS MIRABILIS for the Work it had to be 1950. Although much had been written about Gurdjieff in the popular press, until his death there were no direct accounts of the system or anything from his own pen—except the disastrous *Herald of Coming Good*—available in any printed form. Ouspensky had planted hints and suggestions about an unknown teaching in *A New Model of the Universe*, in order to draw new recruits, but until that miraculous year, the teaching itself had remained true to its esoteric roots, that is, oral. But now the miraculous, or at least Ouspensky's search for it, was available to the public, who could also take a ride on Gurdjieff's spaceship Karnak and listen in on the conversation between Beelzebub and his grandson, through the courtesy of the publishers Routledge and Kegan Paul. And they could also be introduced to an interpretation of the Gospel parables rather different from the sort that the schoolboy Nicoll had sat through, utterly befuddled, the revelation which had first been given to him then, only now finally coming to its full fruition. In 1950 *The New Man*, published by Vincent Stuart, appeared.

Pogson remarks that the publication of a book he had struggled with endlessly "gave pleasure" to Nicoll.[23] We can be sure that was true, but one suspects this is an understatement. But even more than seeing his work finally become a reality, Nicoll must have got considerable pleasure from some of the reviews; no work of his had received any press since the days of *Dream Psychology*. Not all were positive. The *British Weekly*, which his father founded, tipped their hat to their first editor's son, but, as one might suspect, were not taken with his view of the Gospels as a source of esoteric knowledge. Rom Landau, whose bestselling *God Is My Adventure* (1935) had separate chapters on Gurdjieff and Ouspensky, reviewed *The New Man* with *In Search of the Miraculous* and *Beelzebub's Tales* in a roundup for the *Nineteenth Century*. Landau had met Nicoll's teachers. He respected Ouspensky but his encounter with Gurdjieff was less enlightening.[24] But he knew enough about the Work to recognize a connection between the three books, and to see that the "new man" Nicoll wrote of shared an experience of "awakening" that in different ways was common to all three.

Yet the review that must have given Nicoll some very positive emotions was the glowing appreciation of *The New Man* penned by the mysterious "Diogenes" in *Time and Tide*. Both the reviewer and the periodical were widely respected. *Time and Tide* was an influential literary and political review in the early twentieth century that counted among its contributors George Bernard Shaw, C. S. Lewis, D. H. Lawrence, Wyndham Lewis, and Graham Greene, to name only a few of its illustrious bylines. It started out with a radical perspective, supporting causes such as the suffragettes, but gradually veered more to the right with a heavily Christian bias. Exactly who Diogenes was remains debatable, but most opinion suggests it was the pen name of W. J. Brown, an independent member of Parliament, who, it turns out, was also a student of Ouspensky.[25]

It this is true it isn't clear if Nicoll knew of Diogenes's identity. Neither Pogson or Copley mention that he did, so his pleasure at receiving the kind of review every writer dreams of may have been accompanied by genuine surprise. Yet, if Nicoll *did* know that the book was being reviewed by another student of the Fourth Way, he still wouldn't necessarily have expected praise. Indeed, a good test of his not being "identified" with the book would have been to have received a bad review from this source and been forced to swallow it. (That would have been a proper Gurdjieffian roasting.) Yet knowing that Diogenes was a student of Ouspensky—if he was—does put a different slant on the review. A positive review coming from a respected literary doyen outside the Work would certainly carry more "force" than one written from within the fold. The fact that Diogenes wrote an equally glowing review of *The Fourth Way* on its appearance in 1957 may be taken as circumstantial evidence in favor of his being in the Work, as may the fact that he spoke highly of Nicoll's other work when it appeared.[26]

In any case, whoever he was, Diogenes certainly liked the book. And given that his outing as a follower of the Fourth Way—again, if indeed he was—happened well after the fact, the praise Nicoll received would have certainly drawn attention to it. Diogenes put *The New Man* in the same category as the *Bhagavad Gita* and the *Yoga Sutras of Patanjali*, two classics of Eastern wisdom literature. This was no small praise. In his opinion, no other book on "the mind and teaching of Jesus" was more valuable, and no other book had given him more "instruction and pleasure."[27] Vincent Stuart could not have asked for a better send off.*

Yet not everyone agreed with Diogenes's assessment. It is understandable that Nicoll would have wanted *The New Man* to make some impact on the religious world. But is it surprising that a book suggesting that what people have believed Christianity to be about was wrong, prompted at best a cool reception from the clergy? In his review for the

---

*The book received further support from outright Fourth Way followers. Gorham Munson, the literary critic and student of Orage, released an American edition through his Hermitage House Press. And Rodney Collin's Ediciones Sol published Spanish editions in Mexico and South America.

Nineteenth Century, Rom Landau said that *The New Man* would be criticized by the church and ignored by science. He was certainly accurate about the first part of this prediction; and given the absence of any response from the scientific world, he seems to have hit the mark with the second part as well.

Yet one review, not of *The New Man* and coming from an unmistakable source in the Work, must have certainly pleased Nicoll. In July of his annus mirabilis he received a letter from Jeanne de Salzmann, praising what she had read in the *Commentaries*. A copy of the privately printed edition had reached her, and she commended Nicoll for presenting the ideas "in the genuine order in which they were given out with the exact formulation without any distortion."[28] If Nicoll had ever worried if he had done his duty by the Work, or was concerned that he had failed to hand on the ideas "just as they were taught," he could now breathe a sigh of relief. The imprimatur of the person carrying on as de facto head of the Work following Gurdjieff's death must have meant something to him, even if he did not think it worthwhile going "back to his mother's womb" during Gurdjieff's last days. De Salzmann mentioned that she would be in London, giving a demonstration at Colet House of some of the last movements Gurdjieff had taught, and she invited Nicoll to attend. Whether it was his health that prevented him from accepting or a bit of Fourth Way diplomacy, we don't know. But the upshot was an invitation for her to visit Great Amwell House, which de Salzmann accepted. If Nicoll had felt he had been slighted in the to-ing and fro-ing following Ouspensky's death, this gesture of inclusion must have provided some conciliation.

Another letter Nicoll received around this time sounded a less enthusiastic note about the *Commentaries*. As mentioned earlier, in April 1950, Jung wrote to Nicoll, asking him to confirm his memories of the "noteworthy adventure" involving Jung's experience of the ghost in the cottage in Aylesbury years before. Nicoll had sent Jung one of the privately printed copies of the *Commentaries,* and in his letter Jung acknowledged receipt of them. He apologizes for not "having had the time to go into them."[29] But one suspects his real reason for not finding the time was that, as he reminded Nicoll, he "was not particularly fond of the things that smell of metaphysics," something, alas, Jung had to point out to his critics practically throughout his career. His reason for this, he explained, was that "Possibilities get too limitless when you open the door to unconscious vastness."[30]

One can only imagine how Jung would have reacted to *Beelzebub*, although Jung's own *Red Book* certainly opens quite a few doors to a vast unconscious. One also wonders how Jung responded to the letter from Nicoll that accompanied his gift. In it Nicoll tells his old mentor that he stood "at the beginning of his awakening." "I love you," Nicoll wrote, "and have never not done so in my heart." Unlike Ouspensky, who apparently hoped to either avoid or alter significantly his meeting with Gurdjieff the next time around, Nicoll assured Jung that he deeply hoped to meet him in recurrence. It seems that Nicoll had regrets regarding his relationship with Jung similar to the misgivings he had about his "slandering" of Ouspensky. Whether Jung felt the same about meeting in recurrence is unknown.

Jung had difficulty with his relationships with men, and he may have found Nicoll's emotional tone off-putting.[31] Nicoll sent Jung a copy of *The New Man* when it appeared. Jung didn't reply but Emma did, thanking Nicoll for the book and saying that it was a "very original idea to interpret the Evangelists in that way," and that it made "the writings of the Bible come alive again."[32] Nicoll sent Jung copies of his other books as they were published, but it was Emma, not his former teacher, who replied.

WHAT WAS IT ABOUT *The New Man* that the clergy objected to, but Emma Jung found so "original"? It is a shame that Jung most likely did not look at the book. Aside from his own interest in Christ as an archetype of the Self, Nicoll's symbolic reading of the parables may have caught his attention.* My own feeling is that we can profit from Nicoll's general insight into the need to read the parables—and other sacred texts—symbolically, without having to accept the explicit meanings he assigns to them.

"All sacred writings," Nicoll begins, "contain an outer and an inner meaning. Behind the literal words lies another range of meaning, another form of knowledge."[33] This knowledge, for Nicoll, is of a higher type than the literal. It conveys a deeper sense of significance, and when we *see* this, when we grasp the meaning of a parable, the understanding that comes to us affects us, *changes* us in some way. It lifts us out of the immediate sensory world, the world of "fact," and reveals a world that is *invisible*, that is, not of the senses. This is the change in being that Nicoll seeks, the transformation that will produce the New Man.

Nicoll tells us that, according to an "age-old tradition, Man was once in touch with this inner knowledge and inner meaning."[34] At an earlier time, the language of this other way of knowing was itself more known, unlike today, when it has fallen into obscurity. Precisely because we are unaware of this other way of knowing and other kind of meaning, literal-minded people see the parables as meaningless. Or, as Nicoll's father did, they accept the surface meaning of the Gospels as the "literal truth," and demand faith rather than insight.

But the literal character of the parables is only their *persona*, so to speak. Below this is a level of deeper significance, their "real self" or "essence," what Nicoll calls their "psychological meaning."[35] This is arrived at via Ouspensky's "psychological method," which, we remember, accepts that "perceptions change according to the powers and properties of the perceiving apparatus."

The literal-minded, Nicoll writes, ask why parables are necessary to

---

*See, for example, his strange work *Aion: Researches into the Phenomenology of the Self* (1951).

convey this knowledge. "Why not say directly what is meant?" They see it as simply mystification. But the knowledge conveyed is not a fact, something that could be stated explicitly, but a recognition that "must be seen . . . *internally*."[36] When this happens, there is a moment of *gnosis*, direct knowing, not mediated by the senses or reason. The fundamental significance of this is that it introduces you to *the reality of your inner world*. Of, in fact, "you." This is precisely the experience Nicoll had when he realized that his headmaster knew nothing. It is a moment of "self-remembering," of coming to one's self as an irreducible reality, albeit an *invisible* one. This cannot be proven, only *experienced*. To evoke this experience is the aim of esoteric writings.

The basic aim of the parable, Nicoll tells us, is to connect the lower levels of reality with the higher, linking "below" with "above." This is equivalent in our psychology to connecting "outer" and "inner," which we can see as "personality" and "essence," or "persona" and "self." It is through this that the "rebirth" that is the purpose of the Gospels, the essence of the "glad tidings," can come about. It is the "inner man," as Swedenborg says, who is, or can be, reborn. The Gospels are exercises aimed at triggering a "definite inner evolution" in those who can grasp this. That evolution proceeds by widening and enlivening one's understanding. As Nicoll writes, "*A man is his understanding*."[37]

We can say that this process or transformation takes one at the literal level, and through the psychological method introduces a deeper understanding, which leads to the recognition of the esoteric meaning behind the parables. This transformation is the second birth, that of the spirit, as distinguished from our first birth, which is of the flesh. It is also the essence of the alchemical transformation of water into wine that takes place at the Marriage at Cana. As noted, turning water into wine was something that occupied Nicoll in his diaries. It was a transformation he sought in himself.

How do Nicoll's specific interpretations of the parables hold up to what we might call his esoteric hermeneutics? Early on he gives us an example not from the parables but from the commandments, which, he tells us, have a literal meaning but also a psychological one. The literal meaning of "thou shalt not kill" is self-evident. Its psychological meaning also seems fairly clear. Not only should you not murder anyone literally, you should also not do so "in thy heart."[38] Harboring murderous thoughts against someone commits the literal crime psychologically. If the law didn't prevent you or if you could get away with it, you might actually do it. So in the eyes of the Lord, you *are* a murderer.

But what of "thou shalt not commit adultery?" Shouldn't we also not commit adultery in our heart, or at least in our imagination? I may not actually sleep with my neighbor's wife, but I may fantasize about doing so, which is the sexual equivalent of murdering someone in my imagination. This seems pretty obvious and is in fact part of Christian teaching. But Nicoll's reading is rather different. The psychological meaning of the sixth commandment apparently has nothing to do with lusting after your neighbor's wife. It is about "mixing different doctrines, different teachings," and explains the biblical saying that people went "whoring after other gods," something that may not seem immediately clear to an unprepared reader.[39] This is also true of the psychological meaning of "thou shalt not steal," which, Nicoll tells us, means "to think that you do everything *from yourself,* by your own powers, not realising that you do not know who you are or how you think or feel, or how you even move."[40]

What are we to make of this? The point isn't whether it is true that we don't know who we are or how we think and so on. I take it that we don't. But is this *really* what "thou shalt not steal" means "psychologically"? It could mean to not pick up opinions or ideas from others and claim them as your own, to claim to possess knowledge without actually acquiring it genuinely. Or possibly something else.

An unprepared reader, with no knowledge of esotericism, may be intrigued by Nicoll's interpretations, but I do not think he will immediately get the connection. And to a reader, like myself, who knows that

Nicoll wants to fit Scripture to the teaching of the Work, it can often seem that he is trying to make the facts fit the theory, rather in the way that a strict Freudian will bend over backward to interpret a dream according to psychoanalytic ideology; a strict Jungian might do the same. The esoteric interpretation can often seem just as arbitrary. The fact that you should not claim to do anything "from yourself," because you "do not know who you are or how you think or feel, or even move," is strict Work doctrine. But unless you know this, I don't think the psychological meaning Nicoll provides here is as apparent as he would like it to be.

Nicoll applies his esoteric hermeneutic to well-known parables, such as those of the Marriage at Cana, the Good Samaritan, the Laborers in the Vineyard, and also to the Sermon on the Mount, and to his interpretation of the Kingdom of Heaven as a change in being. He also brings in Swedenborg's doctrine that Good is higher than Truth. (If we were good, Nicoll told his flock, we would not need the truth, a remark that might raise some contemporary eyebrows.) Swedenborgian ideas blend with those of the Work throughout *The New Man*, too intimately to pick apart here, and in general Nicoll's writing in many ways takes on a Swedenborgian character. I mean that he often presents his readings as "just so," and often labors the reader with long sections of prose without paragraph breaks. (Many of the *Commentaries* are written in this way. It makes for repetition and a certain breathless character.)

The reader will have to decide for himself if Nicoll's interpretations "fit," much as an analysand must decide if his analyst's interpretations of his dreams hit or miss the mark. To me, some of Nicoll's readings work, in the sense that they suggest new possibilities of meaning, while others seem a bit forced. So, relating the "five porches" at the pool of Bethesda to the five senses, and the difficulty of our sense-bound literal minds in understanding the meaning of esoteric truth—the revivifying water of the pool—works for me.[41] I am not so sure about equating the Greek φρόνιμος, "wise," with the practical street-smarts Nicoll, following Gurdjieff, said was necessary for the Work.[42]

If you accept the claim that the Gospels *are* the work of "conscious men" in the Gurdjieffian sense, and that they present an early CE version of the Fourth Way, then Nicoll's interpretations will certainly make the parables "come alive again," as they did for Emma Jung. If you don't, you can still find much in Nicoll's take on Scripture to stimulate your faculty for grasping things psychologically (that is, symbolically, metaphorically). This, I think, is the real benefit of Nicoll's hermeneutic. The shift to a more than literal perception—whether of the parables or anything else—can in itself prompt profound changes in the person experiencing it.* Whether or not this leads to the kind of specific "definite inner evolution" stemming from the "definite teaching"—the Work—to which Nicoll wants to bring his readers is a different question.

Perhaps the single most important parable to grasp psychologically, Nicoll tells us, is that of the Sower. It is "the parable of parables," and unless it is understood, the other parables will not be.[43] All the parables are about the Kingdom of Heaven; that is, the change in being needed for our evolution. The parable of the Sower relates to the idea that psychologically, Man—human beings—are understood as "undeveloped seeds."[44] We have the potential to grow *inward*, to achieve the second birth, but this is not guaranteed. In fact, as stated many times, there is a cosmic law preventing everyone from so developing. Not all seeds germinate and grow.

"Man is a seed sown on earth to grow into the Kingdom of Heaven," Nicoll writes.[45] That is, we are created as beings with the possibility

---

*Nicoll's psychological reading has much in common with the "spiritual hermeneutics" of Henry Corbin. Corbin speaks of practicing *ta'wil*, which is a methodological practice of "looking through" phenomena, whether a text or in the natural world, and going below the surface—what he calls, following the Arabic, *zahir*—to reach the depth, the *batin*. Lachman, *Lost Knowledge of the Imagination* (Edinburgh: Floris Books, 2017), 90.

of self-evolution. Whether we do evolve or not depends on a number of things. And just as some seeds fall on fallow ground, so too does the esoteric teaching of the Kingdom of Heaven, necessary for our self-evolution, fall on those too literal to grasp it—that is, on stony soil. There is also the danger that even the good seed that falls on good soil may be thwarted by envious people who sow "tares" among the wheat. Psychologically, this means the same as "thou shalt not commit adultery," a mixing of teachings and doctrines. That is, the true seed, the true wheat, is obscured by tares, a weed that looks like wheat when it first appears. So too the true teaching is easily surrounded by the false, and the true wheat must grow amid weeds. As always, discrimination is essential.

Nicoll expresses the idea that in the parables the literal is symbolized by stone in a variety of ways. Christ gave the apostle Simon a new name, Peter, and said he would be the stone on which he would build his church. This is the literal Petrine Church, the exoteric teaching. The tablets of its law, the commandments, are of stone. But the literal teaching is not enough; it must be made less rigid and opaque through the liquifying power of the psychological method—water is fluid and transparent—and through this, the esoteric knowledge, the living truth, can be revealed. This is the water that, having once drunk of it, you will never again know thirst, as Jesus told the Samaritan woman. At Cana, the miracle at the wedding feast was the transformation of water into wine. That is, according to Nicoll, when the wine at the wedding feast ran out Jesus had the stone vessels (the literal truth) filled with water (its psychological content) and in the end transformed into wine, that is, the change of being that grants us entry into the kingdom heaven.*[46]

---

*There are parallels here with the ancient Gnostic typology that posits three levels of spiritual understanding: the hylic (literal/stone), the psychic (psychological/water), and the pneumatic (spiritual/wine). The pneumatics have an experience of *gnosis*, which we've seen is equivalent to self-remembering. Nicoll would have come across this tripartite typology through his reading for *Living Time*, 111.

NICOLL MAY HAVE KNOWN that his last days had come, but life went on at Amwell. In December 1948, he and Catherine became grand-parents when Jane gave birth to a daughter. It was a sign, perhaps, that the future was moving on, that while one time-body was reaching its end, others were just at their start. New octaves were beginning. Yet it was unmistakably a time of closure. Many of the old guard were fall-ing away. Fulford Bush had died. Soon so would Colonel Butler and Nicoll's old housemate Maud Hoffman, and Jack Edwards, a longtime member of the group. Nicoll, who would follow them, felt their loss. But what was undoubtedly most painful was to learn of Catherine's own illness. She had kept it to herself, but during the months of Nicoll's decline, Catherine had been receiving treatment for what was eventu-ally diagnosed as breast cancer. The trouble was thought to have gone, but the pain in her shoulder and arm had returned, and in the sum-mer of 1952, a year before Nicoll's death, she announced that she would have to have an operation; one assumes it was a mastectomy, although details are scant.

It must have been a tremendous blow to Nicoll. The year before, in summer 1951, he had been taken to Guy's Hospital in London for an emergency operation. He was diagnosed with cancer and given only a few years to live, five at best. We've seen that even before this, when he first announced to the group that he felt his end was near, he had hoped that Catherine would carry on the Work. At the time, Catherine's London group was well under way; other subgroups had also started—Pogson had one—and her operation was thought to be successful. Nicoll could die believing she would long succeed him. Sadly this was not the case. Catherine's operation wasn't successful. Three months after Nicoll's death, she would die too.

Understandably, after the news of Nicoll's cancer reached the group, "it was not always easy to know how to behave," as one new member described the atmosphere in a house where one never really did know how to behave.[47] Nicoll made himself as available as he could, continuing to make impressions on new students that would last the rest of their lives. One new arrival, Diana Pettavel, had come to Amwell by way of Vincent Stuart. As many had said before, when she was introduced to Nicoll, she felt that she had "met a man unlike anyone" she had ever met. "It is impossible," she wrote in her recollections of Great Amwell in Nicoll's last days, "to give any just description of someone of Dr. Nicoll's calibre."[48]

Her first encounters with Nicoll were, if not abrasive, certainly not smooth. When they met Nicoll told her that she was "like a small tree without any branches." At Amwell House, trying to observe herself, she took to dusting. When Nicoll came across her at this, he asked why she was doing it. Was it really necessary? Wasn't there anything better she could do? Although his own health was failing, Nicoll believed he could still give advice on that of another. He practically ordered Pettavel to drink a Pernod when she was recovering from jaundice, although her doctor had strictly forbidden alcohol.[49] Illness, he told her, was a way to enter the time-body. True or not, the drink did her good. He also upbraided her on not knowing more about wine, as he had once Sam Copley for his lack of nautical knowledge.[50]

At another occasion he asked why she took everything so tragically. If she continued to do so, he told her, "life is there to catch you and steal your force."[51] Was this why "down here at Amwell, we laugh a lot, play a lot," and "take nothing seriously except the Work"?[52]

Nicoll seems to have taken to giving nicknames to new students, a tactic perhaps inspired by Kenneth Walker's account of proceedings at Gurdjieff's table. If Ms. Pettavel was a branchless tree, there was also Antelope, a very shy newcomer, the Champagne Lady, who seemed always dressed to the nines, and Ivy, a woman with the habit of covering other people's lives with her own.[53] Something else clear from Pettavel's account is that Nicoll's interest in Jung and Swedenborg was not muted. Nicoll made use of the fourfold cross diagram Jung used to show the division of the "psychological functions," with thinking

and feeling forming the vertical arm and intuition and sensation forming the horizontal.[54] She also tells us that Nicoll assigned Swedenborg's
The Doctrine of Uses to some in the group. Swedenborg believed that
there are no free lunches, that everything has a purpose and a use. Even
in heaven the angels are put to work, something Gurdjieff would have
approved of. When one student expressed confusion about his own use,
saying he had no task, Nicoll replied "No use? No task? Remember
yourself! How's that?"[55]

Pettavel was also privy to some of Nicoll's unbuttoned remarks about
his old teachers' students. Ouspensky's people, Nicoll said, were "will
worshippers," no doubt referring to the strenuous efforts to remember
themselves that one of them, Kenneth Walker, we know commented
on. They practiced "fakir stuff." "Why," Nicoll asked rhetorically, "did
they not observe themselves internally and notice their suspicion and
envy?"[56] Their suspicion may be chalked up to Ouspensky's paranoia
about the police, but envy? About what or of whom, one wants to ask.
One also wonders if remarks like these constitute the "slander" that
Nicoll felt he had committed against Ouspensky.

Yet if illness is a way of entering the time-body, Nicoll was certainly
entering his. Kenneth Walker, who visited him regularly at this time,
told him that he should rest, to stop his activities. If Nicoll had, he
might have lived the three to five years his doctors had granted him.
But Nicoll was determined to carry on as long as he could. There
was still much to do, much left unfinished. He continued writing the
Commentaries that would appear, after his death, as volumes 4 and 5.
He also worked on the material that would be posthumously published
as *The Mark*. He tried to keep up his correspondence, but this had to
be abandoned in order to conserve strength for his writing. Yet it was
clear to those around him that this work was carried out, as Pogson
writes, under a sentence of death. Dr. Johnson, Nicoll's favorite writer,
had long ago opined that the knowledge that one was to be hanged in
a fortnight, would "concentrate the mind wonderfully." The time left

to Nicoll was a bit more than a fortnight, but the knowledge that his death was near seemed to have concentrated his mind nonetheless.

As was said to have happened around Ouspensky during his own last days—at least as reported by Rodney Collin—the atmosphere in Great Amwell House seemed to have opened up to the "invisible world," or at least was allowing it to shine through the material one. Nicoll himself spoke of his death simply. If we can go by Pogson's account, he seemed to look forward to it. After Ouspensky's death, Nicoll confided in his diary that he suspected his teacher had been glad to be free of his body. One suspects Nicoll, who was never really fond of his mortal form, felt the same. Catherine told Pogson that Nicoll was being "brave and cheerful," and that he laughed when he asked, "What is the flesh anyway?" He later told Pogson that he hoped that after death, he "would be given the work of being an invisible guardian," protecting people from their negative emotions, becoming in effect a guardian angel. (Strangely this was an afterlife occupation Collin believed Ouspensky had taken up.[57])

Nicoll also hoped that when he recurred, he would be able to gather together all the people he had worked with in this life, those who had "served the teaching," so that they could continue to do so together in his—and one assumes their—next recurrence. Nicoll seemed to share the idea that groups of people with a spiritual connection, recur together at different periods in time.* This was in order to work toward the regeneration of the age. In *The New Man* and elsewhere, Nicoll spoke of the "end of the world" not as some cataclysmic destruction, as so many of our blockbuster films today trip over themselves to portray, but the end of a way of thinking, a form of belief, an age. He had

---

*This was an idea shared by his younger contemporary and fellow psychiatrist Arthur Guirdham. In a series of books starting with *The Cathars and Reincarnation* (London: Neville Spearman, 1970), Guirdham claimed to have discovered that he and some of his patients had a past life together in thirteenth-century France as members of the heretical Christian sect the Cathars.

worked toward a new vision of this in this life, had formed an ark and saved what he could. He would, he believed, do so in the next.

Yet it was inevitable that he would slow down and that the pace at Amwell would change. Diana Pettavel records that at the last meetings, Nicoll "seemed to have reached a different level of himself where no one dared approach."[58] The sorts of questions that he might have allowed to take up time earlier were now rejected outright, an echo of Ouspensky's impatience with trivialities. "Enough of the sub-group questions," Nicoll would say. "Does no one have a real question?" "A deeper note was struck," as Pogson remarks.[59] Nicoll was occupied with more "interior thinking," and no doubt this, and his diminishing strength, led to longer silences at the meetings and to him gently brushing away concerns that he might have indulged at another time. The evening discussions were now severely limited; at them Nicoll was reduced to drinking Ribena, a sugary fruit drink, while his followers enjoyed the wine of old. If he thought ruefully of the miracle of turning water into wine as he nursed his insipid black currant cordial, we cannot blame him.

After a time Nicoll retired to his room, which he now rarely left. He had an intercom system installed so that he could communicate with different parts of the house. Nicoll enjoyed sounding the buzzer, making comic remarks, and surprising his housemates, playing a kind of peekaboo, rather as he enjoyed setting up his electric toys and gizmos at Bay Tree Lodge when a boy. Occasionally a newcomer or old-timer would visit him in his room. He especially liked to have young people to talk with. He enjoyed the company of their relatively fresh minds, free of a lifetime of associations.

Although he did his best, Nicoll couldn't attend all of the weekend meetings that, ironically, were drawing more people now than ever. In 1952, Vincent Stuart published the first three volumes of the *Commentaries*, making them available to the general reading public. In his review of them, not surprisingly Kenneth Walker said that the *Commentaries* would "remain the standard work on the subject for as long as these ideas are of interest to mankind." Their publication brought much correspondence and many new visitors to Amwell House, wanting an audience with Nicoll. Nicoll could not see them all and some left disappointed, no doubt under a heavy cloud of inner considering. But the patient and persistent were often rewarded with a brief talk with the teacher.

Vincent Stuart also published *Living Time* in 1952, a book Nicoll had completed many years earlier but had held back from publication because of the general ban on any Work-related writing prior to Gurdjieff's death. *Living Time*, however, draws on Ouspensky's published ideas about time and recurrence, even his "weakness," *Tertium Organum*, not the Work, although as Ouspensky did, it does make veiled references to it.

Living Time gathers together the material on the Gnostics, Hermeticists, Plato, Swedenborg, and quite a few other mystic sources that Nicoll's American secretary, Frances Ney, had ransacked the British Museum to collect all those years ago. It starts with the revelation that came to Nicoll as a boy and that is at the heart of all spiritual and mystical teachings: that our true self, the inner man who is capable of becoming something more than a clever animal, is *invisible*, outside space, time, and the material world.[60] Its main argument is that eternity is not some endless extension in time, as the universe appears to be an endless extension in space, Einstein notwithstanding. Nor is the "eternal life" promised by religion a similarly extended afterlife, luxuriating amid clouds and chubby cherubs. Both really refer to a change in consciousness, a shift in being, that can happen *now*, in *this* life.

This is the elevation of ourselves out of the horizontal stream of "tick tock" time—the perpetual becoming of "life"—and into the vertical level of being, the "timeless time" that Ouspensky mapped out in *Tertium Organum* and *A New Model of the Universe*. It is the "eternal now," the "living time" an experience of which the Work is designed to induce. It is the "higher order of reality . . . beyond the process of time," that awakening to our true "I," our true self, reveals.[61] To support his insight Nicoll marshals a sometimes overwhelming number of sources including, along with those already mentioned, Meister Eckhart, Schopenhauer, Nietzsche, the theologian Karl Barth, the alchemist Robert Fludd, the mathematician Eugene Minkowski, the opium ecstasies of Thomas De Quincey and the ether visions of Sir William Ramsay, the Scottish Nobel Prize–winning chemist and discoverer of the noble gasses.

As often happens with Jung, the reader sometimes loses the forest for the trees—Nicoll is not at his best when organizing an argument—but the general idea gets across. Most important, the reader can feel Nicoll's excitement about the power of *ideas* to change our perceptions, of the positive use of imagination to extend our vision beyond the immediately given, just as the "psychological method" reveals the deeper meaning below the surface of a literal text. This energizing of the mind through the effort of grasping a new way of thinking—one, as Ouspensky said, that uses "different categories"—is itself a means of awakening consciousness, of self-remembering. As much as any psychological exercise or meditation, it is a means of grasping the reality of the invisible world of *meaning*, whose locus is the human mind.

Someone who grasped this was Kenneth Walker. Walker admitted to "certain inner reservations" about *The New Man*; exactly what they were is unclear.[62] And although he recognized the *Commentaries* for the remarkable source that they are, he had always felt that Nicoll "had never produced anything adequate to [his] genius." Now with *Living Time* it seemed that Nicoll finally had. Walker had read some chapters from the book years earlier, and was not particularly impressed. But now all that had changed. In a letter Walker told his old friend that the book was the "best thing" he had ever done. It was his "*chef d'oeuvre.*" Walker was able to communicate his high estimate of the book to a wider public, in his review of it for the Sunday *Times*. He told his readers that it was "one of those rare books which may have a lasting effect on the reader's thinking and give new meaning to the Universe, to himself, and to life in general."

We might excuse Walker for pitching his praise a bit high, wanting his friend to leave this vale of tears with a sense of true accomplishment, if indeed that was his intent. Yet the reviewer for the *Times Literary Supplement* would have felt no emotional bond with Nicoll. And, as far as I can tell, he was not in the Work. So the praise he gave the book was genuine and deserving, calling it "throughout a triumph of clarity and good writing." Diogenes (or W. J. Brown) in *Time and Tide* agreed. For him the book contained "some of the most significant writing of our time." And for the *Spectator*, a conservative cultural journal, it was "a work in which intellect and emotion are justly balanced." This last assessment must have pleased Nicoll, for whom achieving such a balance was a lifetime's work. One of the central metaphors in the *Commentaries* is that of the pendulum, our inner state, forever swinging between extremes, and the need to catch it at the midpoint, the still moment, when perfect balance is achieved.

TOWARD THE END, Nicoll spent his time in his room, reading Swedenborg and the Gospels, writing the last of the *Commentaries,* and working on the material for *The Mark*. The "final act of the drama" of his life, as Pogson writes, had begun. Around this time Nicoll had a dream that affected him deeply and that eventually found its way into *The Mark* as "The New Will."[63] In the dream Nicoll is pushed up a grassy slope, to the edge of a ditch. The distance to the other side is not great and a plank is there, ready to cross. But some "restraining power" holds him back. The ditch itself is immeasurably deep, an abyss filled with the bones of prehistoric creatures, violent beasts. Fear stops him from crossing the chasm, and then, suddenly, he is already across. On the other side he sees a man drilling some troops, new raw recruits. There is nothing marvelous in this; it is just everyday work. The man smiles, and somehow communicates to Nicoll that he "does not necessarily expect to get any results from what he is doing." The recruits are unruly and useless and his efforts seem pointless, but the man doesn't mind. He is indifferent to their taunts and sneers, and knows that "one must give them help, though they don't want it," rather as Jesus forgave his executioners because they knew not what they did.

Nicoll woke from the dream feeling that what the man in it was doing was "utterly contrary" to anything he would do. It seemed so futile. In order to so act, Nicoll understood, he would require a "new will," one that did not aim for results or act out of the self. That was the way of the old will, the way of violence, the way of the past, symbolized by the abyss of bones. In the new world, on the other side of the abyss, one acted from a higher will, not to gain reward or assert one's personal will. That was how the man acted; he was, Nicoll understood, "a man without violence." In the dream the sea beckoned in the distance, which Nicoll understood to mean that the man would travel on once his work was done, perhaps to train others elsewhere. Nicoll believed that he still had much more work to do to reach the kind of "new will" he had caught a glimpse of in the dream. Those around him in his last days may be excused for disagreeing with him, and believing that when he reached the other side, he would be teaching new recruits there, just as he had taught them here.

Nicoll saw visitors almost until the end, although what took place during these meetings was not always obvious. The subject of conversation might seem "trivial," but Nicoll still had a way of drawing deep insight from apparently inconsequential things. One visitor received significant personal observations through Nicoll's appreciation of a clockwork toy mule.[64] A remark about detective stories or gardening could be read with much profit in a nonliteral way. Of Nicoll, one visitor said, as so many had before, that he "had met a *man* for the first time."[65] His remarks may have been gruff, but the "strange mixture of fierceness, humour, leg-pulling, relaxation," that his visitors found in Nicoll had nothing of "earnestness, or piousness." As Diana Pettavel remarked, Nicoll "often behaved in a way which totally discouraged any form of guru worship."[66] He had always taken serious things lightly; he was not going to stop now.

Nicoll had prayed that if he was granted more time he would not misuse it. It would be difficult to prove that his prayer was answered, but it is clear that whatever time he had left he did not waste. But opportunities are not endless, and neither is one's time. As the end approached, Nicoll seemed in an almost celebratory mood. One visitor who saw Nicoll not long before he died reported that he was "smiling, carefree, and radiant." When she asked if he was not afraid of death, he replied "slowly and with great serenity," "No, I am not afraid." "Cast your burdens upon the Lord," was his advice. "That's all. Stop thinking. Cast your burdens upon the Lord."[67] As was reported during Ouspensky's last days, there were signs and portents, or at least what Jung would have called a synchronicity. On July 26, just more than a month before Nicoll's death, there was a lunar eclipse; during it, a swallow flew into the room in which a meeting was being held. Nicoll smiled and said that the others must think it a bad omen, although in Northern Europe, swallows are generally seen as symbolizing good fortune. This time, however, may have been an exception. Not long after this, Catherine's illness returned. It was the pain of her having to suffer that, according to Pogson, left Nicoll with little will to live.

Nicoll gave his last meeting on August 16. Pogson and Vincent Stuart read the paper, which developed the theme of Nicoll's dream. He warned against keeping what were known as "internal accounts," the feeling that one was "owed" something by the Work for one's efforts.[68] One must work without reward, Nicoll impressed upon the group, just as the man in his dream had taught his recruits without promise of success. One must learn how to do a thing for its own sake, for the sheer joy of doing it well. And one must work against the "subhuman monkey conceit" that prevents one from understanding this. A man *is* his understanding. This was a point Nicoll had worked to get across to them from the beginning. One cannot be forced or compelled to understand.[69] No one can understand something for someone else. Only one's own understanding can lead to that state of quiet joy called "inner happiness."

During the discussion after the paper had been read, it seemed that for that last meeting, Nicoll had thrown off his illness, had "cast his burden upon the Lord." It was as if it were "Dr. Nicoll as we had known him of old who was sitting there."[70] He spoke once again of the need for humility, of the danger of vanity, and of the way of service to the Work. Pogson had an intuition that this was his last meeting and the last time he would address the group. Most likely Nicoll did too. He pointed out that if people did not learn to do the Work through their own understanding, if they did not learn how to see themselves, how to work through their negative emotions and mechanical reactions, he could not use them. Only those who could do this could teach the Work. If nothing else, people must recognize that they occupy better or worse states of mind, that they wander through better or worse neighborhoods in their inner worlds, and that they need to have a map of these interior spaces, something he had learned from Swedenborg long ago.

He was "speaking to those who know there is something wrong with them," and hoping that they have "caught" some of what he was sending their way all these years.[71] "What use has your life been to you," he asked them, "if you have never caught a glimpse of the way to inner happiness and are bitter and have done little else than make internal accounts against others and understand nothing about yourself or what you have to learn?"[72] To know thyself is simple wisdom. To spend a lifetime trying to do so is another matter.

Nicoll started another paper, returning to these themes, but he was unable to finish it. Not long after, he fell into a coma from which he did not awaken. On August 30, 1953, the time-body of Dr. Maurice Nicoll came around full circle. One's life is one's time, Ouspensky said, and for Nicoll both had come to an end. But if there is any truth to recurrence, he is back at work again.

EPILOGUE

Hitting the Mark

After Nicoll's death his body lay in state for a time in his room at Great Amwell House. When Diana Pettavel came to pay her respects, she sat for a time with Nicoll in his room, where before so many had sought his counsel. "It was not only his body lying there," she remarked.[1] His "presence in the room was strong," that presence that Fulford Bush and others recognized, as almost everyone did, practically the moment they met Nicoll. Death may have put an end to Nicoll's physical activity, but whatever intangible something survives that biological full stop, it was there, making itself known. All Pettavel could think to say was "Thank you," which was no doubt all Nicoll would have wanted to hear, if even that. Later that night she had a dream in which Nicoll spoke with her. He told her to look after Catherine, that she needed her now, and he added that he was "going back to . . ." Pettavel could not remember the date in the dream Nicoll had mentioned, but she wondered if it was 1884, the year of his birth.[2]

But it was not only Nicoll's time-body that had made its round and was now, if the doctrine of eternal recurrence was true, somehow starting again. Great Amwell House too had reached its end. This particular ark would sail on the waters of life no more. One of the last things Catherine said to the group was "You must sell this house. It is

403

founded on the being of my husband. And you must find a new way of working."[3]

Another charge Catherine gave was to Beryl Pogson that she write a book about her husband. *Maurice Nicoll: A Portrait* is that book. Catherine didn't live to see it, although one suspects she would have been happy with the respect if not adoration her husband's secretary showed to him and herself. Three months after Nicoll's death, Catherine was dead too. Nicoll's hope that she would be able to carry on their work was unfulfilled, and, in general, the Work that had taken on a "perceptible Nicoll character" at Great Amwell House would not survive the death of its namesake. After Nicoll's cremation, his ashes were scattered at Sidlesham, where Ouspensky could hear the world turning and, ironically, where he could sleep better than anywhere else. Nicoll, I think, would have appreciated the joke. A memorial service was held at Lumsden Church, where a plaque was erected "To the Glory of God and in Loving and Eternal Memory" of Maurice and Catherine.

As Catherine said, many did find a new way of working. According to Bob Hunter, a student of Pogson's, at the end of his ministry, Nicoll's congregation numbered some six hundred parishioners.[4] As generally happens after the death of a guru—which, to all intents and purposes, is what Nicoll was to his devotees—this large body broke up into smaller groups. Some people, like Samuel Copley, made their way to the Gurdjieff Society, where they were able to carry on their work, as Copley did until his death in 2002. Some drifted away from the "Work life" entirely, or found a new spiritual path to follow. And some, like Pogson, tried to carry on working along what we might call "perceptible Nicoll lines."

Pogson did not drift to the Gurdjieff Society, just as Nicoll had not drifted to Gurdjieff. She started her own groups—she had already led a subgroup—and founded a "Nicoll-like" community in Upper Dicker, in Sussex, south of London. In a large house named The Dicker, she led groups and continued the arts-and-crafts approach to the Work that so characterized Nicoll's own brand of it. She died in 1967. What remains of her efforts, and the last expression of the Work informed with the "perceptible Nicoll character," are her books, which, like the *Commentaries*, are mostly transcripts of talks she gave.

Nicoll was right. He did not build for posterity. Long ago Gurdjieff had told him that. Soon everything would be different, the master had said to his kitchen boy as they looked out on the Prieuré with its inmates scurrying about. Everyone would be somewhere else. The Work would have no permanent home. Did Nicoll understand then what that meant? Did the people he was leaving now understand it? Copley said that what Nicoll "said and wrote was of great importance." But "what he was and how he manifested his being was of greater importance."[5] "It surely must have been the same with Gurdjieff," Copley added, perhaps remembering Nicoll's claim to have been Gurdjieff's "subtype."

Yet, while a living teacher suffused with presence can create a unique and unmistakable effect, something no number of lectures or diagrams may do, the opposite is also true. Once the teacher is gone, the teachings alone are not enough. That Ouspensky's line of the Work ground to halt, with the only possible hope of renewal coming from an unlikely contact with the Inner Circle of Humanity, is evidence enough of this. Ouspensky was brilliant, but whatever charm and charisma he possessed in his early, more "poetic" days, had long been drummed out of him via the Gurdjieff treatment. "The spirit of the Work," Copley writes, "requires the 'Being' of its teachers to give it the vibrations of life." No teacher, no being, no life, no Work.

Yet one could be forgiven for disagreeing with Copley and suggesting that what Nicoll wrote was, if not of greater importance than his own personal being, certainly of equal stature. Because today, this is the only way anyone will get any idea of what the Work with a "perceptible Nicoll character" was like. And if meeting Nicoll was a unique and unforgettable experience—as many who met him described it as being—readers today can still meet him in his books. This, indeed, is how most readers meet their authors, and it is an introduction often preferable to one in the flesh.

Some who met Nicoll this way were certainly enriched by the acquaintance. One such was E. F. Schumacher, the German-British economist most famous for his bestselling book *Small Is Beautiful* (1977), a look at the benefits of decentralization years ahead of the fashion for "downsizing." Schumacher became interested in the Gurdjieff Work in postwar Germany; a study of it led to his translating *The New Man* into German with his mother.[6] He first came across the Fourth Way through the unlikely offices of the British National Coal Board. J. G. Bennett was running the British Coal Utilisation Research Association and at weekends "the BCURA laboratories at Coombe Springs were transformed into a center for spiritual seekers who met to explore the meanings and implications of Gurdjieff's teachings."[7] Schumacher was one of these seekers. What he learned at Coombe Springs later informed his own educational efforts. In the summer of 1953, just as Nicoll was dying, Schumacher came upon *The New Man,* and it made a powerful impression on him.

Years later, in his short book about the "perennial philosophy," *A Guide for the Perplexed* (1977), Schumacher featured Nicoll along with Ouspensky, Étienne Gilson, Jacques Maritain, René Guenon, Martin Lings, and other "Traditionalist" philosophers in an aptly brief but effective argument for an "hierarchy of being" and the need for a consciousness adequate to its higher levels. *Living Time* and the *Commentaries* are referenced throughout.[8] Although not as successful as *Small Is Beautiful, A Guide for the Perplexed* was well received; Arthur Koestler, a mainstream figure gone over to the parapsychological camp, reviewed it positively. This was at a time when the Fourth Way, and spiritual traditions in general, were receiving much popular attention. To have Schumacher and, by association Koestler, speaking well of his work, must have turned some readers in Nicoll's direction.

Someone else who did the same for Nicoll a decade or so earlier was J. B. Priestley. In 1950, Nicoll wrote to Priestley, suggesting that he write a play along the lines of the plot for the aborted *Pelican Hotel*. Priestley, we know, was famous for his "time plays," into which he incorporated some of Ouspensky's ideas about recurrence. "Could you write a play of a man, say of sixty, 'visiting' himself as he was say a lad of twenty at Cambridge and seeing what he could advise this lad to do?" Nicoll asked the world-famous playwright. "To move through the 'Time-Body' was one of the exercises I was taught by Gurdjieff," Nicoll mentioned. "Only you, with your fine dramatic sense, could do this play."[9]

We don't know if Priestley replied, but we do know that he didn't write such a play. What he did do, not long after receiving Nicoll's letter, was turn to the *Commentaries* for help during the difficult breakup of his second marriage. According to his biographer Vincent Brome, during his split up with Jane Bannerman, Priestley "used to read a bit of Maurice Nicoll's *Commentaries* . . . every night and . . . found them most helpful, particularly the idea of non-identification."[10] Apparently, trying not to identify with his anger made it easier for Priestley to cope with the difficulties of a divorce, although some members of the family seemed to have thought otherwise. Priestley also had well-thumbed copies of *The New Man* and *Living Time*.*

Years later, Priestley made a more public show of his appreciation of Nicoll's work, by including him with Ouspensky and Bennett and other "time-haunted men" in his classic and highly popular study *Man and Time* (1964). In the chapter "Esoteric School," along with looking at Ouspensky's ideas about recurrence—which he rejects—and Bennett's notions about "freedom" being the domain of the "fifth dimension of time," Priestley mentions the *Commentaries* and devotes several pages to *Living Time*. It is, he wrote, "a plea, eloquent and enriched by

---

*A correspondent, Nicholas Colloff, came into some of Priestley's library sometime after his death. Among the books were *The New Man* and *Living Time* in the Vincent Stuart editions.

quotations from a wide range of authors for our self-deliverance from the domination of 'passing-time.'"[11]

This is a phrase from *Living Time* that Priestley freely admits to appropriating, just as he also borrowed the notion of "time alive" that runs through his Fourth Way–inspired novel *The Magicians* (1954), which features a character that to my reading is based on Gurdjieff.[12] In *Man and Time* he remarks on Nicoll's advocacy of the "supremacy of the invisible," and, as Schumacher will, provides long quotations from Nicoll's work.[13] He also compares it favorably to H. G. Wells's last book, *Mind at the End of Its Tether* (1946), written, as Priestley believed *Living Time* was, at the end of Wells's life. Wells, we know, was the original "time-traveler," his debut novel *The Time Machine* (1895), putting both himself and "time travel" on the map. In his last days, Wells lost his hope for a future scientific social utopia, and succumbed to a kind of existential despair. His last work, Priestley said, was a "dark little dead end," while Nicoll's offered "liberation" and "light."[14]

Time certainly haunted Priestley. In one of his own last books, *Over the Long High Wall* (1972), subtitled *Some Reflections and Speculations on Life, Death, and Time*, Priestley returned again to Nicoll. Here he was a bit more critical of Nicoll's "time writing," remarking that for all its eloquence and sensitivity, *Living Time* "suffers from a certain vagueness." This is because Nicoll's approach is "deliberately unsystematic" but also because he nowhere discusses "the probable structure of multi-dimensional Time," unlike Ouspensky, who manages to include eternal recurrence within a six-dimensional time, and goes to some trouble to explain exactly how this could work.[15] As Priestley points out, Nicoll nowhere does this, aside from a nod at recurrence that, as Priestley suggests, Nicoll seems to present in a half-hearted way. Nicoll's, Priestley says, is rightly a psychological approach, not a metaphysical one. Priestley also suggests that Nicoll perhaps leaned too heavily on quotations from "the mystics," whom he seemed to regard as "the spokesmen of an esoteric tradition," which Priestley did not. As for the

Fourth Way, it without doubt "deserves our admiring attention," but "we don't have to agree with all of it," which strikes me as the most commonsense attitude to have. I should say that Priestley was also a great reader of Jung.

Another reader of *Living Time* with a more committed attitude toward the Fourth Way was the philosopher Jacob Needleman, who has brought some of Gurdjieff's ideas and that of the Traditionalist branch of esoteric philosophy into the context of mainstream education. Needleman included *The New Man* among the esoteric writings he presented in paperback editions for Penguin Books in the 1970s. Years later, in *Time and the Soul*, a title Nicoll might have used himself, Needleman explores ways of moving out of what Nicoll called "passing-time," into more meaningful and purposeful temporal dimensions having little to do with the clock. In his suggestions for further reading on the subject he writes of *Living Time* that, "If I had to recommend one title, it would be this one." It is a "life-changing book of great profundity and clarity about the mystery of time," one that also "unlocks many doors to the inner teachings of Christianity and the spiritual philosophies of the West."[16]

But perhaps the posthumous acquaintanceship with Nicoll that he would have most appreciated was that developed by the comedian John Cleese, of *Monty Python's Flying Circus* fame. In an article in the *Week* for February 5, 2017, among his six favorite books, Cleese included Nicoll's *Commentaries*, which pulled in at no. 5. Nicoll is in some high-caliber company, sharing column space with the philosopher Karl Popper and Leo Tolstoy. At the top of his list Cleese puts *The Master and His Emissary*, by Iain McGilchrist, a book that reboots the question of the relationship between our two cerebral hemispheres, which we know interested Nicoll in his last years, and that he no doubt would have wanted to read. Cleese has engaged with McGilchrist in interviews on YouTube, and what has emerged is Cleese's deep interest in spirituality. Cleese commended the *Commentaries* for providing "the best advice on understanding one's own psychology as looked at through the Esoteric Christian tradition."[17]

In an article for *Harper's Magazine* for November 2018, Cleese went into more detail about his appreciation of Nicoll. In a long account of his approach to spirituality, in which he quotes from Aldous Huxley and Sogyal Rinpoche, author of *The Tibetan Book of Living and Dying*, Cleese inserts long quotations from the *Commentaries* and speaks about "the Work" in ways that suggest a personal experience of it. Talking about the need to "chip away at our egotistical shells," Cleese declares that, "The best stuff I have ever read" about how to go about doing this, "was written by a British psychiatrist, Maurice Nicoll, who studied with Georges Ivanovitch Gurdjieff."[18] And at the webpage John Cleese Quotes we find this:

> The neurologist and psychologist Maurice Nicoll told how he had once asked his headmaster about a passage in the Bible, and after he had listened to the answer for some time, he realized that the man had no idea what he was talking about. What I admire about Nicoll is that he made this discovery when he was only ten. It took me another forty-five years before the penny dropped: very, very few people have any idea what they are talking about.[19]

One can only hope that somehow, through some turn in his time-body, Nicoll is aware that there is very funny person around today who agrees with him wholeheartedly that serious things must be taken in a humorous way.

Acknowledgments

I'd like to thank Jeffrey Adams for suggesting I write a book about Nicoll and for providing an enormous amount of indispensable material toward doing so. I'd also like to thank John Willmett for his research into Nicoll's life and for what must have been the considerable effort involved in transcribing his diaries. Needless to say, my reading of Nicoll's diaries is strictly my own and does not reflect either Jeffrey's or John's interpretation of them. I'd like to thank Nicholas Colloff for providing important material about J. B. Priestley's interest in Nicoll. I'd also like to thank my colleagues Mitch Horowitz and Richard Smoley for answering important questions. As always, my thanks go to the staff of the British Library, which remains a haven in dark times. My greatest thanks, though, go to my friend James Hamilton, a longtime practitioner of the Work, who passed away not long after I completed this book. No doubt, he has moved on to another level of the octave. He will be missed.

Notes

Introduction. Essence and Shadow

1. J. G. Bennett, *Gurdjieff: Making a New World.*
2. Kenneth Walker, *Venture with Ideas*, and *A Study of Gurdjieff's Teaching.*
3. Beryl Pogson, *Maurice Nicoll: A Portrait*, 24.
4. Walker, *Venture with Ideas*, 70.
5. P. D. Ouspensky, *A New Model of the Universe*, 451–76.
6. P. D. Ouspensky, *In Search of the Miraculous*, 55.
7. Marsha Keith Schuchard, *Why Mrs. Blake Cried.*

Chapter One. Unclean Thoughts

1. Ouspensky, *In Search of the Miraculous*, 161.
2. Ouspensky, *In Search of the Miraculous*, 200.
3. Ouspensky, *In Search of the Miraculous*, 201.
4. P. D. Ouspensky, *Tertium Organum*, 38–39.
5. Pogson, *Maurice Nicoll*, xiii.
6. Pogson, *Maurice Nicoll*, xiii.
7. Pogson, *Maurice Nicoll*, xiii.
8. Samuel Copley, *Portrait of a Vertical Man*, 20–21.
9. "Informal Work Talks and Teachings, 1940–1950," September 20, 1942, Nicoll Archive, Edinburgh University Library.
10. Pogson, *Maurice Nicoll*, 8.
11. "Where Did Robert Louis Stevenson Live in Hampstead?" spookyisles.com
12. Copley, *Portrait of a Vertical Man*, 2.
13. Copley, *Portrait of a Vertical Man*, 2.
14. Ouspensky, *In Search of the Miraculous*, 3.
15. Pogson, *Maurice Nicoll*, 3.

16. Pogson, *Maurice Nicoll,* 194–95. For the links between Kammerer's "seriality" and Jung's "synchronicity," both of which were of special interest to Nicoll, see my *Dreaming Ahead of Time: Experiences with Precognitive Dreams, Synchronicity and Coincidence.*

17. Copley, *Portrait of a Vertical Man,* 1.

18. Maurice Nicoll, *Psychological Commentaries on the Teachings of Gurdjieff and Ouspensky,* 1:8.

19. Nicoll, *Psychological Commentaries,* 5:1765.

20. Copley, *Portrait of a Vertical Man,* 3.

21. Copley, *Portrait of a Vertical Man,* 1.

22. Copley, *Portrait of a Vertical Man,* 4.

23. Pogson, *Maurice Nicoll,* 10.

24. Pogson, *Maurice Nicoll,* 3.

25. Maurice Nicoll, "Unclean Thoughts," in Early Diary 1919-21.

26. Nicoll, "Unclean Thoughts," Early Diary 1919-21.

27. Nicoll, "Unclean Thoughts," Poe's "Alone:"
    From childhood's hour I have not been
    As others were—I have not seen
    As others saw—I could not bring
    My passions from a common spring . . .

28. Nicoll, "Unclean Thoughts," Early Diary 1919-21.

29. Pogson, *Maurice Nicoll,* 21.

30. Nicoll, *Commentaries* vol. 19.

31. Nicoll, *Commentaries* 1:9.

32. Nicoll, *Commentaries* 1:8.

33. Nicoll "Unclean Thoughts," Early Diary 1919-21.

34. Maurice Nicoll, *Living Time,* 1.

35. Pogson, *Maurice Nicoll,* 13.

36. Pogson, *Maurice Nicoll,* 11.

37. Pogson, *Maurice Nicoll,* 12.

38. Pogson, *Maurice Nicoll,* 25.

39. Copley, *Portrait of a Vertical Man,* 8.

40. Pogson, *Maurice Nicoll,* 14.

41. "Lord Richard in the Pantry," bfi.or.uk.

42. Gary Lachman, *Madame Blavatsky: The Mother of Modern Spirituality,* 244–45.

43. Charles Higham, *The Adventures of Conan Doyle,* 50.

Chapter Two. The Sins of the Father

1. Pogson, *Maurice Nicoll*, 14.
2. Peter Gay, *Freud: A Life for Our Time*, 184.
3. Gary Lachman, *Jung the Mystic*, 91–92.
4. John Kerr, *A Dangerous Method*.
5. Gay, *Freud*, 184.
6. William McGuire, ed. *The Freud/Jung Letters*, 164.
7. William James, openlibrary.org, "The Energies of Men."
8. Colin Wilson, *Frankenstein's Castle*, 31–34.
9. W. B. Yeats, "Under Ben Bulben."
10. Pogson, *Maurice Nicoll*, 18.
11. C. G. Jung, *Memories, Dreams, Reflections*, 172.
12. Jung, *Memories, Dreams, Reflections*, 173.
13. Anthony Storr, *The Dynamics of Creation*, 1–2.
14. Gary Lachman, gary-lachman.com, "Was Freud Afraid of the Occult?"
15. Lachman, *Jung the Mystic*, 75–78.
16. Pogson, *Maurice Nicoll*, 19.
17. C. G. Jung, *Collected Papers on Analytical Psychology*, 156. Jung worked on this paper and a later version appeared in 1949.
18. Jung, *Collected Papers on Analytical Psychology*, 156.
19. Jung, *Collected Papers on Analytical Psychology*, 172.
20. Friedrich Nietzsche, *Beyond Good and Evil*, 73.
21. Pogson, *Maurice Nicoll*, 19.
22. Colin Wilson, *A Criminal History of Mankind*, 64–75.
23. Pogson, *Maurice Nicoll*, 19.
24. Copley, *Portrait of a Vertical Man*, 8.
25. Pogson, *Maurice Nicoll*, 20.
26. Jack Adrian, ed., *Strange Tales from the "Strand" Magazine*.
27. Pogson, *Maurice Nicoll*, 22.
28. Pogson, *Maurice Nicoll*, 22.
29. Richard Noll, *The Jung Cult*.
30. Noll, *The Jung Cult*.
31. Pogson, *Maurice Nicoll*, 23.
32. Pogson, *Maurice Nicoll*, 23.
33. Pogson, *Maurice Nicoll*, 31.
34. From Rupert Brooke's "Peace." See www.poetryfoundation.org.
35. Pogson, *Maurice Nicoll*, 33.
36. Ouspensky, *In Search of the Miraculous*, 4.

37. Ouspensky, *In Search of the Miraculous,* 4.

38. Ouspensky, *In Search of the Miraculous,* 3.

Chapter Three. Shell-Shocked

1. Pogson, *Maurice Nicoll,* 32.

2. Pogson, *Maurice Nicoll,* 32.

3. G. I. Gurdjieff, *Meetings with Remarkable Men.*

4. Martin Swayne, *In Mesopotamia,* a copy can be found at www.gutenberg.org.

5. Swayne, *In Mesopotamia,* chapter 4, "Heat Stroke."

6. Nicoll, *Commentaries* 1:13.

7. Pogson, *Maurice Nicoll,* 59.

8. Swayne, *In Mesopotamia,* chapter 6, "The Day's Work."

9. Swayne, *In Mesopotamia,* chapter 6, "The Day's Work."

10. "Contribution to the Psychology of Rumour," in *Collected Papers on Analytical Psychology,* 176–90.

11. Viktor Frankl, *Man's Search for Meaning.*

12. Swayne, *In Mesopotamia,* chapter 8, "Amara."

13. Pogson, *Maurice Nicoll,* 59.

14. Pogson, *Maurice Nicoll,* 50.

15. Pogson, *Maurice Nicoll,* 58.

16. Ean Begg, "Jung's Lost Lieutenant."

17. Pogson, *Maurice Nicoll,* 57.

18. Maurice Nicoll, *Dream Psychology.*

19. Begg, "Jung's Lost Lieutenant." For Sonu Shamdasani, *Dream Psychology* is "the first didactic presentation of Jung's psychology." Shamdasani, *Jung and the Making of Modern Psychology* (Cambridge: Cambridge University Press, 2003), 147.

20. Begg, "Jung's Lost Lieutenant."

21. Nicoll, *Dream Psychology,* vi.

22. Nicoll, *Dream Psychology,* 24.

23. Nicoll, *Dream Psychology,* 15–16.

24. Nicoll, *Dream Psychology,* 112.

25. Nicoll, *Dream Psychology,* 76.

26. Nicoll, *Dream Psychology,* 72.

27. Martin Swayne, *The Blue Germ,* 13.

28. Swayne, *The Blue Germ,* 27.

29. Gary Lachman, *The Return of Holy Russia,* 296, 347.

30. Swayne, *The Blue Germ,* 72.

31. Swayne, *The Blue Germ,* 126

32. Swayne, *The Blue Germ,* 145.

33. Swayne, *The Blue Germ,* 204, 220.

34. Swayne, *The Blue Germ,* 225.

35. Annie Besant and C. W. Leadbeater, *Thought Forms.*

36. Swayne, *The Blue Germ,* 226.

37. Swayne, *The Blue Germ,* 128.

Chapter Four. A Taste for the Forbidden

1. Stephan Hoeller, *The Gnostic Jung and the Seven Sermons to the Dead.*

2. Colin Wilson, *Origins of the Sexual Impulse,* 159, 167.

3. Colin Wilson, *The Misfits: A Study of Sexual Outsiders,* 87–88.

4. Nicolai Berdyaev, *The Meaning of the Creative Act,* 168.

5. Maurice Nicoll, "Unclean Thoughts," Early Diary, 1919–1921.

6. See Monica Furlong, *Genuine Fake.*

7. Wilson, *Origins of the Sexual Impulse,* 171.

8. Colin Wilson, *New Pathways in Psychology,* 30.

9. Wilson, *Origins of the Sexual Impulse,* 96.

10. Wilson, *Origins of the Sexual Impulse,* 98.

11. Colin Wilson, *Order of Assassins,* 65–77.

12. Quoted in Wilson, 1975, 58.

Chapter Five. Dark Nights of the Soul

1. Maurice Nicoll, Early Diary 1919-21, June 18, 1919.

2. Nicoll, Early Diary 1919-21, June 19, 1919.

3. Nicoll, Early Diary 1919-21, June 25, 1919.

4. Nicoll, Early Diary 1919-21, June 25, 1919.

5. Nicoll, Early Diary 1919-21, July 10, 1919.

6. Gary Lachman, *Jung the Mystic,* 72–75.

7. Nicoll, Early Diary 1919-21, August 3, 1919.

8. Gary Lachman, *Aleister Crowley: Magick, Rock and Roll, and the Wickedest Man in the World.*

9. Nicoll, Early Diary 1919-21, July 13, 1919.

10. Pogson, *Maurice Nicoll,* 64.

11. C. G. Jung, *Memories, Dreams, Reflections,* 215–16.

12. Nicoll, Early Diary 1919-21, July 16, 1919.

13. Nicoll, Early Diary 1919-21, July 17, 1919.

14. Nicoll, Early Diary 1919-21, July 29, 1919.

15. Nicoll, Early Diary 1919-21, August 10, 1919.

16. Nicoll, Early Diary 1919-21, October 20, 1919.

17. Nicoll, Early Diary 1919-21, October 20, 1919.

18. Novalis, *Heinrich von Ofterdingen* (1842).

19. Nicoll, Early Diary 1919-21, June 25, 1919.

20. P. D. Ouspensky, *Letters From Russia 1919*, 2–3.

21. A. R. Orage, *Readers and Writers (1917–1921)*, see "Psycho-Analysis," "Psycho-Analysis and the Mysteries," and "Gently with Psycho-Analysis," 151–57.

22. A. R. Orage, *Consciousness: Animal, Human, Superman.*

23. Philip Mairet, *A. R. Orage,* xiii.

24. Nicoll, Early Diary 1919-21, October 16, 1919.

25. Nicoll, Early Diary 1919-21, October 16, 1919.

26. Edwin Muir, *An Autobiography,* 150.

27. Pogson, *Maurice Nicoll,* 67.

28. Pogson, *Maurice Nicoll,* 68.

29. Pogson, *Maurice Nicoll,* 71.

30. Pogson, *Maurice Nicoll,* 72.

31. Pogson, *Maurice Nicoll,* 79.

32. Pogson, *Maurice Nicoll,* 79.

33. Pogson, *Maurice Nicoll,* 84.

34. Pogson, *Maurice Nicoll,* 84.

35. Pogson, *Maurice Nicoll,* 68.

36. Nicoll, Early Diary 1919-21, December 5, 1920.

37. Nicoll, Early Diary 1919-21, November 28, 1920.

38. Nicoll, Early Diary 1919-21, November 27, 1920.

39. Nicoll, Early Diary 1919-21, November 27, 1920.

40. Erich Neumann, *The Origins and History of Consciousness,* 152.

41. Nicoll, Early Diary 1919-21, May 25, 1920.

42. Nicoll, Early Diary 1919-21, April 30, 1920.

43. Nicoll, Early Diary 1919-21, May 25, 1920.

44. Nicoll, Early Diary 1919-21, May 25, 1920.

45. Nicoll, Early Diary 1919-21, August 25. 1920.

46. Nicoll, Early Diary 1919-21, August 25, 1920.

47. Nicoll, Early Diary 1919-21, August 25, 1920.

48. Nicoll, Early Diary 1919-21, August 30, 1920.

49. Nicoll, Early Diary 1919-21, September 15, 1920.

50. Nicoll, Early Diary 1919-21, September 18, 1920.

51. Nicoll, Early Diary 1919-21, September 18, 1920.

52. Nicoll, Early Diary 1919-21, September 18, 1920.

53. Nicoll, Early Diary 1919-21, September 18, 1920.

54. Nicoll, Early Diary 1919-21, September 18, 1920.

55. Nicoll, Early Diary 1919-21, September 18, 1920.

Chapter Six. Breaking Up Is Hard to Do

1. Paul Bishop, *The Dionysian Self: C. G. Jung's Reception of Friedrich Nietzsche*, 244.

2. Gerhard Wehr, *Jung: A Biography*, 218.

3. Arthur John Hubbard's *The Authentic Dreams of Peter Blobbs* can be found online at anotherurl.com.

4. Hubbard, *The Authentic Dreams of Peter Blobbs*.

5. Hubbard, *The Authentic Dreams of Peter Blobbs*.

6. Maggy Anthony, *The Valkyries*, 45.

7. Nicoll, Early Diary 1919-21, September 20, 1920.

8. Nicoll, Early Diary 1919-21, September 20, 1920.

9. Nicoll, Early Diary 1919-21, September 20, 1920.

10. Nicoll, Early Diary 1919-21, September 20, 1920.

11. Nicoll, Early Diary 1919-21, September 20, 1920.

12. Nicoll, Early Diary 1919-21, September 20, 1920.

13. Nicoll, Early Diary 1919-21, September 30, 1920.

14. Nicoll, Early Diary 1919-21, September 30, 1920.

15. Nicoll, Early Diary 1919-21, September 30, 1920.

16. Nicoll, Early Diary 1919-21, September 30, 1920.

17. Nicoll, Early Diary 1919-21, September 20, 1920.

18. Nicoll, Early Diary 1919-21, September 20, 1920.

19. Nicoll, Early Diary 1919-21, October 7, 1920.

20. Nicoll, Early Diary 1919-21, October 7, 1920.

21. Nicoll, Early Diary 1919-21, October 2, 1920.

22. Nicoll, Early Diary 1919-21, October 2, 1920.

23. Nicoll, Early Diary 1919-21, October 7, 1920.

24. Nicoll, Early Diary 1919-21, October 7, 1920.

25. Nicoll, Early Diary 1919-21, September 30, 1920.

26. Nicoll, Early Diary 1919-21, October 8, 1920.

27. Nicoll, Early Diary 1919-21, October 8, 1920.

28. Nicoll, Early Diary 1919-21, October 11, 1920.

29. Nicoll, Early Diary 1919-21, October 11, 1920.

30. Nicoll, Early Diary 1919-21, October 11, 1920.

31. Nicoll, Early Diary 1919-21, October 11, 1920.

32. Nicoll, Early Diary 1919-21, October 7, 1920.

33. Nicoll, Early Diary 1919-21, October 17, 1920.

34. Nicoll, Early Diary 1919-21, October 17, 1920.

35. Nicoll, Early Diary 1919-21, October 17, 1920.

36. Nicoll, Early Diary 1919-21, October 17, 1920.

37. Nicoll, Early Diary 1919-21, October 17, 1920.

38. Nicoll, Early Diary 1919-21, May 4, 1921.

39. Nicoll, Early Diary 1919-21, October 17, 1920.

40. Nicoll, Early Diary 1919-21, October 19, 1920.

41. Nicoll, Early Diary 1919-21, October 24, 1920.

42. Nicoll, Early Diary 1919-21, December 11, 1920.

43. Nicoll, Early Diary 1919-21, April 24, 1921.

44. Nicoll, Early Diary 1919-21, April 22, 1921.

45. Nicoll, Early Diary 1919-21, November 23, 1920.

46. Nicoll, Early Diary 1919-21, November 14, 1920.

47. Nicoll, Early Diary 1919-21, November 26, 1920.

48. Nicoll, Early Diary 1919-21, April 2, 1921.

49. Nicoll, Early Diary 1919-21, April 9, 1920.

50. Nicoll, Early Diary 1919-21, April 9, 1920.

51. Nicoll, Early Diary 1919-21, May 4, 1921.

52. Nicoll, Early Diary 1919-21, May 12, 1921.

53. Nicoll, Early Diary 1919-21, June 9, 1921.

54. Nicoll, Early Diary 1919-21, June 9, 1921.

55. Nicoll, Early Diary 1919-21, June 9, 1921.

56. Nicoll, Early Diary 1919-21, June 9, 1921.

57. Nicoll, Early Diary 1919-21, June 9, 1921.

58. Nicoll, Early Diary 1919-21, June 9, 1921.

59. Nicoll, Early Diary 1919-21, October 29, 1921.

60. Nicoll, Early Diary 1919-21, July 3, 1921.

61. Nicoll, Early Diary 1919-21, June 12, 1921.

62. Nicoll, Early Diary 1919-21, July 4, 1921.

63. Nicoll, Early Diary 1919-21, August 6, 1921.

64. Nicoll, Early Diary 1919-21, June 30, 1921.

65. Nicoll, Early Diary 1919-21, August 6, 1921.

66. Nicoll, Early Diary 1919-21, August 6, 1921.

67. Nicoll, Early Diary 1919-21, September 14, 1921.

68. Nicoll, Early Diary 1919-21, September 14, 1921.

69. Nicoll, Early Diary 1919-21, September 14, 1921.

70. Nicoll, Early Diary 1919-21, August 17, 1921.

71. Pogson, *Maurice Nicoll,* 70.

72. Nicoll, Early Diary 1919-21, September 15, 1921.

73. Colin Wilson and Donald Seaman, *Scandal!,* 8–9.

74. Nicoll, Early Diary 1919-21, September 15, 1921.

75. Nicoll, Early Diary 1919-21, September 18, 1921.

Chapter Seven. Finding the Miraculous

1. Claude Bragdon, introduction to P. D. Ouspensky, *Tertium Organum,* (Rochester, NY: Manas Press, 1920) p. vii.

2. Colin Wilson, *The Strange Life of P. D. Ouspensky,* 88.

3. David Garnett. *The Flowers of the Forest* (London: Chatto & Windus, 1955), 226.

4. Paul Selver. *Orage and the New Age Circle* (London: George Allen & Unwin, 1959), 72.

5. Algernon Blackwood, "Passport to the Next Dimension," *Prediction* (March 1948).

6. Claude Bragdon. *The Secret Springs* (London: Andrew Dakers, 1938), 320.

7. Nicoll, Early Diary 1919-21, September 24, 1921.

8. Nicoll, Early Diary 1919-21, September 25, 1921.

9. See Gary Lachman, *The Quest for Hermes Trismegistus.*

10. Ouspensky, *In Search of the Miraculous,* 302.

11. Nicoll, Early Diary 1919-21, September 27, 1921.

12. Nicoll, Early Diary 1919-21, October 2, 1921.

13. Nicoll, Early Diary 1919-21, October 9, 1921.

14. Nicoll, Early Diary 1919-21, October 9, 1921.

15. Nicoll, Early Diary 1919-21, October 9, 1921.

16. Wilson, *Origins of the Sexual Impulse,* 96.

17. Nicoll, Early Diary 1919-21, October 9, 1921.

18. Pogson, *Maurice Nicoll,* 70.

19. James Webb, *The Harmonious Circle,* 219.

20. Pogson, *Maurice Nicoll,* 71.

21. Nicoll, Early Diary 1919-21, November 13, 1921.

22. Nicoll, Early Diary 1919-21, November 10, 1921.

23. Nicoll, Early Diary 1919-21, November 18, 1921.

24. Webb, *The Harmonious Circle,* 219.

25. Nicoll, Early Diary 1919-21, November 28, 1921.

26. Nicoll, Early Diary 1919-21, January 1, 1922.

27. Walker, *Venture with Ideas,* 24–26.

28. Nicoll, Early Diary 1919-21, January 1, 1922.

29. G. I. Gurdjieff, *Life Is Real Only Then, When "I Am,"* 25.

30. Walker, *A Study of Gurdjieff's Teaching,* 13.

31. Wilson, *The Strange Life of P. D. Ouspensky,* 94.

32. Peter Washington, *Madame Blavatsky's Baboon,* 173–74.

Chapter Eight. *Sonnez Fort!*

1. Ouspensky, *In Search of the Miraculous,* 44.

2. Ouspensky, *In Search of the Miraculous,* 47.

3. Ouspensky, *In Search of the Miraculous,* 49.

4. Thomas de Hartmann, *Our Life with Mr. Gurdjieff,* 103.

5. De Hartmann, *Our Life with Mr. Gurdjieff,* 103.

6. Webb, *The Harmonious Circle,* 233.

7. C. S. Nott, *Teachings of Gurdjieff,* 28.

8. Nott, *Teachings of Gurdjieff,* 28.

9. Mairet, *A. R. Orage,* 92.

10. Webb, *The Harmonious Circle,* 260.

11. Nott, *Teachings of Gurdjieff,* 28.

12. Mairet, *A. R. Orage,* 92.

13. J. G. Bennett, *Witness,* 105.

14. Bennett, *Witness,* 114–17.

15. James Moore, *Gurdjieff and Mansfield,* 137.

16. Ouspensky, *In Search of the Miraculous,* 385.

17. Ouspensky, *In Search of the Miraculous,* 386.

18. Bennett, *Witness,* 110.

19. Washington, *Madame Blavatsky's Baboon,* 241, 201, 239.

20. Pogson, Naurice Nicoll, 75.

21. Bennett, *Witness,* 107–8.

22. Bennett, *Witness,* 107–8.

23. Pogson, *Maurice Nicoll,* 81.

24. Peters, *My Journey with a Mystic,* 15.

25. Bennett, *Witness,* 109.

26. Pogson, *Maurice Nicoll,* 81.

27. Pogson, *Maurice Nicoll,* 89.

28. Bennett, *Witness,* 120.

29. Pogson, *Maurice Nicoll,* 89.

30. Pogson, *Maurice Nicoll,* 90.
31. Bennett, *Witness,* 111.
32. Webb, *The Harmonious Circle,* 244.
33. Bennett, *Witness,* 113.
34. Anthony Storr, *Feet of Clay: A Study of Gurus,* 26.
35. Pogson, *Maurice Nicoll,* 89. The lecture, given on August 21, 1923, can be found in *Views from the Real World: Early Talks of Gurdjieff,* 107–11.
36. James Young, "Experiment at Fontainebleau," *The New Adelphi* 1921.
37. Bennett, *Witness,* 106.
38. Nicoll, *Commentaries,* 1:13.
39. Webb, *The Harmonious Circle,* 235.
40. Pogson, *Maurice Nicoll,* 83.
41. Webb, *The Harmonious Circle,* 243.
42. Pogson, *Maurice Nicoll,* 92.
43. Pogson, *Maurice Nicoll,* 90.
44. Ouspensky, *Tertium Organum,* 128–29.
45. Nicoll, letter to Jung, April 9, 1923, ETH archive Zürich.
46. Pogson, *Maurice Nicoll,* 89.

Chapter Nine. "Go Away—and Teach the System!"

1. Walker, *Venture with Ideas,* 15.
2. Walker, *The Log of the Ark,* Constable & Co., 1923.
3. Walker, *Venture with Ideas,* 16.
4. Walker, *Venture with Ideas,* 16.
5. Walker, *Venture with Ideas,* 17.
6. Walker, *Venture with Ideas,* 30.
7. Walker, *Venture with Ideas,* 43.
8. J. H. Reyner, *Ouspensky: The Unsung Genius,* 86.
9. Walker, *Venture with Ideas,* 26.
10. Walker, *Venture with Ideas,* 20.
11. Washington, *Madame Blavatsky's Baboon,* 174.
12. Walker, *Venture with Ideas,* 22.
13. Walker, *Venture with Ideas,* 23.
14. Gurdjieff, *Life Is Real Only Then, When "I Am,"* 132.
15. T. S. Eliot, *The Family Reunion,* in *The Complete Poems and Plays of T. S. Eliot* (London: Faber & Faber, 2004).
16. Walker, *Venture with Ideas,* 27.
17. Walker, *Venture with Ideas,* 69.

18. Ouspensky, *In Search of the Miraculous,* 167. Jung, too, saw great value in secrets. Lachman, *Jung the Mystic,* 24.
19. Walker, *Venture with Ideas,* 64.
20. Walker, *Venture with Ideas,* 65.
21. Bennett, *Witness,* 119.
22. Ouspensky, *In Search of the Miraculous,* 170–76.
23. Walker, *Venture with Ideas,* 66.
24. Walker, *Venture with Ideas,* 67.
25. Walker, *Venture with Ideas,* 68.
26. Gurdjieff, *Life Is Real Only Then, When "I Am,"* 153.
27. Gurdjieff, *Life Is Real Only Then, When "I Am,"* 153.
28. Wilson, *The Strange Life of P. D. Ouspensky,* 9.
29. Ouspensky, *In Search of the Miraculous,* ix.
30. See Rodney Collin, *The Theory of Celestial Influence,* and J. G. Bennett, *The Masters of Wisdom.*
31. Pogson, *Maurice Nicoll,* 95.
32. Ouspensky, *A New Model of the Universe,* 131.
33. Ouspensky, *A New Model of the Universe,* 131.
34. Ouspensky, *A New Model of the Universe,* 12.
35. Ouspensky, *A New Model of the Universe,* 132.
36. Ouspensky, *A New Model of the Universe,* 133.
37. Walker, *Venture with Ideas,* 132.
38. Walker, *Venture with Ideas,* 132.
39. Bennett, *Witness,* 260.
40. Bennett, *Witness,* 159.
41. Bennett, *Witness,* 261.
42. Rom Landau, *God Is My Adventure,* 172.
43. Pogson, *Maurice Nicoll,* 97.
44. Gary Lachman, *In Search of P. D. Ouspensky,* 204–10.
45. J. H. Reyner, *Diary of a Modern Alchemist,* 11.
46. Reyner, *Diary of a Modern Alchemist,* 86. Similar inaccuracies pepper his *Ouspensky: The Unsung Genius.*
47. Pogson, *Maurice Nicoll,* 105.
48. Pogson, *Maurice Nicoll,* 105–6.

Chapter Ten. Working at Home

1. Washington, *Madame Blavatsky's Baboon,* 254.
2. Bennett, *Witness,* 154.

3. J. B. Priestley, *"Time and the Conways" and Other Plays*, 86.

4. Copley, *Portrait of a Vertical Man*, 24.

5. Copley, *Portrait of a Vertical Man*, 25.

6. Pogson, *Maurice Nicoll*, 108.

7. Copley, *Portrait of a Vertical Man*, 25.

8. Copley, *Portrait of a Vertical Man*, 27.

9. Pogson, *Maurice Nicoll*, 111.

10. Copley, *Portrait of a Vertical Man*, 27.

11. Copley, *Portrait of a Vertical Man*, 27.

12. Copley, *Portrait of a Vertical Man*, 27.

13. Copley, *Portrait of a Vertical Man*, 39.

14. Pogson, *Maurice Nicoll*, 110.

15. Julius Evola, *The Doctrine of Awakening* (Rochester, VT: Inner Traditions, 1996), 184.

16. "Dr. Nicoll's First Instructions to His Group," in Beryl Pogson, *The Work Life* (Utrecht: Eureka Editions, 2020).

17. Pogson, *Maurice Nicoll*, 94.

18. Lachman, *The Quest for Hermes Trismegistus*.

19. See Colin Wilson, *New Pathways in Psychology*, 201, and especially his novel *The Black Room* (New York: Pyramid Books, 1975).

20. Copley, *Portrait of a Vertical Man*, 23.

21. Copley, *Portrait of a Vertical Man*, 20–21.

22. Bennett, *Witness*, 119.

23. Copley, *Portrait of a Vertical Man*, 21.

24. Copley, *Portrait of a Vertical Man*, 23.

25. Copley, *Portrait of a Vertical Man*, 23.

26. studysociety.org.

27. Copley, *Portrait of a Vertical Man*, 30.

28. Copley, *Portrait of a Vertical Man*, 30.

29. Webb, *The Harmonious Circle*, 411.

30. Walker, *Witness*, 106.

31. Merrily Taylor, *Remembering P. D. Ouspensky*, 37.

32. Robert S. de Ropp, *Warrior's Way*, 101.

33. Copley, *Portrait of a Vertical Man*, 40.

34. Copley, *Portrait of a Vertical Man*, 40.

35. Pogson, *Maurice Nicoll*, 113.

36. Pogson, *Maurice Nicoll*, 114.

37. Pogson, *Maurice Nicoll*, 115.

38. Copley, *Portrait of a Vertical Man,* 31.

39. Pogson, *Maurice Nicoll,* 115.

40. Pogson, *Maurice Nicoll,* 116.

41. Copley, *Portrait of a Vertical Man,* 6.

42. Copley, *Portrait of a Vertical Man,* 32.

Chapter Eleven. "You Are Not Building for Posterity!"

1. Pogson, *Maurice Nicoll,* 120.

2. Pogson, *Maurice Nicoll,* 120.

3. Copley, *Portrait of a Vertical Man,* 37.

4. Copley, *Portrait of a Vertical Man,* 36.

5. Pogson, *Maurice Nicoll,* 121.

6. Copley, *Portrait of a Vertical Man,* 40.

7. Pogson, *Maurice Nicoll,* 122.

8. Pogson, *Maurice Nicoll,* 122.

9. Nicoll, *Psychological Commentaries,* 1:12–13.

10. Pogson, *Maurice Nicoll,* 124.

11. Copley, *Portrait of a Vertical Man,* 37.

12. Copley, *Portrait of a Vertical Man,* 45.

13. Copley, *Portrait of a Vertical Man,* 38.

14. Copley, *Portrait of a Vertical Man,* 38.

15. Copley, *Portrait of a Vertical Man,* 40, 43.

16. Copley, *Portrait of a Vertical Man,* 39.

17. Copley, *Portrait of a Vertical Man,* 48.

18. Copley, *Portrait of a Vertical Man,* 41.

19. Copley, *Portrait of a Vertical Man,* 41.

20. Copley, *Portrait of a Vertical Man,* 42.

21. Pogson, *Maurice Nicoll,* 125.

22. Copley, *Portrait of a Vertical Man,* 48.

23. Copley, *Portrait of a Vertical Man,* 43.

24. Pogson, *Maurice Nicoll,* 124.

25. Copley, *Portrait of a Vertical Man,* 46.

26. Copley, *Portrait of a Vertical Man,* 45.

27. Pogson, *Maurice Nicoll,* 125.

28. C. S. Nott, *Further Teachings of Gurdjieff,* 95.

29. C. S. Nott, *Further Teachings of Gurdjieff,* 96.

30. C. S. Nott, *Further Teachings of Gurdjieff,* 106.

31. C. S. Nott, *Further Teachings of Gurdjieff,* 110.

32. C. S. Nott, *Further Teachings of Gurdjieff,* 110.

33. Pogson, *Maurice Nicoll,* 125.

34. Copley, *Portrait of a Vertical Man,* 44.

35. Copley, *Portrait of a Vertical Man,* 62.

36. Pogson, *Maurice Nicoll,* 126.

37. Pogson, *Maurice Nicoll,* 127.

38. See Gary Lachman, *Dreaming Ahead of Time: Experiences with Precognitive Dreams, Synchronicities, and Coincidence.*

39. Pogson, *Maurice Nicoll,* 132.

40. Pogson, *Maurice Nicoll,* 132.

41. Copley, *Portrait of a Vertical Man,* 47.

42. Marie Seaton, "The Case of P. D. Ouspensky," *Quest,* no.34 (1962), Bombay, India.

43. Ouspensky, *In Search of the Miraculous,* 99.

44. Pogson, *Maurice Nicoll,* 134.

Chapter Twelve. The Home Front

1. Pogson, *Maurice Nicoll,* 138.

2. Pogson, *Maurice Nicoll,* 139.

3. Pogson, *Maurice Nicoll,* 143.

4. See "Gurdjieff and the Rope" on the Gurdjieff Legacy Foundation website; and Maggy Anthony, *The Valkyries: The Women around Jung.*

5. Pogson, *Maurice Nicoll,* 144.

6. Copley, *Portrait of a Vertical Man,* 50.

7. Pogson, *Maurice Nicoll,* 140.

8. See Dion Fortune, *The Magical Battle of Britain* (Cheltenham, UK: Skylight Press, 2012).

9. Bennett, *Witness,* 246–47.

10. Ouspensky, *In Search of the Miraculous,* 31–33.

11. Copley, *Portrait of a Vertical Man,* 52.

12. Gary Lachman, *Swedenborg: An Introduction to His Life and Ideas,* 85–86.

13. Pogson, *Maurice Nicoll,* 140.

14. Pogson, *Maurice Nicoll,* 186.

15. Pogson, *Maurice Nicoll,* 156.

16. Pogson, *Maurice Nicoll,* 145.

17. Pogson, *Maurice Nicoll,* 153.

18. Pogson, *Maurice Nicoll,* 144.

19. Pogson, *Maurice Nicoll,* 146.

20. Pogson, *Maurice Nicoll,* 154.

21. Pogson, *Maurice Nicoll,* 185.

22. Pogson, *Maurice Nicoll,* 153.

23. Pogson, *Maurice Nicoll,* 192.

24. Pogson, *Maurice Nicoll,* 140.

25. Pogson, *Maurice Nicoll,* 174. See C. G. Jung, *Essays on Contemporary Events: The Psychology of Nazism.*

26. Pogson, *Maurice Nicoll,* 150.

27. Pogson, *Maurice Nicoll,* 151.

28. Pogson, *Maurice Nicoll,* 155.

29. Pogson, *Maurice Nicoll,* 169.

30. Pogson, *Maurice Nicoll,* 155.

31. Pogson, *Maurice Nicoll,* 156. It's not clear which books Nicoll has in mind, but one of the leading scientists of the day, J. B. S. Haldane, was an avowed Marxist and was at one point accused of spying for the Soviets. "Geneticist, Gentleman, Spy," claremontreviewofbooks.com.

32. Pogson, *Maurice Nicoll,* 156.

33. Pogson, *Maurice Nicoll,* 156.

34. Pogson, *Maurice Nicoll,* 157.

35. Pogson, *Maurice Nicoll,* 156.

36. Pogson, *Maurice Nicoll,* 163.

37. Pogson, *Maurice Nicoll,* 164.

38. Pogson, *Maurice Nicoll,* 164.

39. Pogson, *Maurice Nicoll,* 160.

40. Pogson, *Maurice Nicoll,* 180.

41. Pogson, *Maurice Nicoll,* 175.

42. P. D. Ouspensky, *A Record of Meetings,* 428.

43. Pogson, *Maurice Nicoll,* 166.

44. Pogson, *Maurice Nicoll,* 161.

45. Pogson, *Maurice Nicoll,* 187.

46. Pogson, *Maurice Nicoll,* 190.

47. C. G. Jung and Wolfgang Pauli, *The Interpretation of Nature and the Psyche,* 31. Jung also mentions the story of Flammarion and the wind, and the classic account of Monsieur Fortgibu and the plum pudding (20–21).

48. Pogson, *Maurice Nicoll,* 161.

49. Arthur Koestler, with Alister Hardy and Robert Harvie, *The Challenge of Chance,* 161.

50. Pogson, *Maurice Nicoll,* 209.

51. Pogson, *Maurice Nicoll*, 209. The book was *Footprints on the Ceiling* (New York: G. P. Putnam's Sons, 1939) by Clayton Rawson.

52. Pogson, *Maurice Nicoll*, 210.

53. See Arthur Koestler, *The Case of the Midwife Toad.*

54. Pogson, *Maurice Nicoll*, 194.

55. Pogson, *Maurice Nicoll*, 195.

56. Nicoll, *Psychological Commentaries* 1:16.

57. Nicoll, *Psychological Commentaries* 1:15.

58. Nicoll, *Psychological Commentaries* 1:16.

59. Nicoll, *Psychological Commentaries* 1:15.

60. G. I. Gurdjieff. *Beelzebub's Tales to His Grandson,* First Book, "Friendly Advice," n.p.

61. C. S. Nott, *Teachings of Gurdjieff,* 125–215.

62. Nicoll, *Psychological Commentaries* 1:11.

63. Nicoll, *Psychological Commentaries* 1:11.

64. Nicoll, *Psychological Commentaries* 1:1.

65. Nicoll, *Psychological Commentaries* 1:1.

66. Nicoll, *Psychological Commentaries* 1:1.

67. Nicoll, *Psychological Commentaries* 1:1.

68. "Forget Domani," by Riz Ortolani and Norman Newell.

69. Nicoll, *Psychological Commentaries* 1:2.

70. Nicoll, *Psychological Commentaries* 1:9.

71. Nicoll, *Psychological Commentaries* 1:9.

72. Nicoll, *Psychological Commentaries* 1:9.

73. See Anthony Storr, ed., *The Essential Jung,* 94–96.

74. T. S. Eliot, "The Love Song of J. Alfred Prufrock."

75. Nicoll, *Psychological Commentaries* 1:5.

76. Nicoll, *Psychological Commentaries* 1:5.

77. Nicoll, *Psychological Commentaries* 1:5.

78. Nicoll, *Psychological Commentaries* 1:4.

79. Nicoll, *Psychological Commentaries* 1:9.

80. Nicoll, *Psychological Commentaries* 1:9.

81. Nicoll, *Psychological Commentaries* 1:10.

82. Nicoll, *Psychological Commentaries* 1:9.

Chapter Thirteen. Working against Time

1. Nicoll, *Psychological Commentaries,*1:5

2. Ouspensky, *In Search of the Miraculous,* 306–7.

3. Nicoll, *Psychological Commentaries* 5:1744.

4. Pogson, *Maurice Nicoll,* 220.

5. Nicoll, Later Diary, 1941-48, March 13, 1945.

6. Nicoll, Later Diary, 1941-48, November 6, 1946.

7. Nicoll, Later Diary, 1941-48, November 14, 1947.

8. Ouspensky, *In Search of the Miraculous,* 154–55.

9. "What is Masturbation Addiction?" verywellmind.com.

10. Nicoll, Later Diary, 1941-48, November 6, 1946.

11. Nicoll, Later Diary, 1941-48, June 14, 1946.

12. "If you already know it is bad and do it, you commit a sin difficult to redress." Gurdjieff, *Life Is Real Only Then, When "I Am,"* 273.

13. Gurdjieff, *Beelzebub's Tales to His Grandson,* 1:275–77.

14. Gurdjieff, *Beelzebub's Tales to His Grandson,* 1:275–77.

15. Ouspensky, *In Search of the Miraculous,* 94.

16. Gurdjieff, *Life Is Real Only Then, When "I Am,"* 276.

17. Ouspensky, *In Search of the Miraculous,* 94.

18. Nicoll, Later Diary, 1941-48, October 2, 1946, and October 14, 1946.

19. Pogson, *Maurice Nicoll,* 179.

20. Nicoll, Later Diary, 1941-48, July 9, 1946.

21. Nicoll, Later Diary, 1941-48, March 22, 1947.

22. Pogson, *Maurice Nicoll,* 246.

23. Copley, *Portrait of a Vertical Man,* 54.

24. Copley, *Portrait of a Vertical Man,* 54.

25. Nicoll, *Psychological Commentaries,*1:153.

26. Pogson, *Maurice Nicoll,* 199.

27. Nicoll, Later Diary, 1941-48, January 15, 1948.

28. Nicoll, Later Diary, 1941-48, September 15, 1948.

29. Nicoll, Later Diary, 1941-48, April 7, 1947.

30. "Anger and Cancer: Is There a Relationship?" psychologytoday.com.

31. Nicoll, *Psychological Commentaries,* 1:95.

32. Nicoll, *Psychological Commentaries,* 1:95.

33. Nicoll, *Psychological Commentaries,* 1:97.

34. Nicoll, Later Diary, 1941-48, December 18, 1942; Nicoll, *Psychological Commentaries,* 1:237; Nicoll, Later Diary, 1941-48, May 13.

35. Copley, *Portrait of a Vertical Man,* 63.

36. Quoted in Wilson, *The War Against Sleep,* 56-57.

37. See Colin Wilson, *Frankenstein's Castle* (Sevenoaks, UK: Ashgrove Press, 1980), and *Access to Inner Worlds* (Berkeley, CA: Celestial Arts, 1990); and

Iain McGilchrist. *The Master and His Emissary* (London: Yale University Press, 2009).

38. Nicoll, *Psychological Commentaries,* 3:1067.

39. Nicoll, Later Diary, 1941-48, May 27.

40. Emanuel Swedenborg, *Heaven and Hell* (New York: Swedenborg Foundation, 1984), 80.

41. Stan Gooch, *The Paranormal* (London: Fontana, 1979), 242.

42. Copley, *Portrait of a Vertical Man,* 54.

43. Pogson, *Maurice Nicoll,* 226.

44. Copley, *Portrait of a Vertical Man,* 54.

45. Copley, *Portrait of a Vertical Man,* 56.

46. Pogson, *Maurice Nicoll,* 233.

47. Pogson, *Maurice Nicoll,* 232.

48. Pogson, *Maurice Nicoll,* 230.

49. Nicoll, Later Diary, 1941-48, March 7, 1946.

50. Pogson, *Maurice Nicoll,* 232.

51. Pogson, *Maurice Nicoll,* 231.

52. Copley, *Portrait of a Vertical Man,* 58.

Chapter Fourteen. The End of an Octave

1. Nicoll, Later Diary, 1941-48, December 8, 1944.

2. Nicoll, Later Diary, 1941-48, December 10, 1944.

3. Nicoll, Later Diary, 1941-48, August 21, 1945.

4. Nicoll, Later Diary, 1941-48, January 30, 1945.

5. Nicoll, Later Diary, 1941-48, November 28, 1946.

6. Nicoll, *Psychological Commentaries,* 4:1475–80.

7. Anthony Stevens, *Archetypes: A Natural History of the Self,* 168.

8. Nicoll, *Psychological Commentaries,* 1:10.

9. Nicoll, Later Diary, 1941-48, March 7, 1945.

10. Nicoll, Later Diary, 1941-48, March 8, 1945.

11. Nicoll, Later Diary, 1941-48, March 8, 1945.

12. Nicoll, Later Diary, 1941-48, March 9, 1945.

13. Nicoll, Later Diary, 1941-48, March 12, 1945.

14. Nicoll, Later Diary, 1941-48, March 26, 1945.

15. Nicoll, Later Diary, 1941-48, April 10, 1945.

16. Nicoll, Later Diary, 1941-48, April 26, 1945.

17. Nicoll, Later Diary, 1941-48, September 12, 1945; November 22, 1945.

18. Nicoll, Later Diary, 1941-48, November 14, 1945.

19. Nicoll, Later Diary, 1941-48, November 14, 1945.

20. Pogson, *Maurice Nicoll*, 253.

21. Pogson, *Maurice Nicoll*, 238.

22. Nicoll, Later Diary, 1941-48, August 19, 1946.

23. Wilson, *The Strange Life of P. D. Ouspensky*, 110.

24. Nicoll, Later Diary, 1941-48, December 30, 1945.

25. Copley, *Portrait of a Vertical Man*, 58.

26. Copley, *Portrait of a Vertical Man*, 58.

27. Copley, *Portrait of a Vertical Man*, 59.

28. Copley, *Portrait of a Vertical Man*, 59.

29. Pogson, *Maurice Nicoll*, 245.

30. Nicoll, *Psychological Commentaries*, 1:11.

31. William Seabrook, *Witchcraft: Its Power in the World Today*, 166.

32. Copley, *Portrait of a Vertical Man*, 72; Nicoll Later Diaries October 4 1946, 426.

33. Pogson, *Maurice Nicoll*, 244.

34. Pogson, *Maurice Nicoll*, 244.

35. See Colin Wilson, *The Devil's Party*.

36. Walker, *Venture with Ideas*, 128.

37. Walker, *Venture with Ideas*, 129.

38. Ouspensky, *A Record of Meetings*, 585–643. The reader can find a transcript of Ouspensky's last talks here, from which I have taken the essence.

39. Nicoll, Later Diary, 1941-48, December 13, 1946.

40. Nicoll, Later Diary, 1941-48, May 29, 1947.

41. Nicoll, Later Diary, 1941-48, September 17, 1947; September 18, 1947,532; November 14, 1947.

42. Walker, *Venture with Ideas*, 129.

43. Walker, *Venture with Ideas*, 130.

44. Walker, *Venture with Ideas*, 131.

45. Rodney Collin, *The Theory of Conscious Harmony*, viii.

46. See Joyce Collin-Smith's letter regarding my article on James Webb in *Fortean Times*, no. 152 (September 2001).

47. See Webb, *The Harmonious Circle*, 439–60 for a full account of Ouspensky's last days.

48. "J. G. Bennett Bio," jgbennett.org.

49. Webb, *The Harmonious Circle*, 494–95.

50. Bennett, *Witness*, 219.

51. Pogson, *Maurice Nicoll*, 248.

52. Nicoll, Later Diary, 1941-48, January 13, 1947.
53. Nicoll, Later Diary, 1941-48, October 2, 1946.
54. Copley, *Portrait of a Vertical Man,* 65.
55. P. D. Ouspensky, *Letters from Russia 1919,* 3.
56. Bennett, *Witness,* 252.
57. Copley, *Portrait of a Vertical Man,* 65.
58. Nicoll, Later Diary, 1941-48, January 15, 1948.
59. Nicoll, Later Diary, 1941-48, September 17, 1947.
60. Nicoll, Later Diary, 1941-48, October 16, 1947.
61. Nicoll, Later Diary, 1941-48, October 19, 1947.
62. Nicoll, Later Diary, 1941-48, January 4, 1947.
63. Nicoll, Later Diary, 1941-48, November 14, 1947.
64. Nicoll, Later Diary, 1941-48, March 22, 1947.
65. Nicoll, Later Diary, 1941-48, April 12, 1947.
66. Nicoll, Later Diary, 1941-48, April 16, 1947.
67. Nicoll, Later Diary, 1941-48, November 1, 1947.
68. Walker, *Venture with Ideas,* 142.
69. Walker, *Venture with Ideas,* 145.
70. Walker, *Venture with Ideas,* 146.
71. Walker, *Venture with Ideas,* 148–49.
72. Walker, *Venture with Ideas,* 150.
73. Walker, *Venture with Ideas,* 164.
74. Kenneth Walker, "Report on G, 21 April 1949," 1.
75. Walker, "Report on G, 21 April 1949," 4.
76. Webb, *The Harmonious Circle,* 466.
77. Walker, *Venture with Ideas,* 173.
78. Walker, "Report on G, 21 April 1949," 1.
79. Walker, "Report on G, 21 April 1949," 1.
80. James Moore, *Gurdjieff: The Anatomy of a Myth,* 293.
81. Walker, "Report on G, 21 April 1949," 1.

Chapter Fifteen. Last Days

1. Nicoll, Later Diary 1941-48, January 8, 1946.
2. Lachman, *Swedenborg,* 122–23.
3. Nicoll, Later Diary 1941-48, January 9, 1946.
4. Nicoll, Later Diary 1941-48, April 4, 1946.
5. Nicoll, Later Diary 1941-48, April 6, 1946.
6. Nicoll, Later Diary 1941-48, February 12, 1947.

7. Nicoll, Later Diary 1941-48, July 18, 1947.

8. Nicoll, Later Diary 1941-48, January 19, 1948.

9. Nicoll, Later Diary 1941-48, July 30, 1948; Lachman, *Swedenborg,* 85–86.

10. Nicoll, Later Diary 1941-48, June 15, 1946.

11. Nicoll, Later Diary 1941-48, August 17, 1948.

12. Nicoll Later Diary 1941-48, June 30, 1947.

13. Nicoll, Later Diary 1941-48, April 8, 1948.

14. Nicoll, Later Diary 1941-48, April 8, 1948. Jung's notion of individuation is also opposite to the kind of immersion in the divine that Ramakrishna experienced.

15. Pogson, *Maurice Nicoll,* 256.

16. Pogson, *Maurice Nicoll,* 260.

17. Pogson, *Maurice Nicoll,* 257.

18. Pogson, *Maurice Nicoll,* 258.

19. Pogson, *Maurice Nicoll,* 258.

20. Pogson, *Maurice Nicoll,* 261.

21. Pogson, *Maurice Nicoll,* 261.

22. Pogson, *Maurice Nicoll,* 262.

23. Pogson, *Maurice Nicoll,* 262.

24. Rom Landau, *God Is My Adventure,* 181–203.

25. "Diogenes in Time and Tide," archives.yale.edu.

26. "Diogenes in Time and Tide," archives.yale.edu.

27. Quoted in Pogson, *Maurice Nicoll,* 256.

28. Pogson, *Maurice Nicoll,* 263.

29. Letter from Jung to Nicoll, April 29, 1950.

30. Letter from Jung to Nicoll, April 29, 1950.

31. See Vincent Brome, *Jung: Man and Myth.*

32. Letter from Emma Jung to Nicoll, July 30, 1950.

33. Maurice Nicoll, *The New Man,* 1.

34. Nicoll, *The New Man,* 1.

35. Nicoll, *The New Man,* 2.

36. Nicoll, *The New Man,* 2.

37. Nicoll, *The New Man,* 4.

38. Nicoll, *The New Man,* 2.

39. Nicoll, *The New Man,* 2.

40. Nicoll, *The New Man,* 3.

41. Nicoll, *The New Man,* 52–54. It may do so because it recalls Blake's lines

opening his "Europe: A Prophecy": "Five windows light the caverned mind," the windows, as with the porches, being the senses.

42. Nicoll, *The New Man,* 79–80.

43. Nicoll, *The New Man,* 158.

44. Nicoll, *The New Man,* 8.

45. Nicoll, *The New Man,* 158.

46. Nicoll, *The New Man,* 34.

47. Pogson, *Maurice Nicoll,* 274.

48. Diana Pettavel, *A Few Recollections of Dr. Nicoll and of Amwell 1949–1953,* 4.

49. Pettavel, *A Few Recollections,* 8.

50. Pettavel, *A Few Recollections,* 19.

51. Pettavel, *A Few Recollections,* 5.

52. Pettavel, *A Few Recollections,* 15.

53. Pettavel, *A Few Recollections,* 19.

54. Pettavel, *A Few Recollections,* 6.

55. Pettavel, *A Few Recollections,* 21.

56. Pettavel, *A Few Recollections,* 19.

57. Rodney Collin, *The Theory of Eternal Life,* 116.

58. Pettavel, *A Few Recollections,* 22.

59. Pogson, *Maurice Nicoll,* 269.

60. Maurice Nicoll, *Living Time,* 1.

61. Nicoll, *Living Time,* 121–22.

62. Quoted in Pogson, *Maurice Nicoll,* 266.

63. Maurice Nicoll, *The Mark,* 195–96.

64. Pogson, *Maurice Nicoll,* 273.

65. Pogson, *Maurice Nicoll,* 274.

66. Pettavel, *A Few Recollections,* 20.

67. Pogson, *Maurice Nicoll,* 277.

68. Nicoll, *Psychological Commentaries,* 5:1737.

69. Nicoll, *Psychological Commentaries,* 1:1739.

70. Pogson, *Maurice Nicoll,* 279.

71. Pogson, *Maurice Nicoll,* 280.

72. Nicoll, *Psychological Commentaries,* 5:1739.

Epilogue. Hitting the Mark

1. Pettavel, *A Few Recollections,* 22.

2. Pettavel, *A Few Recollections,* 23.

3. Pettavel, *A Few Recollections,* 23.

4. Bob Hunter, *P. D. Ouspensky: Pioneer of the Fourth Way,* 9–10.

5. Copley, *Portrait of a Vertical Man,* 77.

6. Barbara Wood, *E. F. Schumacher: His Life and Thought,* 233.

7. Wood, *E. F. Schumacher,* 231.

8. E. F. Schumacher, *A Guide for the Perplexed,* 4, 32, 48, 95–98.

9. Pogson, *Maurice Nicoll,* 252.

10. Vincent Brome, *J. B. Priestley,* 348.

11. J. B. Priestley, *Man and Time,* 279.

12. J. B. Priestley, *The Magicians,* 42. This is the Balkan Perperek, who speaks atrocious English, is fat, and is also a remarkable cook. His tall and reticent companion strikes me as a kind of Ouspensky.

13. Priestley, *Man and Time,* 279–80.

14. Priestley, *Man and Time,* 281–82.

15. J. B. Priestley, *Over the Long High Wall,* 113–15.

16. Jacob Needleman, *Time and the Soul,* 156–57.

17. "John Clesse's Six Favorite Books," theweek.com.

18. "A Divine Pat," harpers.org.

19. "The neurologist and psychologist Maurice Nicoll," quotefancy.com.

Selected Bibliography

WORKS BY MAURICE NICOLL

Dream Psychology. London: Hodder and Stoughton, 1917.

Early Diary 1919-21, transcribed by Dr. John Willmett, Edinburgh University Archives, 2018-20.

Later Diary 1941-48, transcribed by Dr. John Willmett, Edinburgh University Archives, 2018-20.

The New Man. New York: Penguin Books, 1976.

Living Time. London: Watkins, 1981.

Psychological Commentaries on the Teaching of Gurdjieff and Ouspensky. Vols. 1–5 London: Watkins, 1980.

The Mark. London: Watkins, 1981.

WORKS BY MARTIN SWAYNE

Lord Richard in the Pantry. London: Methuen and Co., 1911.

The Sporting Instinct. London: Hodder and Stoughton, 1912.

Cupid Goes North. London: Hodder and Stoughton, 1913.

In Mesopotamia, London: Hodder and Stoughton, 1917.

The Blue Germ. London: Hodder and Stoughton, 1918.

WORKS BY P. D. OUSPENSKY

Tertium Organum. New York: Alfred A. Knopf, 1981.

A New Model of the Universe. New York: Alfred A. Knopf, 1969.

In Search of the Miraculous. New York: Harcourt, Brace and Company, 1949.

The Psychology of Man's Possible Evolution. New York: Alfred A. Knopf, 1954.

Strange Life of Ivan Osokin. New York: Hermitage House, 1955.

The Fourth Way. New York: Alfred A. Knopf, 1957.

Letters from Russia 1919. London: Penguin Books, 1991.

A Record of Meetings. London: Arkana, 1992.

WORKS BY G. I. GURDJIEFF

Beelzebub's Tales to His Grandson. New York: E. P. Dutton, 1978.

Meetings with Remarkable Men. London: Penguin Modern Classics, 2015.

Life Is Real Only Then, When "I Am." New York: E. P. Dutton Triangle Editions, 1975.

Views from the Real World: Early Talks of Gurdjieff. New York: E. P. Dutton, 1975.

WORKS CITED

Adams, Jeffrey. *Arcana in Plain Sight: The Influence of Emanuel Swedenborg's 'New Christianity' on Maurice Nicoll's Esoteric Christianity,* Master of Arts thesis submitted to the Graduate Theological Union, 2020 (unpublished).

Adrian, Jack, ed. *Strange Tales from the "Strand" Magazine.* Oxford: Oxford Paperbacks, 1992.

Anthony, Maggy. *The Valkyries: The Women around Jung.* Shaftesbury, UK: Element Books, 1990.

Begg, Ean. "Jung's Lost Lieutenant: Jung's Friendship with Maurice Nicoll." *Journal of Analytical Psychology,* Harvest, 1977.

Bennett, J. G. *Gurdjieff: Making a New World.* New York: Harper and Row, 1973.

———. *The Masters of Wisdom.* New York: HarperCollins, 1980.

———. *Witness.* Tucson, AZ: Omen Press, 1974.

Berdyaev, Nicolai. *The Meaning of the Creative Act.* New York: Colliers, 1962.

Besant, Annie, and Charles Leadbeater. *Thought Forms.* London: Theosophical Publishing House, 1901.

Bishop, Paul. *The Dionysian Self: C. G. Jung's Reception of Nietzsche.* Berlin: De Gruyter, 1995.

Brome, Vincent. *J. B. Priestley.* London: Hamish Hamilton, 1988.

———. *Jung: Man and Myth.* London: Paladin Books, 1985.

Butkovsky-Hewitt, Anna. *With Gurdjieff and Ouspensky in St. Petersburg and Paris.* London: Routledge & Kegan Paul, 1978.

Collin, Rodney. *The Theory of Celestial Influence.* London: Watkins Books, 1980.

———. *The Theory of Conscious Harmony.* London: Watkins Books, 1958.

————. *The Theory of Eternal Life*. Boulder, CO: Shambhala Books, 1989.

Copley, Samuel. *Portrait of a Vertical Man*. London: Swayne Publications, 1989.

De Hartmann, Thomas. *Our Life with Mr. Gurdjieff*. Harmondsworth, UK: Penguin Books, 1972.

De Ropp, Robert S. *Warrior's Way*. London: George Allen and Unwin, 1980.

Frankl, Viktor. *Man's Search for Meaning*. New York: Touchstone Books, 1984.

Furlong, Monica. *Genuine Fake*. London: Unwin Paperback, 1987.

Gay, Peter. *Freud: A Life for Our Time*. London: Little Books, Ltd., 2006.

Higham, Charles. *The Adventures of Conan Doyle*. New York: W. W. Norton, 1976.

Hoeller, Stephan. *The Gnostic Jung and the Seven Sermons to the Dead*. Wheaton, IL: Quest Books, 1982.

Hunter, Bob. *P. D. Ouspensky: Pioneer of the Fourth Way*. Utrecht, Netherlands: Eureka Editions, 2000.

Jung, C. G. *Aion: Researches into the Phenomenology of the Self*. Princeton, NJ: Princeton University Press, 1959.

————. *Collected Papers on Analytical Psychology*. Translated by Constance Long. New York: Moffat, Yard and Co., 1916.

————. *Essays on Contemporary Events: The Psychology of Nazism*. Princeton, NJ: Princeton University Press, 1989.

————. *Letters, Volume I: 1906–1950*. Princeton, NJ: Princeton University Press, 1973.

————. *Memories, Dreams, Reflections*. London: Fontana Books, 1989.

————. *The Red Book*. New York: W. W. Norton & Co., 2009.

————. *Symbols of Transformation*. Princeton, NJ: Princeton University Press, 1976.

Jung, C. G., and Wolfgang Pauli. *The Interpretation of Nature and the Psyche*. New York: Pantheon Books, 1955.

Kerr, John. *A Dangerous Method*. London: Atlantic Books, 2012.

Koestler, Arthur. *The Case of the Midwife Toad*. New York: Random House, 1971.

————. *The Ghost in The Machine*. New York: Macmillan, 1968.

Koestler, Arthur, with Alister Hardy and Robert Harvey. *The Challenge of Chance*. London: Hutchinson, 1973.

Lachman, Gary. *Aleister Crowley: Magick, Rock and Roll, and the Wickedest Man in the World*. New York: Tarcher/Penguin, 2014.

————. *A Dark Muse*. New York: Thunder's Mouth Press, 2005.

———. *Dark Star Rising: Magick and Power in the Age of Trump*. New York: Tarcher Perigee, 2018.

———. *Dreaming Ahead of Time: Experiences with Precognitive Dreams, Synchronicities, and Coincidence*. Edinburgh: Floris Books, 2022.

———. *In Search of P. D. Ouspensky*. Wheaton, IL: Quest Books, 2006.

———. *Introducing Swedenborg: Correspondences*. London: Swedenborg Society, 2021.

———. *Jung the Mystic*. New York: Tarcher/Penguin, 2010.

———. *Madame Blavatsky: The Mother of Modern Spirituality*. New York: Tarcher/Penguin, 2012.

———. *The Quest for Hermes Trismegistus*. Edinburgh: Floris Books, 2011.

———. *The Return of Holy Russia*. Rochester, VT: Inner Traditions, 2020.

———. *Swedenborg: An Introduction to His Life and Ideas*. New York: Tarcher/Penguin, 2012.

Landau, Rom. *God Is My Adventure*. London: Faber and Faber, 1935.

Lawrence, T. E. *The Seven Pillars of Wisdom*. Harmondsworth, UK: Penguin Books, 1979.

Mairet, Philip. *A. R. Orage*. New York: University Books, 1966.

McGilchrist, Iain. *The Master and His Emissary*. London: Yale University Press, 2009.

McGuire, William, ed. *The Freud/Jung Letters*. London: Hogarth Press and Routledge & Kegan Paul, 1977.

Moore, James. *Gurdjieff and Mansfield*. London: Routledge & Kegan Paul, 1980.

———. *Gurdjieff: The Anatomy of a Myth*. Shaftesbury, UK: Element Books, 1991.

Muir, Edwin. *An Autobiography*. Edinburgh: Canongate, 1993.

Needleman, Jacob. *Time and the Soul*. New York: Doubleday Currency, 1998,

Neumann, Erich. *The Origins and History of Consciousness*. Princeton, NJ: Princeton University Press, 1973.

Nietzsche, Friedrich. *Beyond Good and Evil*. Translated by R. J. Hollingdale. Harmondsworth, UK: Penguin Books, 1977.

Noll, Richard. *The Jung Cult*. London: HarperCollins, 1996.

Nott, C. S. *Further Teachings of Gurdjieff*. Routledge & Kegan Paul, 1978.

———. *Teachings of Gurdjieff*. New York: Samuel Weiser, 1971.

Orage, A. R. *Consciousness: Animal, Human, Superman*. New York: Samuel Weiser, 1974.

————. *Readers and Writers 1917–1921*. Freeport, NY: Books for Libraries Press, 1969.

Peters, Fritz. *My Journey with a Mystic*. Laguna Niguel, CA: Tale Weaver Publishing, 1986.

Pogson, Beryl. *Maurice Nicoll: A Portrait*. New York: Fourth Way Books, 1987.

Priestley, J. B. *The Magicians*. Richmond, VA: Valancourt Books, 2014.

————. *Man and Time*. London: Aldus Books, 1964.

————. *Over the Long High Wall; Some Reflections and Speculations on Life, Death, and Time*. London: William Heineman, 1972.

————. *"Time and the Conways" and Other Plays*. London: Penguin Books, 1969.

Reyner, J. H. *Diary of a Modern Alchemist*. London: Neville Spearman, 1974.

————. *Ouspensky: The Unsung Genius*. London: George Allen and Unwin, 1981.

Schuchard, Marsha Keith. *Why Mrs. Blake Cried*. London: Century, 2006.

Schumacher, E. F. *A Guide for the Perplexed*. New York: Harper & Row, 1973.

Seabrook, William. *Witchcraft: Its Power in the World Today*. New York: Harcourt, Brace and Co. 1940.

Shaw, George Bernard. *Back to Methuselah*. London: Penguin Classics, 1987.

Shiel, M. P. *The Young Men Are Coming*. London: Allen & Unwin, 1937.

Stevens, Anthony. *Archetypes: A Natural History of the Self*. London: Routledge & Kegan Paul, 1990.

Storr, Anthony. *The Dynamics of Creation*. New York: Atheneum, 1972.

————, ed. *The Essential Jung*. London: Fontana Press, 1998.

————. *Feet of Clay: A Study of Gurus*. London: HarperCollins, 1996.

Taylor, Merrily, ed. *Remembering P. D. Ouspensky*. New Haven, CT: Yale University Library, 1978.

Walker, Kenneth. *A Study of Gurdjieff's Teaching*. London: Jonathan Cape, 1973.

————. "Report on G, 21 April 1949" archives.yale.edu "Maurice Nicoll papers."

————. *Venture with Ideas*. New York, Samuel Weiser, 1972.

Washington, Peter. *Madame Blavatsky's Baboon*. London: Secker and Warburg, 1993.

Webb, James. *The Harmonious Circle*. New York: Putman's, 1980.

Wehr, Gerhard. *Jung: A Biography*. Boston, MA: Shambhala Books, 1987.

Willmett, John, "Maurice Nicoll and the Kingdom of Heaven: a study of the psychological basis of 'esoteric Christianity' as described in Nicoll's writings," Doctoral Thesis, University of Edinburgh, https://era.ed.ac.uk>handle>Willmett 2018.

Wilson, Colin. *Access to Inner Worlds*. Berkeley, CA: Celestial Arts, 1990.

———. *A Criminal History of Mankind*. New York: G. P. Putnam's Sons, 1984.

———. *The Devil's Party*. London: Virgin Publications Ltd., 2000.

———. *Frankenstein's Castle*. Sevenoaks, Kent, UK: Ashgrove Press, 1980.

———. *The Misfits: A Study of Sexual Outsiders*. London: Grafton, 1988.

———. *New Pathways in Psychology*. New York: Taplinger Publishing Co., 1972.

———. *Order of Assassins*. St. Albans, UK: Granada, 1975.

———. *Origins of the Sexual Impulse*. New York: G. P. Putnam's Sons, 1963.

———. *The Strange Life of P. D. Ouspensky*. London: The Aquarian Press, 1993.

———. *The War Against Sleep* Wellingborough, UK: The Aquarian Press, 1980.

Wilson, Colin, and Donald Seaman. *Scandal!* London: George Weidenfeld and Nicholson, Ltd., 1986.

Wood, Barbara. *E. F. Schumacher: His Life and Thought*. New York: Harper & Row, 1984.

Wyndham, John. *Trouble with Lichen*. London: Penguin Books, 2008.

❖

Readers wishing to pursue research into Nicoll and his milieu can consult the Maurice Nicoll papers at the Archives at Yale University, archives.yale.edu.

Index

About the Author

Gary Lachman is the author of many books about consciousness, culture, and the Western esoteric tradition, including *Dreaming Ahead of Time, The Return of Holy Russia, Dark Star Rising: Magick and Power in the Age of Trump, Lost Knowledge of the Imagination,* and *Beyond the Robot: The Life and Work of Colin Wilson.* He has written biographies of C. G. Jung, Madame Blavatsky, Rudolf Steiner, Emanuel Swedenborg, P. D. Ouspensky, and Aleister Crowley. He writes for several journals in the United States, United Kingdom, and Europe, lectures around the world, and his work has been translated into more than a dozen languages. In a former life he was a founding member of the pop group Blondie and in 2006 was inducted into the Rock and Roll Hall of Fame. Before moving to London in 1996 and becoming a full-time writer, Lachman studied philosophy, managed a metaphysical book shop, taught English literature, and was Science Writer for UCLA. He is an adjunct professor of transformative studies at the California Institute of Integral Studies. He can be reached at

gary-lachman.com
facebook.com/GVLachman
twitter.com/GaryLachman

BOOKS OF RELATED INTEREST

The Return of Holy Russia
Apocalyptic History, Mystical Awakening,
and the Struggle for the Soul of the World
by Gary Lachman

Occulture
The Unseen Forces That Drive Culture Forward
by Carl Abrahamsson
Foreword by Gary Lachman

Deconstructing Gurdjieff
Biography of a Spiritual Magician
by Tobias Churton

Gnostic Philosophy
From Ancient Persia to Modern Times
by Tobias Churton

Occult Russia
Pagan, Esoteric, and Mystical Traditions
by Christopher McIntosh

John Dee and the Empire of Angels
Enochian Magick and the Occult Roots of the Modern World
by Jason Louv

The Bavarian Illuminati
The Rise and Fall of the World's Most Secret Society
by René Le Forestier
Translated by Jon E. Graham

Lords of the Left-Hand Path
Forbidden Practices and Spiritual Heresies
by Stephen E. Flowers, Ph.D.

INNER TRADITIONS • BEAR & COMPANY
P.O. Box 388
Rochester, VT 05767
1-800-246-8648
www.InnerTraditions.com
Or contact your local bookseller